Trade, Tariffs and Growth

Trade, Tariffs and Growth

Essays in International Economics

JAGDISH BHAGWATI

Professor of Economics,
Massachusetts Institute of
Technology

Weidenfeld and Nicolson
5 Winsley Street, London, W1

For Padma

SBN 297 17829 6

Printed in Great Britain by
C. Tinling & Co. Ltd., London and Prescot

Contents

Preface

The essays collected in this volume have been written over a period of nearly nine years. These years were spent at different universities: Cambridge, MIT, Chicago, Oxford, Indian Statistical Institute, Delhi School of Economics and Columbia University. I have profited much from numerous teachers, students and colleagues during this period. I should like to acknowledge particularly my considerable intellectual indebtedness to three distinguished teachers: Professors Harry G. Johnson, Charles P. Kindleberger and Paul A. Samuelson. I also recall with great pleasure the intellectual stimulus provided by my thesis supervisors at Oxford, Professor J. R. Hicks and Sir Donald Mac-Dougall.

The essays are almost exclusively on issues in the pure theory of international trade, although empirical exercises of some interest are included within Chapters 1 and 10.

Part One contains two papers. Chapter 1, a full-length Survey, was commissioned by the Royal Economic Society for publication in the *Economic Journal*, as part of a series of surveys of economic theory planned by the Society with the American Economic Association. It was finished around mid-1962, published in March 1964 and eventually reprinted in *Collected Economic Surveys* (Macmillan, London, 1965). The Addendum has been written subsequently, to bring the Survey reasonably up to date. Chapter 2 was written with Harry Johnson and published in the *Economic Journal*, March 1960. It considers four historical controversies in the theory of international trade. Aside from its historical interest, the paper has stimulated further research on measurement of the cost of protection and controversy concerning 'elasticity pessimism' in the analysis of the efficacy of exchange rate changes.

Part Two contains three recent papers on propositions relating to the gains from trade while the fourth (Chapter 6), reprinted from the *Economic Journal*, March 1967, essentially provides a useful statement of the proofs of the Ricardian and Heckscher–Ohlin theorems of comparative advantage construed as explanations of the pattern of trade. Chapter 3 is reprinted from the *Oxford Economic Papers*, July 1968; Chapter 4 from the *Quarterly Journal of Economics*, May 1969; and Chapter 5 from the *Journal of Political Economy*, October 1967.

Part Three contains five papers relating to tariffs, quotas and subsidies and covers both 'positive' and welfare aspects of trade theory. Chapter 7, reprinted from the *Economic Journal*, December 1959, is a systematization and extension of the analysis of the effects of protection on real wages of factors, initiated by Stolper and Samuelson in a classic paper in 1941. Chapter 8, reprinted from the *Oxford Economic Papers*, October 1961, generalizes the results of this analysis to cases involving variable factor supplies and income-distributional changes, among others. Chapter 9 is an amalgamated paper, based on a paper of the same title in the Haberler Festschrift Volume, *Trade, Growth, and the Balance of Payments*, edited by Caves, Johnson and Kenen (Rand McNally, Chicago), and a subsequent extension in 'More on the Equivalence of Tariffs and Quotas', *American Economic Review*, March 1968. It examines the well-known proposition of equivalence between tariffs and quotas and shows its critical dependence on the universal assumption of perfect competition in demand, production and importation. Chapter 10 is again a merged version of two papers in the *Bulletin of the Oxford University Institute of Statistics*: 'On the Under-invoicing of Imports', November 1964; and 'Fiscal Policies, the Faking of Foreign Trade Declarations, and the Balance of Payments', Vol. 29, No. 1, 1967. Chapter 11, reprinted from the *Journal of Political Economy*, February 1963, develops the important proposition that the optimal intervention in the case of domestic distortions requires domestic rather than trade policy instruments.

Part Four contains four papers on growth and development. Chapter 12 reprints an early paper in the *American Economic Review*, which analyses the effect of economic growth on trade within the framework of a two-factor two-commodity model, first developed by Harry Johnson. Chapter 13 is a contemporary note, published originally in the *Review of Economic Studies*, June 1958, where I explored the conditions under which growth could lead to a sufficiently acute deterioration in the terms of trade to outweigh the primary gain in real income from the growth and thus result in 'immiserizing growth'. In Chapter 14, reprinted from the *Review of Economic Studies*, December 1968, I show that this paradoxical phenomenon of immiserizing growth can arise whenever there are distortions, endogenous or policy-imposed, in the economic system. Chapter 15, reprinted from *Value, Capital and Growth* (Edinburgh UP), is largely an exercise in political economy and demonstrates how empirical phenomena, such as the insistence on reciprocity in tariff bargaining and the pattern of international-trade behaviour of the less developed countries, can be explained by adapting trade theory so as to allow for industrial production as an argument in the social welfare function. The implication of this modified theory for the GATT rules governing international trade relations is also examined.

Aside from the major alterations already noted, only a few minor changes have been occasionally made. Thanks are due to the following for permission to reprint the essays: the *Review of Economic Studies*, the *Economic Journal*, the *American Economic Review*, the *Journal of Political Economy* and the University of Chicago Press, the *Oxford Economic Papers*, the *Bulletin of the Oxford University Institute of Statistics* and Basil Blackwell Ltd, Harvard University Press (for permission to reprint from the *Quarterly Journal of Economics*), the Edinburgh University Press, Macmillan and Co. Ltd, and Rand McNally and Co.

March 1969   JAGDISH BHAGWATI

PART ONE

Survey and Controversies

1 The Pure Theory of International Trade: A Survey[1]

This Survey[2] covers that branch of international trade theory which, following Marshall, is generally described as 'pure'. This epithet separates it from 'monetary' theory. It is *not* to be taken to imply exceptional esotericism and abstraction from the problems of the real world. Indeed, I propose to give prominence to that part of the growing, new literature in pure theory which attempts explicitly to bring the theory on to the ground – through empirical verification of testable propositions, through measurement of the gains and losses from changes in trade policy and through the formulation of analytical and operational models to assist the developmental planning that is becoming a characteristic of the developing nations.

The pure theory of international trade represents essentially the application of the theories of value and welfare to questions of international economics.[3] Although the distinction between them has not always been clear in many writings, it is none the less true that two different species of problems have been the subject of analysis in pure theory. There are questions of 'positive' or 'objective' analysis: for instance, what determines the composition of trade; how will tariffs affect factor prices; what is the effect of trade on the terms of trade?

[1] This is the fourth of the series of Surveys supported by the Rockefeller Foundation.

[2] This Survey was partly written when I was with the Indian Statistical Institute. For correspondence and/or discussions, I am thankful to Professors H. G. Johnson, R. W. Jones, C. P. Kindleberger, B. S. Minhas, P. A. Samuelson and T. N. Srinivasan. V. Balasubramanian and R. Tagat have assisted with the computational work.

[3] The pure theory of trade thus differs structurally from general theory in the kinds of questions asked, rather than in the kinds of assumptions made. This vexed question has been considered at length by Haberler [4, Chapter 1].

On the other hand, there are questions in 'welfare' or 'normative' economics: among them, does free trade maximize world real income; are tariffs superior to free trade from the viewpoint of national advantage; how do tariffs compare with subsidies as forms of State intervention?[1]

The range of questions that have been asked is impressive. The recent literature which is addressed to them runs into several dozen books and over two hundred papers. This makes a brief survey exceptionally difficult, even if confined to the developments in the last two or three decades.[2] This difficulty is compounded by the fact that the subject has already been extensively, frequently and recently surveyed. We currently have a cogent and lucid survey in a brief monograph by Haberler [4], revised only in 1961; a nearly exhaustive, full-length account in a 1960 volume by Caves [3]; an excellent, theoretical survey of some of the central analytical propositions of pure theory by Mundell [11] in 1960; and, most embarrassingly, a survey of some of the more impressive recent developments in pure theory by myself [1] as recently as 1961.[3]

To collapse the immense literature into a concise survey, to exercise the inevitable selectivity (with respect to both authors and problems of analysis) to maximum advantage, it is necessary to have a precise, logical frame. The structure of this paper is built squarely on the

[1] The distinction between 'positive' and 'welfare' questions is recent in trade theory and appears to have been stated explicitly and emphatically only as late as 1933 by Ohlin [34]. Ohlin, who distinguished between these two aspects, criticized the classical economists for muddling them. As Haberler [4, p. 3], however, has charmingly pointed out: 'That his demand for not just a clear distinction between political evaluation and theoretical explanation, but for actual separation of these two areas by putting them into separate books or chapters, is easier postulated than accomplished is demonstrated by Ohlin himself. Thus, in an early passage of his celebrated treatise, in the midst of "objective theory", he proves in typical classical manner that interregional trade and division of labour results in an increased social product without making it clear that this statement implies a value judgment on his part and is not merely "objective analysis".'

[2] Thus Lipsey's [7] concise and brilliant review of the theory of customs unions (part of the theory of discriminatory tariff changes) in this *Journal* runs into several pages. And it deals with a comparatively recent field which forms only a small segment of the literature on pure theory.

[3] To these may be added Meade's celebrated works [8, 9, 10], which cover the entire field and the writings of Johnson [5, 6], which have done much to synthesize the literature on many aspects of trade theory. Mention may also be made of two papers: Lipsey's [7] 1960 survey of customs-union theory and the review in 1960 by myself and Johnson]2] of certain historical controversies in pure theory, reprinted as chapter 2.

clear distinction between 'positive' and 'normative' pure theory.

Under positive theory, in turn, a distinction has been drawn between: (1) the propositions of 'statics', which describe the properties of an equilibrium situation at *any given point* of time; (2) the propositions of 'comparative statics', which concern the *differences* in the equilibrium values of variables between situations at *two different points of* (conceptual) time; and (3) the propositions of 'dynamics', which involve time in an essential way.

The static propositions which have attracted the greatest analytical interest concern: (1) the pattern of trade: the determination of commodities as exports and imports; and (2) the configuration of factor prices. The analysis of the former question has further been enriched greatly by a recent, noticeable trend towards empirical verification. The propositions of comparative statics (which continue to be almost exclusively deductive) fall again into two classes: (1) those that concern the effect, on equilibrium prices and quantities, *under a pre-defined trade policy*, of an autonomous change in one of the following data: production functions, demand and factor supply; and (2) those that relate to the effect, on equilibrium prices and quantities, of a change in trade policy itself, while other data are constant. The development of pure theory has witnessed a synthesis and simplification of these propositions in comparative statics which eludes the few, though diverse, attempts at dynamic analysis. This synthesis has also been accomplished in terms of an analytical framework characterized by primary factors of production and integrated processes of production. This constitutes a central limitation of the theory in a theoretical world where this conceptualization has been replaced generally by the more general approach of process analysis and in a real world where a large portion of the world trade consists of intermediates and capital goods and an increasing number of developing nations' imports are coming to consist almost exclusively of these commodities.

The parts of this paper dealing with positive theory have therefore been divided into the following five groups:

1 Section 1: *Theorems in Statics: The Pattern of Trade.*
2 Section 2: *Theorems in Statics: Factor Price-Equalization.*
3 Section 3: *Theorems in Comparative Statics.*
4 Section 4: *Theorems in Dynamics.*
5 Section 5: *Central Limitations of Pure Theory: Intermediates and Capital Goods.*

In the theory of welfare and trade the classification has been easier. There is, on the one hand, the 'traditional' theory which is addressed to *qualitative* propositions that rank different trade policies (*e.g.*, free trade is superior to no trade) and can be classified according to whether they satisfy Samuelson's superior-for-all-income-distributions criterion. On the other hand, there is a growing, important segment of the literature which aims at *quantitative* measures of costs and benefits – prompted by the objective of making economic analysis policy-oriented. At the same time the growth of centralized planning in many developing countries has raised the interesting questions of the *operational* use of trade theory's welfare insights and results as part of the complement of planning techniques; and some useful experience has been obtained.

The survey of welfare propositions in trade theory, therefore, has been divided into three major groups:

1 Section 6: *Welfare Propositions: Gains from Trade.*
2 Section 7: *Measurement of Welfare.*
3 Section 8: *Trade Theory and Development Planning.*[1]

1. THEOREMS IN STATICS: THE PATTERN OF TRADE

The theory of comparative advantage (or cost), which concerns the determination of the pattern of trade, constitutes perhaps the oldest set of analytical propositions in pure theory. It belongs to the realm of 'statics' because traditionally it has been formulated as a theorem concerning the determination of (traded) commodities into exports and imports in a static, analytical framework. This is certainly true of the two major theories, Ricardian and Heckscher–Ohlin [1], that have dominated this field.

There are, no doubt, different possible ways in which an 'international economy' may be simulated by a theorist. Each such 'model' could be used to deduce analytical propositions. Indeed, the literature on pure theory contains a large number of such idealizations, among the most celebrated being those of Yntema, Mosak and Graham [3].[2]

---

[1] Although the paper falls neatly into these eight sections, there are inevitably some overlaps. None the less, I would maintain that the proposed classification is the most advantageous from the viewpoint of assessing the current state, limitations and trends of the pure theory of trade.

[2] For a summary statement of these and other models, Caves [3] is an excellent reference. A cataloguing of such models, however, is of limited interest as any number of models can be put down as one wishes. Only those models are of

From the viewpoint of propositions concerning the pattern of trade, the two models of significance are those of Ricardo and Heckscher–Ohlin [19, 34]. Not merely have these models been used to derive 'logically true' theorems concerning the trade pattern.[1] These theorems have also now been adapted to formulate testable hypotheses (based on factors stressed in the respective models). And these hypotheses have been subjected to empirical verification in a series of excellent papers. In consequence, new theories have now been devised, which provide *alternative* explanations of the pattern of trade. Prominent among these are the analyses of Kravis [22] and Linder [27]. These four theories concerning the pattern of international specialization are discussed here, distinguishing clearly between the formulations as deductive, analytical propositions (which are logically true under a specified set of sufficient conditions) and formulations as testable hypotheses.

The Ricardian Theory

The Ricardian Theory can be construed in either of two ways: (1) as a highly simplified model which was intended to be, and served as, an eminently successful instrument for demonstrating the welfare proposition that trade is beneficial; or (2) as a serious attempt at isolating the crucial variables which can be used to 'explain' the pattern of trade. There is little doubt that the former view is plausible. A careful study of the original texts yields supporting evidence; the most persuasive element is the fact that when both Ricardo and Mill discussed the 'positive' (as opposed to 'normative') proposition relating to the effects of cheap corn *imports* from the colonies on profits, wages and rents, and thence on the approach of the stationary state, they were using the full-fledged classical model characterized by three factors and diminishing returns [1]. And yet the impact of the Ricardian 'constant cost' model in recent literature has been predominantly as an idealization which affords a significant clue to the structure of foreign trade.[2]

---

significance which have been used to yield theorems; and then it is only in considering those theorems that they are best discussed.

[1] The phrase 'logically true' is used there in the strict mathematical sense: a statement that is true in every logically possible case is said to be *logically true*.

[2] This has been the result of two factors: (i) traditionally the question whether the Ricardian theory should be construed as positive or normative has rarely been raised; it has always seemed 'natural' to construe Ricardo as though he were

On the latter interpretation the Ricardian theory can be deduced directly from the celebrated England–Portugal example in Ricardo's *Principles*. If it is assumed that there are two commodities, a single factor (labour) and constant returns to scale (in each activity),[1] the pre-trade commodity price ratio will be a function exclusively of the (scale-free) output-factor ratios contained in the production functions. The combination of a single factor with constant returns to scale ensures that neither demand nor the level of factor supply makes any difference to the equilibrium commodity price ratio in a closed economy.[2] Since Ricardo assumes a similar model for each country, it follows that the pre-trade commodity price ratio, and hence the composition of trade, is exclusively determined by international differences in relative output-factor ratios. If a_1 and a_2 are the output-factor ratios for country I and b_1 and b_2 for country II in activities 1 and 2 respectively, country I will export commodity 1 and import commodity 2 if $a_1/a_2 > b_1/b_2$ (as this will imply that commodity 1 will be cheaper, and commodity 2 dearer, in country I than in country II *prior to trade*). The algebraic condition is frequently written as $a_1/b_1 > a_2/b_2$, which states the condition in terms of 'comparative factor productivities'. If, however, the number of commodities is increased beyond two, while maintaining the two-country assumption, it is no longer possible to derive the 'strong' Ricardian theorem that the trade pattern is determined exclusively by international differences in production functions (*i.e.*, by comparative factor productivities). The model now implies a weaker proposition: there will be a chain in which all commodities are ranked in terms of their comparative factor-productivity ratios such that *it will always be true that each of a country's exports will have a higher factor-productivity ratio than each of its imports*. The precise composition of exports and imports (*i.e.*, where the chain will be cut, dividing the exports and

genuinely attempting to explain the pattern of trade with his simple model; and (ii) the Ricardian 'demonstration' of the benefits of trade, long since challenged as inadequate by Barrett Whale, has now been superseded by the elegant and more rigorous formulations of the new welfare economics and Samuelson's classic proof of 1939 – so that it is no longer easy to see that the Ricardian preoccupation was predominantly with normative aspects.

[1] The last assumption listed here need not be implicit in the preceding one, since fixed factors like land may well be subsumed in the shape of the production function.

[2] The reason is that the resulting production possibility curve is non-strictly convex and characterized by a constant rate of transformation.

the imports) can be determined only by bringing demand into the model [20]. This proposition will continue to hold also in the more general framework of many countries and commodities, which represents a generalization of Ricardo's two-country model by Graham. In an elegant generalization of Ricardo's theory, drawing upon McKenzie's earlier work [78], Jones [69] has shown that, taking each pair of countries, only comparing the labour cost ratios of the commodities they are producing in specialization, the Ricardian bilateral cost comparisons are necessarily satisfied. (These propositions relate, more generally, to the location of production in a free-trade world: their implications for the trade pattern are in conformity with the Ricardian theory.)

When international trade economists have attempted to formulate hypotheses, based on the Ricardian theory, and test whether observable trade conforms to the postulated pattern, the real difficulty has been that of trying to adapt the one-factor, Ricardian approach to the multi-factor real world. Two ways in which this adaptation may be made can be distinguished.

One way would be to focus on the fact that the Ricardian model emphasizes the crucial role of comparative differences in *production functions* so that the testable proposition should be developed in these terms. For instance, if the technology in activity i could be characterized by $Q_i = \lambda_i^I Q_i(K_i; L_i)$ for country I and by $Q_i = \lambda_i^{II} Q_i(K_i; L_i)$ for country II so that the *only* difference between the two countries' production functions for an identical activity is a multiplicative scalar ($\lambda_i^{II}/\lambda_i^I$ in this case), then the Ricardian testable hypothesis could be construed to mean that

$$\frac{\lambda_i^{II}}{\lambda_i^{I}} > \frac{\lambda_j^{II}}{\lambda_j^{I}}$$

$$i = 1, 2, \ldots m \quad j = m+1, \ldots n$$

where commodities $i = 1, 2, \ldots m$ are country II's exports and commodities $j = m + 1, \ldots n$ are its imports. This would be a Ricardian hypothesis – as much as any other.[1] The possibility of testing such a

[1] The conditions under which this proposition is logically true could be established by an extension of the theoretical work on the Heckscher–Ohlin theory and on the effects of neutral technical progress [5, Chapters I and III]. For instance, if all the assumptions which are shown to be sufficient for the logical validity of the Heckscher–Ohlin theorem are made with the *only* difference that the production functions are not identical, but differ between countries in the manner postulated in the text, it follows that the (Ricardian-type) hypothesis in the text concerning the pattern of trade will be logically true (provided, of course, that international differences in relative factor endowments are ruled out).

hypothesis is not, by any means, remote. Minhas [33, p. 154] states, in
a brilliant paper on the Heckscher–Ohlin theory, that 'the isoquants
in different countries, except for a pure scale change, look alike;
and the marginal rates of substitution are unchanged at given capital:
labour ratios' when homohypallagic production functions are fitted
to the data for certain comparable industries in Japan and the United
States. This empirical evidence seems to provide the means to test the
kind of Ricardian hypothesis formulated here.[1]

The most frequent interpretation for the purpose of formulating a
testable proposition, however, has been in terms of the factor productivities themselves. The comparative factor productivities, defined
in terms of an arbitrarily chosen factor (almost always labour),[2] have
been taken as providing the necessary clue to the trade pattern.

The intuitive and ultimate rationale behind this interpretation is
easily stated (and, as will be evident later, has an important bearing
on the procedure of testing). Since exports will take place only when
domestic (pre-trade) prices are lower than abroad, it follows that

$$\frac{P_i^{\mathrm{I}}}{P_i^{\mathrm{II}}} > 1$$

$$i = 1, 2, \ldots m$$

where $\frac{P_i^{\mathrm{I}}}{P_i^{\mathrm{II}}}$ refers to the price-ratio of commodity i, exported by country
I, *prior to trade*.[3] Similarly,

---

[1] Minhas comes close to doing this, but does not see the problem in this way
because he is focusing on the implications of such 'neutral' differences in production functions for the Heckscher–Ohlin theorem. Credit must be given to him,
however, for having seen the possibility of construing the Ricardian approach in
the broader way (of differences in production functions) suggested here, as
against the narrower approach of labour productivity ratios that is to be found
in the literature.

[2] There is nothing in the basic *structure* of the Ricardian model which requires
that this single factor be labour. It could be anything else. However, it has mostly
been taken to be labour. The reasons for this exclusive preference may be that:
(i) the historical context of the labour theory of value, in terms of which Ricardo's
comparative cost doctrine has usually been understood, makes it inevitable that
the formal identity between labour and any other factor, as noted here, should
have been missed, and (ii) there has been, until recently, also a widespread tendency, in economic literature generally, to take labour productivity as the index
of 'productivity' rather than, say, capital productivity.

[3] Where transport costs are present, lower pre-trade prices are only a *necessary*
condition for exports; where transport costs (and similar cost-raising factors) are
ignored, lower pre-trade prices also become a *sufficient* condition.

$$\frac{P_j^{\mathrm{I}}}{P_j^{\mathrm{II}}} > 1$$

$$= m + 1, \ldots n$$

where the commodity j is exported by country II. Hence.

$$\frac{P_i^{\mathrm{I}}}{P_i^{\mathrm{II}}} < \frac{P_j^{\mathrm{I}}}{P_j^{\mathrm{II}}}$$

$$i = 1, \ldots m \quad j = m + 1, \ldots n$$

Now it is possible to write these prices (defined as equal to costs) in terms of three component factors:

$$P_i = a_i \cdot \frac{W_i}{L_i} \cdot \frac{TC_i}{W_i}$$

where a_i is the labour:output ratio, W_i is the wage bill (so that $\frac{W_i}{L_i} = w_i$ is the wage-rate) and TC_i the total cost (inclusive of profits, by definition) in activity i. If we now argue that it is, in practice, enough to focus attention on a_i and to ignore the other two factors (on the ground that either they are insignificant *or* they are identical between countries individually or as a product), then we could substitute a_i for p_i in the above price-comparison. We could also alternatively assume that the inter-industrial pattern of wage rates (w_i) and the total-cost/wages ratio $\left(\frac{TC_i}{W_i}\right)$ is identical internationally. We would then get the condition

$$\frac{a_i^{\mathrm{I}}}{a_i^{\mathrm{II}}} < \frac{a_j^{\mathrm{I}}}{a_j^{\mathrm{II}}} \qquad \qquad (1)$$

$$i = 1, 2, \ldots m \quad j = m + 1, \ldots n$$

This is, in fact, the condition stated frequently as the Ricardian hypothesis.

This chain of reasoning also leads to a further formulation. It is possible to advance a variation of the hypothesis, which brings into the picture the structure of the wage-rates as well. This can be done by rewriting the previous hypothesis thus:

$$\frac{a_i^{\mathrm{I}}}{a_i^{\mathrm{II}}} \cdot \frac{w_i^{\mathrm{I}}}{w_i^{\mathrm{II}}} < \frac{a_j^{\mathrm{I}}}{a_j^{\mathrm{II}}} \cdot \frac{w_j^{\mathrm{I}}}{w_j^{\mathrm{II}}} \qquad \qquad (2)$$

$$i = 1, 2, \ldots m \quad j = m + 1, \ldots n$$

This is, in fact, a statement of the Ricardian hypothesis which is in terms of comparative *unit labour costs* and not *labour productivity*. It is the hypothesis which is to be found in much of the empirical literature [1].

Although it appears relatively simple to go on from these formulations to their tests, there are some points of interest that need to be spelled out.

(1) To begin with, 'indirect' tests of these hypotheses readily suggest themselves but can be treacherous. For instance, it has been customary to argue through an attempted demonstration of the international 'similarity' of the inter-industrial wage-rate structure and the pattern of the total-cost/wages ratio. Caves [3, p. 272] has cited Kravis' [21, pp. 145–6] empirical results, which show that the ranking of industries by hourly earnings of workers is almost identical between Japan and the United States, to argue that these data lend force to the Ricardian hypothesis in terms of comparative labour productivity differences (as the determinants of relative price differences).[1] However, such a deduction leaves out of reckoning the possibility that the structure of the costs–wages ratio may be largely dissimilar between trading countries and makes implicitly an unverified assumption of 'similarity' of this structure. This procedure, in any case, is unsound, since, although each of the two structures (costs–wages and wage-rates) may be internationally 'dissimilar', their product may be similar as a result of these dissimilarities being offsetting. A method which proceeds in terms of investigating the similarities of individual structures will leave out this possibility and thereby constitute an unduly restrictive and false test for the empirical verification of the Ricardian hypothesis in question.

(2) But then, if a direct test of the Ricardian hypotheses were adopted, examining whether the labour productivity or unit wage–cost ratios for the exports and imports for two countries (taken bilaterally) conform to the postulated relationships, would that be enough? I do not think so. Let me cast my argument in terms of hypothesis (1), which relates to labour productivity ratios – it is equally valid for hypothesis (2) relating to unit wage–cost ratios.

It will be recalled that hypothesis (1) is derived in two steps. (a) First, it is argued that the (pre-trade) prices are such that the relative price (defined as the domestic over the foreign price) of an exported good

---

[1] Similar data, showing similarity of industrial wage structures, have been produced for the United States, United Kingdom, Canada and (only a little less successfully) Sweden by Lebergott [23]. None of this, however, adds up to anything impressive, since the coverage in terms of both activities and nations is severely limited.

must be lower than the relative price of an imported good. This is a natural assumption to make; it merely reflects the assumption that the profit motive will direct the pattern of trade.[1] This, however, relates to the *pre-trade* prices. But the observed prices are inevitably *post-trade* prices. This should have posed an impossible difficulty in testing any proposition concerning the pattern of trade and prices. However, it is easy to get around the problem when one reckons with the fact of transport (and other) costs that lead to a difference in the post-trade f.o.b. and c.i.f. (landed) prices. This difference in f.o.b. and c.i.f. prices means that the price–trade proposition that the relative price of an exported good must be lower than that of an imported good will continue necessarily to hold (with the domestic price of a good defined f.o.b. and the foreign prices c.i.f. for exported goods). The proposition is necessarily valid empirically in a world which is characterized by natural and artificial cost-raising factors. It therefore calls for no conscious attempt at verification. This is indeed a great gain. It is, however, an advantage not shared by the other postulate that must be made before the Ricardian hypothesis can be derived. *(b)* This other assumption consists in arguing that prices can be approximated by labour productivities. This proposition takes generally the strong form that the linear regression equation fitted to observed labour productivity ratios (for each activity in both countries) and corresponding price ratios would yield a 45 degree line from the origin.[2] This strong assumption, which is equivalent to arguing that the inter-industry structure of the total cost per unit labour is identical between the trading countries, is only a sufficient condition for yielding, along with the price–trade assumption, the required Ricardian hypothesis. It is also the condition that is most frequently found in the literature on Ricardian theories [3, Chapter X]. A weaker, but still sufficient, assumption would be to make labour productivity ratios a monotonically increasing function of price ratios. But the

[1] Theoretically, of course, one can think of cases where the pattern of trade does not conform to this rule. For instance, the contrary possibility can arise if there are domestic distortions (i.e. divergence of the domestic rate of transformation in production from the commodity price-ratios) [112]. In anticipation, I may point out that this qualification does not apply to the *post-trade*, relative price comparison for exportables and importables, to which I proceed immediately in the text.

[2] The labour productivity ratio here must be defined as the foreign labour productivity divided by the domestic; and the price ratio is defined as the domestic price divided by the foreign.

weaker this assumption gets, the more difficult it becomes to interpret it in meaningful, economic terms.[1]

Since one does want to know why it is that the trade pattern is characterized, if at all, by the comparative labour productivity ranking postulated by Ricardian hypothesis (1), I would argue that it is also necessary to supplement such a direct verification by a further verification of whether labour productivity ratios exhibit the (underlying) hypothesized relationship with price ratios.[1] Unfortunately, neither the direct verification of the rankings of exports and imports (for a pair of trading countries) in terms of their comparative labour productivities or unit wage–cost ratios nor the necessary, supplementary test of the implied relationship between price ratios and labour productivity or unit wage–cost ratios has yet been attempted.

The empirical literature that exists, in some abundance, concerns itself with really different kinds of testable propositions concerning trade. These hypotheses do have some overlap with the Ricardian hypothesis (1) and (2), with the unfortunate consequence that the surprisingly good results that attempts at verifying them have turned up have been construed frequently as validating the Ricardian approach [3, Chapter X]. The pioneering study in this field is by MacDougall [28, 29], with follow-up by Balassa [13], Stern [40] and MacDougall [30] himself.

Taking American and British exports of similar commodities to third markets, MacDougall [28, 29] has conducted analysis which is

---

[1] In the tests of this assumption which I later attempt in this paper even the weaker hypothesis does not get through: the linear regressions yield very poor fits.

[2] Concerning the derivation of the Ricardian hypothesis (1) in this two-step fashion, however, there is just a little more that may be said. It may be contended that labour productivities approximate the *pre-trade* prices but that trade leads to boosted profits in the export industries with no imputation to wages and no impact on labour productivities. If so, one *could* find evidence for the trade pattern exhibiting the Ricardian ranking in terms of comparative labour productivities and/or unit wage–cost ratios, but *not* necessarily for the productivity or unit wage–cost ratios being related in any way to the price ratios. While, of course, this is theoretically possible (and such a theory would have its own further implications which should then be tested), I do not find it plausible. Why should labour productivity ratios, for instance, be a good approximation to relative prices before trade but cease to be so after trade? This asymmetry seems to have no rationale. In any case, the particular chain of reasoning used in the text, aside from being more plausible, is also the one generally subscribed to; and hence its implications have been fully spelled out.

tantamount to investigating three hypotheses: $\dfrac{a_i^{\mathrm{II}}}{a_i^{\mathrm{I}}}$ is positively correlated with

$$\frac{E_i^{\mathrm{I}}}{E_i^{\mathrm{II}}}, \quad (i = 1, \ldots k); \qquad \qquad (3)$$

if

$$\frac{a_i^{\mathrm{II}}}{a_i^{\mathrm{I}}} \cdot \frac{w_i^{\mathrm{II}}}{w_i^{\mathrm{I}}} > 1,$$

then

$$\frac{E_i^{\mathrm{I}}}{E_i^{\mathrm{II}}} > 1, \quad (i = 1, \ldots k): \qquad \qquad (4)$$

and $\dfrac{a_i^{\mathrm{II}}}{a_i^{\mathrm{I}}} \cdot \dfrac{w_i^{\mathrm{II}}}{w_i^{\mathrm{I}}}$ is positively correlated with

$$\frac{E_i^{\mathrm{I}}}{E_i^{\mathrm{II}}}, \quad (i = 1, \ldots k) \qquad \qquad (5)$$

where $E_i^{\mathrm{I}}/E_i^{\mathrm{II}}$ is the ratio of exports of commodity i by countries I and II respectively to third markets.[1] Stern has recently followed Mac-Dougall's hypotheses and procedures closely, but introduced more recent data on productivity. MacDougall [30] has done the same. Balassa has tested hypothesis (3), using again the same new data on productivity, but does not consider hypothesis (4) and approaches hypothesis (5) differently, through multiple-correlatoin analysis.

Now, each of these three hypotheses has two main elements: (a) the adequacy of labour productivity (or unit labour-cost) ratios as an approximation to price ratios; and (b) the relation of price ratios (between prices of similar commodities exported to third markets by the United States and the United Kingdom) to quantity-ratios (of United States and United Kingdom exports of similar commodities). It is easy to recognize the former as a proposition borrowed from the Ricardian analysis. The latter proposition, however, represents a departure from the Ricardian price–trade assumption. The assumption that the relative prices of exported goods will be lower than those of imported goods is now replaced by the postulation of some relationship between (United States–United Kingdom) price ratios of third-market exports and (United States–United Kingdom) shares in third markets. In hypotheses (3) and (5), for instance, the relationship takes the form of a negative correlation between the relative export prices

---

[1] Hypothesis (3) is clearly inspired by Ricardian hypothesis (1) and hypotheses (4) and (5) by Ricardian hypothesis (2). It should be made clear here that Mac-Dougall's papers contain much *other* analysis of considerable interest and that the papers neither are confined to testing the hypotheses listed here nor approach those questions in the same formal manner as set out here.

and shares; in hypothesis (4) the form is shifted: a country's exports are postulated to be greater when its price is relatively cheaper than its rival's, but nothing is stated about the effects of different degrees of relative price advantage on export shares.

Neither of the hypothesized price–trade relationships, however, seems to be plausible. It is difficult to see, for instance, the theoretical reason why the ratio of two rivals' third-market exports should, in a cross-section analysis, turn out to increase as the corresponding price ratio falls. The argument that relative prices of similar commodities and their relative sales can be correlated in *cross-section analysis* cannot be justified on the presumption that, for *any given industry*, a reduction in the relative price of a competitor will increase its relative sales. It is difficult to imagine that this presumption can be extended to cross-section data where different commodities will have varying 'elasticities of substitution', depending on different degrees of product differentiation, quality differences, etc., as between different sources of origin (the United States and the United Kingdom in the present example).[1]

Despite these difficulties with the hypotheses (3), (4) and (5), the empirical verification is remarkably successful.[2] And yet, as already

[1] This is perhaps what Caves [3, p. 269] also is hinting at in his critique of the MacDougall papers.

[2] If one examines the evidence MacDougall [28, pp. 715–17] has produced one is astonished at the empirical support which is turned up for this hypothesis. For United States: United Kingdom export shares and price ratios, MacDougall produces supporting evidence, with twenty-three regressions and correlations, from 1913 to 1948; the lowest two correlation coefficients are -0.73. Fairly high correlation coefficients, with nicely negative regression slopes, are turned up, moreover, for United States : United Kingdom, United States : Japan, United States : Germany, United States : France, United Kingdom : France, France : Japan, France : Germany, United Kingdom : Japan and United Kingdom : Germany. As for the evidence on hypotheses (3), (4) and (5) themselves, the results can be systematized as follows:

I. *Hypothesis (3).* The results of MacDougall, Stern and Balassa can be stated briefly (*see table on opposite page*).

[a] x and y refer to the logarithms of the United States : United Kingdom export ratio and United States : United Kingdom labour productivity ratio respectively. x^* and y^* in the last regression refer to the ratios themselves. MacDougall does not state his 1937 regression equation.

[b] The productivity data refer to 1950 and the source is the same as that used by MacDougall and Stern. However, the export data refer to values instead of quantities and are for 1951 instead of 1950. For the latter, the reason is that 1950 was an 'abnormal' year. For the former, the reason is that it is very tricky to

Author		Sample	Year	Regression equation[a]	Correlation coefficient
MacDougall	(1)	25 industries	1937	Regression slope $= -4$	-0.70
	(2)	39 ,,	1950	$x = -2.19 + 1.89y$	0.61
Stern	(3)	24 ($=$ MacDougall 1937 sample)	1950	$x = 0.98 + 1.65y$ (0.57)	0.52
	(4)	39 industries	1950	$x = -0.68 + 1.27y$ (0.43)	0.44
	(5)	25 ,,	1950	$x = 0.91 + 1.49y$ (0.59)	0.46
Balassa[b]	(6)	28 ,,	1950 and	$x = -1.761 + 1.594y$ (0.181)	0.86
	(7)	28 ,,	1951	$x^* = -53.32 + 0.721y^*$ (0.103)	0.80

separate export prices and quantities. Balassa prefers to work with values and justifies this choice on the ground that, with the estimates of elasticity of substitution being high in general, a positive correlation between productivity and export quantities will exist, so that the tests proposed are not vitiated. This argument, however, rests on the estimates of high elasticities of substitution – which, in turn, are based upon the very same separation of prices and quantities which Balassa is shying away from.

The results, on the whole, seem clearly to support the stated hypothesis mildly.

II. *Hypothesis (4)*. Here only MacDougall and Stern have produced evidence. Two different approaches can be distinguished. (1) One is to examine the industries directly and see how many conform to the pattern laid down by the hypothesis. (*a*) Using only the *average* wage levels for the United States and the United Kingdom (instead of individual industry wages), MacDougall found for 1937 that 'where American output for worker was more than twice the British, the United States had in general the bulk of the export market, while for products where it was less than twice as high the bulk of the market was held by Britain' [28, p. 698], while the average American wage was twice as high as the British wage. Thus, out of 25 industries investigated, 20 conformed and 2 more would have if the measure of productivity were suitably adjusted. (*b*) Stern, with the average American wage 3·4 times the British wage in 1950, found that from 24 industries (comparable to MacDougall's 25), 20 conformed to the expected pattern. (*c*) For the larger sample of 39 industries, the exceptions were only 5. These three strikingly favourable results were obtained when the *average* American and British wages were taken. Both MacDougall and Stern, however, attempted to analyse the effect of taking individual wages for different products as well. (*d*) Owing to data limitations, MacDougall could attempt this only for 13 industries. His results showed a slight improvement: cigarettes became an exception, whereas pig-iron, glass containers and hosiery held the line. (*e*) Stern, using the same sample, found a slight deterioration, although the expected pattern still continued.

(2) The other approach to examining hypothesis (4) is through statistical estimation procedures. Both MacDougall and Stern have estimated regression

equations for logarithms of labour productivity ratios and export ratios, already listed earlier here. These are used to estimate the validity of hypothesis (4). (a) For instance, MacDougall found that his regression line, fitted to the 1937 data plotted on a double logarithmic scale, passed through the horizontal dividing line of 2 (i.e. American output per worker twice the British) at a point considerably to the left of a vertical dividing line at unity, marking the point of equality in the two countries' exports. This implied that America tended to export only about *two-fifths* as much as Britain in 1937, when the American advantage in output per worker was exactly offset by the inferiority in advantage in average wage. (b) For the same sample of industries, Stern found in 1950 that America tended to export only about four-fifths as much as Britain when American output per worker and average wage-rates were 3·4 times higher. This clearly came closer to hypothesis (4). (c) For 39 industries, Stern's regression line passed almost exactly through the 3·4 point, appearing to verify hypothesis (4) totally. All these estimates are for data using *average* wage-rates. While this approach, on the whole and especially for 1950, appears to support hypothesis (4), it must be admitted that it represents an inadequate test from the viewpoint of hypothesis (4) itself: even though all observations conform to the postulated pattern, the estimated regression may register a deviation (from the point of intersection of the dividing lines); whereas the regression line may pass exactly through the point of intersection while the observed points deviate from the postulated pattern.

III. *Hypothesis (5)*. This hypothesis, relating unit labour cost ratios and export shares, has been tested directly only by Stern and, with a different formulation, by Balassa. (a) For *average* wage data, of course, the regression and correlation coefficients for the estimated regression equations in the labour productivity hypothesis (3) should hold again, because all that happens is that the productivity ratios get each multiplied by a scalar (equal to the wage ratio). The results derived earlier, therefore, hold. (b) Stern, however, has produced the regression equation

$$x = 0.01 - 1.40y, \; r = -0.43$$
$$(0.38)$$

(where y is the logarithm of unit costs ratio), which lends some, though not very strong, support to the hypothesis being tested. (c) Balassa approaches the problem in terms of the question whether the introduction of the wage ratios as an *additional* explanatory variable (in a multiple correlation analysis) improves the explanation of export shares. Balassa's regression equation is

$$x^* = -181.2 + 0.691y^* + 0.140z^*$$
$$(0.167) \qquad (0.102)$$

where x^* is the export ratio, y^* the productivity ratio and z^* the wage ratio. The multiple correlation coefficient is 0·81 (as against 0·80 in the simple correlation). The partial coefficients are 0·77 (for x^* and y^*) and 0·24 (for x^* and z^*); the latter is not significant at the 5% level. For logarithms, Balassa's regression equation is:

$$x = -5.164 + 1.457y + 1.250z$$
$$(0.328) \quad (0.566)$$

The multiple correlation coefficient is 0·88 (as against the simple coefficient of 0·86). The partials are 0·84 (x and y) and 0·11 (x and z); the latter is not significant at the 5% level. The explanation which comparative labour productivities

argued, this has little to do with the empirical verification of the Ricardian hypotheses (1) and (2). While this is true, the authors of these empirical exercises have turned up a great deal of data on export prices and on labour productivities and unit wage-costs. These data can be used to examine the proposition that relative prices can be approximated by comparative labour productivities and/or unit wage–cost ratios. This can only result in the verification (or refutation, as it turns out) of the prop on which the Ricardian hypotheses (1) and (2) are generally rested. A full-blooded test of these hypotheses, directly examining the ranking of (bilateral) exports and imports by comparative labour productivities and/or unit wage–cost ratios, is

TABLE 1 *Labour Productivity Ratios and Export Price Ratios (United States/United Kingdom) for 1937 and 1950*

Industry	1937		1950	
	Output per worker, US/UK	Price of exports, US/UK	Output per worker, US/UK	Price of exports, US/UK
1 Tin cans	5·25	0·68	—	—
2 Pig iron	3·60	0·84	4·10	1·33
3 Wireless sets	3·50	0·64	4·00	0·95
4 Motor cars	3·10	0·91	2·40	2·63
5 Glass containers	2·40	0·69	—	—
6 Paper	2·20	0·72	3·40	0·90
7 Beer	2·00	1·30	3·00	1·00
8 Linoleum and oil cloth	1·90	1·04	2·60	1·11
9 Coke	1·90	1·08	1·90	1·36
10 Hosiery	1·80	1·24	—	—
11 Cigarettes	1·70	1·08	2·50	1·08
12 Rayon weaving and making	1·50	1·19	—	—
13 Cotton spinning and weaving	1·50	1·03	—	—
14 Leather footwear	1·40	1·31	1·70	1·28
15 Woollen and worsted	1·35	1·42	1·80	1·44
16 Margarine	1·20	1·34	1·80	1·46
17 Cement	1·10	2·12	1·20	1·33
18 Electric lamps	5·40	0·51	3·60	0·92
19 Biscuits	3·10	1·01	2·40	1·24
20 Matches	3·10	0·86	—	—
21 Rubber tyres	2·70	1·12	2·40	1·42
22 Soap	2·70	1·24	2·50	1·10

Source: Stern [40, p. 278].

provide is not improved by adding wage ratios as an additional explanatory variable. (It follows, therefore, that wage-structure differences between ratios do not have any systematic relationship with price differences.)

impossible to carry out with this information and must await further research.

For the limited test outlined here, I have used two sets of data. For the MacDougall sample of 25 industries (reduced to 24 in Stern's calculations for 1950), the necessary data are available for 22 industries for 1937 and for 16 of these for 1950 (Table 1). There is a slightly larger and different sample of 25 industries, used by Stern for 1950 (Table 2). There are certainly many limitations to these data. The most serious ones, from the viewpoint of the current analysis, are three: (i) the f.o.b. price reflects gross value, whereas the labour

TABLE 2 *Labour Productivity Ratios, Export Price Ratios, Unit Labour Cost Ratios and Wage Ratios (United States/United Kingdom) for 1950*

	Export prices, US/UK	Output per worker, US/UK	Unit labour costs, US/UK	Wage-rates US/UK
1 Cement	1·33	1·16	2·33	2·70
2 Sugar factories and refineries	1·32	1·48	1·89	2·79
3 Tanneries	1·01	1·68	1·92	3·23
4 Footwear (except rubber)	1·28	1·71	1·68	2·88
5 Woollen and worsted	1·33	1·85	1·96	3·63
6 Metal-working machinery	2·64	2·21	1·79	3·96
7 Rayon, nylon and silk	1·15	2·26	1·51	3·42
8 Generators, motors and transformers	2·63	2·39	1·49	3·56
9 Tyres and tubes	1·23	2·41	1·50	3·62
10 Wirework	1·28	2·44	1·52	3·72
11 Soap, candles and glycerine	1·18	2·49	1·58	3·93
12 Rubber products (excluding tyres and footwear)	1·31	2·50	1·45	3·62
13 Tobacco manufactures	1·08	2·51	1·02	2·56
14 Linoleum and leather cloth	1·11	2·56	1·27	3·25
15 Bolts, nuts, rivets and screws	2·06	2·56	1·71	4·31
14 Breweries and manufacturing of malt	1·00	3·00	1·33	3·99
17 Pulp, paper and board	0·90	3·38	1·08	3·65
18 Electronic tubes	0·68	3·55	1·10	3·91
19 Electric-light bulbs	0·92	3·56	1·10	3·92
20 Paint and varnish	0·09	3·63	0·96	3·50
21 Basic industrial chemicals	0·95	3·72	0·91	3·38
22 Radio	0·95	4·00	0·85	3·39
23 Blast furnaces	1·33	4·08	0·72	2·96
24 Electrical household equipment	1·70	4·12	0·96	3·95
25 Containers, paper and card	1·12	4·28	0·96	4·09

Source: Stern [408]., p. 28

productivity refers to the final, value-adding industry; the results would surely be more in conformity with the spirit of the Ricardian approach if the *indirect* labour productivities were also computed; (ii) the f.o.b. prices also include transport and other costs which add to the ex-factory price, whereas the labour productivity figures are not adjusted for this when necessary; and (iii) in most exporting industries a differential is observable between the average domestic price and the average foreign price [3, p. 281], so that the approximation of labour productivity ratios to relative (export) prices may have to be adjusted analytically for this phenomenon. Notwithstanding these limitations, however, I have carried out the analysis in consonance with the tradition of economists to catalogue the difficulties and thereafter to ignore them. The results, as already hinted at, are seriously prejudicial to the usefulness of the Ricardian approach: though, it should be emphasized, the verdict cannot be final in the absence of better and fuller tests.[1]

The linear regressions of export price ratios on labour productivity ratios are almost entirely hopeless, whether we take logarithms or not. The six regressions, listed in Table 3, uniformly fail to be significant except for the unlogged, MacDougall sample for 1937. The failures clearly overwhelm the success in verification.

Testing the relationship between comparative unit labour-costs and export price ratios, we find the results to be equally disappointing.

TABLE 3 *Relationship between Labour Productivity Ratios and Export Price Ratios*

Data	Regression equation*	Coefficients	
1937 (Table 1)	$Y = 1 \cdot 72 \quad - 0 \cdot 211 X$ $(0 \cdot 2291) \quad (0 \cdot 0450)$	$r^2 =$	$0 \cdot 525$
		$r = -0 \cdot 724$	
1937 (Table 1)	$\log Y = 0 \cdot 252 \quad - 0 \cdot 525 \log X$ $(0 \cdot 1925) \quad (0 \cdot 432)$	$r^2 =$	$0 \cdot 0686$
		$r = -0 \cdot 262$	
1950 (Table 1)	$Y = 1 \cdot 58 \quad - 0 \cdot 169 \ X$ $(0 \cdot 32605) \quad (0 \cdot 1204)$	$r^2 =$	$0 \cdot 129$
		$r = -0 \cdot 359$	
1950 (Table 1)	$\log Y = 0 \cdot 264 \quad - 0 \cdot 611 \log X$ $(0 \cdot 3769) \quad (0 \cdot 5155)$	$r^2 =$	$0 \cdot 0912$
		$r = -0 \cdot 302$	
1950 (Table 2)	$Y = 1 \cdot 7044 \quad - 0 \cdot 1470 X$ $(0 \cdot 3291) \quad (0 \cdot 1095)$	$r^2 =$	$0 \cdot 0728$
		$r = -0 \cdot 2698$	
1950 (Table 2)	$\log Y = 0 \cdot 2056 \quad - 0 \cdot 2773 \log X$ $(0 \cdot 0816) \quad (0 \cdot 1831)$	$r^2 =$	$0 \cdot 0906$
		$r = -0 \cdot 301$	

* $Y =$ Export price ratio, and $X =$ Labour productivity ratio.

[1] I am indebted to B. S. Minhas for assistance with the statistical analysis in this paper. The responsibility for any errors, however, is entirely mine.

Table 4 lists the two linear regression equations for the 1950 data (Table 2). Both relationships are insignificant (though they register a negligible improvement over the regressions for export price-ratios and labour productivity ratios alone).

TABLE 4 *Relationship between Unit Labour Cost Ratios and Export Price Ratios*

Data	Regression Equations*	Coefficients
1950 (Table 2)	$Y = 0.7227 + 0.4141X$ $(0.33194)\quad(0.23021)$	$r^2 = 0.1233$ $r = 0.3512$
1950 (Table 2)	$\log Y = 0.03785 + 0.42113 \log X$ $(0.0335)\quad(0.1997)$	$r^2 = 0.162$ $r = 0.40248$

* Y = export price ratio, and X = unit labour cost ratio.

Handling the influence of relative inter-country wage-rates alternatively through the introduction of wage ratios as an additional explanatory variable in a multiple correlation analysis, further, we find that the results for the available data are again poor (Table 5). The correlations continue to be insignificant (though they register a slight improvement over the simple correlation, for the same data, between export price ratios and labour productivity ratios alone).

TABLE 5 *Multiple Regressions between Export Price Ratios, Labour Productivity Ratios and Wage Ratios*

Data	Multiple regression equation*	Coefficients	
1950 (Table 2)	$Y = 0.5572 - 0.2286\,X_1 + 0.3905\,X_2$ $(7.8)\quad(0.1140)\quad(0.2182)$	$r^2 =$ $r =$ Partial: $X_1 =$ $X_2 =$	0.191 0.437 -0.3931 0.3564
1950 (Table 2)	$\log Y = 0.1646 - 0.4304 \log X_1 + 0.8011 \log X_2$ $(0.0599)\quad(0.2015)\quad(0.5018)$	$r^2 =$ $r =$ Partial: $X_1 =$ $X_2 =$	0.1850 0.4301 -0.4143 0.3220

* Y = export price ratio; X_1 = labour productivity ratio, and
X_2 = wage-rate ratio.

These results, limited as they are, cast sufficient doubt on the usefulness of the Ricardian approach (as generally understood). Contrary, therefore, to the general impression (based on the Mac-Dougall, Balassa and Stern results), there is as yet no evidence in favour of the Ricardian hypotheses. This is perhaps not as unfortunate as it seems. For ultimately the practical utility of the Ricardian hypotheses is somewhat limited. Labour productivity, after all, is not a datum in the sense that production functions are. The reliance of the prediction on labour productivity unaccompanied by any explanation of why the labour productivity is what it is, and how therefore it may be expected to change, restricts the utility of the prediction. Moreover, even if we could forecast changes in labour productivity, we could not tell exclusively therefrom that the pattern of imports and exports would change in a specified manner; all we could say is that, if the pattern of exports and imports changes in any way, the new pattern will also be characterized by the postulated Ricardian ranking in terms of comparative labour productivities and/or unit wage ratios.[1]

The Heckscher–Ohlin Theory

An alternative approach to explaining the pattern of trade is attributed to the works of Heckscher [19] and Ohlin [34], but owes much to the work of Samuelson [38, 91]. Indeed, in its current form it has discarded so many of the variables which Ohlin explicitly listed as significant that it is almost certainly liable to be rejected by Ohlin as an adequate version of his original analysis!

This approach breaks away from the Ricardian model and works in terms of an analytical framework which is in striking contrast to its predecessor. As we saw, the Ricardian model assumes one factor, and therewith (through the supporting assumption of constant returns to scale) makes the factor supply irrelevant in determining the trade pattern;[2] on the other hand, as we shall soon see, the Heckscher–Ohlin model assumes two factors and makes international differences in factor endowments the crucial and sole factor determining comparative advantage.[3] Moreover, whereas the former attributes to

[1] I would not claim that *any* type of prediction concerning change in the pattern of trade is impossible. But even apparently simple predictions are not possible. For instance, if labour productivity increases in an export industry we *cannot* necessarily predict that the industry will continue to export its product (even if all other autonomous change in the trading countries is ruled out).

[2] This is, strictly speaking, not true in a model with more than two commodities. In this case demand must be brought in to 'break the chain' of ranked commodities into exports and imports. But demand itself will be a function of the level of income, which will depend, among other things, on the factor supply.

[3] Viner [44] has attempted to demonstrate that the factor endowment approach is to be found in classical writings. But his contention is not persuasive, based as it is on fragmentary remarks which do not add up to systematic analysis.

international differences in production functions the explanation of comparative advantage, the latter explicitly postulates the international identity of production functions.[1] The Heckscher–Ohlin theory is also different from the Ricardian analysis in having been presented *explicitly* as a contribution to the 'positive' theory, as an attempt at explaining the structure of foreign trade, rather than with a view to establishing the welfare propositions of trade theory.

The Heckscher–Ohlin theorem states that *a country's exports use intensively the country's abundant factor*. This is an eminently 'plausible-looking' proposition. One would expect that a country should be able to produce more cheaply those goods that are intensive in the use of a factor when that factor of production is (physically) abundant in the country relative to its trading partner. Of course one can think of some exceptions immediately. For instance, it is clear that this presumption rests on the similarity of production conditions between trading countries. There could obviously be a contradiction of the Heckscher–Ohlin proposition if *production functions* for individual industries were different between countries. Alternatively, the country may quite well have an offsetting preference for the *consumption* of these commodities – so that the pre-trade (relative) prices of commodities may turn out to be higher (rather than lower) abroad – thus refuting the Heckscher–Ohlin proposition. Some qualifications are less intuitively seen. One of the theoretically interesting qualifications[2] follows from the fact that although, technologically, the production function for an activity may be identical between countries, the operative segments of it may be intensive in the use of a different factor in each country. Where such 'reversals of factor-intensity' can

---

[1] It should be emphasized that these contrasts, which are based partly on the distinction between production functions and factors of production, raise the well-known question as to the proper definitions of these two concepts. It is interesting, in this connection, to recall that Ohlin appears to have taken it as apparent that production functions would be the same everywhere, because the same causes everywhere (and at any time) produce the same effects. However, as Haberler [4, p. 19] has pointed out, 'if the concept of the production function is to be a useful tool of analysis, it cannot be identified with, or derived from, such unverifiable metaphysical propositions as "the constancy of the laws of nature". By hypothesizing every conceivable circumstance which may affect output as a separate factor, the production function can, no doubt, be endowed with constancy, invariability, homogeneity, and what not, but at the price of emptying the theory of all empirical content and reducing it to a useless tautological system.'

[2] It is also empirically possible, as Minhas' [33] study shows.

occur the effect can be similar to that of differences in production functions and the Heckscher–Ohlin proposition need not hold.

Theorists have established a set of conditions which ensure the 'logical truth' of the Heckscher–Ohlin theorem. These conditions differ, depending on the definition of 'factor abundance'. It is possible to choose between two definitions: the physical and the price definitions. Under the former, country I is abundant in factor x and country II in factor y when $(X/Y)^I > (X/Y)^{II}$, where X and Y refer to the quantities of factors x and y respectively and the superscripts to the countries.[1] Under the latter, the countries are similarly described when $(Rx/Ry)^I < (Rx/Ry)^{II}$ prior to trade where Rx and Ry refer to the rentals on factors x and y respectively.

When the physical definition is used the set of sufficient conditions for the logical truth of the Heckscher–Ohlin proposition is: (1) international identity of production functions; (2) non-reversibility of factor-intensities, such that a given commodity is factor x-intensive in relation to another at *all* relevant factor price-ratios; (3) constant returns to scale and diminishing returns (along isoquants) in each production function; and (4) identity of the consumption pattern between countries at each relevant commodity price ratio.[2] Samuelson [38, 39] has established that, under perfect competition and profit maximization in perfect markets, condition (3) will suffice to generate a strictly convex production possibility curve, characterized by a unique relationship between factor and commodity price ratios (except at positions of complete specialization in production). Using

[1] The physical definition raises serious conceptual difficulties when applied to the factor 'capital'. As is obvious, it is impossible to collapse different varieties of capital equipment into a single index of 'capital' in the same way as we reduce labour to man-hours. Of course, even with labour, the element of 'human capital' raises equally knotty issues.

[2] Identity of tastes, i.e. the aggregate preference map, is not adequate, since two countries may be at different levels of income and hence at different positions on their preference maps. Unless, therefore, the maps have homothetic isoquants the result can be different consumption patterns at identical price ratios. For a disaggregated economy, with many individuals, the conditions which give rise to such aggregate identity of tastes are quite restrictive [66, 67]. It is also necessary, of course, that transport costs for individual commodities are not such as would shatter this chain of comparative advantage when the c.i.f. prices are considered (as they have to be from the viewpoint of the determination of the trade pattern). The trade theorists generally disregard transport costs; the omission of 'distance' as a factor in most trade models represents a serious deficiency which vitiates the utility of many conclusions.

these propositions, it is possible to demonstrate in a two-commodity system that where two countries, with identical production functions for each activity (condition 1) and non-reversible factor intensities (condition 2) have different capital:labour ratios in the aggregate, the capital-abundant country will have a higher ratio of capital-intensive:labour-intensive outputs at *each* commodity price ratio. When condition (4) is added to this result it follows that the pre-trade commodity price ratios will be such that the capital-intensive commodity will be cheaper in the capital-abundant country. Hence the Heckscher–Ohlin theorem will be logically true. This result is valid for a multi-commodity model as well:[1] as Jones [20] has demonstrated, commodities can still be ranked, from technological and factor-supply data, in terms of factor ratios, and are thereby uniquely ranked also in terms of comparative advantage, with demand being introduced (as in the Ricardian system) to 'break the chain' into exports and imports.

(ii)   When the price definition of factor abundance is chosen we can dispense with the condition of identity of consumption patterns. This is because, when the other assumptions are made, a country which is capital-abundant will, by virtue of the unique Samuelsonian relationship between commodity and factor price ratios, necessarily have cheaper capital-intensive output. The use of the price definition, while it has this advantage over the physical definition, correspondingly leaves less scope for 'explanation'.[2]

Where the theory is deficient is in its not having been extended to a multi-country, multi-commodity framework. The prediction holds when there are many commodities and two countries. However, when there are many countries and commodities it is not clear, in the absence of theoretical analysis, what conditions will suffice to make the Heckscher–Ohlin hypothesis true – in any of the several alternative versions that are possible in a multi-country framework: (1) the comparison of factor endowments may be between country I and the sum of *all* the other countries of the world; or (2) it may be between country I and the *sum* of *all* the countries directly in trade with it; or

---

[1] The definitions of 'factor abundance' and 'factor-intensity' in a multi-factor model, however, are not so intuitive; but one can always adopt a convention [35, 53]. The results, however, are both more restrictive and less intuitive.

[2] Lancaster has proposed inadvertently a third definition which states that a country is abundant in that factor which is used intensively in the exportable industry [14]. From the viewpoint of the Heckscher-Ohlin theory, this is totally tautologous and leaves *no* scope for 'explanation'.

(3) between country I and the sum of *all* the countries directly or indirectly in trade with it; or (4) between country I and *each* of the countries in direct trade with it, so that the Heckscher–Ohlin hypotheses would hold for *each* pair of countries (*bilaterally*). There is little in the traditional analysis of the Heckscher–Ohlin hypotheses which affords a reliable clue to a meaningful choice among these different ways in which a Heckscher–Ohlin hypothesis can be interpreted in a multi-country framework. Nor need we expect the conditions under which each of these hypotheses will be logically true to be identical either with each other *or* with those that have been spelled out for the restrictive traditional frameworks.[1] This amounts to a deficiency in the literature (especially from the viewpoint of empirical testing, since the real world unfortunately constitutes a multi-country, multi-commodity international economy).

Empirical testing of the Heckscher–Ohlin hypotheses has indeed been attempted in the literature, starting with Leontief's pioneer attempt at ascertaining the factor-intensities of the average exports and competitive imports in the United States [25]. It is typical of his and other contributions that, while factor-intensities are carefully ascertained, the factor-abundance of the country in question is usually left uninvestigated, except tangentially and vaguely. The result has been a failure to face up to the question raised by multi-country, multi-commodity analysis: how is factor-abundance to be interpreted? By *implication*, Leontief [25, pp. 386, 399] seems to favour the

---

[1] For instance, it is clear that if country I is K-abundant in relation to country II and L-abundant in relation to country III, and the Heckscher–Ohlin hypothesis holds for each pair of countries (say, I and II, II and III), then it is *impossible* that the export and import commodities of country I can be ranked in terms of K : L ratios such that all exports are K-intensive in relation to all imports. The export and import commodities inevitably criss-cross, fouling up the strictly ordered chain on which the traditional Heckscher–Ohlin hypothesis and proof depend. However, if this chain cannot criss-cross under the usual assumptions, as Jones has demonstrated, we have a contradiction *in terms of the traditional model* and apparently the pattern of international specialization in production and in trade will necessarily have to turn out such that the bilateral formulation of the Heckscher–Ohlin hypothesis holds in a multi-country world. Of course, what I have argued here is not intended to be a proof, in the strict sense, of an extension of the Heckscher–Ohlin hypothesis to the bilateral, multi-country formulation within the fold of traditional postulates concerning technology, etc. The point I am making is really that the analysis of the Heckscher–Ohlin variety of hypotheses, in any or all of their possible versions in a multi-country framework, is not yet available and represents a serious lacuna in the literature.

bilateral interpretation: 'A comprehensive, two-sided explanation of our economic relationships with the rest-of-the-world will not, of course, be possible before the internal economic structure of at least one of the most important of our trading partners has been studied as fully as that of our own'. Recent studies by Bharadwaj [16] for India, Tatemoto and Ichimura [42] for Japan and Wahl [45] for Canada have also implicitly adopted the bilateral interpretation by considering, in addition to the factor intensities of the average *aggregate* exports and competitive imports (which necessitates viewing the country's factor-abundance in a non-bilateral way), the factor-intensities of the average exports to and competitive imports from *specific* trading countries or regions.[1]

While Leontief [25], and nearly all of his many followers, have left this crucial aspect unsatisfactory, Leontief's attempted test has been of significance – for the perverse reason that it turned up the startling result that the United States exports are labour-intensive and its competitive imports capital-intensive.[2] Since the United States may be conceded to be capital abundant by any definition, this result did seem to contradict the Heckscher–Ohlin hypothesis – provided the statistical information and procedure could be accepted. There *were* objections on statistical grounds. For instance, the agricultural capital–output ratio was considered unreliable [18], but recomputation under different assumptions did not reverse the findings. Balogh [12] voiced compelling doubts concerning the implications of aggregation in the input–output matrix (used to compute indirect capital–labour ratios). Thus, the labour-intensity of the American export industries might be spurious and attributable to the aggregation of capital-intensive exportable products with 'similar', non-export, labour-intensive activities. No evidence was produced to support this objection [1]: yet, it leaves a degree of doubt.

While Leontief's exercise spurred the majority of the theorists on to a re-examination of the sufficient conditions for the Heckscher–Ohlin hypothesis [20, 36, 37], the plausibility of the Heckscher–Ohlin

[1] In each of these instances, however, there is no discussion either of the alternative ways in which the Heckscher–Ohlin hypothesis can be interpreted or of the theoretical implication of the specific (bilateral) form of the hypothesis that is chosen or suggested.

[2] The tests have uniformly used the two factors, capital and labour. This choice, as also the definition of capital, is necessarily arbitrary. This arbitrariness is inevitable, and its justification lies in the argument that the theory being tested represents an abstraction.

propositions is so powerful that some ingenuity was addressed to the task of rescuing it from the refutation that had emerged from Leontief's exercises (Leontief himself being one of this small group of analysts).[1] This task is not entirely hopeless, since, although Leontief's results may be accepted, it is possible for the economist, *not* to change the form of the hypothesis, but to retain this form while redefining the concepts used. This is a perfectly valid, scientific procedure: the hypothesis, with redefined concepts, can once again be subjected to empirical verification [1]. This is precisely what may be done with the Heckscher–Ohlin hypothesis, in the expectation that Leontief's United States results may be reversed.

There are many ways in which this can be done. For instance, one could argue that the factor-abundance comparison should refer to the quantities of factors employed in the traded-goods sector, since the original formulation of the Heckscher–Ohlin theorem is logically deduced in a framework assuming no non-traded goods [1]. Or it could be argued that, since the traded-goods sector in some countries represents merely a geographical extension of a country's activities, these sectors being really foreign enclaves based on foreign capital

---

[1] Leontief also produced subsequently another paper [26] which reworked the calculations in the light of criticism addressed to his original work. For instance, instead of the inversion of only a 50-sector matrix earlier, he inverted a 192-sector matrix. Adjustments were carried out concerning agricultural data. None of this, however, reversed the findings concerning the refutation of the (unadjusted) Heckscher–Ohlin hypothesis. Leontief also went into some theoretical issues, such as the examination of a linear, input–output model for international trade. This has unfortunately been responsible for some confusion concerning the limitations of the empirical verification of the Heckscher–Ohlin hypothesis itself. For instance, Valavanis-Vail [3, p. 279] has objected to Leontief's exercise on the ground that 'input–output models (except with rare luck) are logically incompatible with international trade'. Whatever the analytical support for (any interpretation of) this statement, it is really irrelevant to the objective of Leontief's exercise and the methods used by him to achieve it. The input–output table is used by Leontief (along with the labour and capital coefficients matrices) merely to *compute* the indirect capital and labour requirements for unit exports and imports. The assumptions of input–output *analysis* are *not* necessary. Although Leontief loosely talks of 'reducing' exports by a million dollars and seeing what capital and labour are 'released' thereby, this is *not* what is actually required. All that is necessary, and this is really how Leontief's exercise should be construed, is to compute the total capital and labour requirements of the *current* (level and composition of) exports. And this can be done by a purely 'notional reduction' of (a representative bundle of) exports and the corresponding, computed notional 'release' of capital and labour.

and dominated by foreign economic considerations, it is sensible in such cases to merge these enclaves with the foreign country in question for obtaining the data for the Heckscher–Ohlin test [18].[1] The most interesting attempts, however, have centred around the fact that labour embodies (human) capital, and its implications for both factor-abundance and factor-intensity.

The easiest way of handling this has been to argue that the human capital element should be allowed for in the factor-intensity comparisons. For the United States, this seems to provide an important escape from the refutation of the Heckscher–Ohlin hypothesis. As many of the commentators have noted: (i) American export industries employ relatively more non-agricultural labour,[2] and agricultural labour is likely to be less educated and trained than non-agricultural labour [18]; and (ii) American export industries pay an average wage in excess of the national wage (suggesting that they intensively use skilled labour)[3] [21]. Thus, this computation of human capital (from an analysis of the labour inputs in the exporting and import-competing industries) added to the capital employed in measuring factor-intensities may quite possibly reverse the factor-intensity findings for the United States. However, we should also have to adjust correspondingly the measurement of factor endowments, adding the computed human capital to the measure of capital stock: a procedure which highlights the great conceptual difficulties that attend on both measuring capital meaningfully and comparing it between countries.

An alternative way in which the fact of labour efficiency differences between countries has been handled is by adjusting the labour supply

[1] It is not necessarily correct to use such an adaptation of the Heckscher-Ohlin hypothesis. For the latter, what is relevant is the *availability* of factors of production *regardless of their ownership*. It is only in the extreme case where the investment is accompanied by full, complementary migration of other necessary factors to a piece of foreign territory (which itself does not serve as a factor of production) that it would be proper, from the Heckscher–Ohlin viewpoint, to adopt this approach. Not otherwise.

[2] The breakdown of labour (for a million dollars of exports and import replacements) between agricultural and non-agricultural labour was given by Leontief [25] as follows:

	Exports	Import replacements
Agricultural labour, man years	22·436	40·394
Non-agricultural labour, man years	159·872	127·069

[3] An alternative explanation, of course, is that they are the 'dynamic' innovating industries, and hence pay higher wages.

itself by an efficiency factor.[1] Leontief [25, p. 26], in his original paper, argued that 'labour' should be defined in 'standard' units, after adjusting for varying degrees of efficiency. On this basis he asserted that the average American worker is three times as efficient as elsewhere and that 'spread thrice as thinly as the unadjusted figures suggest the American capital supply per 'equivalent worker' turns out to be comparatively smaller, rather than larger, than that of many other countries'.[2] Hence, the Heckscher–Ohlin theory could be rescued from an apparent refutation (on the implicit assumption that this efficiency factor concerning labour is not neutralized by a similar efficiency factor attributable to the other factor of production).

Leontief's procedure, however, is not valid, although his suggestion is valuable. He does not state how the efficiency factor of three was arrived at. Leontief's argument in support of the assumed efficiency factor of three is that if it were not so it would be impossible to 'explain the comparative surplus of labour which our figures unmistakably reveal' [25, p. 28]. This argument is unpersuasive because (as I have already argued elsewhere [1]) 'it already assumes that the Heckscher–Ohlin theorem provides a valid explanation of the American pattern of trade when, in fact, the question being asked is precisely whether it does'; and (2) 'it also assumes that only the hypothesis about three-fold efficiency of American labour can reconcile the results with the Heckscher–Ohlin type hypothesis when, in fact, there *are* other ways in which such reconciliation could be attempted'. The most interesting analysis, which has a bearing on this issue, is by Minhas [33]. As noted earlier, Arrow, Chenery, Solow and he continuously found that for individual industries in different countries the only significant difference between the estimated homohypallagic (CES) production functions consisted of an overall efficiency term, which meant that whereas the isoquants continued to remain more or less the same, the scale factor changed. This means, as Minhas concluded [33, p. 159], that Leontief's requirement that the efficiency factor can be attributed

---

[1] This method adjusts the measurement of the labour input, whereas the earlier method alters the measurement of the capital stock.

[2] In the original paper [25] Leontief argued for this threefold efficiency, but did not make any differential adjustment for the efficiency factor in export- and import-competing industries. This implicit assumption of an identical efficiency factor for labour in both these sectors was removed by Leontief in his later exercise [26] by an explicit weighting of labour in each sector by its average wage.

to one factor *alone* is unsupported by his specific investigations.[1]
While these different ways in which the definitions of capital and
labour have been adjusted, to explore the possibility of reconciling the
United States pattern of trade with the Heckscher–Ohlin hypothesis,
are of interest, perhaps the more significant innovations have emerged
from the work of those who proceeded to apply Leontief's methods to
the trade patterns of other countries. There have been four Leontief-
type studies so far: Bharadwaj [15, 16] on India, Stolper and Roskamp
[41] for East Germany, Tatemoto and Ichimura [42] for Japan and
Wahl [45] for Canada. These have now given us a larger range of
evidence with which to attempt an assessment of the Heckscher–Ohlin
hypothesis. For Japan, exports are capital-intensive and imports are
labour-intensive – on the surface again, a black mark against the
tested hypothesis. For East Germany exports are capital-intensive
and imports are labour-intensive – the authors find this consistent
with the stated hypothesis, since the East German trade is three-
quarters with the Communist block, where she is probably among the
most industrialized of these nations. For Canada, exports are capital-
intensive and imports are labour-intensive – presumably an un-
successful verification, as Canadian trade is primarily United States-
orientated.

Where many of these studies innovate is in departing from the
Leontief method of taking the *aggregate* exports and competitive imports. They begin to explore the possibility of defining the Heckscher–

---

[1] Diab [18] also has attempted to test Leontief's conjecture, using Colin Clark's
data. His results appear to sustain this conjecture. Diab's methods show that the
United States has, in terms of 'standard' labour, a lower capital : labour ratio
than Canada, Great Britain, Netherlands, France and Norway. The procedure
by which this conclusion is reached, however, is arbitrary. Diab assumes that:
(1) labour is the factor which has to be reduced to 'standard' units in each country;
and (2) the Cobb–Douglas production function, identical for all countries studied,
is known for national output, in terms of capital and 'standard' labour. With this
production function, national output and capital known, it is then easy to determine the single unknown, 'standard' labour, with the one equation [1]. Diab
postulates a hypothetical production function (with 'standard' labour), uses
observed values of output and capital to deduce his 'standard' labour and then
attributes the discrepancy between the quantities of 'standard' and observed
labour to an 'efficiency' factor. This is surely an arbitrary procedure, which can
yield no acceptable results. For instance, one could well use the procedure,
assuming that capital, and not labour, is the factor which should be reduced to
'standard' units. Out of curiosity, I did this: the United States turned out to be
overwhelmingly 'capital'-intensive [1]!

Ohlin hypothesis in the *bilateral* form[1] (*i.e., for each pair of countries*) rather than in terms of one country and (presumably) the rest of the world. Thus, Bharadwaj [16] goes on from the aggregative analysis to work out the factor-intensities of Indian trade with the United States, Wahl works with Canada–United States and Canada–United Kingdom trade, and the Tatemoto–Ichimura result is interpreted in terms of the geographic composition of Japanese trade. In the Indian case, when the Indo–United States trade is isolated for analysis, the factor-intensities are the *reverse* of those that obtain for total Indian trade. The Indian exports to the United States turn out to be capital-intensive and imports from the United States are labour-intensive, thus appearing to refute the Heckscher–Ohlin hypothesis. For Canada, the results again are identical with the aggregate results and refutation continues. For Japan, however, the result of disaggregation is beneficial. In the Japanese case the aggregative result is supposed to be attributable to the fact that 75% of Japanese exports go to the (presumably labour-abundant) underdeveloped areas and only 25% to the (presumably capital-abundant) advanced countries. It is widely accepted in Japan that the Japanese economy is somewhere in the middle of the advanced and underdeveloped countries and the 'disaggregated' explanation is only a logical consequence. Tatemoto and Ichimura have computed the capital–labour ratios of Japanese exports to the United States and imports from the United States and find the latter higher than the former. Unlike the Indian case, therefore, a disaggregated approach *supports* the Heckscher–Ohlin approach in the Japanese study. The Japanese result thus demonstrates the possibility of profitably adapting the Heckscher–Ohlin hypothesis so as to state it in terms of *each pair of trading countries* (instead of in aggregate terms).

When these diverse bits of evidence and arguments are added up there is little doubt that an attitude of agnosticism is certain to be left in the reader's mind concerning Leontief's original refutation of the Heckscher–Ohlin theorem.[2] Meanwhile, the empirical verification is

[1] This bilateral formulation, it may be recalled, is only one of several formulations of the Heckscher–Ohlin hypothesis that we can have in a multi-country world.

[2] It is of interest to note that the Ricardian hypothesis (in terms of comparative labour productivities) may be verified and yet the result may equally be in conformity with the Heckscher–Ohlin hypothesis. Thus, for instance, a capital-abundant country I may be exporting capital-intensive commodity x to country II in exchange for commodity y. Then, if transport costs are introduced and the

progressing apace and evidence is accumulating on either side. The most interesting recent result has been Minhas' [33] demonstration that, far from being a theoretical curiosum (as Samuelson [38, 39] believed it to be), the reversal of factor-intensity is an empirical possibility of some significance. Since his data relate to the United States and Japan, the results appear to furnish additional ammunition to those who are sceptical of the utility of the Heckscher–Ohlin approach.[1]

The Kravis Theory

While the Ricardian and the Heckscher–Ohlin approaches have dominated the thinking on comparative advantage for many decades, recently some original theories have appeared in the field. Kravis [22], for instance, in the early period of gloom after Leontief's paper [25], argued that the commodity composition of trade is determined primarily by 'availability'. Trade tends to be confined to goods which

---

necessary technological assumptions which underlie the Heckscher–Ohlin theorem are made, the capital–labour ratio in x will be higher in country I than in country II and therefore the output–labour ratio in x will also be higher in I than II. Similarly, the output–labour ratio in y will be lower in I than in II. Therefore, *both* the Ricardian and the Heckscher–Ohlin hypotheses will be valid in this case. A similar example can also be produced for the more sophisticated Ricardian hypothesis stated in the text (involving comparisons of production functions). For instance, assume that the production function is identical for commodity y in both countries and that country I has 'neutral' advantage in producing commodity x such that the same capital and labour produce λ times more of x in I than in II. Assume x to be capital-intensive at all factor price ratios and I to be capital abundant. Then if the Heckscher–Ohlin thesis holds, so does the sophisticated Ricardian hypothesis automatically. Further, it follows that in free trade equilibrium (with zero transport costs), the capital–labour ratios in I will be lower in each activity than in II. Since constant returns to scale are being assumed, the labour productivity in both x and y would be lower in I than in II, except that the efficiency factor λ in the production of x in I would offset the fall in labour productivity due to lower capital–labour ratio. Assuming that this offset leaves the labour productivity in x greater in I than in II, the comparative labour productivity ratio in x will be greater for I than in y. Hence the Ricardian hypothesis will be sustained in its comparative labour productivity form as well.

[1] Minhas' demonstration of the possibility of factor-intensity reversals is quite serious, since it contradicts one of the premises on which the Heckscher–Ohlin hypothesis is traditionally based. In fact, the damage it does is fatal because, if factor-intensities *are* reversed between two trading countries, for exports and imports, it is logically *impossible* for *both* countries' trading patterns to pass the Heckscher–Ohlin test (though, of course, one will).

are 'not available at home' [22, p. 143]. By this phrase, Kravis intended to describe goods which are 'unavailable in the absolute sense (for example, diamonds)', and goods where 'an increase in output can be achieved only at much higher cost (that is, the domestic supply is inelastic)'. The reason for trade to be restricted to items characterized by such unavailability is that tariff policies, transport costs, cartelization, etc., tend to eliminate from trade those commodities which are available through domestic production, although at 'slightly' higher cost. The reasons cited for unavailability, as defined, are: lack of natural resources (relative to demand) or technical change and product differentiation which confer temporary monopoly of production on the innovating country (until the trading partners have learnt to imitate).

The theory appears attractive. However, it is noticeable that Kravis does not get down to stating precise, testable hypotheses. While he fails to do so, one can still derive several from his suggestive ideas. (1) For instance, one could seize on his idea of the 'inelasticity' of domestic supply and state the refutable proposition that *a country's imports will be characterized by domestic inelasticity of supply.* (Such an hypothesis would, naturally have to be backed by an explicit definition of 'inelasticity'.) (2) Another hypothesis, based also on the concept of inelasticity, might be that *a country's imports will be characterized by the excess of foreign over domestic elasticity of supply.*[1] Both these hypotheses, and related formulations, however, neither get down below the surface *qua* explanations nor are capable of being tested without elaborate econometric estimates of supply elasticities. (3) A more interesting way of formulating Kravis-type hypotheses seems to be to go *directly* to the scarcities of natural resources and temporary scarcities through innovations. Kravis himself indicates that *a country's export-industries will show rates of technical progress higher than the national average.* (4) This could be turned into an alternative, plausible proposition, with traces of Ricardo [1]: *a country's export-industries will show higher rates of technical progress than the same industries in the trading partners.* (5) Perhaps the most promising approach would be to utilize Kravis' distinction between 'unavailability' due to scarce natural resources and due to innovation. Thus, to the preceding two propositions, one could add a further clause: *or, will be intensive in the use, or consist, of raw materials which*

[1]Cf. Kravis' remark: 'it is the elasticity of supply abroad and its inelasticity at home that gives rise to [the United States imports].' [22, p. 150].

are relatively abundant in the country.[1] Such Kravis-type hypotheses have, however, neither been clearly formulated and analysed so far nor tested systematically with empirical evidence.

The Linder Theory

Another novel and ingenious approach is attributable to a recent Swedish author, Linder [27]. He begins by attempting to explain the pattern of trade, but ends up by doing something quite different – and it is precisely in this way that Linder makes a contribution of some significance.

Linder starts with the distinction between trade in primary products and in manufactures. The former is natural resource-intensive, and Linder accepts the thesis that such trade must be explained in terms of 'relative natural-resources endowments' [27, p. 92].[2] Trade in manufactures, however, cannot be so explained. Linder explicitly rejects the analogy.

He despairs, however, of being able to predict the *precise* composition of trade in manufactures. This is a function of many factors: 'technological superiority, managerial skills and economies of scale are perhaps the most important . . .' [27, p. 103]. The results cannot be congealed into a precise, predictable pattern.[3] Economists, when confronted with questions that they could not answer, have usually changed the question. Linder likewise virtually gives up the traditional inquiry and argues that, while the precise composition of trade in manufactures cannot be forecast, what one *can* have instead is a theory

[1] This, of course, begs the question of defining relative abundance. Some working definition would have to be devised. In practice, of course, it is relatively easy to identify the industries whose advantage consists in access to raw materials; although, once again, the distinction between abundance in terms of price and physical units is relevant. For an interesting attempt at estimating the 'resource-intensiveness' of activities entering trade in the United States see Vanek [43].

[2] Linder construes this as consistent with the Heckscher–Ohlin theory because he accepts the original Ohlin statement of his theory, which mentioned a whole host of factors of production, *inclusive* of natural resources. Of course, to the extent that other factors of production are also brought in, the theory both becomes less impressive as an abstraction and is less successfully tractable analytically because of the consequences, for the definitions of 'factor-abundance' and 'factor-intensity', of more than two factors of production.

[3] Linder, while he admits this, does not quite reconcile himself to the conclusion. He feels that *something* can still be said about the trade pattern. But his observations (e.g. that Sweden will export paper because of forest resources or that Eskimos are unlikely to export refrigerators) do *not* constitute a theory.

concerning the *volume* of trade (as proportion of national income) between different pairs of trading nations.

Linder's central thesis is that the *volume of trade in manufactures of a country with each of her trading partners, when taken as a proportion of the corresponding national incomes of these countries, will be higher, the greater the similarity in the demand patterns of the pair of trading countries.* The 'similarity of demand patterns' would be associated with the similarity of incomes *per capita* – although income distribution and similarity of taste patterns are additional variables. However, tastes are internationally not very dissimilar according to recent evidence [27, p. 95]. Hence, provided income distribution is ignored, the last clause in the thesis can be rewritten to state: '*the closer the pair of trading countries in their incomes* per capita'.

Although Linder has not rigorously formulated his analytical framework, the chain of reasoning which leads to this hypothesis is available. (1) The pre-condition for a non-primary commodity to emerge as an export is the presence of 'home demand'. This is attributed to several reasons: foreign trade is only an extension of domestic trade; innovation centres on existing industries and gives them export possibility; etc.[1] (2) The existence of industry catering for internal demand implies that the internal demand pattern will determine the range of commodities that constitute potential exports. (Linder tries here to introduce the concept of 'representative demand' – to narrow down the range of potential exports. The intention is to exclude those commodities for which the internal production is presumably not 'large enough'. But Linder really leaves this idea hanging in the air, without chiselling it down into clarity and precision.) (3) Where the overlap in the commodity-composition of the potential-export range of any pair of trading countries is *greater*, the possibility of a *larger* volume of trade will obtain. (4) The potential volume of trade will be larger, the larger the income-level of either trading country [27, p. 111]. (5) Where the potential volume of trade is larger, the actual volume of trade will also be larger (though tariffs, transport costs, political connections which prompt discriminatory trade promotion, etc., may 'distort' the relationship). (6) A similar set of arguments applies to imports. Linder qualifies only to the extent of stating that

[1] One might add: the foreign market is risky (through QRs and the possibility of entry which cannot be 'controlled' with tariffs as in the domestic market) and the home market is not, so that producers generally do not wish to rely on the foreign market alone.

his 'representative demand' concept is no longer necessary: this hardly matters, however, in view of its imprecision. (7) Hence the Linder thesis.

Many questions inevitably come to one's mind. Aside from, and related to, the looseness of concepts such as 'representative demand', there is lack of precision concerning the concept of the potential-export range. Is it to be defined entirely in terms of the number of commodities with domestic production, or is one to assign weights to commodities in terms of their relative size in terms of some relevant index? What are the conditions under which the size of the trading countries can be expected to affect the volume of trade? And so on.[1] But, despite these limitations (which inevitably attend on pioneering analyses), Linder's work remains significant.

Our survey thus demonstrates that the theory of comparative advantage has been greatly advanced recently. New theories have emerged. And it has been the vehicle of the significant, recent trends towards empirical verification. This trend has synchronized with a more general investigation of the empirical validity of traditional theses about the structure of the international economy: among the prominent contributions being Michaely's [31] study of concentration in world trade and Coppock's [17] analysis of the incidence of economic instability among the trading nations.

Meanwhile, analytical theory of the 'traditionalist' persuasion, concerned with the statement of 'logically true' theorems, has proliferated at a great pace. To this, we must now turn.

2. THEOREMS IN STATICS: FACTOR PRICE EQUALIZATION[2]

The problem which has engaged the attention of many of the most distinguished trade theorists concerns the relationship between factor prices in different countries, under free trade in goods but factor

---

[1] Linder's brief attempt at empirical verification is also not fully satisfactory. The trade figures relate to aggregate imports, instead of imports of manufacture goods. The relationship investigated is with respect to *per capital* income, with no attempt at examining whether the explanation improves with additional variables like regional or fractile equations. Linder's hypothesis, while brilliantly suggestive, awaits both rigorous analytical formulation and empirical verification.

[2] I have had the invaluable opportunity of corresponding with Professor P. A. Samuelson in writing this Section. Although I have drawn freely on this correspondence, especially for the general case of many goods and many factors, the responsibility for any errors is entirely mine.

immobility between countries.[1] The question dates back to the writings of Heckscher [19] and Ohlin [34]. They considered trade to be an equalizing factor with respect to factor returns in trading countries, though they cited several reasons why *full* factor price equalization would not occur in practice. In 1948 Samuelson [38] initiated the rigorous investigation of the conditions under which complete factor price equalization would follow.

Samuelson [38, 39] stated everything that has ever been said subsequently as far as the restrictive case of two goods and two factors is concerned and, subject to certain sufficient assumptions to be noted shortly, managed to prove factor-price equalization by establishing a *unique* relationship between (relative) factor and commodity prices. In 1953 Samuelson [53], preceded by an investigation of Meade [50] into the two-factor, three-product case, offered the first serious analysis of the general case of many goods (n) and many factors (r), thereby extending the analysis to all the $n \geqslant 2 \leqslant r$ cases. In the process it turned out that the more general analysis was limited by the non-existence of the required mathematics, Samuelson having to content himself with the formulation of what were clearly overly-strong sufficiency conditions for uniqueness in the large (for $n = r > 2$). Subsequent to Samuelson's 1953 analysis, progress has been registered in this area in the following respects: (1) Kuhn [47] has added an alternative sufficiency condition for uniqueness when $n = r \geqslant 2$;[2] (2) McKenzie [49] has provided a basic theorem which seems to overlap with Samuelson's 1953 sufficiency theorem, without either

---

[1] I have referred only tangentially in Section 7 to one other problem, on which there is some, though scant, literature. This is the question of the pattern of international specialization in *production* (as distinct from *trade*). The papers of McKenzie [78] and Jones [69] discuss this problem most elegantly in a Ricardo–Graham model with one primary factor of production and many countries. While I am on the subject of omissions, I should also note that I have not dealt at any length with the question of the stability of trade equilibrium, although I might have included it in Section 4. The interested reader will find useful and adequate discussion of the problem in the papers of Mundell [11] and myself and Johnson [2, Section 4] and in the volumes by Meade [9] and Vanek [93].

[2] Pearce [51], in an excellent paper which brings out the essence of the problem in an extremely simple fashion, has attempted to provide alternative sufficiency conditions. But apparently Professor McKenzie has produced an example which contradicts Pearce's conjecture and the mathematical results of Nikaido and Gale also have had a similar effect. Mention may also be made of Reiter's [52] contribution which demonstrates the intuitive, inverse theorem that identical production functions are implied by 'universally observed factor price equalization'.

implying or being implied by it; (3) Nikaido and Gale are reported to have discovered a basic flaw in Samuelson's mathematical proof of the sufficiency condition for the uniqueness of equilibrium in the large; and (4) Samuelson [54] has extended the analysis to an investigation of the conditions under which free trade would equalize not merely rentals but also interest rates between countries.

In contrast to the difficulties of the general case, the case where $n = r = 2$ is strikingly simple and, since Samuelson's pioneering analysis, has been extensively surveyed [5, Chapter I; 3, Chapter III]. Samuelson used the following assumptions, which proved to be sufficient for the purpose: (1) linear, homogeneous production functions in each good; (2) diminishing returns along isoquants for each good; (3) non-reversible and different factor-intensities of the two goods at all (relevant) factor prices; (4) identity of production functions for each good between countries; (5) perfect competition and valuation of factors according to marginal value productivity; (6) incomplete specialization in production in each country; and (7) absence of transport costs. The last assumption ensures commodity price equalization, under free trade, between countries. The first five assumptions ensure a unique relationship between commodity and factor prices, under incomplete specialization in production, which obtains identically between countries. With assumption (6), ruling out complete specialization, therefore, commodity price equalization necessarily entails factor price equalization.[1]

When the general case, $n \geqslant 2 \leqslant r$, is considered the analysis is the simplest for the case $n = r > 2$. The kernel of the argument can be summarized easily.[2] If x_{ij} is the quantity of the ith factor used in the production of the jth good, ϕ_j the output of the jth good and q_j its selling price, constant returns to scale ensure that

$$\sum_{i=1}^{n} p_i x_{ij} = q_j \phi_i \quad (j = 1, 2, \ldots n)$$

The quantities x_{ij} of factors used are determined by factor prices p_i and commodity prices q_j so that the n equations can be thought of as

[1] Of all these assumptions, the postulate concerning the non-reversal of factor-intensities has aroused the greatest analytical and econometric interest. The principal analyses in this direction were noted earlier, in Section 7, when discussing the Heckscher–Ohlin theorem.

[2] Samuelson's [53] Appendix contains a lucid account of the argument concerning uniqueness. Pearce's [51] paper contains an easily comprehensible account, from which I have borrowed.

equations in $2n$ variables, p_i and q_j. For uniqueness, therefore, it is necessary that there be only one set of p_i corresponding to each set of q_j, and vice versa. It can then be shown that uniqueness follows if $|x_{ij}| \neq 0$, which constitutes a sufficient condition for factor-price equalization in the small. It should be noted that, in the $n = r = 2$ case, $|x_{ij}| \neq 0$ turns into the familiar factor-intensity-difference condition, and uniqueness can be established *both* in the small and in the large because every element of the determinant is essentially one-signed. For the $n = r > 2$ case, however, Samuelson [53] argued that the condition that $|x_{ij}| \neq 0$ was not sufficient and an *additional* sufficiency condition would be that there should be *some* numbering of factors such that the leading principal minors of $|x_{ij}|$ of *every* order should be non-zero. It is this 'strong factor-intensity' condition which has recently been reportedly re-examined by Nikaido and Gale and found to be inadequate. However, a further strengthening of the factor-intensity postulate, such that *every* principal minor is non-zero (for *all* naturally ordered sets, as distinct from only one, corresponding to *all* numbering of factors), appears to constitute a sufficient condition for uniqueness in the large (as per Samuelson's correspondence).

The cases where $n \neq r$ are more difficult and the results of the analysis more devastating to the prospects for factor price equalization. Samuelson's results are most conveniently summarized as follows. Let the observed number of goods actually produced in both countries be $n^* < n$ and the factors actually used in production of these goods, and with positive prices, be r^*. Then, if $n^* \geqslant r^*$, and if for *some* subset of r^* goods of the n^* goods, the strong factor-intensity conditions of Samuelson–Nikaido–Gale (or alternatively Kuhn and McKenzie, not detailed here) are realized, then equalized goods prices imply equalized factor prices. If, however, $r^* > n^*$, factor price equalization is generally not implied (though it may obtain under certain strong and bizarre assumptions).[1]

Although the bulk of the analysis has been centred on the question of the equalization of the *rentals* earned by factors of production in a Walrasian general equilibrium system (with extension to intermediate products), the effect of free trade on *interest rate* equalization has recently been subjected to analysis by Samuelson [54] in a hitherto unpublished paper. The analysis supports the inference that rental

---

[1] Several illustrative examples could be produced. For instance, if $n = 1$ and $r = 2$, factor price equalization will generally be forbidden.

equalization (except in certain limiting situations) will be accompanied by interest rate equalization.[1] The possibility of introducing intermediate products without invalidating the factor price equalization theorem, while demonstrated by Samuelson generally in his 1953 analysis, has further been recently demonstrated by Vanek [55], whose $n = r = 2$ analysis dovetails neatly into Samuelson's more powerful work.[2] Laing [48] has, on the other hand, opened up the investigation of the effects of increasing returns to scale; his results serve to underline the implication of Samuelson's analysis that constant returns to scale cannot be given up without invalidating the logical truth of the factor price equalization theorem. Although the subject is, therefore, both of historic interest and still continues to attract fresh minds, one cannot help feeling that perhaps too great a proportion of the intellectual energy of trade theorists has been directed towards a question of limited utility. Of greater importance are the propositions in comparative statics which we must now discuss.

3. THEOREMS IN COMPARATIVE STATICS

The bulk of the analytical literature in pure theory is concerned with the implications of *differences* between two general equilibrium situations – or putting it differently, with the effects of specific *changes* in a given general equilibrium situation.

Two classes of questions can be distinguished. (1) On the one hand, the effects of a change in *trade policy* are considered while assuming as given, for the trading country, the general equilibrium 'data' (*i.e.*, tastes, the distribution of ownership or resources and transfer claims, factor supplies, production functions and general economic policy plus a specific trade policy from the outside world

[1] The inapplicability of the traditional models (used to examine factor prices equalization) for the purpose of analysing the effect of trade on interest rates was suggested originally, by a reading of Harrod's [46] paper, to V. K. Ramaswami and myself at Oxford in 1958. We noticed Harrod's unwarranted transition from rental to interest-rate equalization, while operating within the framework of Samuelson's 1948 and 1953 models. I wrote subsequently to Samuelson concerning this question, and he worked out the required analysis. Ramaswami also wrote independently a paper which is yet unpublished.

[2] Samuelson has drawn my attention to the fact that Vanek [55] has managed to prove the following intuitive theorem: that (where $n = r = 2$ and both goods also serve as intermediates) if the *direct* factor-intensities are in one direction, then the *total* factor-intensities (including indirect factor requirements as well) will always be in the same direction.

such that the precise offers of trade at varying terms of trade which the country has open to it are known and given): for instance, the effect of a change in a country's tariff rate on its terms of trade may be analysed. (2) On the other hand, the effects of a change in these 'data' may be considered, while assuming the trade policy as given: for instance, the effect of capital accumulation on the terms of trade may be investigated.

Naturally it is not true, *strictly speaking*, that trade theorists have always considered the given 'data' (trade policy), in the context of which the stipulated change in trade policy (data) takes place, as independent of the change itself. Thus, for instance, Myint [83] has argued that a change in trade policy from no trade to some trade will change the country's taste pattern itself – though no formal analysis is founded on this observation. An interesting illustration of the change in trade policy when the 'data' shift is furnished by Kindleberger's [73] brilliant study of the trade policy reaction of different European governments to the influx of cheap American corn in the 1870s. The only other, and the most formal, example of such interaction is provided by the analysis of tariff retaliation. A change in trade policy prompts retaliation which alters the trade possibilities open to the country. A full, sequential analysis is usually presented, with the response mechanisms of each country specified, which properly belongs to the next section on dynamic analysis [5, Chapter II]. Aside from these instances, the last of which belongs elsewhere, while the others are not formalized into theorems, it does continue to be true that the interactions between changes in trade policy and in 'data' have not been the object of serious analysis in the comparative statics of pure theory.

The effects of the shifts in trade policy and in data have been studied generally with reference to certain variables which recur with varying frequency in the numerous analyses. The terms of trade, the internal commodity price-ratios, the factor price ratio, output levels, the composition of trade and the levels of individual exports and imports are among those that turn up almost regularly. Yet, even among them, frequently important extensions of theory have bypassed the analysis of the impact on some variables, leaving many gaps in the literature (which merely need patient and much tiresome work to be filled out).

The models in terms of which the effects of the stipulated changes on these variables are studied vary as well. And yet, it is true that, in the last three decades, an astonishing amount of synthesis has been effected and a large number of theorems worked out in terms of the model (already used in Section 7) which, while inspired by the work of Ohlin and Heckscher, is very much the creation of Samuelson, springing directly out of his early work on the factor price equalization theorem [38, 39] and, with Stolper, on the effect of protection on factor rewards [91].

This Heckscher–Ohlin–Samuelson (HOS) model is characterized by two countries and (within each country) two commodities, two factors of production, production functions characterized in each activity by constant returns to scale and diminishing returns along isoquants, perfect competition and full employment of the given supply of the factors of production.[1] The supply of each commodity, in this system, is exclusively a function of the terms of trade between the two commodities. On the other hand, the demand for each commodity is taken to be determined by both the terms of trade and the level of domestic expenditure. A detailed specification of an HOS type model for the international economy (but omitting the specifications concerning the number of factors) has been provided recently by Mundell [11], who has also furnished therewith an excellent summary of many of the principal results (excluding those that depend upon the HOS specification concerning the number of factors) in comparative statics of the pure theory of trade. Meade's [9] work on trade and welfare contains many formal statements and applications of the HOS model.[2] Recently the HOS model has been strikingly extended, with many of its 'restrictive' characteristics removed. Among the more significant of these extensions are: (1) the investigation of the *multiple country* (and multiple-commodity) case by Mundell [11, pp. 101–9] drawing upon Mosak's earlier work; (2) the analysis of demand explicitly in terms of the pattern of income distribution associated with an equilibrium situation, in contrast to the standard HOS practice of assigning to aggregate, community demand the same properties as to individual demand – an extension introduced independently by Meade [9] and Johnson [66, 67]; and (3) the relaxa-

---

[1] For certain limited purposes, the assumption of international identity of production functions for each activity is sometimes made.

[2] On the other hand, the *geometrical* applications of the HOS model are innumerable. Much ingenuity has also been expended on alternative geometrical depictions. I am afraid this runs into rapidly diminishing returns, and I have deliberately refrained from entering into a survey of these geometrical techniques.

tion of the assumption of fixed factor supply to include the classical case of factors *in elastic supply* with respect to their rentals by several writers: Walsh [95], Vanek [92], Kemp and Jones [72], and myself and Johnson [60].

The theorems derived with the HOS model (and its recent extensions) and others, can be surveyed under the two main heads:[1] (A) *shifts in data (other than trade policy)*; (B) *shifts in trade policy*. Under the former the analysis subdivides further into shifts in data internal and external to the trading country. Among the internal shifts are: (1) *changes in demand*; (2) *changes in factor supply*; (3) *technological change*; and (4) *changes in (non-trade) economic policy*. The external shift in data involves some shift in the foreign offers to trade and may be prompted by changes internal to foreign countries or by changes in trade policy abroad. Such external shifts are classified generally as (5) *changes in international demand*. Under shifts in trade policy, I shall consider mainly tariff policy, distinguishing between: (1) *non-discriminatory tariff change*, and (2) *discriminatory tariff change*. The literature on other forms of trade policy is either largely symmetrical with tariff analysis (as in respect of quotas and subsidies) or limited (as with state trading) so that it will be surveyed only tangentially in the course of the analysis of tariffs which dominate the analysis in the pure theory of commercial policy.

A. *Shifts in Data (other than Trade Policy)*

(i) *Changes in Demand*

Problems relating to the changes in demand in trade theory have to be carefully defined, since demand is frequently understood by trade theorists as 'international demand', which is different from demand *per se*. By international demand is meant the demand for imports (and supply of exports) at some given terms of trade.[2] This demand for imports represents the excess of domestic consumption over domestic production of *importables* corresponding to the defined terms of trade. A shift in international demand is therefore to be traced to a shift in domestic consumption and/or production (which, in turn,

---

[1] Since the literature using the HOS model is admirably synthesized, I shall focus largely on this, while noting the main respects in which other types of models, which have been employed, differ in assumptions and/or conclusions. A fuller survey is ruled out by limitations of space.

[2] The locus of these international demands is nothing but the Marshallian 'offer curve'. International demand is also Mill's 'reciprocal demand'.

may be autonomous or induced by policy). International demand therefore reflects, and is to be distinguished from, internal (overall) demand. Internal demand in turn reflects individual tastes and the level and distribution of purchasing power. Shifts in internal demand therefore must be distinguished again from changes in individual tastes and in the level and distribution of (earned and unearned) income.

The propositions of pure theory have very nearly sidestepped the question of the effects of changes in *internal* demand. There is no formal analysis associated with the effects of changes in a country's tastes. The changes in the internal distribution of income have been brought into the fold of economic analysis only in so far as they *result* from changes in trade policy rather than as autonomous changes whose effects are spelled out. The only striking contrast is provided by the analysis of the effects of changes in the *level* of expenditure (and its accompanying effects on demand). This is nothing but the celebrated '*transfer problem*' which concerns the analysis of the effects on the terms of trade of a transfer of expenditure from one country to another. As for changes in 'international' demand, trade theory is well endowed with controversies and literature concerning the effects on the terms of trade when the foreign reciprocal demand shifts while the country's own demand for the foreign product is unchanged. In the following summary I proceed to the transfer problem, leaving shifts in international demand (which relate to changes in the external data given to the country) to be treated in a later sub-section.

The effect of a transfer on the terms of trade has been of interest because a deterioration in these terms, from the viewpoint of the transferor country, would represent a 'secondary burden' supplementary to the principal burden implicit in the transfer itself. Ignoring transport costs and using the HOS model (without the assumptions with respect to the factors of production and competition), the answer is immediately obvious: the terms of trade will deteriorate or improve according as $m_a + m_b \lessgtr 1$, where m_a is the marginal propensity to spend on importables in the transferor country A and m_b in the transferee country B [11, 88, 89].[1] Since the propensity to spend on exportables, x_a and x_b, is here merely unity minus the propensity

[1] It need hardly be stressed that the full-blooded HOS model is not necessary for the present analysis. Only the stability conditions have to be assumed, to determine the direction of the terms of trade change purely in terms of the marginal propensities to spend on importables with respect to expenditure change.

to spend on importables, the criterion can be rewritten in any number of alternative forms such as $m_a \lessgtr x_b$. Where tariffs obtain, and it is assumed that the tariff proceeds are redistributed and spent by private consumers as part of their income, the proportion of the transfer eventually turning up as expenditure on imports will be naturally smaller than m_b, since there is a 'leakage' each time the revenue is earned from expenditure directed at imports. The criterion thus changes to whether the sum of the marginal propensities to spend on importables is greater or less than a value which is greater than unity [5, Chapter VII, p. 173]. Where transport costs are incurred, the formula must change again, except in the extreme case when the transport cost is incurred in the form of the exported good itself. Where the transport cost is incurred, at least, partially, in the form of the imported good, it follows that the entire import expenditure does *not* accrue to the foreigner and, therefore, the criterion would again have to be that the sum of the marginal propensities to spend on importables be greater or less than a value greater than unity [89; 5, p. 174].[1] Mundell [11, p. 107] has extended the analysis to the multi-country case where a transfer from country i to country j will rearrange demand throughout the international economy – for commodities exported from countries other than i and j. The resulting formula does not admit of any *a priori* generalization.[2]

[1] Economists have a propensity to answer impossible questions, and they have done so in the context of the transfer problem. There has been a great deal of discussion as to whether, in the *real world*, the classical proposition that the terms of trade would turn against the transferor country still remains a '*presumption*'. Fundamentally, this seems to be the wrong question to pose *until* one has *first* investigated the empirical applicability of the analytical model used. The failure to ask this key question seems to me to vitiate the utility of the entire discussion concerning what is 'plausible' as a prediction. I also wonder whether it is useful to discuss what is generally 'likely' when economic analysis and empirical work can enable us, subject to errors of interpretation and estimation, to make a precise prediction whenever necessary.

[2] Johnson [5, p. 176] anticipates this conclusion in a literary analysis. He also proceeds to introduce additional commodities differently – as non-traded goods in the two countries. However, the analysis is again not presented with full algebraic treatment and it is merely stated that: 'The introduction of non-traded goods does alter the criteria, since changes in demand for such goods must be classed either as changes in (virtual) demand for exportables or as changes in (virtual) demand for imports, according to whether they are more substitutable in production and consumption for one or the other. In both these cases, however, the direction of change of the commodity terms of trade is not uniquely determined by whether the transfer is undereffected or overffected at constant prices.'

While these criteria are devised in a full-employment framework Johnson [5, pp. 177–83], drawing upon earlier work by Meade, Harberger, Metzler, and others, has synthesized and extended the analysis for a Keynesian framework where output in each country is in perfectly elastic supply at a fixed domestic-currency price level, so that output, income and employment are determined by the aggregate demand for output. The resulting criterion involves, in the most general formulation, not merely the marginal propensities to spend on imports and exportables but also now the marginal propensities to save out of both pre-transfer and transfer income. As with the full-employment case, the criterion permits the transfer again to be under-effected or over-effected at constant terms of trade.[1]

(ii) *Changes in Factor Supply*

There are three ways in which changes in factor supply enter the analysis in pure theory: (i) The effect of an *autonomous* change in factor supply has been analysed. We know now, for instance, how capital accumulation or population expansion will affect the terms and volume of trade. (ii) The effect of a *shift* in a factor of production from one country to its trading partner, on the terms and volume of trade, has also been investigated. (iii) Finally, changes in factor supply *resulting* from changes in trade policy, when the supply of factors is elastic with respect to their rentals, have also been considered. These, however, are properly treated with the analysis of the effects of changes in trade policy.

(i) *Autonomous Changes in Factor Supply*. In surveying the literature on this problem, two central difficulties arise. Firstly, there is the difficulty of distinguishing models of growth into 'static' and 'dynamic'; only the former belong here. Sometimes a model is presented with factors increasing at a steady rate over time, and the resulting time-paths of several variables are worked out. And yet the analysis does

---

[1] The transfer will be under-effected or over-effected according as

$$\left(m_a' + m_b' - \frac{m_a}{s_a} \cdot s'_a - \frac{m_b}{s_b} \cdot s'_b - 1 \right) \lessgtr 0$$

where the transferor is country A and the transferee country B and $m_a' + m_b'$ is the sum of the proportions of the transfer by which expenditure on imports is altered by the financing and disposal of the transfer, m_a and m_b are the (non-transfer-income) marginal propensities to import in A and B respectively, s_a and s_b are the marginal propensities to save (from non-transfer incomes) in A and B and s_a' and s_b' are the proportions of the transfer by which savings are altered [5, p. 179].

not really involve time in any essential way except with respect to the 'disturbance' itself. Basically, what is involved is working out, for each unit of time, the effects of the factor expansion and then repeating the analysis for each other period: time merely defines the nature of the 'disturbance' (*i.e.*, the increase in the factor supply) which is itself independent of the equilibrium parametric values of the preceding periods. Surely it is sensible to treat such models as 'static' in nature. The second difficulty consists in separating out models that refer to increase in factor supply and those that concern technical change. Frequently the same authors, for instance Johnson [5, Chapter III], analyse both questions in the same framework. Sometimes, however, the two are not even distinguished and merely 'productivity increases' defined as increases in output (attributable naturally to either cause) are discussed, as by Mundell [11], or shifts in demand and supply schedules over time are defined without explicit distinction between different causes, as by Black [59]. Where these models are discussed is inevitably arbitrary, and I have brought them in under the present sub-section.

The simplest and yet the most influential analysis of the effects of economic expansion accruing through increased factor supply is that of Johnson [5, Chapter III], who uses the HOS model.[1] There is a great flood of subsequent contributions, among them by Corden [61], which explores the HOS model further on this issue. The analysis of the effect on the terms of trade proceeds simply by noting that the excess demand for imports (*dm*) at unchanged terms of trade would equal the difference between the change in the demand for importables (*dc*) and in their supply (*dp*).[2] If this excess demand for imports is positive, then the terms of trade will shift against the growing country provided the stability condition is satisfied. And the precise change in

[1] Historically, the contributions occurred as a result of the interest in the causes of dollar shortage in the post-war world. The explanation of the shortage, first propounded by Balogh [58], was in terms of the rapidly increasing productivity in the United States. Translated in terms of the HOS model, with the adjustment mechanism defined in terms of the terms of trade, the explanation was inevitably formalized into a theory of the effect of growth (due to capital accumulation and technical change) on the terms of trade. The connecting link between Johnson's important contributions and the less formal writings of Balogh and others is a seminal paper of Hicks [3, p. 154] which reflects all the difficulties of a pioneering contribution.

[2] In the HOS model the excess demand for imports implies an equivalent excess supply of exports, and the analysis can proceed in terms of *either* good.

the terms of trade can be obtained by equating the excess demand for imports due to growth with their excess supply due to adverse terms of trade [11, 111].

Since $dm = dc - dp$, the question of the properties of dc and dp has been raised. The former involves merely a weighted sum of the individual marginal propensities to consume importables. The latter, however, has prompted interesting analytical contributions. A proposition of Rybczynski [87] states that $dp \gtreqqless 0$ according as importables are factor K-intensive or factor L-intensive as the supply of K increases. Where the two commodities postulated have different factor-intensities, the output of the commodity intensive in the use of a factor will decrease absolutely as the supply of the other factor rises at unchanged terms of trade.[1] A taxonomic exercise, therefore, can be carried out, using such theorems to define the possible properties of dc and dp [5, Chapter III].

In an influential paper, written prior to the analysis discussed hitherto, Johnson [5, Chapter IV] used a model which assumed that each country consumed and exported one commodity and imported, but did not produce, the other.[2] In this model, which amounts to only a special case of the HOS model, $dp = 0$, and it follows that dm must necessarily be positive unless the consumption of importables

---

[1] This proposition follows immediately as follows. $\frac{K}{L} \equiv \frac{Kx}{Lx} \cdot \frac{Lx}{L} + \frac{Ky}{Ly} \cdot \frac{Ly}{fL}$, which states that the aggregate factor endowment ratio is a weighted sum of the factor ratios in the two activities, X and Y. If the terms of trade are kept fixed so are the factor proportions in the model used. Therefore, $\frac{Kx}{Lx}$ and $\frac{Ky}{Ly}$ are fixed. So is L. Let K now increase. The resulting increase in $\frac{K}{L}$ can be accommodated then *only* by reducing Ly and increasing Lx if X is the K-intensive activity, such that $\frac{Kx}{Lx} > \frac{Ky}{Ly}$. Thus, the output of Y, the L-intensive activity, falls when K increases at unchanged terms of trade [61]. Since this argument is in terms of the relative factor endowments, it is easy to generalize the argument to the case where both factors increase in supply. Thus, for instance, if both factors increase at the same rate there will be a uniform expansion of the outputs of X and Y. If K increases more rapidly the analysis implies notionally a uniform expansion of X and Y (at the rate of growth of L) plus a *reduction* in the output of Y from this expanded level (resulting from the *excess* growth of K). And so on.

[2] Johnson [5, Chapter IV] formulated his analysis in terms of exchange-rate adjustment. In the model used by him, however, it is obvious that this is tantamount to terms-of-trade adjustment. An extension to the n-country case is also available.

falls as output increases with factor expansion. Although it is tempting to say this is ruled out if there is no inferior good, it should be noted that although the good is not inferior in any *individual's* consumption, it *may* be for the economy in the aggregate owing to changing income distribution (associated with a changed factor supply).[1]

Three other contributions are of interest – by Mundell [11], Ramaswami [86] and Black [59]. Mundell has extended Johnson's analysis to the multi-country case, noted earlier here. The same conclusions hold as in Johnson's [5, Chapter III] analysis, provided gross complementarity among the exports of different countries is ruled out.[2]

More novel is the analysis of Ramaswami [86], who has recently attempted to distinguish between the effects of 'completed' accumulation and accumulation-in-progress on the terms of trade. Characterizing the analyses of Johnson and others as relating to the latter question, Ramaswami deploys altogether four models to explore the former problem. These models reduce to two basic 'types'. (1) One of the two goods in Johnson's model is assumed to play a dual role – as a consumer and also as a capital good, and accumulation is conceived as a demand shift, at constant prices, from consumption to investment goods. The model is simple and can be easily put through the various paces. For instance, any investment increase means increased demand for the dual-role good. If the reduction in consumption exclusively falls on that good there is no reason to expect the terms of trade to shift. If not, adjustment is clearly necessary. (2) The other approach is to assume a *third* industry ('tools') which serves as the capital good. The analysis is a little more complex but still manageable. The relative ranking of the factor ratios in the three industries adds to the scope for interesting taxonomic analysis.

While the analyses of Johnson, Mundell and Ramaswami are in the general equilibrium framework, Black [59] has produced a model which is strictly partial-equilibrium in its approach and correspondingly of lesser significance.[3] Using the partial-equilibrium supply

---

[1] Mundell [11], in his otherwise excellent survey, does not make this point clear and relies on the 'non-inferiority' of goods to give him necessarily positive terms.

[2] It is necessarily ruled out in the two-good model, for these two goods have to be substitutes. Gross substitutability among goods is shown by Mundell to guarantee the equivalence of the two-country and multi-country (-cum-multicommodity) case.

[3] Black describes his approach as Marshallian because his model essentially amounts to using the Marshall–Lerner devaluation analysis and introducing

and demand schedules for commodities in a four-commodity (an export and domestic good for each country), two-country model, he introduces trend-shifts in these schedules to derive changes over time in the balance of payments and terms of trade. In contrast to the general equilibrium models, however, this approach leaves untouched the crucial question of how exactly these schedules may be expected to shift in response to accumulation (technical change, etc.).

(ii) *Transfers of Factors between Countries.* Trade theory has also examined the impact of transfers of factors of production between trading countries. The analyses fall into two classes: (1) either the movement of a factor between countries is made contingent upon the presence of an international differential in its rental and the equilibrium condition postulates the elimination of international factor movements when international factor returns are equalized; or (2) an autonomous shift in a factor's location is analysed. The former is clearly more relevant when there is perfect freedom for factor mobility between countries; the latter is more appropriate to modern conditions where this freedom does not exist and the international migration of factors is subject to political decision-making.

Practically the only rigorous analysis in the former class is by Mundell [82], who uses the HOS model. Mundell postulates a tariff imposed on a situation characterized by international equality of factor rentals. The tariff raises the rental of the factor intensively used (in the strict Samuelson sense) and thereby precipitates a movement of that factor from the other into the tariff-imposing country.[1] Ultimately, the factor prices are equalized, factor movement eliminated and commodity prices are also equalized. The tariff is redundant and can be removed without affecting the new equilibrium reached. Mundell has merely turned the factor price-equalization theorem on its head and effectively proved a commodity price-equalization theorem (when factor mobility is perfect but commodity mobility is not, thanks

---

trend-shifts in the supply and demand schedules. The Marshallian analysis can be interpreted, of course, in a partial sense or as an unhelpful general equilibrium approach (where the elasticities are *total* elasticities). Black is interpreting the Marshallian approach in the former sense.

[1] It is equally possible to argue that the other factor may also more in the contrary direction. In fact, multiple (indeed, an infinite number of) solutions are possible, characterized by different international distributions of factors of production.

to the tariff). The terms of trade and factor prices will be identical in the new equilibrium as prior to the tariff.[1]

Of greater interest than this variation on the factor price-equalization theorem is the analysis by Johnson [5, Chapter III] of the effects of *given* transfers of productive factors between trading countries. It represents essentially an extension of the analysis of the effect of growth on the volume and terms of trade: a transfer of factors can be analysed as a simultaneous (and equal) increase and decrease in the two countries' factor supply. Aside from the inevitable taxonomy, using propositions such as Rybczynski's, Johnson carefully argues that an income transfer may be associated with the factor shift. Thus, for instance, profit remittances may follow upon capital transfer. Or gifts may attend upon labour migration. The 'transfer problem' analysis may thus have to be super-imposed upon the 'growth and trade' analysis to get a *total* picture. Meade [9, Chapter XIX] has presented a more elaborate model, permitting international differences in production functions for each activity.[2] However, his formal analysis excludes the 'transfer problem' aspects of the question.[3]

(iii) *Technological Change*

Although recent writings have underlined the desirability of treating technical change integrally with capital accumulation, trade theory is cast in the neo-classical tradition which separates them out. The formal analyses of changes in technology again divide into those that treat such changes as autonomous and those which concern the transfer of technical knowledge from one trading country to another.

In the former category there are several contributions. Using the HOS model, on the technological side, Johnson [5, Chapter III] has formulated the proposition that 'neutral' change in an activity will decrease the output level in the other activity, at constant commodity prices.[4] This proposition can be used to define the sign of dp

---

[1] This is easy enough to see when the factor-losing country has no monopoly power in trade. When the terms of trade can vary, the result still continues to hold.

[2] This extension is of considerable significance, since the formal HOS model, with the assumption of internationally identical production functions, rules out one of the central reasons why international factor migration may be *desirable*.

[3] Caves [3, Chapter V] includes several Continental and other writings on capital movements in his survey. It is difficult, however, to extract anything formally rigorous from these writings.

[4] Unlike with the Rybczynski proposition, the factor prices will change although the commodity prices are held constant.

and the taxonomic analysis thereon is similar to that for the change in factor supply, considered in the earlier sub-section. Findlay and Grubert [62] have extended the analysis of the effects of technical change, on output-composition at constant commodity prices, to the case of biased change. For two factors, say land and labour, they have shown that for labour-saving technical change in the labour-intensive activity there will be an absolute decrease in the output of the land-intensive activity. And that, for land-saving change in the labour-intensive activity, the fall in the output of the other activity does not necessarily follow. In general terms, there will be a fall in the output of an activity when there is technical progress in the other activity which saves on the factor used intensively in that activity.[1] Intuitively, these results are obvious. For instance, land-saving invention in the land-intensive activity has two effects: (1) the technical change, conceived *neutrally*, decreases the output of the other activity (Johnson proposition); and (2) the 'notional' release of land reduces the output of the other, labour-intensive activity as well (Rybczynski proposition). The two effects thus reinforce the fall in the other activity's output. On the other hand, they oppose each other when the invention saves on the factor in which the activity is *not* intensive.[2]

Seton [90] has produced an alternative model to analyse the effects of technical change on the terms of trade. It has practically all the features of Johnson's [5, Chapter III] model, but Seton formulates his analysis in terms of concepts which underline the significance of the 'weight' of the trading countries in international trade.[3] A distinguishing feature is his defining technical change exclusively as the 'neutral' change discussed earlier, though Seton does not establish any propositions concerning its effect, at constant commodity prices, on the composition of output.

[1] The definitions of 'neutral', 'labour-saving' and 'land-saving' are in terms of technology alone. Neutral change merely amounts to multiplying the numbers on the isoquants by a scalar. Under 'labour-saving' invention, at the *same* factor price-ratio, the land–labour ratio is increased; and for 'land-saving' progress the land–labour ratio is decreased.

[2] Johnson [65] has ingeniously combined the analysis of technical change with a disaggregated-economy assumption to trace the effects of different types of technical change on the sign of *dc*.

[3] Seton's analysis is lucid, but the results are quite cumbersome, largely by virtue of the novel concepts used by him and his use of proportionate rather than absolute changes. I suspect, since his propositions are consistent with those deducible from Johnson's analysis, that Seton's formulae could be reduced to forms made familiar by the other models.

Kemp's [71] is practically the only other contribution of some interest in this field. He departs from the preceding analyses in introducing Keynesian unemployment. This renders the supply curves of exports and domestic goods perfectly elastic in his four-good model (with an export and a domestic good in each of the two trading countries).[1] The results of the analysis are worked out for technological progress in both the domestic and export industries.

(iv) Changes in Non-trade Policy

A shift in 'data' can also come from a change in the (non-trade) economic policy pursued by the government. For instance, the government may decide to impose a tax on *importables* (instead of on imports via a tariff) in an open economy engaged in free trade. How will this affect the volume and terms of trade? Such questions have rarely been posed directly in trade theory. They have, no doubt, been raised tangentially – mostly in relation to *welfare* analysis. For instance, Meade [9, Chapters V and VI] has analysed the choice between an import duty and a consumption tax, and between an export duty and a production tax, as a means of raising revenue, the preference function being defined with respect to world advantage. These analyses indirectly involve contributions to pure theory.

Practically the only *direct* analysis of such problems, however, is due to Mundell [11], who has extended his survey of pure theory to include an original contribution on the effect of consumption and production taxes on the terms of trade (at market prices and factor cost). For instance, a consumption tax on the imported good (with the revenue redistributed as income subsidy to consumers) will always improve a country's terms of trade because its net effect is to reduce the demand for imports by the product of the compensated elasticity of demand for importables and the tax change. This proposition is intuitively obvious, since the tax can be expected normally to reduce the world demand for importables. Mundell also notes the interesting fact that tariffs and (trade) subsidies can always be simulated in their 'real' effects by taxes and subsidies on commodities. Thus, for instance, a tariff on Y (or an export duty on X) is equivalent,

---

[1] In this respect Kemp's analysis comes close to that of Asimakopoulos [56], who has investigated the effects of a third non-traded good in a constant-cost model which is otherwise analogous to the Johnson model. Kemp's analysis, however, is rigorous, whereas that of Asimakopoulos lacks in formal rigour in so far as the formal model is not fully specified.

among several other combinations, to a consumption tax on Y plus a production tax on X or a consumption tax on Y plus a production subsidy on Y.

(v) *Changes in International Demand*

Until now, the autonomous shift has been located within the trading country itself. But the problem can also be posed in terms of an *external* shift – *i.e.*, a shift in the *foreign offer curve* (which represents a schedule of trade offers to the trading country at varying terms of trade).[1] There is indeed a considerable literature on the effect of such shifts on a trading country's terms and volume of trade. This literature was sparked off by an apparent contradiction, in the results reached by Marshall and Graham, which has now been traced to different *definitions* of a shift in the offer curve.[2]

Naturally the results will vary with the definitions chosen; and, as Kemp [70] and Oliver [84] have demonstrated by analysing the effects of three different definitions, any number of definitions may be devised as one wishes. From the viewpoint of the usefulness of the economic analysis, however, the two definitions, adopted each by Marshall and Graham, appear to be the most meaningful and have their counterpart in the standard analysis of value. Marshall's analysis defines the change in international demand in terms of a change in the price at which the given quantity (of imports) is demanded; whereas Graham's definition is in terms of a change in the quantity demanded at given terms of trade. Johnson and myself [2] have argued that each of these approaches has utility in the analysis of trade problems, and hence merits retention in the repertoire of trade theorists.[3]

[1] This shift will naturally be *internal* to the foreign country itself and will reflect any or more of the four types of changes discussed earlier and or a trade-policy change. By the same token, the analysis of this sub-section is of limited interest.

[2] In their analysis, however, the shift was in the country's *own* offer curve, the *foreign* country's offer curve remaining unchanged.

[3] I may quote [2, pp. 78–9]: 'Broadly speaking, Graham's approach is likely to be more convenient when . . . the direction of change of international equilibrium can be predicted from the effect of the change on quantity demanded at the initial price. Examples are the transfer problem and the effect of economic expansion on international trade equilibrium. Marshall's approach, on the other hand, is likely to be more convenient when the problem concerns the effects of a change in a country's commercial policy on its equilibrium prices and quantities, since the direction of change of this equilibrium can be predicted from the effect of the tariff on the quantity of imports demanded at the initial internal price, and

B. *Shifts in Trade Policy*

So far I have surveyed much of the central analysis of pure theory which concerns the effects of shifts in 'data' while the trade policy (usually free trade) is assumed unchanged between the two situations being compared. However, many of the principal questions in trade theory have related to the effects of a shift in the trade policy itself. This is quite natural in view of the traditional preoccupation with the choice of commercial policy. Moreover, the trade policy most frequently analysed is tariff policy.

(i) *Non-discriminatory tariff change.* Within tariff theory, further, the analysis of non-discriminatory tariff change has received a disproportionate attention. Indeed, from the viewpoint of *systematic* theoretical analysis in its positive aspects, non-discriminatory tariff change is practically the only type of tariff change to have been analysed. As with all other positive analysis of trade policy, the theory of non-discriminatory tariff changes has sprung directly out of concern with questions of trade and welfare.

The assertion of the vulgar protectionists that tariffs would increase the share of labour in the national income has, in fact, prompted a thorough analysis, in terms of the HOS model,[1] of the entire question of the effects of non-discriminatory tariffs on commodity prices, factor prices, and the absolute and relative shares of either factor in national income. In a classic analysis Stolper and Samuelson [91] revived the controversy concerning the effect of protection on the real incomes of factors and focused on the issue which was baffling most discussants – namely, how anything definitive could be said concerning the question posed *unless* the consumption pattern of the factors was specified. In an ingenious exercise, within the framework of the HOS model, the authors successfully demonstrated that conditions *could* be specified under which the impact of protection on the absolute and relative shares of factors could be definitively predicted without reference to the consumption pattern of the factors. This was accomplished via the analysis of the impact of tariffs on factor prices. Since, in the HOS model, a unique relationship exists between factor

---

of the corresponding reduction of the external price on the quantity of imports the foreigner would supply. Marshall himself used this technique for the analysis of tariffs and subsidies; . . .'

[1] The assumptions concerning the factors of production are, however, not necessary to the analysis.

and commodity prices, Stolper and Samuelson opened up, in effect, the entire modern analysis of the effects of tariffs on commodity and factor prices and on absolute and relative shares of factors in national income. Metzler [80, 81] has subsequently extended the analysis to the 'paradoxical' case where a tariff *reduces* the (relative) price of the importable commodity in the tariff-imposing country. The analysis has been further extended with respect to an elastic factor supply by Kemp and Jones [72] and myself and Johnson [60], the interdependence of public and private consumption by Baldwin [57] and myself and Johnson [60], changes in income distribution by Johnson [67, 60] and the multi-country case by Mundell [11].

In the analysis the distinction between a prohibitive (*i.e.*, trade-eliminating) and a non-prohibitive tariff is of crucial importance, for two reasons: (i) with a prohibitive tariff, starting from free trade, the price of importables cannot be lowered by the imposition of the tariff (in the specified HOS model), whereas it can be when the tariff is non-prohibitive; and (ii) a prohibitive tariff generates no revenue, whereas a non-prohibitive tariff does, creating the necessity to make some assumption about the revenue disposal. The assumption about revenue disposal is, in turn, of significance, since the results of the analysis depend upon it. The two common assumptions in tariff theory are that *either* the government spends it directly *or* that the revenue is re-distributed as an income-subsidy to the consumers, who then spend it like earned income. (The results vary unless the government spends the revenue at internal prices in the same way as consumers do and government consumption does not alter private consumption.)

Subject to these further specifications, the HOS model can be readily employed to work out a large number of formulae concerning the impact of tariff change on domestic and international terms of trade (and hence also on the absolute and relative shares in national income of each of the two classes of factors) [11, 60]. It would be tedious to record the numerous results here; besides, a fairly exhaustive survey has been provided by me elsewhere [1]. I would merely note here that the results under the strict HOS model naturally get modified when any of the assumptions is changed. For instance, letting one of the factors vary in response to its rental complicates the analysis considerably [60, p. 245]. Thus, in this case, the proposition that, when the tariff proceeds are spent by the private sector, the terms of trade will *necessarily* improve for the tariff-imposing country (which follows from the fact that, at constant terms of trade, there is an excess supply of importables measured by the product of the compensated elasticity of demand for imports and the tariff change), is no longer valid and the terms of trade can deteriorate, even though this condition is satisfied [60, p. 246].[1] Similarly, for the case of a disaggregated private sector where changes in income distribution are allowed to play a role in determining the pattern of demand, the net result of such disaggregation is to make the aggregate marginal propensity to spend on imports a weighted sum of these propensities for the different individuals constituting the economy [60, pp. 235-8]. The extension to the multi-country case by Mundell [11], however, does not destroy the simple elegance of the traditional conclusions, for instance, with respect to the effects on the external and internal terms of trade. Gross substitutability among the exports of different countries to the tariff-imposing country is sufficient to sustain the two-country result; further restrictions need not be imposed on the pattern of expenditure out of redistributed revenue [68]. Kemp has also re-examined the standard HOS conclusions in the framework of Keynesian unemployment [3, p. 74], establishing the conditions under which Metzler's 'paradoxical' result would continue to hold.[2] Of some interest is also the recent analysis by MacDougall [75, 76], which utilizes the flood of empirical studies on the international price mechanism to investigate the empirical 'likelihood' of Metzler's results and deduce the conclusion that it is relatively small.

(ii) *Discriminatory Tariff Changes.* Discriminatory tariff changes can be distinguished according as the discrimination is between countries or between commodities. Any particular tariff may

---

[1] Kemp and Jones [72] have examined additionally the question of the levels of importable production and the variable factor's supply.

[2] (1) Under competitive conditions quotas are identical with tariffs (with redistributed revenue) and the analysis in the text is valid for them as well. Each tariff implies an equivalent quota and the other way round. Where, however, the quota system confers a domestic monopoly, the results are different. (2) Subsidies are perfectly symmetrical with the case where tariff proceeds are redistributed to the private sector. However, there is no sensible counterpart to the case where the Government spends the tariff proceeds itself [11]. (3) State trading can be easily analysed as well, for it merely turns tariff analysis on its head. Where tariff theory analyses the effect of specific tariffs (and subsidies) on the volume and terms of trade, the theory of state trading is concerned with the investigation, in effect, of the tariffs (and subsidies) which must be imposed to make a particular volume and terms of trade feasible [9]. (It may be remembered that *trade* taxes and subsidies can be reduced invariably to equivalent *production* and *consumption* taxes and subsidies.)

discriminate in both ways, of course, as when it is levied on a commodity which is imported only from a single foreign source.

In contrast to the analysis of non-discriminatory tariff changes, the theory of discriminatory tariff changes, in its positive aspects, is singularly lacking in formal propositions concerning the determinants of behaviour of equilibrium variables. This is to be accounted for partly by the analytical dominance of the two-good, two-country (HOS) model, which rules out the possibility of discriminatory tariff changes. Partly it is also the result of the preoccupation of discriminatory tariff analysts with welfare analysis. For instance, the formal analysis of preferential tariff reduction, prompted by the post-war interest in customs unions and free-trade areas, has been almost exclusively oriented towards questions like: will a customs union increase world welfare? rather than towards problems like: how will the terms of trade of the non-member countries be affected? No doubt, welfare analysis must be founded on positive analysis. But it happens that the kind of positive analysis that is subsumed in these welfare exercises in tariff discrimination rarely has the formal neatness that is now associated with the theory of non-discriminatory tariff changes.[1]

The formal theory of customs union begins with Viner's [94] examination of the assertion that a customs union, by virtue of its being a move towards free trade, would *improve* welfare. The models employed were not fully stated, but the arguments have none the less proved seminal. Viner considered merely shifts in the given production (of a single commodity), in an essentially three-country model, from one country to another. (Where the union results in the shift of imports from the lower-cost outside country to the higher-cost partner country, he described the shift as trade-diversion. Where the preferential tariff reduction merely eliminates the inefficient, domestic industry and replaces it with imports from the member country, he named the change trade-creation.) Lipsey [121] and Meade [79] have subsequently elaborated upon these basic concepts,

---

[1] This is itself attributable frequently to the way in which welfare analysis has been pursued. For instance, Lipsey [121], in a brilliant paper on customs union theory, is content with demonstrating a *possibility* (that despite 'trade diversion', both national and international welfare may be improved by a customs union) and does not carry the analysis through to a formal algebraic statement of the conditions under which the possibility will occur. Further again, Meade's [79] analysis is more in the nature of the demonstration of a method than a fully taxonomic and formal exercise.

stating their models more fully and introducing both the possibility of an *increase* in the volume of imports (as distinct from a mere shift in their origin) due to their cheapening domestically, as also the existence of imperfectly elastic supply curves. This has been done in the context of both a simple formalization of Viner's (implicit) model into a two-good, three-country model [121] and a more complex version with more than two goods which admits of complementarity between imports from different sources [7, 79].

Unfortunately, all these analyses are welfare-orientated and, for reasons outlined earlier, fail to contribute, in their extant form, anything systematic and substantive to positive theory. It is only recently that Vanek [93] has directly posed the questions of positive theory in an interesting extension of the standard, Marshallian offer-curve analysis to the case of preferential tariff reductions in a two-commodity, three-country model. However, he halts his analysis short of the derivation of the conditions under which the possibilities stated by him will occur.[1] In a real sense, therefore, the question of discriminatory tariff change invites systematic and fresh analysis – in its positive aspects.[2]

---

[1] However, see his later work on customs union theory.

[2] Part of the difficulty in systematically analysing the customs-union problems consists in the vast number of possible cases which logically must be catalogued and analysed. For instance, even in the extremely simplified two-good, three-country model we have seven logically different possibilities (as distinct from four mentioned by Vanek [93]), catalogued in the following matrix, *presented in terms of a single commodity* which may be an export (X) or import (M) of, or not traded (O) by, a country and where the three countries are the home country (H) the partner country (P) and the non-member country (N). The categorization is in terms of the pre-customs-union position.

	H	P	N
(1)	X	M	M
(2)	M	X	X
(3)	M	M	X
(4)	X	X	M
(5)	O	O	O
(6)	M	O	X
(7)	X	M	O

From the viewpoint of economic analysis, cases (1) and (2) are identical in structure; so are cases (3) and (4), so that the number of distinct cases may be considered to reduce to five. For the three-commodity model the possibilities are greater in number, and depend further on relations of substitution and complementarity between different goods.

4. THEOREMS IN DYNAMICS

In contrast to the general richness and synthesized character of much of pure theory in its comparative statics, dynamic propositions in international trade are comparatively few and bear no trace of any uniform design, each having been developed in virtual isolation. Dynamic trade theory, where it exists, has grown up in an essentially *ad hoc* fashion and has witnessed none of the interaction of analysis which usually accompanies the development of an area of knowledge and produces a common design, a unifying frame.

At the same time there is no dearth of interest in the dynamic aspects of trade theory, and a vast amount of non-rigorous but suggestive literature is available [3, Chapter IX]. This is supplemented by the occasional attempts of growth theorists to include international trade in their models ('for completeness', and more frequently to 'show that it does not affect the validity of the approach and/or conclusions') – as, for instance, by Chakravarty [137]. I have kept away from either kind of literature – from the former because these unverified conjectures provide a fertile source for fresh theoretical analysis but themselves do not constitute it;[1] and from the latter because the trade aspects of the models are frequently the least interesting, for they are also treated as the least important.

Broadly speaking, the scant formal literature on dynamic propositions divides itself into: (1) those analyses where the inquiry concerns the effects of an *initial* change in the *trade policy*, and (2) those where the effects of an *initial* change in other *data* are being considered.[2]

1. *Change in Trade Policy*

Perhaps the neatest dynamic analysis of the effects of a change in trade policy concerns that involving adaptive, mutual and sequential changes in tariffs. Starting with the imposition of an optimum tariff, levied by a country in a two-country world, the Cournot-type adjustment mechanism where each country alternatively imposes an optimum tariff leads eventually to the two possibilities demonstrated

---

[1] There are a few exceptions that I have made, partly to illustrate the non-rigorous character of these analyses, but mostly because they come close enough to formal analysis to merit brief comment.

[2] The initial change itself may be defined to be a *continuing* one: for instance, a change in the rate of saving may be *permanent*.

by Johnson [5, Chapter II]: (i) an eventual equilibrium where the optimum tariff of each country is the existing tariff; or (ii) each country moves into a 'tariff cycle' such that the two countries oscillate between a pair of own tariffs. While the possibility of generalizing the theory by changing the postulated reaction mechanism has been recognized previously, Panchmukhi [124] has recently formulated the theory of tariff retaliation in explicitly game-theoretic terms. It is highly improbable, however, that tariff retaliation can be studied profitably on the assumption that tariffs are levied, autonomously or in retaliation, to maximize the tariff-imposing country's advantage. Surely, the tariff levels *and* structure are prompted by distributional considerations (operating through pressure groups) rather than by considerations of national advantage.[1]

By contrast, the literature on the effects of changes in trade policy in the absence of retaliation is characterized by less sophistication, though greater relevance. Practically all the analyses relate to the effect of trade on the rate of growth of income – but the mechanisms postulated vary considerably, and so do the clarity and rigour that attend these contributions.

The earliest of these, and analytically impressive for its time, is the classical analysis of the effect of cheap food imports from the colonies on the approach of the Stationary State. Among the clearest exponents of this theory was Mill [32], who attempted to demonstrate how, through the consequential increase in the rate of profit and hence in the accumulation of savings and capital, the approach of the Stationary State would be put off. What is not available, however, is the *precision* that we have now come to expect in theoretical writing; and unfortunately the recent mathematical formulations of the Ricardian systems (by Samuelson and Pasinetti) leave out international trade altogether, although Ricardo traced out the essence of the sequence that Mill elaborated. Other ways in which such a dynamic link between trade and growth has been established are: (i) via the effect of trade on the marginal capital–output ratio by virtue of the proposition that (free) trade increases real income [27, 132]; (ii) via the effect of trade on the distribution of income and hence on the average savings ratio [97, 99, 100]; and (iii) via the effect of trade through factor price rigidity on the level of employment, hence on real income

---

[1] The question of tariff retaliation is considered at greater length in Section 6, since it has important implications for welfare analysis.

and savings [27].[1] None of these analyses is fully rigorous. For instance, the analysts who argue via the effects on the distribution of income and hence on the average savings ratio never specify a model. And yet the sequence is clear and the models are easy to invent.[2]

2. *Change in Data*

The most interesting (though insufficiently formal) model, designed to analyse the effects of continuous accumulation on the trade pattern, has been presented by Bensusan-Butt [96]. He operates in a two-country, multi-commodity framework, with a simplified production technology such that each commodity has two alternative processes, one with and the other without machinery, which are known in both countries. Starting with a situation where no accumulation has previously taken place, and the cost and price structure is identical between countries, and trade is absent in consequence, Bensusan-Butt unfolds a sequence in which the steady accumulation of capital in one country leads to progressive mechanization, and emergence as exports, of industries in the accumulating country. The resulting improvement in the other country's real income (initially through the rise of trade and subsequently through the postulated improvement in the terms of trade as the accumulation proceeds) is linked with the emergence of savings there, and the effect of this on the pattern of trade is examined.

While Bensusan-Butt's analysis examines the structure of trade, as

[1] Linder [27] considers his model applicable to underdeveloped countries and uses it to turn up immiserating growth paths of output. The model is, in fact, quite symmetrical between movement from free trade to no trade and a reverse movement. For any change will bring about unemployment (due to factor-price rigidity) in the industry which should contract, and hence the contraction of real income and possible reduction in the rate of growth. The model, not being mathematically formulated, does not specify *where* the incremental output is allocated and whether the mechanism of factor allocation envisaged would be compatible with the factor-price rigidity assumption. Also, it would be pertinent to consider whether it is right to ignore the effects of change brought about by increased output: it may well be that the change implicit in trade may *offset* the change involved by growth. The analysis offered by Linder is thus not fully satisfactory.

[2] For example, a model where tractors produce tractors and corn, and corn is exchanged for toys when trade opens, could easily be used to demonstrate how the possibility of trade can reduce the marginal capital–output ratio and raise the rate of growth (with given average savings ratio). For a treatment of several types of causal links between trade and growth in a historical context, Kindleberger [101] is an excellent reference.

it *evolves* sequentially, the rest of the dynamic analyses in the literature are concerned instead with the equilibrium time-paths of variables such as output, real income and terms of trade in a growing economy engaged in a *pre-defined* pattern of trade.

Srinivasan [104] has constructed an interesting two-country, three-commodity model where one country produces two goods (a consumer good and a capital good which produces all goods in the system) and the other country produces the other (consumer) good. Assuming: (1) the Paretian allocation mechanism to allocate the fully employed factors, labour and capital (good); (2) a fixed trade pattern involving the exchange of the former country's capital good with the latter country's consumer good; and (3) international lending predetermined by a linear relationship between exports and import values, Srinivasan introduces growth into the system by letting labour grow exponentially, capital accumulate through savings and neutral technical progress characterize industries in both countries. The equilibrium time-paths of income, terms of trade and comparative factor rewards are analysed.

While in Srinivasan's model the import demand functions are ingeniously implicit in the production and trade patterns specified, Johnson [5, Chapter V] has used the more conventional approach of specifying marginal propensities to import (and spend on imports) and used them in the context of a Harrod–Domar type of flow-analysis extended to the international economy. Johnson explores, in effect, the behaviour of the equilibrium rate of growth of output and income of a country over time under the assumption of international lending and also under the more realistic postulate of exchange-rate adjustment (when the time profile of the terms of trade becomes relevant).[1]

Far more complex, and for the same reason ineffective as theory, is the analysis of Brems [98], who, using a 52-equations system (among whose novelties is trade in producers' goods), solves it to derive two *L*-order difference equations (where *L* is the durability, in years, of capital goods). These yield solutions which establish relations, over

---

[1] Verdoorn [105] has attempted a rigorous analysis, of similar intent, but under the restrictive assumptions of: (1) fixed coefficients of production, and (2) independence of the foreign rate of growth from the rate of growth of the economy under consideration. Johnson [5, Chapter V] eliminates the former type of analysis altogether (because he operates with the concept of the marginal propensity to import), while his analysis is fully general on the latter question.

the time-path, between the equilibrium values of variables such as the growth rates of the two trading countries.

These analyses nearly exhaust the literature on dynamic theory – except for the 'omissions' justified earlier.[1] There is little doubt that, in contrast to the comparative statics of pure theory, dynamic trade theory still calls for further systematic analysis and synthesis.

5. Central Limitations: Intermediates and Capital Goods

Of greater significance is the negligible dent made so far by intermediate and capital goods in the theoretical models employed by analysts of international trade. To state this is *not* to assert that the present stock of knowledge will not survive the required change in the formulation of the models. In fact, we do know, from such little analysis as already obtains in this direction, that the survival rate tends to be quite high! More important, however, is the fact that a vast range of interesting problems, applicable to economies using intermediate and (produced) capital goods, cannot get within the range of analysis until the theorists get away from the traditional picture of primary factors and integrated processes of production (with the inevitable concomitant feature of trade in consumer goods).

The introduction of intermediates and (produced) capital goods can be accomplished in principle in either of the following alternative ways: either these enter only domestic processes but not trade or they enter trade as well. For instance, a sector producing capital goods may exist though capital goods do not enter trade. The existing theoretical analyses in trade theory exhibit the entire range of these possibilities. For example, Samuelson's [54] interest-rate equalization model has produced but untraded capital goods. So has Ramaswami's [86] model, which analyses the effect of trade on growth. On the other hand, Srinivasan's [104] dynamic model has a capital good which is both produced and traded. As for intermediate goods, the models used by McKenzie [78, 108] and Jones [69], which explore the pattern of trade in a Ricardo–Graham framework, distinguish between the cases where intermediate goods are traded and where

---

[1] Perhaps the only omission that I regret is that of some Japanese analyses that seem extremely interesting, though the sources I have been able to consult in English [102, 103] do not give enough formal account of these theories. I refer to the analysis of the 'Marxist' economists, S. Tsuru and H. Ktamura, which links cyclical fluctuations with the *pattern* of trade [102].

they are not. Vanek [55], on the other hand, uses a two-sector model where the intermediates are identical with the final goods which enter trade.

A large number of propositions continue to be valid despite the introduction of intermediates and/or capital goods in the analytical models. For instance, as Samuelson [125] and Kemp [120] have shown, the proposition that free trade is superior to no trade is valid even when intermediates exist and enter trade. Similarly, Jones [69] has shown that the pattern of efficient specialization in the Ricardo–Graham model will continue to satisfy the bilateral comparative cost rankings postulated by Ricardo, even when intermediates enter trade. The factor price equalization theorem again has been examined, in the light of traded intermediate goods, by Samuelson [53] and Vanek [55] without leading to any qualitative change in the traditional propositions. On the other hand, certain propositions *do* change. For instance, the *exact* pattern of specialization in the Ricardo–Graham model naturally changes with the possibility of trade in intermediate goods [69, 78]. The effect of growth on the terms of trade again is shown by Ramaswami [86] to change qualitatively with the introduction of a (produced) capital-goods sector.

Of far greater significance, however, is the fact that a whole range of interesting and important questions slip through the analyst's hands unless intermediates and (produced) capital goods are introduced into the formal models. For instance, the recent GATT [107] discussions on the exports of 'new manufactures' from the industrializing underdeveloped countries have drawn attention to the disparity between tariffs levied on unprocessed and semi-processed items (on which tariffs are relatively lower) and those on finished manufactures. It is surely interesting to examine the effects, in both positive and welfare terms, of such tariff discrimination. But the analysis just cannot get off the ground with the traditional types of analytical models![1] Let me take another important illustration. The traditional multiplier analysis in trade theory (which has already been discussed

[1] We may note the related point that an apparently non-discriminatory tariff adjustment on all imports (say, 10% reduction in the tariffs on both alumina and aluminium) would be *de facto* discriminatory in its effects when the imports consist of both the raw material and the finished product. The effective reduction in the protective effect would be greater on the raw material. Incidentally, an analysis of the problem discussed in the text would call for some method of demarcating intermediates in a world where circularities in the Leontief flow-matrix may prevent an easy solution.

earlier in relation to the Keynesian treatment of the transfer problem) postulates the impact of exports and/or autonomous investments on the balance of payments and the levels of domestic output and employment. But there is an extension to the concept of the *import multiplier* as well, when one considers the situation frequently experienced by economies importing raw materials, when excess capacity develops due to the shortage of foreign exchange. An extra unit of exchange (say, through foreign aid) will then increase the level of domestic output directly by a multiple which is the ratio of value added to imported inputs (the latter being the only constraint). If, however, this output enters as input into other processes lying idle for want of materials, one can easily work out (through the input–output mechanism) a whole chain of increased outputs which, on summation, yields a multiplier-measure of the increased output attributable to the incremental unit of imports. This idea has been independently formulated in various writings, by Stolper [109, 110], several Japanese economists such as Akamatsu [106] and Kojima [103], and writers on the Indian balance of payments in recent years. It demonstrates forcefully how the exclusion of intermediates from analysis would rule out from examination one of the most significant aspects of the international trade problems besetting many economies. Since imported intermediates may also lead to extra output of domestically produced capital goods which may help break other bottlenecks at a future date, or the incremental exchange may be used to import capital goods which create capacity to break bottlenecks to domestic utilization of capacity in other sectors of use, this whole notion of the import multiplier has a further time dimension to it and equally illustrates the role of produced and traded capital goods in any realistic analysis of the trade phenomena in the real world.

6. WELFARE PROPOSITIONS: GAINS FROM TRADE

Welfare propositions are among the oldest in pure theory. Trade theory developed in the effort to demonstrate the fallacy of the protectionist prescriptions of the Mercantilist School. Today the range of analytical questions has increased astonishingly beyond the early preoccupation with the comparison of free trade with protection. To seek design and order in this vast literature is no mean ambition.

It is useful to start with the basic proposition that the aim of policy-orientated welfare economics is to provide a *ranking of policies*. This ranking may relate to *trade* policies (while the general equilibrium parameters and relationships, such as the known technology, are given). For instance, is a zero tariff (*i.e.*, free trade) superior to no trade? Is a 15% (non-discriminatory) tariff superior to a 20% tariff? Would an increase in the tariff rate be beneficial? On the other hand, the ranking may refer to policies relating to the general equilibrium *parameters and relationships*, such as the factor supply level (given the trade policy). For instance, for an open economy engaged in free trade, is migration desirable? Should the increment in capital stock be absorbed as domestic or foreign investment?[1]

The ranking of policies in pure theory further divides into two classes of propositions: (1) those that relate to *national* advantage; and (2) those that concern *international* advantage. Thus, for instance, the proposition that free trade is superior to no trade is sought to be established from both national and international standpoints. On the other hand, the proposition that (for a variable tariff rate) the optimum tariff is superior to free trade concerns only national advantage.

These rankings can further be classified according to the *criterion of welfare* employed. The Samuelsonian superior-for-all-income-distributions criterion has been widely used in the early development of the theory subsequent to the new welfare economics. On the other hand, it has been replaced extensively in recent years by criteria which handle the problem of income-distribution in a non-purist fashion. Among them, two approaches can be distinguished, which divide mainly on the issue of the measurability of utility.

The *ordinalist* method sets up a community welfare function which *assumes* that the State adopts a policy of lump-sum transfers to fix

---

[1] Although I have not done so in the text, the ranking of policies could also be classified into the ranking of *specific measures* and of *general forms of policy intervention*. Under the former, a characteristic illustration would be the ranking of two rates of tariffs. For instance, would a 5% tariff be inferior to a 3% tariff? Would a marginal reduction in the tariff rate increase welfare? Under the latter, a typical example would be the ranking of a tariff policy (without specifying a specific tariff rate) and free-trade policy. For instance, the proposition that an optimum tariff is superior to free trade is not formulated in terms of a unique tariff-rate comparison, but is rather valid in the sense that, corresponding to any income distribution chosen, there will be an optimum tariff rate which will be superior to free trade so that the utility possibility curve for an optimum tariff situation, with variable tariff rates, will lie outside (though it may touch) that for the free-trade situation.

the income-distribution at some 'desired' level. The properties of
this welfare function are then assumed to be parallel to those which
are taken normally (with some 'plausibility') to characterize individual
welfare functions. It is only recently that Samuelson [126] has established the exact conditions under which 'social indifference curves'
will enjoy these properties – so that, in effect, the trade theorist must
assume, *ipso facto*, these conditions to obtain if he uses a social-welfare
function with those properties.[1] The ranking of trade policies can then
be carried out in terms of such a community preference function,
corresponding to any 'desired' income distribution.

The other, alternative method of handling the problem of income
distribution so as to achieve a unique ranking of policies has been that
extensively used by Meade [8, 9]. He explicitly combines equity and
efficiency in a single welfare function by assuming *cardinality* and the
possibility of *interpersonal comparisons of welfare* (through assigned
weights). This method enables the analyst to judge the change in
welfare between two situations for the actual market income-
distributions achieved and without having to conjure up a state of
lump-sum transfers (which itself may be construed to be an advantage,
from the ethical and practical viewpoints, over both the Samuelson
criterion and the ordinalist method sketched earlier).[2]

---

[1] Often trade theorists omit mentioning the problem of lump-sum transfers and
use community preference functions as if the community were an individual.
This procedure is clearly sloppy. It is also not uncommon for some theorists to
assume that the economy is composed of individuals with identical tastes and
income (kept equal presumably by lump-sum transfers). This, however, is
tantamount to assuming a single individual and, only in a limited, formal sense
can one concede the 'reduced restrictiveness' of such an assumption! It is also
sometimes stated that the state 'ignores the question of income distribution' and
then the analyst proceeds to operate with the community indifference curves
[129, p. 329]. This, however, is open to objection because: (1) the assumptions
under which the community preference function would be characterized by the
required properties (*e.g.*, convexity) would still have to be specified; and (2) the
position implied by the statement is untenable. In what sense can one be 'indif-
ferent' to income distribution? The only meaning that can possibly be attributed
is that the state attaches equal weight to the marginal utility of each individual –
in which case the analyst ceases to be an ordinalist!

[2] Caves' [3, pp. 233–4] neat summary of Meade's method is useful. 'Suppose
that a change is made somewhere in the economy, such as the elimination of a
monopoly position. There will be a primary gain in economic efficiency, because
consumers now receive extra units of this particular product which they value
above the cost to the suppliers. In addition, because of relations of substitutability
and complementarity between this and other products, both in consumption and

Aside from the possible preferences on ethical and practical grounds, however, the shift in favour of these less-restrictive criteria has been prompted essentially by a change in the kinds of questions that economists are willing to accept from policy makers. The traditional analysis concerned itself with the ranking of specific policy measures (themselves distortionary) under otherwise 'first-best' assumptions or, in ranking forms of policy intervention, compared only policies achieving fully optimal situations with those resulting in sub-optimal ones. In the former category, for instance, is the proposition that a higher tariff is inferior to a lower tariff. In the latter class the most prominent proposition has always been that an optimum tariff (which attains the first best solution) is superior to free trade (which leads to a sub-optimal solution when the country can influence its terms of trade). These rankings satisfy the Samuelson welfare criterion. Now, however, the range of policy questions has increased enormously. The policy-makers wish to know the answers to questions which inevitably involve comparing sub-optimal situations. Problems are posed such that 'second-best' assumptions as also sub-optimal comparisons have to be made.[1] For instance, some distortionary

---

production, expenditure patterns will change throughout the economy. Spending on products with no cost-value divergence may rise; spending on other products with very large divergences may fall. Changes of this type represent secondary losses; their opposites would represent secondary gains. The process of summing these changes over the whole economic system is shown by the expression:

$$u = \sum_{i=1}^{n} \sum_{j=1}^{n} \sum_{s=1}^{s} (U_{ij} D_{ijs} - 1) \mu_j R_{js} \lambda_{ijs}$$

where the net change in utility (u) represents a summation, over all sellers, buyers, and commodities, of the unit revenue from each commodity (R) times the change in the quantity of that commodity exchanged (x), times the rate at which the marginal value to the purchaser exceeds the marginal cost to the seller ($D-1$). Subscript s denotes a commodity, i a buyer, j a seller. In addition, distributional weights appear as μ_j, the weight attached to marginal income for the seller, and U_{ij}, which stands for the ratio μ_i/μ_j.'

[1] Second-best assumptions imply that, from the entire set of assumptions that are made to demonstrate the Pareto optimality of the competitive solution, one (or more) does not obtain. Given this definition of second-best assumptions, it is useful to classify these constraints, the departures from first-best assumptions, into two categories: (1) *Behavioural* constraints; and (2) *Environmental* constraints. In the former class we can consider non-utility maximization and non-profit maximization by decision-making units. In the latter category we may further distinguish between (i) *state-imposed* constraints and (ii) *others*. Among the state-imposed constraints, we have the imposition of direct and indirect taxes, subsidies,

tariffs, restrictions of output levels, etc. The other constraints divide broadly into *'market imperfections'* (for instance, the presence of monopoly, a distortionary wage differential between sectors, divergence of the shadow rental to a factor from its actual rental, and national monopoly power in trade), *'technological characteristics'* (for instance, increasing returns to scale, and non-convexity of isoquants) and *'interdependence'* (for instance, externalities in production and in consumption).

Corresponding to the notion of second-best *assumptions* is the concept of second-best *solutions*. The difference between first-best and second-best solutions is, I suggest, best comprehended if it is founded on a distinction between those second-best assumptions that are *meaningfully* looked upon as removable (*in principle*) by intervention and those that are not. For instance, one can look upon a tax as removable and a wage differential as capable of being offset by a tax-cum-subsidy-on-labour-use, etc., so that the *standard first-best solution* (with all the first-best assumptions holding) is restorable. On the other hand, inter-dependence of utilities of consumers or increasing returns to scale or monopoly power in trade are not second-best assumptions which can be looked upon as capable of 'elimination' so as to restore the *standard* first-best situation. With this distinction in principle, between the different types of second-best assumptions, we can define the respective first-best and second-best solutions.

In the *former* class, where the second-best constraint is removable, the first-best solution is that which would obtain if the constraint *were* removed, *i.e.* it is the standard first-best solution. The functional forms (of the optimizing conditions), as also the values of the solution, will naturally be identical with those obtaining for the standard first-best solution. In the *latter* case, whree the second-best assumption is irremovable, the *first-best solution is that obtained by maximization subject to the second-best assumption.* This solution may have the same functional form (of the optimizing conditions) as for the solution under standard first-best assumptions. In general, the functional forms *will*, however, differ from those of the conditions for the *standard first-best solution.* Thus, for instance, where consumption externality obtains, it would be necessary for a consumer to take into account the impact of his utility on the other consumers. Or there may be produc-tion externality, for instance, under which a producer's decision concerning the level of production may be a function of another producer's level of production. Here again, the optimizing condition for producers will differ from that when no such interdependence obtains (yet the utility level reached will be identical under a policy where the state, by policy intervention, assures the fulfilment of this optimizing condition under interdependence, and under the standard first-best solution when no such interdependence obtains). The second-best solution can then be defined in terms of this first-best solution not being available under the postulates made.

We thus have: (1) the *standard first-best solution* (which obtains under universally first-best assumptions); (2) the first-best solution (equivalent to the standard first-best solution) when the second-best assumption is removable in principle; (3) the second-best solution when the second-best assumption, though removable in principle, is not removable and removed in practice; (4) the first-best solution (which may differ from the standard first-best solution in both functional forms of the optimizing conditions and, where comparison is meaningful, in welfare

taxes may have to be admitted into the analysis when two tariff rates
are being compared. The policy-maker is apt to say: 'I cannot take

---

level reached) when the second-best assumptions are irremovable in principle;
and (5) the second-best solution when these second-best assumptions are
irremovable in principle and the corresponding first-best solution cannot be
obtained.

This analytical classification can be supplemented with a further set of remarks
concerning the ways in which the effects of second-best assumptions are (and
often, without clarity, have been) analysed.

(1) To begin with, the precise way in which the second-best solution should be
delimited has to be clarified. For instance, if a country has monopoly power in
trade the first-best solution would involve the imposition of an optimum tariff.
Suppose that this is ruled out; then, is the second-best solution to be determined
on the assumption that no tariff can be levied or on the assumption that only
the optimum tariff cannot be levied? Similarly, if a wage differential cannot be
eliminated entirely, are we to seek a second-best solution on the assumption that
it cannot be offset in any degree or that it cannot be offset fully? There is no
unique answer: it all depends on what restraints the policy-maker wishes to
impose on himself. But the need for a clear definition of the problem must be
underlined.

(2) Secondly, one has to distinguish between the second-best solution, which
may necessitate intervention in a decentralized economy, and the *actual* solution
that would prevail (under the second-best assumptions made) in the absence of
the intervention that is necessary to bring about the second-best solution. Thus,
if a distortionary wage differential between sectors obtains, the actual solution will
be different from the second-best solution [112]; the latter will call for intervention.

(3) It also follows that, starting from any actual solution, under second-best
assumptions one can ask how any intervention (other than that which produces
the second-best solution) will influence the level of welfare. Thus, rather than
investigate what is the second-best solution, the theorist may merely interest
himself in *changes* in welfare resulting from the variation in the use of one or more
policy instruments when second-best assumptions obtain. Or he may even, using
this method, engage in 'partial optimization' and attempt to seek the optimal
level of a particular policy (*e.g.*, the tariff rate) instead of seeking the optimal,
second-best policy from the *entire* range of policy instruments. In trade theory it
is *only* the latter two varieties of approach which have been used extensively;
the question of the second-best solutions has hardly ever been posed.

This long footnote, highlighting different aspects of second-best theory, has
been inserted primarily to gain a clearer grasp of the structure of many contributions to the theory of trade and welfare. I do not claim any special merits for the
analytical classification proposed here over those currently available, except that
it appears consistent and illuminates the logic of second-best analyses purposively.
I am indebted to T. N. Srinivasan for many helpful conversations and for drawing
my attention to, as also making available to me, an important unpublished paper
by Otto Davis and Andrew Whinston on 'Welfare Economics and the Theory of
Second Best' (*Cowles Foundation Discussion Paper*, No. 146).

off certain taxes. Given these taxes, will a reduction in the tariff rate be desirable?' Another familiar illustration is provided by the policy-makers, who argue that they cannot have universal free trade, but that a free-trade area with continuing tariffs on outside countries may be feasible. If so, would a move to a free-trade area be beneficial (to the member countries and/or the world)? Trade theorists have found that, in general, answers to such questions cannot be given, *even for particular cases* (*i.e.*, for instance, the latter question being asked in relation to a *specific* group of countries joining or opting out of a free-trade area rather than being formulated more generally so that the answer must be valid for all possible free-trade areas), unless the income distribution is specified. In general, *both* the particularizing of a question (in the sense just outlined) and the choice of an income distribution are necessary to the ranking of two alternative policies. Since these questions are of interest to policy-makers, the trade theorist has naturally eschewed all Samuelsonian scruples and, in either of the two ways discussed earlier, decided to handle income distribution in a non-purist fashion so as to enable him to get along with the business of ranking the contrasted policies.

This shift towards policy-orientation of a more realistic variety has logically led to the emergence of a new trend towards the *measurement* of losses and gains from changes in policy. Partly this is a result of the shift to the non-purist welfare criteria. Meade's method, for instance, is candidly cardinal, and the sheer process of determining the direction of the welfare change from a shift in policy involves the evaluation of the magnitude of this welfare change. The measurement of losses and gains in welfare, however, has also been given great currency by ordinalists such as Johnson [132, 133], and the principal reason for this has ultimately to be found in the general demand for such measurement by those who debate policies. Policies are maintained or changed largely for non-economic reasons; and the (economic) 'cost' involved is a magnitude that is commonly demanded and bandied about in discussions of public policy. Whether we like it or not, this is what the policy-makers do want; and the trade theorist, in consonance with the best traditions in the profession, has begun to meet this need in an attempt to bring economic analysis closer to fulfilling the objective that provides its ultimate *raison d'être*.[1] The result has been a definite and significant trend, in the welfare analysis of pure theory,

[1] Other interesting and important uses of the measures of gains and losses in welfare will be discussed in Section 7.

towards measurement of welfare change. It is important enough to merit detailed analysis in Section 7.

In the present Section we will survey the qualitative propositions of welfare analysis in pure theory, utilizing the analytical classifications developed so far. A full survey of the entire range of propositions is not necessary; there are endless ways in which the same theoretical principle may be applied so that a full mapping of these applications in the literature would be both tedious and exhausting. The analytical skeleton of the contributions to the analysis of welfare and trade has already been laid bare. All that needs to be done now is to survey the central analyses so that the skeleton acquires flesh.

Ranking of Policies by Samuelson Criterion: National Advantage

Among the simplest rankings by the Samuelson criterion, in relation to national advantage, is the proposition that a *higher tariff rate is inferior to a lower tariff rate*. This is valid under first-best assumptions (inclusive of the absence of national monopoly power in trade) [1]. There are clearly a very large number of such propositions that could be worked out: for instance, that a *lower trade subsidy is superior to a higher trade subsidy* (under first-best assumptions).[1]

The rankings which have traditionally held the stage in the welfare theory of trade are, however, the two celebrated propositions that: (1) *free trade is superior to no trade*; and (2) *an optimum tariff is superior to free trade* (when a country has monopoly power in trade). To these Kemp [120] has recently added the proposition that (3) *restricted trade is superior to no trade*, and Ramaswami and myself [112] have argued that (4) *an optimum subsidy is superior to a tariff policy* (when there are domestic distortions).

The proposition that free trade is superior to no trade was shown by Samuelson [125], in a classic paper, to hold with standard first-best assumptions. However, its validity has subsequently been extended to the case where a country can influence its terms of trade through the exercise of monopoly power [120]. Although there have always been those who erroneously believe, and have sometimes continued to assert despite proofs to the contrary, that the proposition rests on an

---

[1] These listed propositions hold because, in each case, the superior policy represents a 'weakening' of the sole second-best assumption (*i.e.*, a tariff or a subsidy) in an otherwise first-best situation. Throughout the following analysis the statement that a policy is 'superior' to another is to be taken to include whenever necessary the borderline case where the two produce identical welfare.

assumed mobility of factors of production, the proposition rests on no such postulate. Samuelson's 1939 proof [125] is clear on this issue; and Haberler [117] has subsequently provided a supporting geometrical argument which must make the truth accessible to more numerous economists. It is also necessary to note that the proposition, valid for all income distributions, holds only in the situation sense – such that the utility possibility curve corresponding to the free-trade policy will lie uniformly outside (though it may touch) the utility possibility curve corresponding to the no-trade policy [120].[1]

The proposition that restricted trade is superior to no trade, which is also valid in the situation sense, has been shown by Kemp [120] to hold under the standard first-best assumptions (except that the country may have monopoly power in trade). By restricted trade is meant essentially trade restricted in a manner which merely brings about a divergence between foreign and domestic commodity prices. Thus, the trade may be restricted by tariffs, quotas or exchange control. It is *not* correct to infer from this proposition that *any* manner of restricted trade will be beneficial in relation to no trade: for it is easy to conceive of forms of trade, where the volume and/or value of trade is lower than under free trade and yet the net effect is to lower the country's welfare below the no-trade level. Nor should the proposition be read to mean that any trade is superior to no trade. In fact, it can be shown that (subsidy-) expanded trade may, for some income distribution, be inferior to no trade. The proposition refers exclusively, therefore, to restricted trade (of the form defined here).[2]

The third proposition in this class is the celebrated dictum that an optimum tariff is superior to free trade when a country has monopoly power in trade. This proposition was formulated, though not with modern sophistication, as early as Mill's *Principles* [32]. When a country has the ability to influence its terms of trade the marginal

---

[1] It is not possible to demonstrate that the actual bundle of goods obtained by adopting free trade can be redistributed so as to make at least one person better off while leaving others as well off as with the *actual bundle* in the preceding no-trade condition. This has always been understood, although some confusion has cropped up in the literature occasionally. Johnson [66, p. 259] has produced a good example, illustrative of the proposition that the redistribution of the *actual* bundle of goods so as to demonstrate the superiority of free trade over no trade may be impossible.

[2] The analysis in the text could be adapted to develop the proposition that welfare increases to a maximum as restriction decreases to free trade, then falls as trade is increasingly subsidized until welfare has fallen below the no-trade level.

terms of trade diverge from the average terms of trade and a discrepancy arises, under free trade, between the domestic rate of transformation in production and the foreign rate of transformation. This divergence can be eliminated and the equality of these with the domestic rate of substitution in consumption achieved, resulting in the first-best optimum solution, when a suitable tariff rate is levied [5, Chapter II; 118]. This optimum tariff rate will naturally depend on the income distribution chosen. Hence, the proposition holds only for *variable* tariff rates, and in the situation sense. For the multi-commodity case an optimum tariff *structure* will exist, which in turn will vary with the income distribution [118].

The proposition concerning the superiority of the optimum tariff has been sought to be extended to the case where the imposition of the tariff results in retaliation. An investigation of this question requires a behavioural assumption concerning the foreigner's response (mechanism) and another with respect to the country's own method of accommodation to such response. The early assertions that, in the event of retaliation (insufficiently defined), a country could not gain from imposing an (initially, pre-retaliation) optimum tariff have subsequently been rejected as a result of the demonstration that, for any given income distribution, with a Cournot-type adjustment mechanism such that each country imposes an optimum tariff while assuming the other's tariff rate as fixed, it is *possible* (though *not* necessary) that, if and when final equilibrium is achieved with no country under incentive to change the tariff rate, the country imposing the initial optimum tariff may still be better off than under free trade.[1] While this proposition is valid, it should be noted that the result of a retaliatory system depends naturally on the response mechanisms assumed. Alternative 'rules of the game' can be readily imagined. For instance, the retaliation may plausibly be a function of the ability of the affected income group to coalesce into an effective pressure group – as Kindleberger's [73] historical study of the political sociology of the European tariff response to the influx of cheap American corn underlines. In this case, an integration of the protection-and-real-wages theory with the tariff-retaliation theory is called for. The easiest

---

[1] Two other results are of interest: (1) the adjustment process may result in a 'tariff cycle': countries may mill around the same set of tariff rates and not settle down to an equilibrium pair of tariff rates [5, pp. 42–3]; and (2) the equilibrium pair of tariff rates, where existent, will generally differ, depending on which country starts off the process.

way in which one can demonstrate the dependence of the stated proposition on the response-mechanism assumed is to postulate a retaliatory tariff that eliminates trade (for all income distributions). Here the reversion to no trade clearly leaves the country in a position inferior to free trade, *ruling out the possibility* of an improvement over the free-trade situation.

While the preceding propositions rank *trade policies*, the final proposition considered here involves a ranking of one trade policy and another *trade policy in conjunction with a different form of policy intervention*. This proposition is that, when domestic distortions (*i.e.*, a divergence between domestic rates of transformation and domestic price ratios) obtain, an optimum (production) subsidy (with free trade) is superior to any tariff intervention. The former policy equates the foreign rate of transformation (FRT) with the domestic rates of transformation in production (DRT) and of substitution in consumption (DRS), and thus turns out to be superior to a tariff policy which cannot ensure this [112].[1]

Ranking of Policies by Samuelson Criterion: International Advantage
From the viewpoint of international advantage, the proposition that *free trade is superior to any trade policy* is held to be valid [126]. The proposition holds when all the first-best assumptions obtain (though the possession of national monopoly power in trade, as long as not exercised, is permissible). The propositions that *free trade is superior to no trade*, *free trade is superior to expanded trade and free trade is superior to restricted trade* are only special cases of the preceding proposition.[2]

---

[1] I have deliberately refrained from describing the optimum subsidy policy which equates FRT, DRT and DRS as a policy which produces the first-best solution. This is because, whether it does or not, will depend on *which* second-best assumption causes this domestic distortion. Where an external economy produces such a distortion, the optimum subsidy will produce the standard first-best solution [112]. Where, however, it results from a wage differential, for instance, the optimum subsidy *cannot* produce the standard first-best solution, although it will, of course, be superior to any tariff intervention [112]. Incidentally, this also helps to illustrate the undesirability of trying to develop the theory of the second-best in terms of the violations of optimum conditions rather than in terms of the second-best assumptions themselves as proposed here.

[2] Several diagrammatic proofs of these propositions can be found in the literature. Formal mathematical proofs, however, are not easy to come by, although they could be easily devised.

Ranking by Other Criteria: National Advantage

The bulk of the literature in the theory of trade and welfare, however, concerns the ranking of policies, which yield sub-optimal results under second-best assumptions, with the aid of non-purist criteria of welfare change. These analyses can be conveniently divided into those exercises that seek to evaluate the change in welfare when a trade policy is changed and those that concern the welfare change when (the trade policy remaining unchanged) some given parameter or functional relationship (*e.g.*, factor supply, known technology, etc.) shifts.

A. *Trade Policies*

The most frequent way in which the problem is posed involves a primarily negative orientation. For instance, much of the analysis in this area concerns the demonstration that, even if the income distribution is fixed at an arbitrary level, the proposition that free trade is superior to no trade will *not necessarily* hold if there are, say, domestic distortions in the economy. Meade, using his cardinal method, extends his analysis, on the other hand, to deriving the precise conditions (*e.g.*, elasticity of transformation in domestic production, the degree of distortion, etc.) under which the trade policies being compared will rank one way or the other.[1] The analysis is sometimes extended also beyond the ranking of two trade policies. For instance, instead of merely ranking a 5% tariff and zero tariff, using either the cardinal or the ordinal method, the analyst proceeds to ask what tariff rates (constituting the policy instrument available to the policy-maker) will *maximize* welfare. The optimum level at which the available policy instrument should be used is thus the aim of this analysis, which goes beyond a mere ranking of two arbitrarily chosen levels at which the policy instrument may be used.[2] While such analysis represents a process of social-utility maximization, it should be emphasized that, except in the highly restrictive case where *all* other forms of policy intervention are excluded from the range of available policy instruments, this optimum level of the assigned policy instrument will not

[1] Of course, he is concerned with the effects of *marginal* changes in policies, so that his analysis amounts to ranking, say, a given tariff and a marginally increased tariff.

[2] Since Meade's analysis is usually directed at investigating the effect on welfare of a marginal change in some tariff rate (*i.e.*, du/dt where u is the level of social welfare and t the tariff rate), the optimum tariff level can be discovered readily by putting du/dt equal to zero.

generally represent the optimum, second-best solution under the stated, second-best assumptions (irrespective of what welfare criterion is being employed). This is really a point of some importance, since the bulk of the optimizing welfare analysis in trade is constrained by the fact that it has been directed at finding the optimum level at which a *specific* trade policy instrument (*e.g.*, a tariff) should be used rather than the optimum level at which the optimum policy instrument (or combination of instruments) should be used to maximize social utility, subject to the stated assumptions, in an open economy.

The kinds of problems analysed can be divided broadly into two classes according as the second-best assumptions relate to the: (1) domestic, or the (2) foreign sector. In the former category a wide assortment of second-best assumptions has been considered: external economies; monopolies in commodity markets; infant industry arguments; factor-reward differentials between sectors of use; factor-price rigidity and increasing returns to scale. In the latter class the stage is held by the theory of discriminatory tariff reduction. These arguments are briefly discussed here, to illustrate the prefatory analysis.

(a) *External Economies.* Where the standard first-best assumptions obtain, with the exception of externalities in production, the actual market solution will be characterized by a domestic distortion (*i.e.*, a divergence between the commodity price-ratio and DRT). The classic example of such externality is the dependence of honey production on the level of neighbouring apple output. The time-honoured infant-industry argument also involves externality [8].[1] Recently the theoretical interest in the co-ordination of investment decisions has also given us another impressive example of external economies under a régime of decentralized decision-making [97].

The resulting domestic distortions have been shown to invalidate, for instance, the proposition that free trade is (necessarily) superior to no trade [112, 117]. It is no longer possible to rank these two trade policies uniquely, either for all income distributions or (more im-

---

[1] Although the infant industry case has been classified here, it must be admitted that, formally, it has dimensions of dynamic analysis which go beyond the traditional range of external economies. Allowing for this fact, however, the case for assistance to infant industries *does* rest on an assumption of externality, as pointed out by Meade [8] and recently by Johnson [133]. For a different formal description and analysis of the infant-industry case, Haberler [117] may be consulted: his analysis, however, does not bring out the externality aspect as forcefully as it needs to be.

portantly) even with any assigned income distribution for all possible cases.[1] Similarly, it can be shown that no tariff rate may exist, in any given empirical case, which will produce greater welfare than free trade [112]. The reason is obvious. Under free trade, domestic distortions imply that FRT(= FP) = DRS(= DP) ≠ DRT (where DP and FP are the domestic and foreign price ratios respectively). On the other hand, a tariff may equate FRT and DRT, but will disrupt the equality of FRT with DRS. Since two sub-optimal positions are being compared, the conclusions already stated follow readily. The optimal solution for domestic distortions is clearly a production subsidy (or tax-cum-subsidy) which will equate FRT, DRT and DRS, and thereby achieve the first-best solution.[2]

(b) *Monopoly in Product Markets.* The monopoly argument is frequently taken to collapse into a simple case of domestic distortion.

[1] As stated earlier, the ranking will depend, among other things, on the degree of divergence, the elasticity of transformation in production and so on. In this connection it is probably necessary to point out that, in the standard analysis of external economies, it is not made clear that the externality may disappear at certain levels of output of either activity. With apple blossoms and bees, where the former are already too large relative to the latter, any increase in blossoms output by diversion of resources from bee production will not be subjected to externality effects. In terms of the standard geometry (ignored throughout the text of this paper), the production possibility curve, for certain ranges of output combinations, may thus be characterized by the quality of DRT and DP (domestic prices). If, then, free trade carries the economy's production within this range, the domestic distortions will be inapplicable and the standard, first-best solution (*i.e.*, free trade is superior to no trade) will become applicable. Thus, strictly speaking, the analysis in the text requires that the domestic distortions should be within the relevant ranges of production. This, in turn, makes very clear the crucial nature of income distribution: for, with one income distribution, an $x\%$ tariff may bring the economy within the range of domestic distortions, whereas, for another, it may not, thereby influencing the ranking of policies.

[2] In the light of this analysis it is possible to understand the significant qualification introduced by Haberler [4, p. 57] in his discussion of the correct prescription in the infant-industry case: 'It should also be added that it is, *a priori*, probable that in many cases not a customs duty but an export bounty would be in order in as much as external economies may be realizable in the export rather than in import industries. . . . The fact that the infant industry argument is almost exclusively employed to recommend import restrictions and practically never to justify the opposite . . . shows clearly the bias of those who employ it.' Of course, Haberler's case would require, as the optimal solution, an optimum (production) subsidy to the export industry. It cannot be argued, however, that if this is ruled out the trade-subsidy policy (believed guardedly by Haberler to be desirable) will necessarily produce, or will even be 'likely' to produce, better results than any alternative form of trade or other intervention.

Hence, it is regarded as formally equivalent to the external economy argument. It follows, then, that, once again, free trade cannot be shown to be (necessarily) superior to no trade; and also that no tariff may exist, in any given case, which may yield higher welfare than free trade.

Where, however, the monopoly argument differs from the external economy case is in the fact that the degree of monopoly itself may be a function of the rate of tariff [133]. Take, for instance, the extreme case where the introduction of free trade eliminates the monopoly power and turns the domestic monopolist into a perfect competitor. In this case the proposition that free trade is superior to no trade, for instance, will still be valid. The formal identity with the external economy case therefore breaks down.

(c) *Factor-reward Differentials between Sectors.* The presence of a wage differential between sectors (for remunerating the same factor) represents a market imperfection, constituting a departure from first-best assumptions under certain circumstances.[1] Where it is distortionary, there are two immediate consequences. The rate at which this factor and any other factor are being substituted in production in different sectors will no longer be equal. This will result in a reduction in the transformation possibilities. The production possibility curve will 'shrink in'. Further, at each point on the shrunk-in locus the domestic price ratio will diverge from the domestic rate of transformation (*along the shrunk-in locus*), so that we also are in a situation characterized by domestic distortions.

From these two effects, it is easy to see that: (1) free trade is not (necessarily) superior to no trade; (2) an optimum production subsidy (or tax-cum-subsidy) which equates DRS, FRT and DRT (along the shrunk-in transformation locus) is superior to any tariff; and (3) an optimum subsidy on labour-use, which directly offsets the wage differential, produces the standard first-best result.

(d) *Factor-price Rigidity.* Haberler [117] has sharply distinguished between factor immobility and factor-price rigidity, showing that the former leaves the welfare propositions valid under first-best conditions unaffected, whereas the latter manages to invalidate them. By arguing that factor-price rigidity in the face of commodity price-shift will lead

---

[1] A detailed discussion of the conditions under which a wage differential may be regarded as distortionary is contained in the paper by myself and V. K. Ramaswami [112]. The qualifications to which the present analysis is subject are also considered there. Further comments on the problem are found in Johnson [133]. Credit for pioneering the problem belongs to Hagen [118].

to unemployment, Haberler has demonstrated the possibility that free trade, for any assigned income distribution and given empirical situation, may produce a deterioration in welfare in relation to no trade.[1] Haberler's analysis has recently been refined by Johnson [133], who has investigated alternative ways in which factor-price rigidity may be defined and, in turn, combined with assumptions concerning mobility of the factors of production, to produce a varying range of propositions which confirm Haberler's results.

✓(e) *Increasing Returns to Scale.* When an activity in the system is subject to increasing returns to scale the locus of transformation possibilities may lose its convexity. Matthews [123] has demonstrated how, in this case, a country may be worse off under free trade than under no trade. Thus, under this technological assumption, it is not possible to maintain that free trade is (necessarily) superior to no trade.[2]

[1] This is illustrated by Haberler [117], for a given income distribution, as follows. Taking factor immobility as well, he shows production and consumption under no trade at S, with SR as the price ratio between exportables and importables. With free trade at foreign price ratio FP, the production in importables

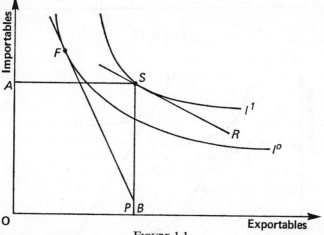

FIGURE 1.1

falls to P and consumption moves to F. The result is a deterioration in welfare. Free trade, for the given income distribution, is inferior to no trade. (It has to be assumed, of course, that the factor-price rigidity is due to institutional rather than voluntary reasons.) I might refer, incidentally, to the analysis of a similar problem [97], where the wage-rate in the agricultural sector is different from the marginal value product (whereas the industrial sector pays according to the marginal productivity principle), the wage-rate being 'rigid' in the agricultural sector.

[2] However, questions of stability of equilibrium arise here which have to be

carefully tackled. Tinbergen [127] has constructed an ingenious example which also illustrates the point in the text. In the accompanying illustration the production associated with free trade happens to be at P (which is a stable point) and the result is welfare deterioration in relation to no trade.

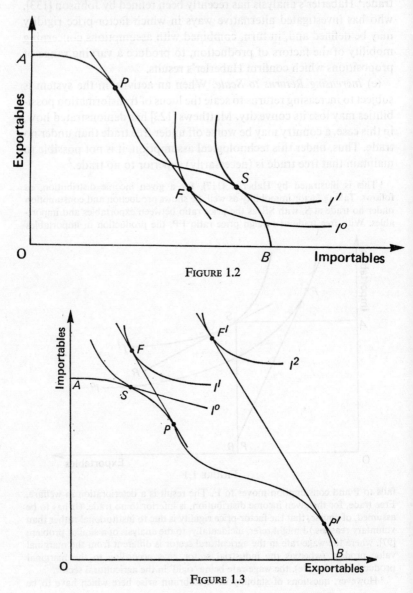

FIGURE 1.2

FIGURE 1.3

Concavity also underlines the fact that the optimizing solutions (and corresponding conditions) strictly imply only local maximization. It can be shown that the optimum optimorum may not be reached by free trade when there is concavity over some (though not the entire) range of the transformation locus, although free trade may continue to be superior to no trade.[1]

(f) *Customs Unions*. So far we have been concerned with departures from first-best assumptions on the domestic side. The welfare problem has, however, also been posed in terms of distortions arising from the presence of tariffs, subsidies and other such policies in foreign trade. Thus, for instance, a typical question has been whether, with tariffs continuing on one country, if the tariffs on another are reduced the national welfare will be increased. For any two tariff rates compared in such a situation, the ranking is subject to the income distribution chosen. Even with the income distribution chosen, no unique ranking is generally possible on an *a priori* basis.

Take, for instance, the model where the home country A can import, without having the power to affect the terms at which it can import, a commodity from either of two countries B and C. For the levels of demands relevant to the defined situation, C supplies M cheaper than B, while A is the highest-cost producer. In the initial situation, assume a tariff rate t_0 which permits C to compete successfully and secure A's market. Suppose, however, that A removes the tariff on imports from B but must continue to impose it on C's exports. If this makes B's export of M to A cheaper than C's, A is shifting its source of supply to a higher-cost producer. The former situation was characterized by DRT = DRS ≠ FRT; the latter is as well (since the most favourable rate at which A can transform its exports into imports is that determined by C's c.i.f. price in A). The choice between them cannot be made on an *a priori* basis; the choice of income distribution will also influence the ranking [7, 121]. For any given income distribution, using the ordinalist method, the ranking can naturally be worked out for any *given* empirical situation. Meade's cardinalist method would also give a unique ranking for a specific *empirical* situation.

There are many other ways in which a similar problem can be set up. One may take a case where A specializes in X and exchanges it

---

[1] Thus, in Figure 1.3, *S* represents the no-trade point, *F* and *P* the consumption and production points corresponding to free trade but representing only a local maximum, while *F'* and *P'* represent the equilibrium points corresponding to the optimum optimorum position under free trade.

for both Y (from B) and Z (from C). There is a uniform tariff rate on the (perfectly elastic supply of) imports of both Y and Z into A. The actual situation, from the viewpoint of A's welfare, is characterized by

$$\left(\frac{P_y}{P_z}\right)_F = \left(\frac{P_y}{P_z}\right)_D \text{ but } \left(\frac{P_x}{P_y}\right)_F \neq \left(\frac{P_x}{P_y}\right)_D \text{ and } \left(\frac{P_x}{P_z}\right)_F \neq \left(\frac{P_x}{P_F}\right)_D$$

where the suffixes F and D refer to foreign and domestic price-ratios in A. Suppose now that the tariff on Z is abolished *while that on Y is continued*. Then the country moves into a situation where

$$\left(\frac{P_x}{P_z}\right)_F = \left(\frac{P_x}{P_z}\right)_D \text{ but } \left(\frac{P_y}{P_z}\right)_F \neq \left(\frac{P_y}{P_z}\right)_D \text{ and } \left(\frac{P_x}{P_y}\right)_F \neq \left(\frac{P_x}{P_y}\right)_D$$

The comparison is again between two sub-optimal situations in this case. No *a priori*, unique ranking is possible [7]; and the income distribution will in general influence the ranking even when a *specific* situation has been defined (with reference to the functional and parametric aspects).

B. *Non-trade Policies*

So far only different trade policies have been compared. However, there is a considerable literature even on the effects of changes in the general equilibrium parameters and functional relationships on national welfare. Among the prominent contributions in this field are analyses of: (1) the effect of change in factor supply, and (2) the effect of technical change on welfare, when the economy is engaged in trade.

In the former category the analysis by Johnson [5, Chapter III] and myself [111] has shown how the effect of a change in factor supply on the growth of real income can be approximated, making allowance for the effect of the adjustment of the terms of trade *when the country has monopoly power in trade*. The analysis has also been extended to establish the conditions under which the growth of factor supply may actually result in the deterioration of the country's welfare through the loss of real income from worsened terms of trade outweighing the direct gain from expansion – a possibility seen independently by Edgeworth, Johnson [5, Chapter V] and myself and now widely known as the case of 'immiserizing growth'. Basically the same analysis can be adapted to the investigation of the impact of transfers of factors of production from one country to another on each's welfare, since the only substantive difference is that the growth of factors of production is, in one case, net for the two countries, while in the latter case there is no addition to the factor supply of the two countries together but only its redistribution [5].

This analysis has also been turned around to examine the relative advantages of absorption of marginal increment in population or capital stock at home or abroad [119, 122].[1] The analysis has further been reworked in relation to the effects of shifts in technology. The results of Findlay and Grubert [62] have been used to examine the effect of different types of technical progress on national welfare, again under the second-best assumption of national monopoly power in trade [2].

Ranking by Less-restrictive Criteria: International Advantage

So far, the rankings have been concerned with national advantage. Largely owing to the nineteenth-century concern with international advantage, however, much interest still continues to be exhibited in questions of international advantage.

The great bulk of the questions have again related to the ranking of trade policies when some second-best assumption obtains. Meade [8, 9] has worked out numerous problems, investigating the optimum level of a specific trade policy under the stated second-best assumptions. There are other contributions, such as Viner's [9] and Lipsey's [121] analyses of customs unions and Ozga's [85] examination of unilateral tariff reduction by a country in a world with other tariffs. These reinforce the proposition that, in general, no *a priori* ranking of policies is possible and that the choice of income distribution can affect the ranking when second-best assumptions obtain and sub-optimal situations are being ranked.

[1] This problem (unlike the others listed here) is of interest even under first-best assumptions for the economy. For instance, if the rental on capital abroad is higher than at home, and reflects the marginal value product, it would appear to be to private and social advantage to invest abroad. However, this is not correct, as what is socially relevant is the marginal return on the investments abroad. If the country already has invested capital abroad a fall in its rate of return through further investment will reduce the previous return, and the net benefit to the country will be *less* than the average rate of return, as Jasay [119] has noted in a valuable contribution. An important practical point may also be that the rate of return on foreign investment will always be less than the marginal-value product abroad because of corporation taxation [122]. And so on. The possibility of affecting the terms of trade differently according as home or foreign investment is chosen, which arises only under the second-best assumption of national monopoly power in trade, introduces still further theoretical questions of interest.

D

Meade's exercises, for instance, range over many such comparisons: (1) A imports Y_1 and Y_2 from B; Y_1 and Y_2 are substitutable or complementary in A's consumption. A duty at $t_2\%$ is levied on the import of Y_2 and cannot be removed. Would a tariff on the import of Y_1 be then worthwhile and, if so, what is its optimum level? (2) A imports Y_1, which is complementary or substitutable in A's consumption with X_2, which A exports to B and on whose exports B levies an import duty. Should a tariff be imposed on the import of Y_1 into A, and if so, what is the optimum level? (3) Or there might be second-best assumptions in the domestic economy of a country. For instance, if there is a divergence in the marginal cost and value of a commodity which competes with imports, would a tariff be worthwhile, and if so, what is its optimum level?

Central Limitations of the Propositions

Regardless of the criterion of welfare change employed, the rankings considered hitherto are valid only in a static context. At least two serious limitations of these propositions spring from the admission of dynamic elements.

(1) The ranking of two tariff rates will be a function of how these two rates are reached. Starting from a current tariff rate of $\alpha\%$, moves to a tariff of $x\%$ and $y\%$ will, in general, rank x and y differently (for the same income distribution) than when the move takes place from an initial tariff rate of $\beta\%$. In fact, even the paths of adjustments from a single current position to each of the pairs of rates of tariffs ultimately reached may not be unique, so that, for different paths chosen, the ultimate ranking may be different. These possibilities, however, are ruled out, for instance, by the restrictive assumption of constant terms of trade (for all tariff rates) in Samuelson's 1939 proof [125] of the proposition that free trade is superior to no trade and, in Kemp's extension [120] of the proof to the case when the terms of trade will vary with the volume of trade, by the (implicit) assumption that the foreign countries' trade offers at different terms of trade are not a function of the trade policy of the country. This restrictiveness is serious in a world where policy changes, especially in international trade, are inevitably accompanied by protracted negotiations concerning the reciprocity of 'benefits', and the interdependence of countries' trade policies is an impressive and irrefutable fact [107].

(2) These propositions are further limited in their reliance on one-period, static criteria. There are undoubtedly ways in which one can

demonstrate that free trade is superior to no trade, for instance, in a multi-period, dynamic, welfare framework. Thus, for instance, it can be established that, for the *same* initial conditions, time profile of consumption in each period, time-horizon and the structural composition of the terminal capital stocks (*e.g.*, the ratio in which they are to be held), free trade will lead to a *greater* quantity of terminal capital stocks than no trade [1].[1] While, however, the conclusions of welfare statics can be sustained in welfare dynamics within certain frameworks, they are also refuted within others. For instance, with a *terminal* preference function (*e.g.*, the income level in the terminal period), savings ratio a function of the income distribution, and the income distribution entirely a function of the market-imputed incomes it is possible for free trade to be *inferior* to no trade.[2]

7. MEASUREMENT OF GAINS AND LOSSES

While, in these significant respects, the welfare propositions of pure theory have continued to be limited, the static methods of welfare analysis have been strikingly extended into the field of measurement of losses and gains (as between the welfare levels reached under the ranked policies). Some of the principal factors motivating this shift have already been analysed: the impact of the shift to less purist criteria of welfare and the general demand for such measurement. To these we must add a third, interesting factor: the analytical use of such measurement in determining a 'scientific tariff' [132]. This itself has its origin in the practice of computing the economic cost of given policies.

Frequently policies are pursued for a specific non-economic objective. For instance, a tariff may be imposed to achieve an assigned level of domestic production of an importable commodity. The cost of that tariff then is the cost of achieving this level of domestic production (which constitutes the non-economic objective). This notion can be extended in two profitable ways.

---

[1] This model, from the seminal work of Dorfman, Solow and Samuelson [113], relies on two main assumptions: (1) perfect foresight; and (2) a centralized authority whose preference function specifies the time-profile of consumption, etc.

[2] I am afraid, therefore, that Caves [3, p. 265] is not correct in arguing that 'static welfare economics is perfectly valid in a dynamic setting for the welfare problems discussed here if the assumption is made that factors of production and commodities are perfectly mobile, that is can be re-allocated with infinite speed and zero cost.'

(1) Suppose that a tariff is the only policy instrument available. However, the non-economic objective, which consists of a *fixed-target* type of assignment (*e.g.*, achievement of a given level of import-competing production or the reduction of imports to a specific value), can be fulfilled in numerous ways. For instance, if the objective is to achieve a given reduction in the value of imports this could be achieved by tariffs on *one* or *more* of the various imported commodities. We have here, then, a problem of choosing that tariff *structure* which *minimizes* the cost of achieving the assigned non-economic objective. This is a familiar problem in economic analysis, with a standard solution.

Johnson [132], in a powerful and ingenious paper, has developed this analysis, christening the minimum-cost tariff structure as 'scientific' [on the (*Oxford English Dictionary*) ground that it is evolved with the aid of expert knowledge]. He uses the notion of the scientific tariff to consider the kinds of tariff structure that would be called for under a wide range of non-economic objectives such as self-sufficiency, promotion of a 'way of life', increased diversification, etc., each such general non-economic objective being reduced to a suitable, operational objective, such as reduction in the value of imports and increase in the value of import-competing production.[1]

(2) But this notion of the tariff structure that minimizes the cost of a fixed-target type of non-economic objective is itself restrictive. For the analysis can be meaningfully extended to the case where the policy-maker is willing to consider a whole range of variables, representing *varying degrees of fulfilment of a non-economic objective*. For instance, a policy-maker interested in reducing the value of

[1] There are two respects, however, in which the analysis, as presented by Johnson, may be misleading. (1) He equates the marginal benefit: marginal cost ratios for tariffs on different imports, as a condition for minimum-cost tariff structure. It should be emphasized that this is only a necessary condition (which would have to be rewritten for cases involving inequalities). (2) Secondly, he frequently talks of 'measuring' a non-economic objective in terms of some observable variable: for instance 'the simplest possible measure of the benefit achieved by such a tariff [to provide national self-sufficiency and independence] in the value of imports excluded by it' [132, p. 342]. This gives the impression that Johnson is setting up an *independent* utility function to *measure* the welfare level reached (with respect to a non-economic objective) by a tariff structure: a procedure which may well be debated. What Johnson really is doing, however, is to translate vague objectives like 'national self-sufficiency' into *precise* and usable objectives such as 'reduction in the value of imports'. And that is both necessary for the analysis to get off the ground and also a valid procedure.

imports may not lay down a specific value of imports as the target, but would like to choose from varying values of imports *after* ascertaining the (*minimum*) costs attached to the tariff structures that lead to these targets. The choice made would then have the usual property (associated with maximizing behaviour): any departure from the selected tariff structure would change the value of imports by an amount which, for the policy-maker, is not worth the change in cost involved. The scientific tariff structure associated with this choice thus exhibits the familiar optimality property from the viewpoint of the policy-maker.[1]

An important limitation of the foregoing analysis is that it specifies a non-economic objective and considers tariffs as the only available instrument variables. While, however, this approach does yield the scientific *tariff* structure, it is possible that the same non-economic objective could have been achieved at a *smaller* cost if the range of policy instruments had been wider. An interesting paper of Corden [128] illustrates this principle tangentially. Working with a two-good model (which eliminates the question of a tariff *structure*) and the fixed-target objective of attaining a *given level* of production of the importable good, Corden has shown that, for unchangeable terms of trade, a (production) subsidy is less expensive than a tariff, whereas, for variable terms of trade, a tariff-and-subsidy measure is superior to either a tariff or a subsidy. Johnson [133], drawing on Young's earlier work, has shown, on the other hand, that, for unchangeable terms of trade, a tariff is more efficient than a subsidy when the non-economic objective is an assigned reduction in the volume of *imports* (in a two-good model). These contributions already begin to pull away in the direction of a scientific *economic* policy, as distinct from a scientific tariff (or even trade) policy.[2]

---

[1] Johnson [132, p. 341] refers to this question of choice among scientific tariff structures in terms of choosing the tariff 'level' (which is presumably to be obtained, in his formulation, by equating the marginal benefits and costs). This may be a little misleading because, in general, the scientific tariff structure for varying degrees of fulfilment of a non-economic objective may *not* be just scalar multiples of each other.

[2] Although the papers by Johnson [131, 132] and Corden [128] have been singled out in the text for their ingenious and path-breaking approach to the analysis of non-economic objectives, there are two other prior contributions which merit mention here. (1) Johnson's [129] analysis of the relationship between the tariff that would produce maximum revenue (a non-economic objective) and the optimum tariff (that equates FRT with DRT and DRS under variable terms of

While the measurement of gains and losses has been used *theoretically* to derive scientific tariffs, its *empirical* application has been for the more pedestrian but surer task of estimating the cost of changes in tariff policies. Among the most striking of these exercises must be reckoned Johnson's [131] attempt at measuring the gain to the United Kingdom from joining the European Common Market and Wemelsfelder's [135] study of the short-term effect of the lowering of import duties in West Germany.[1] These analyses carry the application of the welfare propositions of pure theory of trade very much further than the early, interesting attempts, most prominently that of Marris [134], at estimating the foreign rate of transformation with a view to deriving directional policy conclusions concerning tariffs.[2]

Although these exercises represent a significant, new trend in the welfare analysis of pure theory, they none the less have limitations which reflect essentially the deficiencies of the conceptual framework underlying the measurements employed.

Two different ways in which measurement has been attempted can be distinguished. They reflect, in turn, the ordinalist and cardinalist methods of (non-Samuelsonian) welfare analysis discussed in the previous section.[3]

The former, ordinalist procedure yields several alternative measures as in other applications of 'surplus' theory. The theorist can choose from a large number of possible measures, some of which have been analysed at length by Johnson and myself [2]. Johnson [132] happens to choose Hicks' compensating variation for his measurement.[4]

---

trade) dates back to 1951–2. (2) Meade [9, Chapters V, VI] had also handled, in 1955, two problems which consist in the choice between a tariff and a domestic tax with a specific non-economic objective (of raising given revenue) from the viewpoint of minimizing the loss in world welfare – thereby anticipating the approach in the contributions of Corden [128] and Johnson [133] towards the formulation of policy questions, not just in terms of trade policy, but in more general terms.

[1] There are other, less-impressive estimates by Verdoorn and Scitovsky [7] of the gains from European integration.

[2] Marris' [134] study, while important as a pioneering empirical exercise in trade and welfare, is unpersuasive in interpretation and analysis of the statistical data.

[3] A partial-equilibrium approach to measurement has also been suggested by Corden and Johnson [130], but is subject to well-known drawbacks that are explicitly recognized by these authors.

[4] Hence, the cost of protection, when a tariff is levied, is measured in terms of the compensation that would leave the country as well off, under the tariff, as previously under free trade.

Meade's method, on the other hand, yields a unique measure of the cost of a change in policy. This measure is tantamount to the Marshallian surplus measures, as is evident from the fact that his method estimates gains (losses) as the increase (decrease) in the volume of transactions in each commodity multiplied by the excess of utility derived by the buyer over the utility of that commodity to the seller, a divergence that is measured, for instance, in the case of a tax, by the rate of tax on the assumption that the price paid equals the marginal utility to the buyer and the price received the utility to the seller. Both Johnson's and Meade's measures are identical except for the differences caused by: (1) Meade's assumption of small and Johnson's of large changes,[1] and (2) Meade's Marshallian measure and Johnson's use of the compensating variation.[2]

The identity, except for the differences noted, obtains despite the different views concerning utility measurement because of the fact that, from the present viewpoint, Johnson's assumption of a well-behaved community preference function (enjoying the properties of a *single* individual's preference function) converges on Meade's *de facto* assumption of equal weights for each buyer and seller. In the two respects in which the measurements diverge, Johnson's analysis clearly is an improvement. And yet, from the *operational* viewpoint, Johnson's ordinalist approach runs into an insuperable difficulty. How is the analyst to estimate the contours (albeit at the relevant points) of the hypothesized social indifference map? Meades' (theoretically less attractive) method runs into no such snags (though *other* difficulties of econometric measurement no doubt persist). Since the aim of these exercises is to measure welfare changes *in practice*, operational methods may well be judged to be superior to analytically more impressive results.

Either method, however, leaves out of reckoning, in consonance with the limitations of the conceptual static approach to welfare on which it is based, the dynamic elements in the absence of which the exercises are reduced in their usefulness. For instance, in relation to

[1] This introduces the fraction $\frac{1}{2}$ into Johnson's formulae, stemming from his having to integrate the area under the triangle for large changes.

[2] This leads Johnson to argue in terms of the 'compensated' (*i.e.*, constant-utility) indifference curve and to use a pure substitution term for changed consumption, whereas Meade does not adjust for changed utility and takes the entire change in consumption in his measure of the gain in utility to buyers. Johnson is equally more cautious in trying to adjust for rent in his measure of the production costs.

the estimates of the gains from European integration, it has frequently been noted that these estimates ignore significant considerations like the effects of competition on efficiency, on innovation, etc. They also omit the implications of improved bargaining power in negotiating tariff and other trade concessions.[1]

The most serious limitation springs from the conceptual difficulty of applying the surplus analysis when the economy is producing and/or absorbing commodities for purposes other than consumption. How, for instance, is the 'consumer's surplus' on the purchase of investment goods to be estimated? To assert that this can be done as with consumer goods is to assume that the price paid for investment goods currently reflects the ultimate utility that will accrue from the production resulting from them. This assumption, however, begs a whole lot of questions which are central to the issues of dynamic welfare economics. For instance, the 'correct' valuation of the investment goods will vary in general with the choice of the time-horizon.[2] These issues cannot be conjured away. They are compelling when welfare comparisons are being made.

While these limitations persist, welfare analysis in pure theory has clearly reached a degree of sophistication and feasibility of useful empirical application which is impressive. These developments have brought within the fold of economic analysis many problems with direct policy relevance.

One of the major 'casualties' of this progress has been the historic intellectual dominance of the 'free trader'. The reorientation in the view concerning the role of the analyst – the acceptance of non-economic objectives, the willingness to consider sub-optimal situations instead of strictly utopian prescriptions – has overwhelmed the profession with a new mood of judging 'each case on its merits' and tailoring policies to specific objectives and situations. The few, surviving 'free traders' have, in consequence, been in disarray. At the turn of the century they readily admitted the solitary, twin examples of 'good' tariffs: the optimum (under national monopoly power) and the infant industry tariffs. They even proudly claimed that it was a 'free trader', John Stuart Mill, who foresaw the formal arguments to

---

[1] It should be noted, however, that the authors of the estimates are generally aware of most of these limitations.

[2] Moreover, the decentralization of decision-making adds to the difficulties (*e.g.*, inconsistency and myopia in behaviour) created by imperfect foresight and necessitates a revised approach to the notions of 'rational' decision making, and hence of welfare.

support them. With the breath-taking increase in the 'deviations' from the free-trade case, however, this easy 'theoretical' superiority over the pragmatic protectionists has disappeared.[1] With it, the free traders, greatly reduced in number, have now taken to resting their case exclusively on 'empirical', practical bases. Two varieties of arguments are frequent: (1) The unsophisticated argument is that, in practice, it is impossible to estimate the 'distortions' and hence the tariff structure and level which they justify. Hence, faced with this ignorance, the economist should not advocate a move away from the free-trade situation. This contention must be rejected. Not merely does it ignore the growing trend towards estimation. It also attaches an unacceptable special weight to the situation of a zero-tariff. Indeed, even if the fact of ignorance were admitted, the most one could say was that no ranking of trade policies was possible in practice. Why should the free trader be at an advantage here? If it were contended that a departure from a given position would be incapable of positive justification, and hence free trade should be the policy, the free trader is surely worsted in the debate, since the given situation is almost always characterized by the absence of free trade. This entire approach to the validation of the prescription of free trade is thus unpersuasive. (2) A more sophisticated approach admits that distortions exist and welfare-increasing tariffs may be devised by economists. However, in practice, the way tariffs are politically engineered, they are almost always imposed so as to bring about a deterioration in welfare. This argument admits that the zero-tariff position may not be the optimal one. It merely asserts that the admissibility of tariffs will lead in practice to another sub-optimal position which is inferior. Hence the economist ought to support free trade as a political prescription.[2] It is

[1] I use the objective 'pragmatic' with special emphasis. The theological protectionist is as much at fault as the theological free trader. But whereas the former has always been taken lightly, the latter has traditionally had an intellectual respectability which is now a rapidly wasting asset.

[2] This argument has a long, historical tradition. It is worth quoting the famous passage of Edgeworth, arising out of Bickerdike's discussion of the case for optimum tariffs. 'Thus the direct use of the theory is likely to be small. But it is to be feared that its abuse will be considerable. It affords to unscrupulous advocates of vulgar Protection a peculiarly specious pretext for introducing the thin edge of the wedge. Mr. Bickerdike may be compared to a scientist who, by a new analysis, has discovered that strychnine may be administered in small doses with prospect of advantage in one or two more cases than was previously known; the result of this discovery may be to render the drug more easily procurable by those whose intention is not medicinal. . . . Let us admire the skill of the analyst, but label the subject of his investigation POISON' [4, p. 53].

surely difficult to accept this logic. Surely it is not demonstrable that tariffs will always be 'perverse' or are 'likely' to be perverse. It is equally unpersuasive to assume that politicians will readily accept the free-trade prescription when their revealed preference has continuously been for *some* tariffs (though not for no trade), but that they will reject the prescription concerning the 'correct' tariffs and instead settle for perverse tariffs.[1]

8. TRADE THEORY AND DEVELOPMENTAL PLANNING

While any 'orthodox' survey of international economics would undoubtedly have terminated with the preceding Section, it would be singularly unfortunate if I did not address a few closing remarks to the small but important and growing literature on developmental planning (*in practice*) in its trade aspects. Happily, the subject has been brilliantly analysed in a companion Survey paper by Chenery [139] so that I can confine myself to certain ideas which have value in supplementing Chenery's account.

Broadly speaking, the classes of models that have been used to guide the choice of trade (and production) policy divide conveniently into two sets: (1) the highly simplified, decision models which usually anchor on some striking characteristic of the planned economy; and (2) more elaborate, inter-industry models. The latter, in turn, classify into models that deal with mere consistency and those that also attempt partial or fuller optimization.

Among the class of simple, decision models, several can naturally be identified. The two most interesting, however, appear to be those that are associated with the notions of a wage-goods bottleneck and a capital-goods bottleneck. For instance, a model that postulates the availability of wage-goods (say, food) as the constraint on increased investment and growth (in an overpopulated economy with surplus labour) has prompted in practice a trade policy characterized by imported food/grains and focuses sharply on the role of PL480 variety

---

[1] Ethical arguments are also current. For instance, some free traders claim to be 'internationalists' and object to the optimum tariff argument as purely 'nationalistic' and of the 'beggar-my-neighbour' variety. At the purely ethical level, of course, no argument can be refuted. In this instance, however, one can point out that free trade is optimal internationally only in the situation sense, so that the problem of income distribution does remain with the 'internationalists'. Moreover, the free-trade case does not take cognisance of non-economic objectives *or* dynamic welfare complications.

of foreign aid to developing countries [136]. On the other hand, a two-sector model, with two different investment and consumption goods, helps to highlight the role of developing an adequate capital-goods production base in supporting the targeted rate of investment at some future date (if the economy is faced with a shortfall in exchange earnings currently and prospectively) and hence has resulted in the utilization of exchange to build up capacity in heavy industries [141].[1]

The central limitation of these models, however, is that they can be treacherous in ignoring *other* equally important factors: as in most economic problems, planning is necessarily a complex process. Hence, more detailed, inter-industry models which *permit* the introduction of much other information, have come to be extensively employed in framing developmental plans. Among the operational models actually used, the formulations have generally been limited in being both static and centred on just consistency [140]. Using the Leontief, static-exercise approach, the analyst takes an autonomous export vector and *either* uses the concept of an *import-structure* (involving an import-coefficients matrix analogous to the input-coefficients matrix [142]) to derive the import pattern and total corresponding to the assigned bill of goods *or* derives *imports as residuals* by taking an assigned set of production targets and setting them off against the requirements worked out from the assigned bill of goods. The former approach, using the notion of an import structure, is clearly inappropriate to a planning model which, in looking ahead, need not be tied down to an arbitrary, base-year import structure and, indeed, in doing so, rejects out of hand the important choice (available to the planner) between domestic production and imports. In this respect, the imports-as-residuals approach, used for instance in the Indian planning framework [140], is superior.[2]

---

[1] While these simple models do often serve to make an important point clear, as for instance the necessity to have a capital-goods industry, they fail in giving a clear guide line on the *magnitudes* with which the planners should work. For the latter, more detailed work, involving also other constraints in the system, will be necessary. Reliance on the former alone, therefore, may do far more harm than good. For a discussion of some of the fallacies which have actually sprung from over-reliance on such simplified modes of reasoning, the reader may refer to my paper [97].

[2] Of course, in choosing the assigned domestic production targets themselves, the planner may have *implicitly* made a choice on some sort of 'optimizing' lines. More usually, however, the domestic production targets are in varying degrees 'arbitrary'.

It is possible, however, to introduce explicit optimization into these procedures, at varying levels. The most interesting innovation, from the present viewpoint, is the operational determination of the *shadow exchange rate*, as outlined by Chenery [139] in his Survey and claimed to have been used to determine the choice between imports and domestic production of commodities for Israel by him and Bruno [138] in an excellent paper which develops a useful way of framing *alternative* programmes from which the planner may make his ultimate choice. While the objectives in these exercises are to achieve partial optimization (in limited areas of the economy) and the frameworks are essentially static, the principle of optimization used merely reflects the basic insights of the theory of trade and welfare, and there is every prospect that further work in this area will clear the way for an operational and empirically meaningful use of trade theory in developmental planning.[1]

9. CONCLUDING REMARKS

The overwhelming impression that this survey leaves is one of an area of inquiry which has been unusually active and is witnessing the emergence of many new trends. A growing concern with empirical verification, an explicit introduction of dynamic modes of analysis, the recognition of the importance of intermediates and capital goods, a policy orientation in welfare economics leading to interest in measurement and the attempts at the operational use of trade theory in developmental planning represent, as of today, the gravitational centres towards which the analytical interests of the profession are moving. In some of these respects trade theory is merely modernizing itself, 'catching up' with the advances in theory generally. But in others, as for instance in the measurement of welfare changes, trade theory is the innovator. Indeed, this is the way the subject has always

---

[1] For instance, if there are no distortions of any sort, either internally or externally, a static (traditionalist) optimization procedure, in a programming framework, would yield the equality of FP and DP, and of FRT and DRT. In this sense, the programming approach merely reflects the insights of trade theory. This is, after all, what one would expect, since the proposition that free trade is superior to a tariff (under standard first-best assumptions) is a statement *merely* about the relationship between FP and DP, and *not* about the institutions by which this equality is brought about. The unwary reader, therefore, should note that nothing of what may have been said in favour of *free trade*, for instance, is an argument in favour of *laissez faire*.

grown: in a two-way flow of ideas with the general theory of value and welfare.

ADDENDUM

The preceding Survey was written during 1962, revised during 1963 and published in 1964. Much has been written in the five years since the completion of the Survey: this is inevitable in a rapidly developing field. While the Survey stands intact in the main, certain interesting developments have occurred which require to be noted. This Addendum has been written, therefore, to note briefly, selectively and synoptically the main writings that have appeared since the Survey. In addition to the literature referred to in the text, other recent material has been organized by Sections as in the Survey. The references have been numbered consecutively, beginning (at 143) where the Survey bibliography terminates.

A. Among the major areas in which trade theory has developed recently are precisely those where the Survey had pointed to serious limitations of the existing theories. The Survey had noted the general neglect of dynamic analysis as also the traditional deployment of models which considered trade only in consumer goods produced with primary factors of production. In both these respects, analytical contributions have been accelerated recently. Dynamic models, analysing the pattern of trade involving trade in produced capital goods, have been produced in a series of capital-theoretic, growth models by Uzawa and Oniki [185] and Bardhan [180] [181]. An important capital-theoretic model has been built also by Kenen [154] who has used it to examine familiar issues such as factor price equalization and the pattern of trade. The welfare theory of trade has also been enriched by the extension of the Ramsey analysis to an open economy by Bardhan [179].

Tariff theory has further been extended to consideration of trade in intermediate goods by Corden [188], Travis [192], Balassa [186] and Johnson [189] in a series of papers which look at the effective tariff on processes rather than on products. Among the interesting theoretical analyses, deploying models with trade in intermediates, are McKinnon's [190] examination of the Lerner theorem on the symmetry of export and import taxes and Ramaswami and Srinivasan's [191] analysis of second-best trade policies under additional constraints such as specified levels of importable production and revenue collection.

B. Another set of interesting developments relates to the exploration of models involving the international mobility of factors. Kemp [174] and Jones [173] have recently analysed in depth the question of the optimal policy intervention when monopoly power in trade combines with factor mobility.

C. Finally, a considerable amount of work has continued to be stimulated by Leontief's [25] original test of the Heckscher–Ohlin hypothesis for United States foreign trade. Since, in some respects, this work has qualified the findings reviewed in the Survey besides also opening up new lines of analysis, we treat this set of developments somewhat more fully in this Addendum.

Three areas of analysis, in particular, need to be noted: (1) the seminal and original work of Minhas [33] had demonstrated that factor intensities were reversible in reality within observable ranges of factor price ratios; these results have now been challenged, at both conceptual and empirical levels; (2) the notion of 'human capital' has been deployed to re-estimate the direct and indirect labour and capital coefficients in exports and imports (as also the CES production functions which were estimated by Minhas to demonstrate the empirical possibility of factor intensity reversals); and (3) the role of research and developmental expenditure in determining the US pattern of trade has been systematically investigated.

A. *Factor-Intensity Reversals*

Minhas seemed to have shown that factor intensities were reversible because the CES production functions fitted by him to international data showed elasticities of substitution both significantly different from unity and zero as also from one another; he also had shown, by estimating the production functions, that the reversals were likely to take place within observable ranges of factor endowments internationally. However, the following qualifications must now be listed, on statistical and analytical grounds, to these results.

(i) To begin with, Leontief [159] has pointed out that Minhas inexplicably left much of his data untouched when it came to finding out whether the reversals would take place within observable ranges of factor endowments. On completing the unfinished empirical analysis, using the primary data collected by Minhas himself, Leontief finds that:

Of the theoretically possible 210 crossover points between the 21 lines entered on the graph, only 17 are found to locate within the wide range of factor price ratios, spanned on the one end by those observed in the United States and on the other by those reported from India. Moreover, most of these crossovers occur between industries whose curves run so close together throughout the entire range that for all practical purposes their capital-labor intensities would be considered identical. With two or three exceptions, each one of the twenty-one industries represented can be characterized as capital-intensive, labor-intensive, or as belonging to an intermediate group.

Thus, the evidence from Minhas' work points to a confirmation, rather than a rejection, of the strong factor-intensity hypothesis which rules out intensity-reversals.

(ii) Secondly, the results are derived from an estimating procedure which renders them, in effect, arbitrary and dependent on the choice of the exchange rate or 'conversion factor' assumed for converting local-currency values to a common-dollar basis. The side-relation from which an unbiased estimate of the elasticity of substitution 'σ' would be derived, as Minhas derived it, is:

$$\log \frac{X}{L} = a + b \log \frac{w}{P_x} \quad \cdots \cdots \quad (1)$$

where X is output, L is labour, w is the money wage rate and P_x is the unit price of output, the wage and price being in domestic currency units. However, since the data which are used are in value and do not permit breakdown of output value into unit price and quantity, the actual relation used for estimation is:

$$\log \gamma \cdot \frac{P_x X}{L} = a + b \log \gamma w + [(1 - b) \log \gamma P_x] \quad \cdot \quad (2)$$

from which the last term is again omitted as P_x is not available, with γ being the conversion factor which reduces domestic-currency prices to 'common values'. Now, if we make either the assumption that γP_x and γw are uncorrelated or the assumption that γP_x is constant (which means that the conversion factor γ is so chosen as to equalize converted prices internationally), then it is true that we will get an unbiased estimate of 'b', which is the elasticity of substitution 'σ'. But, precisely because P is not available, neither of these assumptions is verifiable in practice.

The upshot, strictly speaking, is that when Minhas chooses his γ's, in general, so as to correspond to IMF parities and then assumes (what is unverifiable in absence of information on P_x) that, at these γ's, γP_x and γw are uncorrelated, his procedure becomes essentially arbitrary. Thus, an alternative estimator of 'σ', from the *same* data in domestic currency units, could choose an alternative set of γ's, say from random numbers, and assert equally that, at *these* (different) γ's, γP_x and γw are uncorrelated and that therefore the alternative resulting estimate of 'σ' is the true estimate. Whose estimate of 'σ' are we then to choose (when the data on P_x are not available to enable us to choose between the two rival claims of lack of correlation between γP_x and γw) as the true estimate? In fact, there are an infinite number of estimates of 'σ' which can be produced, each generated by an alternative set of γ's, and each prefaced by an (unverifiable) assertion-cum-assumption that, at the γ's chosen, γP_x and γw are uncorrelated. Clearly, therefore, the Minhas estimates must be treated as arbitrary and rejected as evidence in support of the hypothesis that factor intensities are reversible.[1]

(iii) Thirdly, following on Mrs Joan Robinson's [163] earlier lead, Harcourt has pointed out that the elasticity of substitution which Minhas seeks to estimate is that of a

production function which is characterized by disembodied technical progress and *ex-post* variability of factor proportions, so that, at any moment of time, the machines in the capital stock can be treated as if they have been moulded into the form of the latest vintage. But, clearly, the figures for value added relate to the current total production, and those for labour to total employment on machines of *different* vintages in the respective industries of the countries examined, that is, they are observations taken from the *short-run* production functions of the industries in the countries concerned. Moreover, these short-run production functions are likely to be characterized by embodied technical progress and, if not zero, at least extremely limited possibilities of *ex post* substitution.[152, page 227].

This criticism may not be considered serious insofar as economic analysis necessarily proceeds by abstraction; it may be contended that the very fact that the CES production function is fitted significantly indicates that it 'works'. But insofar as direct observation indicates that different countries do have capital equipments of altogether different vintages, and the *ex post* substitution is limited, this counter-argument in defence of Minhas' estimates would appear to rely on a methodological position of the Friedman variety.

(iv) Finally, the observed relationship between labour productivity

[1] This point has emerged as a result of correspondence initiated by the author with Robert Solow, B. S. Minhas and T. N. Srinivasan. The judgment that the estimates presented by Minhas then become arbitrary is, however, entirely mine.

and wage rates, in the same industry across countries, could well run, *not* from the latter to the former but the other way around, and thus may signify merely that, on macro grounds, the real wages are higher where the labour productivity is higher. In fact, this hypothesis is equally consistent with the facts, as Gupta [151] has shown by demonstrating an equally significant linear relationship between wage rates (as the dependent variable) and labour productivity (as the independent variable), even though the data to which this relation was fitted were taken from a different industry for each country. For those who consider the Minhas procedure untenable on grounds such as (iii) preceding, this alternative, macro-type explanation of the observed statistics may appear more persuasive.

Aside from these four points of major importance, there are two others which may be surveyed prior to concluding this area of analysis.

(1) Fuchs [149], who analysed the ACMS data, has argued that separating out the developed and the underdeveloped countries, and introducing a dummy variable, yields estimates of elasticities of substitution which are very close to unity – in contrast to the ACMS results. Fuchs has argued that, with his dummy variable significantly different from zero in most of the industries, the probable explanation is a systematic understatement of wages to labour in the payroll data of one set of countries as against the other. On the other hand, the explanation may well be that labour is not homogeneous between the two sets of countries, in which case we would revert to the original suggestion of Leontief (concerning the 'superiority' of labour in the USA).

(2) Merle Yahr [166], in an interesting recent dissertation, has explored this aspect further, by estimating the CES production function, from international data, with amendment for the possibility that labour is not homogeneous across countries but reflects different levels of training and education. This is done essentially by making the parameters attached to capital and labour in the CES production function dependant, in turn, on an index of human capital, Q. This leads to a modified estimating equation of the following type (if we follow the ACMS procedure):

$$\log\frac{P_x \cdot X}{L} = a + b_1 \log w + b_2 \log Q$$

The resulting estimates of the 'true' elasticity of substitution between labour and capital are close to unity, for 37 three-digit industries,

19 two-digit industries, and 13 industrial categories used by the UN Statistical Office. Thus again the results indicate the non-reversibility of factor-intensities internationally.

While this attempt at differentiating between different types of labour is extremely important, this may not be the best way to set about analysing the problem. The view implicit in the Yahr-formation of the problem is that an Indian structural engineer, for example, is less efficient than a US structural engineer; and the proxy taken for human capital, Q, in the estimation involves elements such as the educational level of the population measured by indices such as the mean level of education of males aged fifteen and over.

The real trouble with this kind of argument is that there is no reason why a lower position for India on such an index should mean that an Indian structural engineer is less efficient than a corresponding US engineer. All that it means is that, while a US and an Indian engineer will be equivalent in quality (as firms operating internationally often testify), the *relative number* of such qualified people will be less, for a country such as India.[1] It seems more sensible to argue that the problem is created, not by the fact that people are less efficient in one country than in another because some such index as used by Yahr is supposed to show it, but that the number of qualified people in some countries is less, in relation to total working population, than elsewhere. Once the problem is posed this way, it may be more fruitful to analyse it directly by introducing a multi-factor production function, distinguishing between different classes of skills as different factors. This could be done even within the framework of CES production functions (although, as Uzawa [165] and Mukerjee [162] have recently pointed out, certain difficulties arise); in which case, the elasticity of substitution among alternative pairs of a multi-factor production function could be measured.

Minhas' pioneering and stimulating work on estimating CES production functions and thereby arguing the possibility of reversals of factor intensity has thus been shown to be subject to important

---

[1] Moreover, lumping all education together, regardless of its quality and content, is surely meaningless for the purpose at hand. More education of the liberal arts variety need not lead to greater industrial efficiency; it may lead to less. Further, unless there is matching capital accumulation, more graduates and hence a higher index of education, *ceteris paribus*, will mean urban unrest and/or work-sharing arrangements, both of which are likely to impair rather than contribute to industrial efficiency.

drawbacks. At the same time, his alternative (and more direct) test of such reversals by examining the rank correlation between two arrays of twenty-four industries for the USA and Japan, each array containing (direct and indirect) capital/labour ratios in descending order, which had shown that factor-intensity rankings were significantly different, has also been re-examined.

Thus, for example, Ball [147] has argued that the Minhas tests are defective because he should not have included primary, agricultural and food-processing industries on the grounds that (i) because of natural resources, they need not have identical production functions; (ii) the categories are so large and broad that the covered items may be strongly dissimilar between countries; and (iii) the measurements of factor use may be defective in these industries. On performing the rank correlation tests, by excluding such industries, Ball finds that the hypothesis of factor intensity reversals is no longer refuted by Minhas' data.

However, Minhas must be defended against such a criticism. While there is something to Ball's last point (to which the correct response should have been to try alternative estimates rather than to drop the industries from the analysis altogether), the first two points are certainly not the distinguishing marks of the industries described as agricultural and food-processing. Within the same finely-defined industry, for example, it is customary to find (within the same country) plants using quite different inputs and processes, even in strictly manufacturing industries such as chemicals. Nor is it possible to argue that the categories in the manufactures left in by Ball are significantly homogeneous as compared to the ones he has chosen to leave out; his choice of what to include and what to exclude is arbitrary in the absence of more detailed empirical analysis. Besides, it is difficult to see why the fact that these industries rely more on natural resources (even were it true, in some sense) should make them subject to different production functions any more than would other primary or produced factors (whose incidence internationally may also be quite diverse, thanks to transport costs and natural endowments) make the other industries subject to different production functions.

Hal Lary's [158] recent examination of international data on thirteen main groups for nine countries (as also three summary groups for twenty countries, for broadly comparable years), has also tended to support the rejection of the reversibility hypothesis.[1] Lary uses value

[1] Lary also undertakes detailed bilateral comparisons for the United States with the United Kingdom, Japan and India.

added per employee data as proxy for capital/labour data, arguing that this is an adequate way of dealing with human capital as well:

> This procedure assumes that there is no such thing in reality as completely 'unskilled labour,' and that, if average earnings are the same in two industries, the average level of human capital per worker is also equal, even though the dispersion around the average is much wider in one case than in the other. For purpose of analysis, however, it is helpful to think of the labour force as if it were composed of units of completely unskilled labour to each of which is added, according to the industry, varying amounts of skill or human capital . . . and of machinery and other physical assets. . . . The higher the value added per employee, the more capital-intensive the industry on both accounts combined; the lower the value added per employee, the more labour-intensive the industry.[1]

While Lary's method represents a rough and interesting way of adjusting for the fact of human capital, there may be difficulties in accepting this index of capital intensity if one remembers that value added may reflect varying rates of monopoly profits and rents which arise from severe controls on imports and entry in less developed countries (such as India). Furthermore, the entire group of tests which seeks to test reversibility of factor intensities by comparison of actual capital-intensity rankings of different industries internationally, requires the assumption that factor price ratios, though they may differ among countries, are everywhere the same within a given country. For, if this is not so, the international comparisons of observed rankings of industries by capital-intensity could demonstrate reversibility which arises, not from reversibility resulting from production function properties, but from the mere fact that factor price ratios facing entrepreneurs are different among industries in a manner which is not similar internationally. This problem may be of some significance in less developed countries where the use of discriminatory taxes between industries and accelerated depreciation or investment allowances (which discriminate *de facto* in favour of capital-intensive processes) are likely to be of importance.[2] Finally, we may note that Lary uses

---

[1] Lary [158, 22].

[2] In view of these and other difficulties arising whenever the analyst has to work with factor rewards data and assume perfect competition to get anywhere, it is surprising that international trade economists, seeking to verify whether production functions can show factor-intensity reversals, have not taken to working straight from engineering data; in this connection, see the interesting paper by Manne and Kurz [160].

direct coefficients, instead of direct and indirect value added per employee data.

B. *Human Capital and Skills*

Leontief's suggestion that labour is not homogeneous across countries has also led to recalculation of the capital and labour coefficients for exports and imports of the United States by Kenen and Yudin [156], of India by Bharadwaj and Bhagwati [148] and of West Germany by Roskamp and McMeekin [164], so as to allow for 'human capital'.

The method used in the Kenen–Yudin and Bharadwaj–Bhagwati exercises is outlined in the Survey. Essentially it consists in treating the difference between skilled labour wage and the unskilled labour wage as an approximate measure of the return to human capital, capitalizing this rental (at alternative rates already computed by Becker and Mincer for the USA and by Harberger and Sahota for India) to secure alternative estimates of the human capital employed in average exports and imports, which are then added to the other capital requirements to arrive at adjusted capital/labour rankings of the US and Indian foreign trade. It is interesting to record that Kenen and Yudin, despite a very large number of alternative assumptions, failed to reverse the Leontief paradox except in a very few cases. For India, the comparative labour intensity of exports was distinctly reduced by this adjustment, but not reversed.

The method used by Roskamp and McMeekin is essentially the same as that used by Kenen–Yudin and Bharadwaj–Bhagwati. However, instead of capitalizing the rental attributed to human capital and then adding it to standard capital estimates, they directly work with the data on returns to factors of production. They treat profits and interest as returns to standard capital (while adjusting them for self-employed incomes and similar complications) and separate out the rental on human capital from wages and salaries by generally treating the average wage as return to labour and wages and salaries in excess thereof as returns to human capital. The adjusted index of comparative labour-intensity then shows a reversal of the earlier, unadjusted finding that West German exports are capital-intensive. Note that the Roskamp–McMeekin variation of the technique deployed by Kenen–Yudin and Bharadwaj–Bhagwati should, in principle, give the same results. However, in an imperfect world, where the valuations of capital in different industries are likely to bear different relationships to the profit and interest incomes observed, the results could be quite sensitive to the actual method of estimation used.[1] In view of this sensitivity, it would be useful to employ *both* methods of estimating relative capital/labour intensities in exports and imports.

Note further that, both in these exercises as also the Yahr-type modification of the estimation of CES production functions, the view taken of differences in homogeneity of labour across countries is that they are attributable to differences in education and training. On the other hand, it may well be the case that sociological factors also account for differences in factor efficiency, as between countries. Thus, for example, Kreinin [157], who undertook a direct examination of Leontief's conjecture (that US labour was thrice as efficient as elsewhere) by asking firms engaged in international operations, found that such differences could indeed be observed, although at a much smaller factor of around 1·4, and were attributed by firms to, not merely inferior training and lack of adequate experience and skills, but also 'lack of motivation and drive', 'union rules' and even 'climate'.[2]

C. *Research and Development*

Another area of research, pursued by Keesing [153] and by Gruber, Mehta and Vernon [150], involves examination of possible relationships between the pattern of trade and intensiveness in 'research and development' (R & D) expenditures. Such an explanation would be, in principle, compatible with two alternative 'theories': (i) that technical progress, induced by this expenditure, lowers costs, pulls resources into these industries, and confers comparative advantage on them; (ii) that such R & D expenditures lead to new products and thus confer temporary 'availability' advantage of the Kravis-type, discussed in the Survey, which leads to comparative advantage.

A considerable amount of evidence in support of the R & D hypothesis, as the relevant explanation of the United States pattern of foreign trade, has been turned up by Keesing and Gruber–Mehta–Vernon. Both use essentially the same data and even similar

---

[1] Quite aside from factor market imperfections, which the Heckscher–Ohlin theory eschews, there could also be simply problems in estimating employed capital correctly.

[2] It may even be argued that Yahr's results are attributable, not to human capital, but to such sociological factors as listed above: that her proxy indices for human capital are themselves correlated with the incidence of such factors, and both in turn to differences in *per capita* incomes. Inefficient work habits and what appear to Western observers as 'lack of drive' are typically related to low income levels, as are low levels of education and literacy.

techniques. Keesing has correlated the 1962 share of US exports in the Group-of-Ten exports for eighteen industries with the January 1961 ratio of R & D scientists and engineers in total employment in each industry, turning up a linear correlation of 0·88 and a Spearman coefficient of rank correlation of 0·94. For twenty-two product-fields, but taking this time the ratio of R & D *expenditures* to value added in 1960, he finds a linear correlation of 0·66 and a Spearman coefficient of 0·78. He further finds that these correlations are stronger than when he substitutes, for R & D factors, indices such as skilled labour, (direct) capital intensity, natural resources and value added per establishment (as a proxy for economies of scale). Using direct coefficients, he also finds that scientists and engineers in R & D represented 2·87 per cent of the labour required to produce US exports but only 1·21 per cent for US imports in 1961. The Gruber–Mehta–Vernon results are broadly similar. They take nineteen industries, using 1962 data. They correlate successfully their two R & D indices, the ratio of R & D expenditure to sales and the ratio of scientists and engineers in R & D to total employment, with alternative indices of US export performance in each industry: the ratio of exports to sales, the ratio of exports minus imports to sales, the ratio of US world exports as a percentage to the exports of OECD countries (including Japan), the UK, West Germany and France, and finally the first two ratios broken down by the trade of the US industries with Europe and non-Europe. As with Keesing, their results generally support the conclusion that, except when other countries with similar R & D orientation (such as UK and Germany) are concerned, the R & D indices correlate pretty well with the different indices of export performance by US industries.

These results are extremely suggestive and are likely to stimulate fresh attempts at relevant theoretical formulations which would incorporate induced technological change as an endogenous factor. It is probably relevant to note, however, that these empirical exercises still fall short of investigation of the R & D indices of partner countries. Furthermore, as these authors recognize, the indices of R & D are crude: for example, the industrywise attribution is made 'according to the main industry of the company performing the task, though firms that perform R & D characteristically spread their efforts over many product fields' [153, page 39].

REFERENCES

The references have been classified into separate groups corresponding to the Sections in the text, while the numbering is consecutive for the groups together. The correspondence between the Sections and the groups is naturally not precise. The works listed do not constitute an exhaustive bibliography; the necessary and sufficient criterion for a work to be cited is that it should have been referred to in the text.

INTRODUCTION

1 Bhagwati, J., 'Some Recent Trends in the Pure Theory of International Trade', Ch. 1, *International Trade Theory in a Developing World* (Ed. Harrod and Hague; London, Macmillan & Co., 1963).

2 Bhagwati, J., and Johnson, H. G., 'Notes on some Controversies in the theory of International Trade', *Economic Journal*, Vol. 70 (March 1960).

3 Caves, R. E., *Trade and Economic Structure* (Cambridge, Mass., Harvard University Press, 1960).

4 Haberler, G., *A Survey of International Trade Theory*, Special papers in International Economics, No. I (International Finance Section, Department of Economics, Princeton University, 1961).

5 Johnson, H. G., *International Trade and Economic Growth*, London (George Allen and Unwin, 1958).

6 Johnson, H. G., *Money, Trade and Growth* (London, George Allen and Unwin, 1962).

7 Lipsey, R. G., 'The Theory of Customs Unions: A General Survey', *Economic Journal*, Vol. 70 (September 1960).

8 Meade, J. E., *Trade and Welfare* (*The Theory of International Economic Policy*, Vol. II) (Oxford, Oxford University Press, 1955).

9 Meade, J. E., *Mathematical Supplement* (*Trade and Welfare*) (Oxford, Oxford University Press, 1955).

10 Meade, J. E., *A Geometry of International Trade* (London, George Allen and Unwin, 1952).

11 Mundell, R. A., 'The Pure Theory of International Trade', *American Economic Review*, Vol. 50 (March 1960).

1

12 Balogh, T., 'Factor Intensities of American Foreign Trade and Technical Progress', *Review of Economics and Statistics*, Vol. 37 (November 1955).

13 Balassa, B., 'An Empirical Demonstration of Classical Comparative Cost Theory,' *Review of Economics and Statistics*, Vol. 45 (August 1963).

14 Bhagwati, J., 'Protection, Real Wages and Real Incomes,' *Economic Journal*, Vol. 69 (December 1959).

15 Bharadwaj, R., *Structural Basis of India's Foreign Trade* (Series in Monetary and International Economics, No. 6) (University of Bombay, 1962).

16 Bharadwaj, R., 'Factor Proportions and the Structure of Indo-US Trade', *Indian Economic Journal*, Vol. 10 (October 1962).

17 Coppock, J., *International Economic Instability* (Economic Handbook Series) (McGraw Hill Book Company Inc., 1962).

18 Diab, M., *The United States Capital Position and the Structure of the Foreign Trade* (Amsterdam, North Holland Publishing Co., 1956).

19 Heckscher, E., 'The Effect of Foreign Trade on the Distribution of Income', *Readings in the Theory of International Trade*, Ed. H. S. Ellis and L. A. Metzler for the American Economic Association (Philadelphia, Blakiston, 1949).

20 Jones, R., 'Factor Proportions and the Heckscher–Ohlin Model', *Review of Economic Studies*, Vol. 24 (1956–7).

21 Kravis, I., 'Wages and Foreign Trade', *Review of Economics and Statistics*, Vol. 38 (February 1956).

22 Kravis, I., 'Availability and other Influences on the Commodity Composition of Trade', *Journal of Polictial Economy*, Vol. 64 (April 1956).

23 Lebergott, S., 'Wage Structures', *Review of Economics and Statistics*, Vol. 29 (November 1947).

24 Leontief, W., 'The Use of Indifference Curves in the Analysis of Foreign Trade', *Quarterly Journal of Economics*, Vol. 47 (May 1933).

25 Leontief, W., 'Domestic Production and Foreign Trade: The American Capital Position Re-examined', *Economia Internazionale*, Vol. 7 (1954).

26 Leontief, W., 'Factor Proportions and the Structure of American Trade: Further Theoretical and Empirical Analysis', *Review of Economics and Statistics*, Vol. 38 (November 1956).

27 Linder, S., *An Essay on Trade and Transformation* (New York, John Wiley and Sons 1961).

28 MacDougall, G. D. A., 'British and American Exports: A Study suggested by the Theory of Comparative Costs, Part I', *Economic Journal*, Vol. 61 (December 1951).

29 MacDougall, G. D. A., 'British and American Exports: A Study Suggested by the Theory of Comparative Costs, Part II', *Economic Journal*, Vol. 62 (September 1952).

30 MacDougall, G. D. A., M. Dowley, P. Fox and S. Pugh, 'British and American Productivity, Prices and Exports: An Addendum', *Oxford Economic Papers*, Vol. 14 (October 1962).

31 Michaely, M., *Concentration in World Trade* (Contributions to Economic Analysis) (Amsterdam, North Holland Publishing Co., 1962).

32 Mill, J. S., *Principles of Political Economy*, Ed. W. J. Ashley (London, Longmans, Green and Co., 1917).

33 Minhas, B. S., 'The Homohypallagic Production Function, Factor Intensity Reversals, and the Heckscher–Ohlin Theorem', *Journal of Political Economy*, Vol. 70 (April 1962).

34 Ohlin, B., *Interregional and International Trade*, Harvard Economic Studies, Vol. 39 (Cambridge, Mass., Harvard University Press, 1933).

35 Pearce, I. F., and James, S. F., 'The Factor Price Equalisation Myth', *Review of Economic Studies*, Vol. 19 (1951–2).

36 Robinson, R., 'Factor Proportions and Comparative Advantage: Part I', *Quarterly Journal of Economics*, Vol. 70 (May 1956).

37 Robinson, R., 'Factor Proportions and Comparative Advantage: Part II', *Quarterly Journal of Economics*, Vol. 70 (August 1956).

38 Samuelson, P. A., 'International Trade and Equalisation of Factor Prices', *Economic Journal*, Vol. 58 (June 1948).

39 Samuelson, P. A., 'International Factor Price Equalisation Once Again', *Economic Journal*, Vol. 59 (June 1949).

40 Stern, R., 'British and American Productivity and Comparative Costs in International Trade', *Oxford Economic Papers*, Vol. 14 (October 1962).

41 Stolper, W., and Roskamp, K., 'Input–Output Table for East Germany with Applications to Foreign Trade', *Bulletin of the Oxford University Institute of Statistics*, Vol. 23 (November 1961).

42 Tatemoto, M., and Ichimura, S., 'Factor Proportions and Foreign Trade: The Case of Japan', *Review of Economics and Statistics*, Vol. 41 (November 1959).

43 Vanek, J., 'The Natural Resource Content of Foreign Trade, 1870–1955, and the Relative Abundance of Natural Resources in the United States', *Review of Economics and Statistics*, Vol. 41 (May 1959).

44 Viner, J., *Studies in the Theory of International Trade* (New York, Harper and Bros., 1937).

45 Wahl, D. F., 'Capital and Labour Requirements for Canada's Foreign Trade', *Canadian Journal of Economics and Political Science*, Vol. 27 (August 1961).

2

46 Harrod, R. F., 'Factor–Price Relations under Free Trade', *Economic Journal*, Vol. 68 (June 1958).

47 Kuhn, H. W., 'Factor Endowments and Factor Prices: Mathematical Appendix,' *Economica*, N.S., Vol. 26 (May 1959).

48 Laing, N., 'Factor Price Equalization in International Trade and Returns to Scale', *Economic Record*, Vol. 37 (September 1961).

49 McKenzie, L., 'Equality of Factor Price in World Trade', *Econometrica*, Vol. 23 (July 1955).

50 Meade, J. E., 'The Equalisation of Factor Prices: the Two-Good, Two-Country Three-product Case', *Metroeconomica*, Vol. 2 (December 1950).

51 Pearce, I. F., 'A Further Note on Factor–Commodity Price Relationships', *Economic Journal*, Vol. 69 (December 1959).

52 Reiter, S., 'Efficient International Trade and Equalisation of Prices', *International Economic Review*, Vol. 2 (January 1961).

53 Samuelson, P. A., 'Prices of Factors and Goods in General Equilibrium', *Review of Economic Studies*, Vol. 21 (1953–4).

54 Samuelson, P. A., 'Equalisation by Trade of the Interest Rate along with the Real Wage', Mimeographed, 1960.

55 Vanek, J., 'Variable Factor Proportions and Inter-Industry Flows in the Theory of International Trade', *Quarterly Journal of Economics*, Vol. 77 (February 1963).

3

56 Asimakopulos, A., 'A Note on Productivity Changes and the Terms of Trade', *Oxford Economic Papers*, N.S., Vol. 9 (June 1957).

57 Baldwin, R. E., 'The Effects of Tariffs on International and Domestic Prices', *Quarterly Journal of Economics*, Vol. 74 (February 1960).

58 Balogh, T., 'The Concept of a Dollar Shortage', *Manchester School*, Vol. 17 (May 1949).

59 Black, J., 'Economic Expansion and International Trade: A Marshallian Approach', *Review of Economic Studies*, Vol. 23 (1955–6).

60 Bhagwati, J., and Johnson, H. G., 'A Generalised Theory of the Effects of Tariffs on the Terms of Trade', *Oxford Economic Papers*, N.S., Vol. 13 (October 1961).

61 Corden, W. M., 'Economic Expansion and International Trade: A Geometrical Approach', *Oxford Economic Papers*, N.S., Vol. 8 (June 1956).

62 Findlay, R., and Grubert, H., 'Factor Intensity, Technological Progress, and the Terms of Trade', *Oxford Economic Papers*, N.S., Vol. II (February 1959).

63 Graham, F. D., 'The Theory of International Values', *Quarterly Journal of Economics*, Vol. 46 (August 1932).

64 Johnson, H. G., 'Economic Development and International Trade', *National Konomick Tidsskript* (Arganj, 1959).

65 Johnson, H. G., 'Effects of Changes in Comparative Cost as Influenced by Technical Change', *Malayan Economic Review*, Vol. 6 (October 1961).

66 Johnson, H. G., 'International Trade, Income Distribution and the Offer Curve', *Manchester School*, Vol. 27 (September 1959).

67 Johnson, H. G., 'Income Distribution, the Offer Curve and the Effects of Tariffs,' *Manchester School*, Vol. 28 (September 1960).

68 Johnson, H. G., 'The Pure Theory of International Trade: Comment', *American Economic Review*, Vol. 50 (September 1960).

69 Jones, R., 'Comparative Advantage and the Theory of Tariffs: A Multi-Country, Multi-Commodity Model', *Review of Economic Studies*, Vol. 28 (June 1961).

70 Kemp, M. C., 'The Relation between Changes in International Demand and the Terms of Trade', *Econometrica*, Vol. 24 (January 1956).

71 Kemp, M. C., 'Technological Change, the Terms of Trade and Welfare', *Economic Journal*, Vol. 65 (September 1955).

72 Kemp, M. C., and Jones, R., 'Variable Labour Supply and the Theory of International Trade', *Journal of Political Economy*, Vol. 70 (February 1962).

73 Kindleberger, C. P., 'Group Behaviour and International Trade', *Journal of Political Economy*, Vol. 59 (February 1951).

74 Lerner, A. P., 'The Symmetry between Import and Export Taxes', *Economica*, N.S., Vol. 3 (August 1936).

75 MacDougall, I., 'Tariffs, Protection and the Terms of Trade', *Economic Record*, Vol. 37 (1961).

76 MacDougall, I., 'A Note on Tariffs, the Terms of Trade, and the Distribution of the National Incomes', *Journal of Political Economy*, Vol. 70 (August 1962).

77 Marshall, A., *The Pure Theory of Foreign Trade* (Reprints of scarce Tracts on Political Economy) (London, London School of Economics, 1930).

78 McKenzie, L., 'Specialization and Efficiency in World Production', *Review of Economic Studies*, Vol. 21 (1953-4).

79 Meade, J. E., *The Theory of Customs Unions* (Amsterdam, North Holland Publishing Co., 1955).

80 Metzler, L., 'Tariffs, the Terms of Trade and the Distribution of National Income', *Journal of Political Economy*, Vol. 57 (February 1949).

81 Metzler, L., 'Tariffs, International Demand and Domestic Prices', *Journal of Political Economy*, Vol. 57 (August 1949).

82 Mundell, R. A., 'International Trade and Factor Mobility', *American Economic Review*, Vol. 47 (June 1957).

83 Myint, H., 'The Classical Theory of International Trade and the Underdeveloped countries', *Economic Journal*, Vol. 68 (June 1958).

84 Oliver, F. R., 'Shifting Demand Schedules and the Terms and Volume of Trade', *Metroeconomica*, Vol. 12 (April 1960).

85 Ozga, S. A., 'An Essay in the Theory of Tariffs', *Journal of Political Economy*, Vol. 63 (December 1955).

86 Ramaswami, V. K., 'The Effects of Accumulation on the Terms of Trade', *Economic Journal*, Vol. 70 (September 1960).

87 Rybczynski, T. N., 'Factor Endowment and Relative Commodity Prices', *Economica*, N.S., Vol. 22 (November 1955).

88 Samuelson, P. A., 'The Transfer Problem and Transport Costs', *Economic Journal*, Vol. 62 (June 1952).

89 Samuelson, P. A., 'The Transfer Problem and Transport Costs', *Economic Journal*, Vol. 62 (June 1952).

90 Seton, F., 'Productivity, Trade Balance and International Structure', *Economic Journal*, Vol. 66 (December 1956).

91 Stolper, W., and Samuelson, P. A., 'Protection and Real Wages', *Review of Economic Studies*, Vol. 9 (November 1941).

92 Vanek, J., 'An Afterthought on the Real Cost–Opportunity Cost Dispute and some Aspects of General Equilibrium under Conditions of Variable Factor Supplies', *Review of Economic Studies*, Vol. 26 (June 1959).

93 Vanek, J., *International Trade: Theory and Economic Policy* (Illinois, Richard D. Irwin Inc., 1962).

94 Viner, J., *The Customs Union Issue* (New York, Carnegie Endowment for International Peace, 1950).

95 Walsh, V. C., 'Leisure and International Trade', *Economica*, N.S., Vol. 23 (August 1956).

4

96 Bensusan-Butt, D. M., 'A Model of Trade and Accumulation', *American Economic Review*, Vol. 44 (September 1954).

97 Bhagwati, J., 'The Theory of Comparative Advantage in the Context of Underdevelopment and Growth', *Pakistan Development Review*, Vol. 2 (Autumn 1962).

98 Brems, H., 'The Foreign Trade Accelerator and International Transmission of Growth', *Econometrica*, Vol. 24 (July 1956).

99 Graham, F. D., 'Some Aspects of Protection Further Considered', *Quarterly Journal of Economics*, Vol 37 (February 1923).

100 Johnson, A., 'Protection and the Formation of Capital', *Political Science Quarterly*, Vol. 23 (June 1908).

101 Kindleberger, C. P., 'Foreign Trade and Economic Growth: Lessons from Britain and France, 1850 to 1913', *Economic History Review*, Vol. 14 (1961).

102 Kitamura, H., *International Economics* (Tokyo), March 1951.

103 Kojima, K., 'A Survey of the Theories on International Economics in Japan', *Japan Science Review* (*Economic Sciences*, No. 1), Japan Union of Associations of Economic Sciences, 1953.

104 Srinivasan, T. N., 'A Two-Country, Three-Commodity, Dynamic Model of International Trade', *Metroeconomica*, forthcoming.

105 Verdoorn, P. J., 'Complementarity and Long-Range Projections', *Econometrica*, Vol. 24 (October 1956).

5

106 Akamatsu, K., 'The Theory of Supply-Multiplier in Reference to the Post-War Economic Situation in Japan', *The Annals of the Hitotsubashi Academy* (October 1950).

107 GATT, *Basic Instruments and Selected Documents, Tenth Supplement* (Geneva, March 1962).

108 McKenzie, L., 'On Equilibrium in Graham's Model of World Trade and Other Competitive Systems', *Econometrica*, Vol. 22 (April 1954).

109 Stolper, W., 'Notes on the Dollar Shortage', *American Economic Review*, Vol. 40 (June 1950).

110 Stolper, W., 'A Note on Multiplier, Flexible Exchanges and the Dollar Shortage', *Economica Internationale*, Vol. 11 (August 1950).

6

111 Bhagwati, J., 'Immiserizing Growth: A Geometrical Note', *Review of Economic Studies*, Vol. 25 (June 1958).

112 Bhagwati, J., and Ramaswami, V. K., 'Domestic Distortions, Tariffs, and the Theory of Optimum Subsidy', *Journal of Political Economy* Vol. 71 (February 1963).

113 Dorfman, R., Samuelson, P. A., and Solow, R. M., *Linear Programming and Economic Analysis* (New York, McGraw Hill, 1958).

114 Fleming, M., 'The Optimal Tariff from an International Standpoint', *Review of Economics and Statistics*, Vol. 38 (February 1956).

115 Gorman, W. M., 'Tariffs, Retaliation and the Elasticity of Demand for Imports,' *Review of Economic Studies*, Vol. 25 (June 1958).

116 Graaff, J., 'On Optimum Tariff Structures', *Review of Economic Studies*, Vol. 17 (1949–50).

117 Haberler, G., 'Some Problems in the Pure Theory of International Trade', *Economic Journal*, Vol. 60 (June 1950).

118 Hagen, E., 'An Economic Justification of Protectionism', *Quarterly Journal of Economics*, Vol. 72 (November 1958).

119 Jasay, A. E., 'The Choice between Home and Foreign Investment', *Economic Journal*, Vol. 70 (March 1960).

120 Kemp, M. C., 'The Gain from International Trade', *Economic Journal*, Vol. 72 (December 1962).

121 Lipsey, R. G., 'The Theory of Customs Unions: Trade Diversion and Welfare', *Economica*, N.S., Vol. 24 (February 1957).

122 MacDougall, G. D. A., 'The Benefits and Costs of Private Investment from Abroad: A Theoretical Approach', *Bulletin of the Oxford University Institute of Statistics*, Vol. 22 (August 1960).

123 Matthews, R. C. O., 'Reciprocal Demand and Increasing Returns', *Review of Economic Studies*, Vol. 17 (1949–50).

124 Panchmukhi, V., 'A Theory for Optimum Tariff Policy', *Indian Economic Journal*, Vol. 9 (October 1961).

125 Samuelson, P. A., 'The Gains from International Trade', *Canadian Journal of Economics and Political Science*, Vol. 5 (May 1939).

126 Samuelson, P. A., 'The Gain from International Trade Once Again', *Economic Journal*, Vol. 62 (December 1962).

127 Tinbergen, J., *International Economic Cooperation* (Amsterdam, 1946).

7

128 Corden, W. M., 'Tariffs, Subsidies and the Terms of Trade', *Economica*, N.S., Vol. 24 (August 1957).

129 Johnson, H. G., 'Optimum Welfare and Maximum Revenue Tariffs', *Review of Economic Studies*, Vol. 19 (1951–2).

130 Johnson, H. G., 'Discriminatory Tariff Reduction: A Marshallian Analysis', *Indian Journal of Economics*, Vol. 38 (July 1957).

131 Johnson, H. G., 'The Gain from Freer Trade with Europe: An Estimate', *Manchester School*, Vol. 26 (September 1958).

132 Johnson, H. G., 'The Cost of Protection and the Scientific Tariff', *Journal of Political Economy*, Vol. 42 (October 1960).

133 Johnson, H. G., 'Optimal Trade Intervention in the Presence of Domestic Distortions', *Money, Trade and Growth: Essays in Honour of G. Haberler* (Ed. Caves, Johnson and Kenen) (Chicago, Rand-McNally, 1965).

134 Marris, R. L., 'The Purchasing Power of British Exports', *Economica*, N.S., Vol. 22 (February 1955).

135 Wemelsfelder, J., 'The Short-term Effect of the Lowering of Import Duties in Germany', *Economic Journal*, Vol. 70 (March 1960).

8

136 Brahmandand, P. R., and Vakil, C. N., *Planning for an Expanding Economy* (Bombay, Vora & Co., 1956).

137 Chakravarty, S., *The Logic of Investment Planning* (North Holland Series) (Amsterdam, North Holland Publishing Co., 1957).

138 Chenery, H., and Bruno, M., 'Development Alternatives in an Open Economy: The Case of Israel', *Economic Journal*, Vol. 72 (March 1962).

139 Chenery, H., 'Comparative Advantage and Development Policy', *American Economic Review*, Vol. 51 (March 1961).

140 Desai, P., 'The Development of the Indian Economy: An Exercise in Economic Planning', *Oxford Economic Papers*, Vol. 15 (October 1963).

141 Mahalanobis, P. C., 'Science and National Planning', *Sankhya*, Vol. 20 (1958).

142 Wonnacott, R., *Canadian–American Dependence* (Contributions to Economic Analysis) (Amsterdam, North Holland Publishing Co., 1961).

ADDENDUM REFERENCES

INTRODUCTION

143 Chipman, J. S., 'A Survey of the Theory of International Trade: Part 1: The Classical Theory; Part 2: The Neo-Classical Theory; Part 3: The Modern Theory', *Econometrica*, Vol. 33, July 1965, October and Vol. 34, January 1966.

144 Corden, W., *Recent Developments in the Theory of International Trade*, International Finance Section, Department of Economics, Princeton University, 1965.

145 Jones, R. W., 'The Structure of Simple General Equilibrium Models', *Journal of Political Economy*, Vol. 73, December 1965.

146 Kemp, M. C., *The Pure Theory of International Trade*, Prentice-Hall, Englewood Cliffs, New Jersey, 1964.

1

147 Ball, D. S., 'Factor Intensity Reversals in International Comparison of Factor Costs and Factor Use', *Journal of Political Economy*, Vol. 74, February 1966.

148 Bharadwaj, R., and Bhagwati, J., 'Human Capital and the Pattern of Foreign Trade: the Indian Case', *Indian Economic Review*, Vol. 2 (New Series), October 1967.

149 Fuchs, V., 'Capital-labor Substitution: A Note', *Review of Economics and Statistics*, Vol. 45, November 1963.

150 Gruber, W., Mehta, D., and Vernon, R., 'The R and D Factor in International Investment of United States Industries', *Journal of Political Economy*, Vol. 75, February 1967.

151 Gupta, S. B., 'Estimating CES Production Functions', *unpublished*, 1966.

152 Harcourt, G. C., 'Biases in Empirical Estimates of the Elasticities of Substitution of C.E.S. Production Functions', *Review of Economic Studies*, Vol. 33, July 1966.

153 Keesing, D., 'The Impact of Research and Development on United States Trade', *Journal of Political Economy*, Vol. 75, February 1967.

154 Kenen, P. B., 'Nature, Capital and Trade', *Journal of Political Economy*, Vol. 73, October 1965; Erratum, December 1965.

155 Kenen, P. B., 'Efficiency Differences and Factor Intensities in the C.E.S. Production Function: An Interpretation', *Journal of Political Economy*, Vol. 74, December 1965. *oct. 1966*

156 Kenen, P. B., and Yudin, E., 'Skills, Human Capital, and U.S. Foreign Trade', *International Economics Workshop*, Columbia University, December 1965.

157 Kreinin, M., 'Comparative Labor Effectiveness and the Leontief

Scarce-factor Paradox', *American Economic Review*, Vol. 55, March 1965.

158 Lary, H., *Imports of Manufactures from Less Developed Countries*, NBER, Columbia University Press, New York, 1968.

√159 Leontief, W., 'An International Comparison of Factor Costs and Factor Use', *American Economic Review*, Vol. 54, June 1964.

160 Manne, A., and Kurz, M., 'Engineering Estimates of Capital-labor Substitution in Metal Machining', *American Economic Review*, Vol. 53, September 1963.

161 Moroney, J., and Walker, J. M., 'A Regional Test of the Heckscher–Ohlin Hypothesis', *Journal of Political Economy*, Vol. 74, December 1966.

162 Mukerjee, V., 'A Generalized S.M.A.C. Function with Constant Ratios of Elasticity of Substitution', *Review of Economic Studies*, Vol. 30, October 1963.

163 Robinson, J., 'International Factor Price Not Equalised', *Quarterly Journal of Economics*, Vol. 78, May 1964.

164 Roskamp, K., and McMeekin, G., 'Factor Proportions, Human Capital and Foreign Trade: The Case of West Germany Reconsidered', *Quarterly Journal of Economics*, Vol. 82, February 1968.

165 Uzawa, H., 'Production Functions with Constant Elasticities of Substitution', *Review of Economic Studies*, Vol. 29, October 1962.

166 Yahr, M., *Estimating the Elasticity of Substitution from International Manufacturing Census Data*, Ph.D. Thesis at Columbia University, 1967.

2

167 McKenzie, L. W., 'The Inversion of Cost Functions: A Counter-example', *International Economic Review*, Vol. 8, October 1967.

168 McKenzie, L. W., 'Theorem and Counter-example', *International Economic Review*, Vol. 8, October 1967.

169 Pearce, I. F., 'More about Factor Price Equalisation', *International Economic Review*, Vol. 8, October 1967.

170 Pearce, I. F., 'Rejoinder to Professor McKenzie', *International Economic Review*, Vol. 8, October 1967.

171 Pearse, I. F., 'Rejoinder to Professor Samuelson's Summary', *International Economic Review*, Vol. 8, October 1967.

172 Samuelson, P. A., 'Summary on Factor-Price Equalisation', *International Economic Review*, Vol. 8, October 1967.

3

173 Jones, R. W., 'International Capital Movements and the Theory of Tariffs and Trade', *Quarterly Journal of Economics*, Vol. 81, February 1967.

174 Kemp, M. C., 'The Gain from International Trade and Investment:

A Neo-Heckscher–Ohlin Approach', *American Economic Review*, Vol. 56, September 1966.

175 Komiya, R., 'Non-traded Goods and the Pure Theory of International Trade', *International Economic Review*, Vol. 8, June 1967.

176 MacDougall, I., 'Non-traded Goods and the Transfer Problem', *Review of Economic Studies*, Vol. 32, January, 1965.

177 Södersten, B., *A Study of Economic Growth and International Trade*, Almqvist and Wiksell, Stockholm, 1964.

178 Takayama, A., 'Economic Growth and International Trade', *Review of Economic Studies*, Vol. 31, June 1964.

4

179 Bardhan, P. K., 'Optimum Accumulation and International Trade', *Review of Economic Studies*, Vol. 32, July 1965.

180 Bardhan, P. K., 'Equilibrium Growth in the International Economy', *Quarterly Journal of Economics*, Vol. 79, August 1965.

181 Bardhan, P. K., 'On Factor Accumulation and the Pattern of International Specialization', *Review of Economic Studies*, Vol. 33, January 1966.

182 Bardhan, P. K., 'Optimum Foreign Borrowing', in Shell, K., ed., *Essays on the Theory of Optimal Economic Growth*, The MIT Press, Cambridge Mass., and London, England, 1967.

183 Kemp, M. C., 'Foreign Investment and the National Advantage', *Economic Record*, Vol. 38, March 1962.

184 Negishi, T., 'Foreign Investment and the Long-run National Advantage', *Economic Record*, Vol. 41, December 1965.

185 Oniki, H., and Uzawa, H., 'Patterns of Trade and Investment in a Dynamic Model of International Trade', *Review of Economic Studies*, Vol. 32, January 1965.

5

186 Balassa, B., 'Tariff Protection in Industrial Countries: An Evaluation', *Journal of Political Economy*, Vol. 73, December 1965.

187 Basevi, G., 'The U.S. Tariff Structures: Estimate of Effective Rates of Protection of U.S. Industries and Industrial Labor', *Review of Economics and Statistics*, Vol. 48, May 1966.

188 Corden, W., 'The Structure of a Tariff System and the Effective Protective Rate', *Journal of Political Economy*, Vol. 74, June 1966.

189 Johnson, H. G., 'The Theory of Tariff Structures, with Special Reference to World Trade and Development', in *Trade and Development*, Institut des Hautes Etudes Internationales, Geneva, 1965.

190 McKinnon, R. I., 'Intermediate Products and Differential Tariffs: A Generalisation of Lerner's Symmetry Theorem', *Quarterly Journal of Economics*, Vol. 80, November 1966.

191 Ramaswami, V. K., and Srinivasan, T. N., 'Optimal Subsidies and Tariffs when Some Factors are Traded', *Journal of Political Economy*, August 1968.

192 Travis, W. P., *On the Theory of Commercial Policy*, Ph.D. Thesis submitted to Harvard University, 1961; pages 214–50.

6

193 Bhagwati, J., 'Non-economic Objectives and the Efficiency Properties of Trade', *Journal of Political Economy*, Vol. 75, October 1967.

194 Bhagwati, J., *The Theory and Practice of Commercial Policy: Departures from Unified Exchange Rates*, Special Papers in International Economics, No. 8, Princeton University, Princeton University Press, 1968.

195 Bhagwati, J., 'The Gains from Trade Once Again', *Oxford Economic Papers*, Vol. 20 (New Series), July 1968.

196 Bhagwati, J., 'Distortions and Immiserizing Growth: A Generalization', *Review of Economic Studies*, Vol. 35, October 1968.

197 Bhagwati, J., and Kemp, M. C., 'Ranking of Tariffs under Monopoly Power in Trade', *Quarterly Journal of Economics*, Vol. 83, February 1969.

198 Bhagwati, J., and Srinivasan, T. N., 'Optimal Intervention to Achieve Non-economic Objectives', *Review of Economic Studies*, Vol. 36, January 1969.

199 Kemp, M. C., 'Tariffs and the Gains from Trade', *Oxford Economic Papers*, Vol. 20 (New Series), July 1968.

200 Kreuger, A. O., and Sonnenschein, H., 'The Terms of Trade, the Gains from Trade and Price Divergence', *International Economic Review*, Vol. 8, February 1967.

7

201 Dardis, R., 'Intermediate Goods and the Gains from Trade', *Review of Economics and Statistics*, Vol. 49, November 1967.

202 Johnson, H. G., 'The Gain from Exploiting Monopoly and Monopsony Power in International Trade', *Economica*, N.S., Vol. 35, May 1968.

203 Wan, H. Y., 'Maximum Bonus – An Alternative Measure for Trading Gains', *Review of Economic Studies*, Vol. 32, January 1965.

8

204 Bruno, M., 'Optimal Patterns of Trade and Development', *Review of Economics and Statistics*, Vol. 49, November 1967.

205 Chenery, H. B., and McEwan, A., 'Optimal Patterns of Growth and Aid: The Case of Pakistan', *Pakistan Development Review*, Vol. 7, Summer 1966.

206 Chenery, H. B., and Strout, A. M., 'Foreign Assistance and Economic Development', *American Economic Review*, Vol. 76, September 1966.

207 Hansen, B., *Long and Short-term Planning in Underdeveloped Countries*, North Holland Publishing Co., Amsterdam, 1968.

208 Tinbergen, J., 'International, National, Regional and Local Industries', in Baldwin and others, *Trade, Growth and the Balance of Payments; Essays in honor of G. Haberler*, Rand McNally, Chicago, and North Holland Publishing Co., Amsterdam, 1965.

2 Notes on Some Controversies in the Theory of International Trade

It is proposed in this paper to review four disputed problems in the theory of international trade.

(1) The first problem concerns the impact of an autonomous shift in international demand on the net barter terms of trade and the volume of trade. Graham disputed the solution that Marshall offered to this problem in *Money, Credit and Commerce*. The contradiction between their rival solutions stems from alternative meanings attached to the 'increase' in demand; this is seen to emerge readily from an extension of recent developments of demand theory.

(2) The second problem concerns Edgeworth's proposition that a reduction in the cost of production of exportables in a country may lead to her impoverishment. Nicholson disputed this proposition on the ground, among others, that the model used to demonstrate the result was very restrictive. It is shown that this possibility, and the conditions under which it will obtain, can be established for less restrictive models.

(3) The third problem relates to Marshall's measure of the 'net benefit' from foreign trade and Viner's objection to it. These rival measures are here evaluated with the aid of an extension of modern welfare economics to the theory of international trade.

(4) The fourth problem relates to Marshall's theorem that, where international demands are sufficiently inelastic for international equilibrium to be unstable, there exists at least one position of stable equilibrium on each side of the unstable equilibrium point.

1. MARSHALL vs. GRAHAM ON CHANGES IN INTERNATIONAL DEMAND, TERMS OF TRADE AND VOLUME OF TRADE

In Chapter VIII of *Money, Credit and Commerce* Marshall discusses the problem of how far the terms of trade and the volume of trade would be changed if 'trade between two countries E and G having been in equilibrium, there is a considerable increase in E's demand for G's goods, unaccompanied by any corresponding increase of demand on the part of G'.[1] His solution, lucidly set out in Appendix J, is that the extent of the deterioration in E's terms of trade will vary directly with E's elasticity of demand for imports and inversely with G's elasticity of demand for imports; and the magnitude of the increase in the volume of trade will vary directly with *both* these elasticities.[2]

Graham, on the other hand, has argued that deterioration in E's terms of trade will vary inversely with *both* these elasticities while the extent of the increase in the volume of trade will vary inversely with E's elasticity and directly with G's elasticity.[3]

(A) *Graham's Solution*

In the following analysis we shall use the two-country (E and G), two-commodity (E-goods and G-goods) 'real' model which both Marshall and Graham were using.

Starting from a position of balanced trade, assume that E's demand for G's goods has increased in the sense that, at each level of the terms

---

[1] Marshall, *Money, Credit and Commerce* (Macmillan, 1923), p. 177.

[2] *Ibid.*, p. 178.

[3] Graham, 'The Theory of International Values', *Quarterly Journal of Economics*, Vol. 46, 1932, pp. 601–2. Viner supports Graham's position in his *Studies in the Theory of International Trade* (Harper & Bros., N.Y., 1937), pp. 543–6. In analysing the Marshall–Graham controversy Viner discards the use of offer curves in favour of diagrams with E-bales on the X-axis and the terms of trade (G-bales per E-bale) on the Y-axis, which leads him easily into construing 'shift in demand' in the traditional, and as we shall see Graham's, sense of change in the quantity of E-bales demanded by G from E at given terms of trade. It should also be mentioned that alternative solutions of the Marshall–Graham controversy are to be found in Allen, 'The Effects on Trade of Shifting Reciprocal Demand Schedules', *American Economic Review*, Vol. 42, 1952, pp. 135–40; and Kemp, 'The Relation between Changes in International Demand and the Terms of Trade', *Econometrica*, Vol. 24, 1956, pp. 41–6. As contrasted with these solutions, however, our approach combines simplicity with the explicit demonstration of the significance of stability conditions, further enabling us to attack directly the Edgeworth–Nicholson controversy in Section 2; we further link the problem to the general theory of value.

of trade, the quantity of imports demanded by E from G has increased in a given proportion; this increase can be represented by an increase in the quantity of imports demanded by E at the initial terms of trade. What will be the resultant impact on the international commodity terms of trade?

Assuming that the terms of trade have been readjusted so as to restore equilibrium in trade, we can analyse the change in the quantity of G-goods imported into E into two components:

(i) The postulated increase in the quantity of G's goods demanded at the initial terms of trade: it may be denoted by $\overline{dM}$, where M refers to E's initial quantity of imports of G's goods.

(ii) The decrease in the quantity of G's goods demanded as the terms of trade move in favour of G-goods to restore equilibrium: this is measured by $M . \alpha . dp$, where $\alpha = -\dfrac{p}{M} . \dfrac{dM}{dp}$ is the elasticity of E's demand for imports, and p is the terms of trade, measured as the price of G-goods divided by the price of E-goods and assumed by choice of units to be unity initially.

The total change in the quantity of G-goods imported into E may thus be measured by:

$$\overline{dM} - M . \alpha . dp \qquad . \qquad . \qquad . \qquad (1)$$

But it can also be measured in terms of the change in the quantity of G-goods supplied by G:

$$M . r_m . dp \qquad . \qquad . \qquad . \qquad (2)$$

where $r_m = \dfrac{p}{M} . \dfrac{dSm}{dp}$ ($Sm \equiv M$ initially) is the elasticity of G's supply of G-goods to E. In equilibrium, (1) = (2). Solving for dp, therefore, we get:

$$dp = \frac{\overline{dM}}{M(r_m + \alpha)} \qquad . \qquad . \qquad . \qquad (3)$$

However, both Marshall and Graham couch their argument, as we have seen, in terms of G's elasticity of demand for E's goods instead of in terms of G's elasticity of supply of her goods to E as we have done. We must, therefore, recast formula (3) accordingly. Let us define G's elasticity of demand for imports of E's goods as $\eta_x = \dfrac{p}{X} . \dfrac{dX}{dp}$, where X is the initial quantity of E-goods imported by

G. Then, by a well-known proposition, $\eta_x - r_m = 1$. Formula (3) thus becomes:

$$dp = \frac{\overline{dM}}{M(\eta_x + \alpha - 1)} \qquad . \qquad . \qquad . \qquad (4)$$

Concerning the change in the terms of trade, therefore, we have emerged with Graham's solution: if we confine ourselves to stable situations ($\eta_x + \alpha - 1 > 0$) the extent to which the terms of trade will become unfavourable to E varies inversely with the elasticities of *both* G and E. It may also be noticed that, provided the stability condition is fulfilled, this conclusion holds even when G's elasticity is less than unity.[1]

The change in the volume of trade is also in conformity with Graham's findings, and can be obtained readily as:

$$M \cdot r_m \cdot dp = \frac{(\eta_x - 1)\,\overline{dM}}{(\eta_x + \alpha - 1)} \qquad . \qquad . \qquad . \qquad (5)$$

For elastic G-demand ($\eta_x > 1$), therefore, the increase in the volume of trade will be greater, the smaller is E's elasticity of demand for imports and the larger is G's elasticity, provided the stability condition is satisfied.

(B) *Marshall's Solution*

It seems surprising that Marshall should, however, have reached a different result. But the puzzle is readily solved when we find that Marshall is construing the increase in E's demand for G's goods to mean that 'the number OM' of her bales, which she will [now] give for PM (or $P'M'$) of G bales, is greater than OM' and that 'there will be an advantage in speaking of OE [E's offer curve] *as moved to the right* by an increase in E's demand'.[2] Marshall clearly means by a 'given' increase in E's demand for G's goods an equi-proportional increase in the quantity of exports E will offer for each quantity of imports received from G; this is the same thing as an equi-proportional increase in the price E will offer for each given quantity of imports.

This being so, the reason for the contradiction in the solutions offered by Marshall and Graham emerges readily. It will be remembered that $\overline{dM}$, which occurs in the earlier formulae, represented

---

[1] Marshall explicitly confined his discussion to the case of elastic demands, although Graham did not. It is best, therefore, to regard the controversy as confined to the case of elastic demands. Cf. Viner, *op. cit.*, pp. 543–6.

[2] Marshall, *op. cit.*, p. 342, Marshall's italics.

the *given* increase in the demand for G's goods, and hence was a datum. Under Marshall's assumption, however, it varies in turn with the elasticity of E's demand for imports. If $\overline{dX}$ is the postulated increase in the quantity of exports of E-goods that E will offer for the initial quantity of G-goods imported from G, $\triangle p = \dfrac{\overline{dX}}{M}$ is the increase in the price E will pay per unit. The increase in the quantity of G-goods E will demand at the initial price is approximately:

$$\overline{dM} = -\frac{M}{p} \cdot \alpha \cdot (-\triangle p) = \alpha \cdot \overline{dX} \qquad . \qquad . \qquad (6)$$

Substituting (6) into (4), we get:

$$dp = \frac{\overline{dX}}{M\left(\dfrac{\eta_x - 1}{\alpha}\right) + 1} \qquad . \qquad . \qquad . \qquad (7)$$

Marshall's solution follows quite readily now. For stable situations and elastic G-demand ($\eta_x > 1$), the extent to which the terms of trade will become unfavourable to E will vary inversely with G's elasticity and directly with E's elasticity. However, when G-demand is inelastic ($\eta_x < 1$) – a case which Marshall excluded by assumption[1] – and the stability condition holds, Marshall's conclusion is inadmissible and the Graham conclusion holds even under the Marshall-type change in international demand.

The change in the volume of trade again is in conformity with Marshall's conclusions and can be obtained readily as:

$$M \cdot r_m \cdot dp = \frac{dX}{\left(\dfrac{1}{\alpha} + \dfrac{1}{\eta_x - 1}\right)} \qquad . \qquad . \qquad . \qquad (8)$$

For stable situations and elastic G-demand the increase in the volume of trade will be greater, the greater are *both* G's and E's elasticities of demand for imports.

We thus see that, where stability obtains and G-demand is elastic, the Graham conclusions hold when the change in international demand is defined in terms of a change in the quantity demanded at given terms of trade; whereas the Marshall conclusions hold when the change in international demand is defined in terms of a change in the price at which the given quantity is demanded.

[1] See footnote 1, p. 126.

(C) *Generalization of the Problem*

Our discussion points directly to a more general proposition in the theory of value, of which the Marshall–Graham controversy is an illustration. This is that the answer to the problem of how the elasticity of demand (supply) affects the extent to which a shift in demand (supply) alters the price and quantity exchanged depends on the precise way in which the shift is defined. There are two possible definitions of such a shift:

(*a*) a change in the quantity demanded (supplied) at a given price; and

(*b*) a change in the price at which a given quantity is demanded (supplied).[1]

According to which definition is chosen, the influence of the elasticity of the shifted curve on the effect of the shift will be different, as follows, if stability is assumed:

(i) An increase in demand will produce a greater increase in quantity exchanged, and a greater increase in price –

(1) on definition (*a*), the *less* elastic is the demand;

(2) on definition (*b*), the *more* elastic is the demand;

and conversely.

(ii) An increase in supply will produce a greater increase in quantity exchanged, and a greater reduction in price –

(1) on definition (*a*), the *less* elastic is the supply;

(2) on definition (*b*), the *more* elastic is the supply;

and conversely.

(D) *Concluding Observations*

Both ways of construing a change in demand – change in quantity demanded at a given price, and change in price at which a given quantity is demanded – may be useful in the analysis of international trade problems. Broadly speaking, Graham's approach is likely to be more convenient when the problem is to examine the effects of some change on the volume and terms of international trade, when the conditions of international competition are assumed constant, since the direction of change of international equilibrium can be predicted from the effect of the change on quantity demanded at the

[1] Definition (*a*) is the Graham-type; definition (*b*) is the Marshall-type. The former corresponds to Hicks' *p*-theory; the latter to Hicks' *q*-theory (Hicks, *A Revision of Demand Theory*, OUP, 1956).

initial price. Examples are the transfer problem and the effect of economic expansion on international trade equilibrium.[1] Marshall's approach, on the other hand, is likely to be more convenient when the problem concerns the effects of a change in a country's commercial policy on its internal equilibrium prices and quantities, since the direction of change of this equilibrium can be predicted from the effect of the tariff on the quantity of imports demanded at the initial internal price, and of the corresponding reduction of the external price on the quantity of imports the foreigner would supply. Marshall himself used this technique for the analysis of tariffs and subsidies; a more recent example of its successful application is Metzler's classic analysis of the case in which a tariff shifts production towards exports.[2]

2. EDGEWORTH vs. NICHOLSON ON THE EFFECT OF AN IMPROVEMENT IN PRODUCTION ON FOREIGN TRADE AND WELFARE

Edgeworth, in the first of his three celebrated articles on 'The Theory of International Values' in the *Economic Journal*, argued that where there has occurred 'a diminution . . . in the cost of production of an exported article', an extension of Mill's analysis indicates that 'the improvement may prove detrimental to the exporting country'. While claiming that his proposition is 'sufficiently supported by common sense', Edgeworth demonstrated it in the context of a model of complete specialization in production of exportables and in consumption of importables, arguing that the foreign elasticity of demand for the country's exportables should be less than unity for such impoverishment to occur in the context of his model.[3]

Nicholson, in his *Principles*, raised objection to Edgeworth's proposition on the ground that 'If, however, we introduce money, this case is seen to work out differently'[4] and that Edgeworth's model was highly restrictive.

[1] H. G. Johnson, *International Trade and Economic Growth*, Allen & Unwin Ltd., 1958, Chapters III and VII. Also J. Bhagwati, 'International Trade and Economic Expansion', *American Economic Review*, Vol. 48, December 1958, pp. 941–53.

[2] Marshall, *op. cit.*, pp. 344–6. Metzler, 'Tariffs, the Terms of Trade and the Distribution of National Income', *Journal of Political Economy*, Vol. 57, February 1949, pp. 1–29.

[3] Edgeworth, 'The Theory of International Values', *Economic Journal*, Vol. 4, 1894. The argument set out in the text is from pp. 40–1.

[4] Nicholson, *The Principles of Political Economy*, Vol. II (London, 1897), p. 311.

Edgeworth returned briefly to the subject in the *Economic Journal* to argue that the introduction of money would not affect the proposition; and, further, that, although his proposition had been demonstrated with respect to his restrictive model, it was clearly not confined to it and should be demonstrable in the context of models of incomplete specialization.[1]

In his *Theory of International Trade* Bastable entered the controversy to argue in favour of Edgeworth, seeking to demonstrate Edgeworth's result, in terms of a model of incomplete specialization in consumption along familiar classical lines, by showing how the country with the postulated improvement may, as a result of inelastic foreign demand, find herself with less of both exportables and importables than prior to the improvement. Bastable then proceeded to state the proposition that: 'It is only where the benefit from improvement is smaller than the advantage of interchange that loss could result from it.'[2]

(A) *Edgeworth Model:*
Complete Specialization in Production and in Consumption

Edgeworth postulates that the country with the improvement in technique produces only exportables and consumes only importables. This remarkable model makes for the simplest, if not the most persuasive, demonstration of Edgeworth's proposition.

Thus, using the notation introduced in Section 1, assume E to be the country with the postulated improvement. Then, the Edgeworth model amounts to arguing: (1) the Marshall-type increment in supply of exports: $\overline{dX}$; (2) that α is unity; and (3) that E's welfare varies directly with the quantity of her imports.

From formula (8) it follows then that E will be impoverished by the improvement if

$$\frac{\overline{dX}(\eta_x - 1)}{\eta_x} < 0 \quad . \qquad . \qquad . \qquad (9)$$

which yields us the Edgeworth condition that $0 < \eta_x < 1$ for the country to be damnified by the improvement.

(B) *Model of Complete Specialization only in Production*

Where, however, consumption of both exportables and importables

---

[1] Edgeworth, 'On a Point in the Theory of International Trade', *Economic Journal*, Vol. 9, 1899, pp. 125–8.

[2] Bastable, *The Theory of International Trade* (Macmillan, 1903), 4th edition (revised), pp. 185 and 186–7. Bastable also correctly dismisses Nicholson's contention that the introduction of money would affect the validity of the result.

obtains, different and more complex analysis becomes necessary to establish Edgeworth's proposition.

What we must now discover is the condition under which, in this model, the gain directly accruing from the improvement is outweighed by the loss from the resultant deterioration in the terms of trade.[1] This can be done readily. Let K be defined as country E's productive capacity, which is always fully employed and is measured in terms of the output of exportables that E would produce at the initial terms of trade. Then $\overline{dK}$ is the increase in real income directly resulting from the postulated improvement. To measure the loss from the deterioration in the terms of trade, we must first discover the change in the terms of trade resulting from the improvement; this is found simply by substituting for $\overline{dM}$ in formula (4) the expression $m \, . \, \overline{dK}$, in which m is the marginal propensity to consume importables. The loss of real income due to this change in the terms of trade is approximately the increase in the cost of the initial volume of imports:

$$M \, . \, dp = \frac{m \, . \, \overline{dK}}{(\eta_x + \alpha - 1)} \qquad . \qquad . \qquad . \qquad (10)$$

It follows, then, that E will be impoverished by the improvement if

$$\overline{dK} < \frac{m \, . \, \overline{dK}}{(\eta_x + \alpha - 1)}$$

i.e., if

$$(\eta_x + \alpha - 1) < m \qquad . \qquad . \qquad . \qquad (11)$$

This condition can be fulfilled without violating the stability condition; hence Nicholson's second objection, concerning the restrictiveness of the model used by Edgeworth, is refuted.

Since α can be decomposed into $m + \varepsilon$, where ε is an expenditure-compensated elasticity of demand, the condition for impoverishment can be rewritten as

$$\eta_x < 1 - \varepsilon \qquad . \qquad . \qquad . \qquad (12)$$

This formula shows, as might be expected, that for impoverishment to ensue both the foreign demand for exports and the domestic (expenditure-compensated) demand for imports must be inelastic.

[1] This argument is to be found in a rudimentary stage in Edgeworth's 1899 *Economic Journal* note, *op. cit.*, as also in his earlier 1894 article, *op. cit.* (p. 41): 'The case of an improvement in the process of manufacture of an article which is both exported and consumed at home . . . is a compound between the certain gain to the native consumer and the possible loss to the home country in the way of foreign trade.'

(C) *Model of Incomplete Specialization in both Production and Consumption*

The analysis resulting in formula (11) can be easily extended to the case where the country is producing and consuming both exportables and importables. All that is required to do is (*i*) to rewrite *m* in equation (11) as $c - h$, the difference between the marginal propensity to consume the importable good (*c*) and the proportion of the increase in productive capacity that would take the form of production of importables if the terms of trade remained at the initial level (*h*); and (*ii*) to recognize that the elasticities of international demand η_x and α now depend on the elasticities of transformation of exportable goods into importables in domestic production, as well as on the elasticities of final demand.[1]

While the possibility of increasing domestic production of importables in response to an increase in their price introduces a factor tending to raise elasticities of international demand and so increase the restrictiveness of the conditions required for the Edgeworth case, the possibility that the improvement may lead to a decrease in domestic production of importables works in the opposite direction. Since *h* can be negative, *m* can exceed unity and impoverishment can occur even if international demands are elastic.

The theoretical analysis of the effects on production of an improvement in technique in an industry, for the standard two-good two-factor constant-returns model of international trade, may be summarized as follows.[2] Assuming initially unchanged factor prices and no change in factor employment in the other industry, technical progress in an industry has two effects: except when it is 'neutral', it releases a quantity of one of the factors from the industry; and it reduces the unit cost of production. At unchanged factor prices the quantity of the factor which is released must be absorbed by an expansion of the industry which uses it relatively intensively, accompanied by a contraction of the other industry (which contraction releases the amount of the other

[1] The actual reworking of the formula along these lines may be found in J. Bhagwati, 'Immiserizing Growth: A Geometrical Note', *Review of Economic Studies*, Vol. 25, June 1958, pp. 201–5; and in H. G. Johnson, *op. cit.*, p. 76.

[2] See H. G. Johnson, *op. cit.*, for the analysis of neutral progress and a brief indication (p. 78, n. 20) of the required line of argument on cases of biased progress; and Findlay and Grubert, 'Factor Intensities, Technological Progress and the Terms of Trade', *Oxford Economic Papers*, Vol. 11, February 1959, pp. 111–21, for the analysis of the effects of biased progress.

factor required to co-operate with the released factor in the com- bination optimal at the given factor prices). At unchanged com- modity prices the reduction of cost in the industry where the improve- ment has occurred must be offset by a shift of resources into that industry out of the other, which will raise the price of the factor used relatively intensively in that industry and cheapen the factor used relatively intensively in the other industry, so restoring the initial comparative cost ratio.[1]

It follows that if progress in an industry is (a) neutral, so that only the second adjustment is called for; (b) saving of the factor used relatively intensively in the industry, so that both adjustments work in the same direction; or (c) not sufficiently saving of the factor used relatively unintensively in the industry for the first adjustment to outweigh the second; then production in the other industry will fall. Conversely, if progress is (d) sufficiently saving of the factor used relatively unintensively in the industry for the first adjustment to outweigh the second, output in the other industry will rise, and in the extreme case output of the industry in which progress occurs will actually decrease.

Thus an improvement in the export industry which is neutral, or saving of the factor used intensively in that industry, will increase demand for imports by both increasing consumption and reducing domestic production of the importable good; and impoverishment may result from such an improvement, even if international demands are elastic.[2] But improvements in the export industry which save the factor used relatively unintensively there do not necessarily give rise to the possibility of impoverishment. On the contrary, improvements sufficiently strongly saving of the factor used relatively unintensively in the export industry may, by increasing domestic production of imports, actually reduce the country's demand for imports. In this case the country will enjoy a double gain – in total output, and through improved terms of trade – instead of a gain in output offset in whole or part by a terms of trade loss.

---

[1] Since the factor used relatively unintensively in the progressing industry falls in price, more than the whole of the benefit of progress goes to the other factor. If the marginal propensities to consume of owners of the two factors differ, this redistribution effect may reduce consumption of one of the goods. This possibility, which could make c negative, is ignored in what follows.

[2] This proposition, and the following ones, assume the fulfilment of the stability condition and the absence of inferior goods.

Edgeworth was therefore incorrect in implying that any improvement which reduced costs in the export industry might prove detrimental to the exporting country. On the other hand, modern analysis points to a possibility not mentioned by Edgeworth, that an improvement in the import-competing industry, if it is sufficiently saving of the factor used relatively intensively in the export industry, will increase the country's demand for imports and so create the possibility of a net loss of welfare from the improvement. Again, this possibility arises even if international demands are elastic.

(D) *Concluding Observations*

We have shown that it is possible, contrary to Nicholson's assertion, to demonstrate the possibility of impoverishment of a country from domestic improvement in the context of models less restrictive than Edgeworth's. Moreover, in the general case of incomplete specialization we have shown that this possibility does not require inelasticity of international demands.

Also, whereas Edgeworth, Nicholson and Bastable confined their discussion (necessarily in view of their models) to improvement in the production of exportables, our analysis of the case of incomplete specialization in production demonstrates, on the one hand, that not all improvements in the export industry will create the possibility of impoverishment, but, on the other hand, that impoverishment is possible even if the improvement occurs in the domestic production of the importable good, and thus further generalizes the scope of Edgeworth's proposition.

Further, since the maximum loss that the country may suffer from adverse terms of trade cannot be greater than her gains from trade, the Bastable proposition follows that the necessary condition for Edgeworth's possibility to arise is that the direct gain from growth is less than the initial gains from trade. Our analysis again proceeds farther and establishes conditions for such impoverishment which are both sufficient and less restrictive.

Finally, it may be noted that Edgeworth correctly argued that where the country is thus damnified by the improvement, it follows 'by parity of reasoning' that it 'may be benefited by a restriction of its exports'.[1] Whatever the model used, it is clear that where impoverishment results from domestic improvement in production, the country can restrict its trade to advantage.

---

[1] Edgeworth, *Economic Journal* (Vol. 4, 1894), p. 40.

3. MARSHALL *vs.* VINER ON MEASUREMENT OF THE 'NET BENEFIT' FROM TRADE

(A) *Marshall's Measure*

In *Money, Credit and Commerce* Marshall measured the 'net benefit' derived by a country from its international trade as the sum of the excesses of the unit prices at which the country would have purchased successive quantities of imports, over the equilibrium 'rate of interchange' established in international trade.[1] In other words, he applied his concept of consumer's surplus to the problem, measuring the gain by the area between the demand curve and the price-line; though the application of the concept to the country's offer curve required considerable geometrical ingenuity, and the prices involved, as well as the surpluses, were expressed in terms of representative bales of export goods rather than money.[2]

Since the representative bales embody unit products of labour and capital, Marshall was able to measure the aggregate gain from trade to the world as a whole in terms of unit products of labour and capital, as the sum of the surpluses of the trading countries, measured in bales of their export goods. In addition, he stated the following proposition concerning a country's (G's) net benefit from trade: 'the surplus is the greater, the more urgent is G's demand for a small amount of E's goods and the more of them she can receive without any great movement of the rate of interchange in her favour'[3] – *i.e.*, the higher the price G will pay for sub-equilibrium quantities, and the more elastic her demand in the sub-equilibrium quantity range.

(B) *Viner's Criticism and Amendment*

Viner's criticism of Marshall's measure, set out in his *Studies in the Theory of International Trade*,[4] runs along lines which are by now familiar. He points out that Marshall's measure assumes that the offer curve is unaffected by whether or not the importing country pays the equilibrium price or the maximum price it is willing to pay for intra-marginal increments in its imports, which in turn implies constancy of the marginal utility of exportables. On the contrary, he argues, the marginal utility of exportables is greater, and therefore

[1] Marshall, *op. cit.*, Appendix J, Section 3, pp. 338–40.
[2] *Ibid.*, p. 339.
[3] *Ibid.*, pp. 339–40.
[4] Viner, *op. cit.*, pp. 570–5.

the price the country will pay for a marginal increment of imports less, the more that has been paid for the previous volume of imports; so that Marshall's measure exaggerates the amount of the surplus the country receives in trade. Because of this exaggeration, Viner claims, Marshall's measure may lead to improbable or meaningless magnitudes of the surplus.

In place of Marshall's measure Viner suggests going behind the offer curve to the country's utility function: deriving from it the offer curve as it would be if the country paid the maximum price it was willing to pay for each successive unit, and measuring the country's benefit from trade as the sum of the excesses (or deficiencies) of the prices shown on this curve for successive quantities of imports over the equilibrium price established in international trade. The offer curve so derived is, of course, the equivalent of the marginal valuation curve in welfare theory; and the measure it leads to is the true Marshallian consumer's surplus (the excess of what the consumer would be willing to pay for the equilibrium volume of imports over what he actually pays) as contrasted with the defective, exaggerated measure of it obtained by integrating the area under the demand curve. Thus Viner's measure is a theoretically sound version of Marshall's consumer's surplus concept, in the context of international exchange.

(C) *Alternative Measures of the Gains from Trade*

Both Marshall and Viner employ the analytical tool of the offer curve – the aggregative version of the demand curve – and both are concerned with measurement according to the concept of benefit from exchange associated with the demand curve: consumer's surplus. Other concepts of benefit from exchange have since been developed, requiring the use of indifference curves for their exposition. The purpose of this section is to apply these concepts to the problem of the benefits derived from international exchange and to develop alternative measures of the gains from trade.

Three alternative approaches to the problem of measuring the gains from trade are available: Marshallian surplus, compensating variation and equivalent variation. The first assumes that the advantage of trade consists in the opportunity to exchange the equilibrium quantity of exports for the equilibrium quantity of imports, and measures the gain from trade by the amount of one good that could be extracted from the country without making it worse off than it would be in the absence of trade. The second and third both assume that the advantage of trade consists in the ability to exchange exports for imports at the equilibrium price ratio; but whereas the second measures the gain from trade by the amount of one good that could be extracted from the country (while leaving it free to trade at the equilibrium price ratio) without making it worse off than it would be in the absence of trade, the third measures the gain by the amount of one good that would have to be donated to the country to make it as well off without trade as it would be when free to trade at the equilibrium price.

Each measure can be made in terms of either of the two goods, exportables and importables. Since, in the world market, the country is a net producer of the former in order to be a net consumer of the latter, measures in terms of exportable goods (the cost of consumption of importables) may be regarded as measures of the country's gain in its capacity as a consumer, while measures in terms of importable goods (the reward for production of exportables) may be regarded as measures of its gain in its capacity as a producer. Consequently, the alternative measurements in terms of the exportable and importable goods may (at the risk of some confusion in the Marshallian terminology) be described as the consumer and producer measurements respectively. Thus there are six possible measures of the gains derived by a country from international trade – Marshallian consumer's and producer's surplus, consumer's and producer's compensating variation, and consumer's and producer's equivalent variation – and twelve in all for the (two-country) world as a whole.

The six measures for each country are illustrated in Figure 1. Country E's exports are measured along OX, country G's along OY; P is the free-trade equilibrium point at which the two countries' offer curves intersect, the slope of OP representing the equilibrium terms of trade. U_o^e and U_o^g represent the no-trade indifference curves, and U_t^e and U_t^g the free-trade equilibrium indifference curves of the two countries.[1] T^e and T^g are the points on the no-trade indifference curves

---

[1] These are to be construed as the trade-indifference curves introduced by Meade, *A Geometry of International Trade* (G. Allen & Unwin, 1952). It is interesting to note that, as Viner records, *op. cit.*, p. 576, Edgeworth, in his 'On the Application of Mathematics to Political Economy', *Journal of the Royal Statistical Society*, Vol. 52, 1889, pp. 555–60, had already introduced, for measuring the net benefit from trade, a 'no-gain from trade' curve, which he called a 'collective utility curve', and had measured the gain from trade (for Germany) by a method exactly identical to our own. Whereas, however, Edgeworth's indifference curve was based purely on exchange analysis, the trade-indifference curve of Meade allows us to admit production into the model.

with slopes equal to the equilibrium terms of trade. The three measures of the gains from trade are denoted by S, C and E respectively; the country whose gain is being measured is denoted by the superscript g or e, and the producer's and consumer's measures by the subscripts p and c respectively.

In the 'normal' case represented in the diagram, with indifference curves strongly convex and neither good inferior, the Marshallian surplus must be less than the compensating variation; the consumer's equivalent variation must be greater than the consumer's compensating variation; and the producer's equivalent variation must be less than the producer's surplus. In other words, in this case the consumer-measures stand in the relationship $S_c < C_c < E_c$; and the producer-measures in the relationship $E_p < S_p < C_p$.[1]

All three types of measures are internationally additive, in the sense that the total gain of the world as a whole can be said to be equal to a certain quantity of one or the other country's export good. But this is a very limited statement, since the measure of total gain is valid only on the assumption that the total quantity is divided between the two countries in a unique proportion corresponding to the distribution of income at the trade equilibrium point.

(D) *Concluding Observations*

The foregoing analysis of alternative measures of the gains from trade suggests some comments on the treatment of the problem by Marshall and Viner, and also leads to a more satisfactory measure of the gains from trade.

(1) All three types of the measures of benefit discussed here employ the no-trade indifference curve as a basis of comparison. It follows that Marshall's proposition concerning the conditions under which the benefit is likely to be large, which runs in terms of the characteristics of the offer curve, must now be reformulated in terms of the properties of the no-trade indifference curve. The revised proposition, about the size of the Marshallian consumer's surplus, must involve the marginal rate of substitution between the goods in the absence of trade, and the

---

[1] Universal non-inferiority means that the slope with reference to the import–good axis of any point on the U_o curve is steeper than that on the U_t curve for the same quantity of exports, and less steep than that on the U_o curve for the same quantity of imports. Hence the distance between the two curves in the export direction increases, and in the import direction decreases, as the point on U_o moves towards the origin.

shape of the indifference curve between the origin and the point corresponding to the equilibrium volume of imports: the consumer's surplus derived from trade will be larger, the greater the difference between the slope of the free-trade terms of trade line (OP) and the slope of the tangent to the no-trade indifference curve at the point of origin, and the higher the elasticity of substitution between the goods (along the no-trade indifference curve). Marshall's own proposition, in terms of the offer curve, is thus clearly incorrect except when the trade-indifference curves are homothetic.

(2) Viner's criticism of Marshall's measure, that 'Marshall's method . . . is capable of producing such improbable results as a surplus, measured in G-bales, many times greater than the total amount of G-bales actually exported, and – if the OG curve is inelastic – may produce such meaningless results as a surplus, measured in G-bales, greater than the total amount of G-bales which G can produce'[1] is both equally applicable to his amended version of Marshall's measure and totally irrelevant. As is easily seen from contemplation of S_c^g in Figure 1, it is perfectly easily conceivable that the gain from trade on Viner's measure (or the other two consumer-measures, though *not* the producer-measures) might exceed the total quantity of goods exported by the country. Nor is the possibility that the gain might exceed the total amount of exportables the country could *produce* ruled out by Viner's measure. This possibility does require that the no-trade indifference curve can be drawn for regions involving exports above the country's productive capacity, implying that the country can value negative consumption of exportables combined with positive consumption of importables; but the fulfilment of this requirement is itself implied by the usual practice of drawing the offer curve through the origin, which assumes that at some finite high price of importables the country becomes a net exporter of such goods. If this possibility is ruled out by assumption, however, the defective Marshallian measure, which exaggerates the true surplus, could still produce the requisite result, so that Viner's argument is justified to that extent.

(3) All three of the measures of gain discussed in the previous section are open to a logical objection. If the quantity of the relevant good which measures the gain were actually extracted from the country the equilibrium volume and terms of trade would be different from their initial equilibrium values: if the gain were extracted in exportable goods the volume would be smaller and the terms of trade more

[1] Viner, *op. cit.*, p. 572.

favourable than initially, and the converse if the gain were extracted in importable goods. The measures are, therefore, in a sense logically inconsistent.

In order to avoid such inconsistency, the gain must be measured by the quantities of the two goods which, if extracted, would leave the international trade equilibrium unchanged. The simplest such measure, illustrated for country G, is T^gQ of G-goods and QP of E-goods, which quantities might be extracted by an income tax, the proceeds of which are spent in buying these amounts of the goods. But T^g is only one point on the no-trade indifference curve, that at which the marginal rate of substitution between the goods is equal to the terms of trade; any of the other points could be reached, in principle at least,[1] by a combination of excise taxes and subsidies (remembering that an income tax is, in this model, equivalent to an excise tax at the same rate on both goods). Thus the gain can be thought of as a transformation curve between the two goods, formed by the no-trade indifference curve referred to the origin P; for simplicity, the curve could be confined to the range bounded by the two Marshallian surpluses, within which the quantity of neither good is negative. By extension of this notion, the value of the opportunity to trade can be regarded as a family of such transformation curves, one for each point on the foreign-offer curve; or as a single curve formed by points on the foreign-offer curve and the points on the no-trade indifference curve at which the marginal rate of substitution between the goods is equal to the terms of trade.

4. MARSHALL'S THEOREM CONCERNING THE STABILITY OF INTERNATIONAL EQUILIBRIUM

Our fourth problem is whether, if international demands are so inelastic in the neighbourhood of an equilibrium point as to make that equilibrium unstable, this necessarily implies the existence of at least two points of stable equilibrium, one at a higher and one at a lower exchange ratio than the (unstable) equilibrium ratio. This problem is rather different from the preceding three, in that no well-recognized controversy over it is embedded in the literature of international trade, though clearly opposed views on it have been stated by different writers.

The proposition that instability of equilibrium implies an odd

---

[1] For instance, by negative purchases of goods.

number of equilibrium prices, alternatively stable and unstable, was stated by Marshall as follows:[1]

> **9.** *On the extreme hypothesis that each of two imaginary countries, in exclusive trade with one another, had an urgent demand for a small quantity of the other's goods, but could find no good use for any large quantity of them, then there might be several positions, alternatively stable and unstable, of equilibrium between them.*
>
> If *OE* and *OG* both belong to this Exceptional Demand class, they may cut one another three (or any other odd number of) times, not counting *O*. The first of these reached from *O* in either direction, will be stable, the second unstable, the third stable and so on. . . .

As is clear from the quotation, Marshall regarded inelasticity of international demand (and therefore instability of equilibrium) as of no conceivable practical relevance. Experience in the 1930s changed opinion on this score, and the conditions required for instability were re-explored in connection with the theory of devaluation and floating exchange rates. But the classic treatments of this subject did not investigate the question of the existence of stable equilibria at all thoroughly, and in *obiter dicta* implied agreement with the Marshallian position. Joan Robinson, in 'The Foreign Exchanges',[2] asserts the existence of a stable lower equilibrium rate of exchange on the grounds that 'a sufficiently violent rise in the price of imports must ultimately choke demand, and even if exports fail to react, in the flurry of the moment, the value of imports must somewhere begin to fall off'. Abba Lerner, in *The Economics of Control*,[3] while arguing generally in terms of constant elasticities which may be too low for stability, implies agreement with the Marshallian proposition in the following passage:

> One country after another is forced off the gold standard, finds its currency appreciating without this affording much relief, and is able to find a stable position only after a long fall in the value of its currency and the introduction of special restrictions on trade have so altered the situation that the elasticities are no longer so low.

On the other hand, Lloyd Metzler, in 'The Theory of International

---

[1] Marshall, *op. cit.*, Appendix J, Section 9, p. 352.

[2] J. Robinson, *Essays in the Theory of Employment* (Oxford, Blackwell, 1947), Part III, p. 201.

[3] A. P. Lerner, *The Economics of Control* (New York, Macmillan, 1944), Chapter 28, p. 380.

Trade',[1] does not mention the Marshallian proposition, but writes as if elasticities of international demand were the same at all levels of price, though increasing with the passage of time. The only explicit attack on the Marshallian proposition known to us is contained in Paul Samuelson's 'Disparity in Postwar Exchange Rates',[2] where it is remarked, *à propos* a restatement of the classical position in Joan Robinson's 'The Pure Theory of International Trade':[3]

At the critical point in her argument she assumes as obvious what is not universally necessarily true. She says, 'at some point the goods become so expensive relative to world money incomes that demand turns elastic . . . and there is some level . . . at which exports fall to zero.' I grant that it is customary to draw demand curves so that at high prices they do touch the price axis and become elastic. Probably this is realistic. But it is not universally necessary as a matter of logic. It is easy to specify indifference curves such that demand is *always* inelastic.

More recently, the Marshallian proposition has been revived as part of the argument for the adoption of flexible exchange rates.[4]

The Marshallian proposition may be illustrated by reference to Figures 2 (*a*) and 2 (*b*). In Figure 2 (*a*), which is based on Figure 20 of Appendix J to *Money, Credit and Commerce*, OE and OG are the reciprocal demand curves of E and G; in Figure 2 (*b*) these are translated into the more familiar concepts of demand and supply for imports as functions of the price of imports, Dd being E's demand for imports and Ss G's supply curve. P is a point of unstable equilibrium and there are stable equilibria at P_H and P_L, representing respectively a higher and a lower price of E's imports than the price at P.

It is at once apparent from the diagrams that the Marshallian proposition is a consequence of the way in which the curves are drawn. Each reciprocal demand curve has two characteristics:

---

[1] *A Survey of Contemporary Economics*, H. S. Ellis ed. (Blakiston, 1948), Chapter 6.

[2] *Foreign Economic Policy for the United States*, Seymour Harris ed. (Harvard UP, 1948), Chapter 22, p. 409, n. 14. In addition, Samuelson makes the theoretically far more important point that, if demand can be financed from an accumulated stock of assets as well as from income, there is no reason why devaluation of any degree should restrict demand to what can be paid for from current income. But we shall restrict our argument to the offer-curve analysis.

[3] *Review of Economic Studies*, Vol. 14, 1946–7, pp. 100–2.

[4] Milton Friedman, 'The Case for Flexible Exchange Rates', *Essays in Positive Economics* (University of Chicago Press, 1953), Chapter 6, p. 160, n. 4.

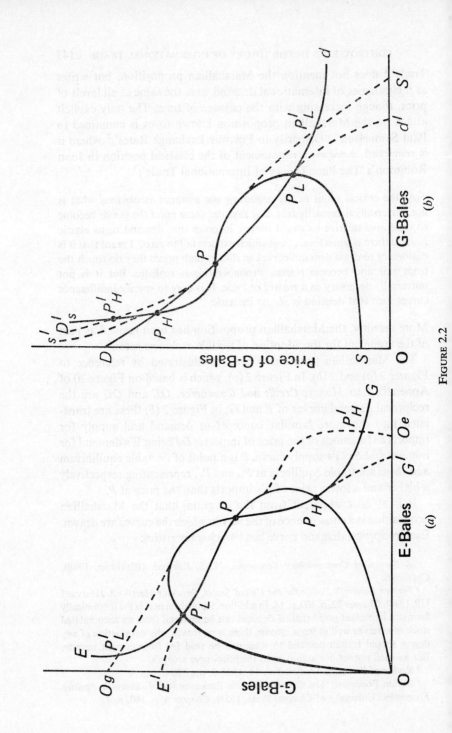

FIGURE 2.2

(i) it passes through the origin, implying that there exists a finite high price of imports which will choke off demand for them; *i.e.*, the demand for imports is terminable;[1]

(ii) it does not join the import-good axis as the price of imports falls, implying that the quantity of imports demanded increases indefinitely as their price falls; *i.e.*, the demand for imports is insatiable.

It is these characteristics which ensure that the reciprocal demand curves (demand and supply curves) intersect at least once above and below the (unstable) equilibrium price. But neither of these characteristics is a necessary logical consequence of demand theory:[2] on the contrary, both are empirical assumptions. Moreover, both characteristics appear inconsistent with Marshall's own assumption that each country has 'an urgent demand for a small quantity of the other's goods, but could find no good use for any large quantity of them'.

If neither assumption holds good for either country, the demand for imports being interminable but satiable in each country, the unstable equilibrium may be the only equilibrium possible at a finite exchange ratio; this possibility is illustrated by the curves $O_e E'$ and $O_g G'$ in Figure 2 (*a*), and $D'd'$ and $S's'$ in Figure 2 (*b*). If one country's demand for imports is satiable but not interminable, while the other country's demand for imports is interminable, there may be only one stable equilibrium possible at a finite exchange ratio, this ratio entailing a higher price for the first country's imports than the unstable equilibrium price ratio. This case is illustrated by the combination of OE' with $O_g G$ or $O_g G'$ and of OG' with $O_e E$ or $O_e E'$ in Figure 2 (*a*), to which correspond the combinations of Dd' with $S's$ or $S's'$ and Ss' with $D'd$ or $D'd'$ in Figure 2 (*b*). If one country's demand for imports is interminable but not satiable, while the other country's demand for imports is both satiable and interminable, there may again be only one stable equilibrium possible at a finite exchange ratio, this ratio entailing a lower price for the first country's imports than the unstable equilibrium price ratio. This case is illustrated by

[1] Each country's reciprocal demand curve must cut its export axis somewhere, as the country cannot spend more than its total national income on imports; but intersection at any other point than the origin implies that an infinitely high price is required to end demand.

[2] Consider, on the one hand, a bread-and-water economy or one relying on imports of a raw material not producible at home; on the other hand, the case of inferior goods.

the combination of $O_e E$ with $O_g G'$ and of $O_g G$ with $O_e E'$ in Figure 2 (a), to which correspond the combinations of $D'd$ with $S's'$ and $S's$ with $D'd'$ in Figure 2 (b). But if the demand for imports is both insatiable and terminable in one country, or satiable but terminable or insatiable but interminable in both, there will be a stable equilibrium at both a higher and a lower exchange ratio than the unstable equilibrium price ratio. These cases are illustrated in Figure 2 (a) respectively by the combinations involving OE or OG, the combination of OE' and OG', and the combination of $O_e E$ and $O_g G$; to these correspond combinations involving Dd or Ss, the combination of Dd' and Ss', and the combination of $D'd$ and $S's$ in Figure 2 (b).

PART TWO

Gains from Trade and Comparative Advantage

3 The Gains from Trade Once Again[1]

In a pair of brilliant, companion papers, Professors Paul Samuelson [6] and Murray Kemp [2] have carried the analysis of the gains from trade (derived by a single country) significantly beyond Samuelson's classic contribution [4] of 1939.

While the majority of the theorems stated in these papers are valid, including the significant extension of the theorem that *free trade is superior to no trade* to the case of countries enjoying monopoly power in trade, the analysis needs to be qualified and can be extended in respect of two important theorems stated (only) by Professor Kemp. More specifically, the following theorem needs to be qualified: that, for a country with neither monopoly power in trade nor domestic distortions, *a higher tariff is inferior to a lower tariff*. Moreover Kemp's remarkable theorem that *restricted trade is superior to no trade* is valid only if the restriction results from tariffs, quotas or exchange restrictions and cannot be sustained as a logically true proposition if taxes and subsidies on domestic production or consumption are introduced, quite legitimately, as possible methods of trade restriction.

Section 1 begins with a restatement of the proof of Samuelson's classic theorem that *free trade is superior to no trade*, stating the proof in a way which brings out certain essential aspects with greater emphasis. Section 2 discusses Kemp's proposition that *restricted trade is superior to no trade* in relation to trade-restricting policies other than tariffs and (equivalent) quotas or exchange restrictions. Section 3 shows Kemp's contention that, for a small country, *a higher*

[1] I wish to thank Professors Murray Kemp and Paul Samuelson for valuable correspondence, and Mr V. K. Ramaswami for discussion of Section 3.

tariff is inferior to a lower tariff, needs to be qualified unless inferiority of the exportable commodity in social consumption is ruled out.

1. Free Trade *vs.* No Trade

The proposition that *free trade* (in the sense of a policy resulting in the equalization of domestic and foreign prices, and hence excluding policies such as trade, production and consumption taxes, subsidies and quotas) *is superior to no trade* has been proved in Samuelson's 1939 [4] and recent [6] papers. The precise sense in which it is valid, and the conditions under which it can be interpreted as an *efficiency rule* by systems not using the price mechanism, are brought out clearly by recasting Samuelson's basic argument along the following lines where a sharp distinction is drawn between technical efficiency and utility improvement and emphasis is pointedly placed on the fact that the proposition that *free trade is superior to no trade* relates to a competitive price system whereas the fact that the *opportunity* to trade (*i.e.*, the trade situation) is superior to the no-trade situation holds regardless of the institutional assumptions made.

For simplicity, assume that the productive factors are fixed in supply, that the country has no monopoly power in trade and that the technology is such as to result in a strictly convex production possibility set.[1] The following three propositions can then be established.

Proposition 1 The trade situation (*i.e.*, the opportunity to trade) is superior to the no-trade situation (*i.e.*, the absence of trade opportunity), from the viewpoint of technical efficiency.

Proposition 2 Under perfect competition, free trade will enable the economy to operate with technical efficiency.

Proposition 3 Under perfect competition, free trade will enable the economy to maximize utility, subject to the given constraints, so that, from the viewpoint of utility-wise ranking as well, free trade is superior to no trade.

For Proposition 1, remember that technical efficiency is defined in

---

[1] The first assumption is not necessary for proving any of the three propositions that follow, as reference to Samuelson [6] and Kemp [2] will show. It is being introduced here merely to simplify the analysis and keep to a geometrical exposition without difficulty. On the other hand, note that the assumption of absence of monopoly power in trade *is* necessary for propositions (2) and (3), because they both refer to the optimality of free trade, which disappears where there is monopoly power in trade (as discussed in footnote 1, p. 153). *However*, free trade, while not being the optimal policy when there is monopoly power in trade, is nonetheless a superior (though sub-optimal) policy to no trade, as Kemp [2] has shown.

the usual, Paretian sense. Hence Proposition 1 merely states that it is *possible* to get more of one good and no less of the other when the opportunity to trade is available than when it is not.

This is readily seen in Figure 1, similar to Samuelson's illustration, where the price-line $CD = EF$ represents the international prices and OAB the production possibility set. If production is set at P and trade is undertaken (as it must be) at the stated international prices, OEF becomes the availability set and EF the availability frontier, the Pareto-efficient locus of available combinations of the two commodities. But if production is set instead at P^*, the availability set is the *largest* possible, at OCD, and CD rperesents the most efficient, Pareto-optimal availability line subject to the domestic and foreign transformation constraints.[1] On the other hand, AB, the production possibility frontier, represents the efficient, availability line in the absence of trade opportunity.

It is thus clear immediately, since CD lies uniformly outside AB (though touching it at P^*), that *any* bundle of commodities which is available by production alone (*i.e.*, in the no-trade situation) *can* be improved upon (with one borderline caes at P^*) by production at P^* and trade therefrom.

Hence, the *opportunity* to trade represents for the economy a superior situation than the absence thereof. In other words, the trade situation is superior to the no-trade situation (in the sense of Paretian, technical efficiency).

Note that this proposition merely states that it is *possible*, if the trade opportunity is exploited in a certain way, to have more of one good and no less of the other(s) under trade than under no trade. The proposition does *not* assert anything as to whether a specific, economic system will in fact manage to utilize the trade opportunity in this technically efficient manner. Of course the proposition that trade *could* expand the economy's availabilities is hardly surprising once one realizes that the possibility of trade really adds yet another 'technological' process of transforming exportables into importables, and this cannot but improve (or, at worst, leave unchanged) the availabilities defined by the *domestic* resource and technological constraints.

---

[1] Note that any shift of production from P^*, and trade therefrom, to production at another point (such as P) and trade from that new point will only *reduce* the availability set open to the economy. Hence, production at P^* represents the most efficient production point from which trade can be conducted.

F

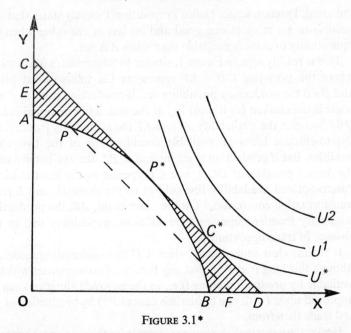

FIGURE 3.1*

* Without trade, $APP*B$ represents the production possibility, and hence availability (or consumption possibility), frontier. If unlimited trade is possible at the world price ratio given by CD's slope, the new availability frontier is given by $CP*D$, the farthest-out line with slope CD that touches the domestic, production possibility frontier. Any domestic welfare function (of the standard, static variety) will be maximized at a point such as $C*$, which gives more welfare than any point within $APP*B$ (save in the singular case where $C*$ and $P*$ happen to coincide).

On the other hand, Proposition 2 relates explicitly to whether an actual, institutional system will operate with *technical* efficiency. It states that, for a competitive price system, free trade *will* in fact enable the economy to exploit the trade opportunity most effectively and thus operate efficiently (*i.e.*, bring production to P* and trade along $CP*D$ in Figure 3·1). The proof of this proposition is straightforward and rests on the fact that with (i) free trade, constituting the equalization of foreign and domestic prices, and (ii) perfect competition, with the assumed technology, assuring the equalization of domestic prices with the marginal rate of transformation in production (on the production possibility frontier), the economy must necessarily end up producing and trading efficiently. To illustrate, under free trade at price $CD = EF$, the economy *will* produce at P^* and trade along CD, thus operating with technical efficiency.

Note further that Proposition 2 can be readily adapted for institutional frameworks other than that of a competitive, price system. Thus, for an economic system which does not use (domestic) prices to guide production, it is conceivable that an alternative way of operating with efficiency would be for planners to follow the rule of *equating foreign prices with the marginal rate of transformation of products in domestic production.*[1] This efficiency rule would ensure the operation of the economy at technical efficiency; in Figure 1, the planners would be guided by the rule to producing at P* and thus trading along CP^*D. Free trade merely happens to be the policy which enables a competitive, price system to implement this efficiency rule.[2]

It is now possible to go beyond questions of technical efficiency and raise the issue of utility-wise ranking of free trade and no trade. If we take a well-ordered, social utility index, Proposition 3 follows immediately.[3] For those not anxious to raise questions about the in-

[1] For a country, however, which enjoys monopoly power in trade, the rule modifies to the well-known prescription to equate the marginal terms of trade with the marginal rate of transformation in domestic production. The rule can be obtained more directly by maximizing the availability of one commodity subject to specified level(s) of the other(s), subject further to the constraints imposed by the implicit, domestic transformation function and the foreign reciprocal demand function.

[2] Following on this, I have found it useful, in the classroom, to tell my Indian students that even a 'Soviet-type' economic system, which may decide to avoid the use of prices to guide domestic allocation of resources, cannot afford to ignore international prices, the reason being that they really represent, from the welfare point of view, a 'technological' datum. I may also add that the distinction between Propositions 2 and 3, based on the distinction between technical efficiency and utility maximization, is also very useful if one is teaching students living in a 'planned' economy; Professor Bent Hansen, who has taught in Cairo for some years, told me some time ago that he has also found it useful to teach free trade optimality in terms of Propositions 1 and 2 above.

[3] Formally, we would be maximizing a function such as $U = U(X, Y)$ where U stands for social welfare, X and Y for the available commodities and the function has the standard properties [5] such as

$$\frac{\partial U}{\partial X} > 0, \quad \frac{\partial U}{\partial Y} > 0, \quad \frac{dX}{dY} < 0 \quad \text{and} \quad \frac{d^2X}{dY^2} > 0$$
$$U = \text{constant} \qquad U = \text{constant}$$

This function would be maximized subject to the implicit, domestic transformation function and the foreign reciprocal demand function. It would then be shown that, under free trade, a perfectly competitive system would satisfy the investigated maximizing conditions.

comparability of different persons' utilities and who are ready to accept a well-ordered social utility index, this procedure is entirely satisfactory.[1] But those who, reluctant to go beyond consideration of utility for each (incomparable) individual, wish to base utility-wise rankings on the superior-for-all-income-distributions criterion may prefer the approach of utility-possibility loci comparisons used by Samuelson [6] and Kemp [2]. They argue, quite correctly, that the

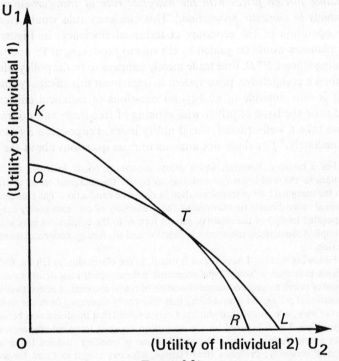

FIGURE 3.2*

* QTR represents the utility possibility curve, in a two-person economy, corresponding to the no-trade situation. KTL represents the utility possibility curve corresponding to the free trade situation. KTL lies uniformly outside QTR (though touching it at T), indicating that the free trade situation is superior (or, at minimum, equivalent) to the no-trade situation from the viewpoint of social welfare.

[1] For those unwilling to assume that *laissez-faire* can be counted on to provide the ethically proper income distribution and yet want to use a social utility index, Samuelson's [6] construction of 'social indifference curves' is the appropriate reference.

fact that *CD*, the availability frontier under free trade, lies uniformly outside (though once touching) *AB*, the availability frontier under no trade, implies that the utility possibility locus for the free trade situation must also lie uniformly outside (though possibly touching) that for the no-trade situation, as illustrated in Figure 3.2 for a two-person economy. This implies that, under free trade, for *any* utility distribution (except at the point(s) where the two loci touch)[1] achieved under no trade, it is possible (*via* ideal lump sum taxes and subsidies) to achieve a higher level for both individuals. Hence, *free trade is* (unambiguously) *superior* (or, at minimum, equal) *to no trade* (for all income distributions).[2]

2. RESTRICTED TRADE *vs.* NO TRADE

Kemp [2] has further argued that, for utility-wise ranking, *restricted trade is superior to no trade*. While all forms of trade cannot be shown

[1] As Professor Samuelson has pointed out to me in correspondence, the free trade possibility locus may even coincide with the no-trade utility possibility locus if all individuals are alike and have unitary income elasticities, and if *C** in Figure 1 coincides with *P**.

[2] Note, however, that while it is correct to argue that (utility-wise) free trade is superior to no trade, it is *not* true that *any kind of trade* is better than no trade.

Samuelson states, in his earlier 1939 paper [4, p. 239], that 'free trade or some trade is to be preferred to *no* trade at all'. In the later, 1962 paper [6] as well, the argument is stated in terms of 'some trade'. 'Some trade', however, is *not* to be interpreted as equivalent to 'any trade'; and it should be noted that Samuelson's method of proof indeed fully supports this presumption. In correspondence Professor Samuelson has pointed out that this is definitely the proper interpretation of his theorem.

It can be easily shown in fact that any kind of trade cannot be shown to be superior to no trade. Take, for example, Figure 3 in the text. It shows that, for an economy with no monopoly power in trade, a production subsidy (or, alternatively tax) on commodity *Y* (or, alternatively *X*) can bring domestic prices for producers to D_P and production to P_T, consumption (at international prices F_P) to C_T and social utility locus U_S ($> U_T$). Thus a policy of trade (involving specifically a production tax-cum-subsidy policy combined with otherwise-free trade) is inferior to that of no trade for the specific income distribution implicit in the social utility index employed, and hence it will be impossible, in this instance, for the gainers in the trade situation to compensate the losers without themselves becoming worse off than in the no-trade situation. This conclusion is readily understandable because, as we know from the theory of Second Best, it is not possible in general to rank uniquely (for all income distributions) two sub-optimal policies: and, trade and no trade are both sub-optimal policies for a country with no monopoly power in trade (unless trade amounts specifically to free trade, which is the optimal policy).

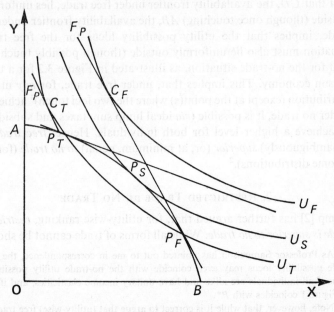

FIGURE 3.3*

* AP_SB represents the domestic, production possibility curve. In the absence of trade, the welfare level is at U_S. Under free trade at the given world price ratio measured by the slope of F_P, welfare will increase ($U_F > U_S$). If, however, an appropriate subsidy (or, alternatively tax) on the production of Y (or, alternatively X) is introduced *along with* otherwise-free trade, production will shift to P_T and consumption to C_T, the volume of trade will be reduced below the free-trade level, and the welfare level reduced *below* that under no trade ($U_T < U_S$), thus demonstrating that restricted trade would, in this instance, be inferior to no trade.

to be (always) superior to no trade,[1] can the classes of trade considered be narrowed down to 'restricted trade' and this sub-set be shown to be superior to no trade?

Kemp is certainly right when the restriction is brought about by three classes of policies: tariffs, quotas and exchange restrictions. Each of these policies will restrict trade by introducing an inequality between foreign prices on the one hand and domestic prices faced by producers and consumers on the other hand. These *are* in fact the policies spelled out by Kemp in his statement of the theorem. Thus he argues [2]:

[1] This has been shown in the preceding footnote.

In the present section I shall argue the more general proposition that compensated free trade or compensated restricted trade is better than no trade. (It is understood, of course, that the restrictions are not prohibitive.) The manner in which trade is restricted is unimportant; the same conclusions hold for tariffs, quantitative commodity controls or exchange restrictions.

But suppose, however, that trade is restricted by a production subsidy (or, alternatively tax) on importables (or, alternatively exportables) – a method which is not merely a theoretical possibility but also frequently in vogue. Kemp's theorem cannot be extended to this case, as seen by reference to Figure 3.3 where a production subsidy (or, alternatively tax) on Y (or, alternatively X) has reduced trade below the free trade level but the welfare level at U_T is below the no trade welfare level at U_S. On the other hand, if productive resources are assumed to be given in supply and monopoly power in trade is absent, Kemp's theorem can be shown to be valid (for utility-wise ranking) even for a production subsidy (tax) on importables (exportables) *as long as* the subsidy is not so large as to increase the domestic production of importables above the no-trade level. A larger subsidy (tax) than this would open up the *possibility*, illustrated by Figure 3.3, of subsidy (tax)-restricted trade being inferior (for the assumed, social utility index) to no trade, such that no lump sum transfers could compensate the losers in the restricted trade situation without leaving the gainers worse off.

Kemp's theorem is again invalid, in general, if we consider yet another way in which trade may be reduced *below* the level of free trade. Even a production subsidy (tax) on exportables (importables) may restrict the volume of trade below the free trade level provided exportables are inferior in social consumption.[1] And, regardless of whether trade is reduced below or increased above the free trade level, a production subsidy (tax) on exportables (importables) can reduce social welfare below the no trade level so that it will, in this case, be impossible to compensate the losers in this restricted trade situation while keeping the gainers at their welfare level in the initial, no trade situation. This is illustrated in Figure 3.4 where the subsidy (tax) is assumed to shift production to P_T, reduce trade below the free trade level and produce welfare level below that under no trade ($U_T < U_S$).

Hence, if subsidies (taxes) on importables and exportables are admitted as possible ways of restricting trade, the theorem that

[1] Such a subsidy (tax) may, of course, reverse the trade pattern as well.

In the [recent section I shall argue the more sound] proposition that compensated free trade or compensated restricted trade is better than no trade. (It is understood, of course, that the restrictions are non-prohibitive.) The manner in which trade [is restricted is irrelevant in this same argument, for tariffs, quantity controls commodity subsidies are defined as] equivalent.

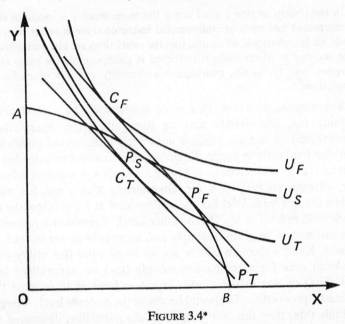

FIGURE 3.4*

* AP_SB represents the domestic, production possibility curve. Free trade at given, world prices measured by the slope of $C_F P_F$, would take production to P_F and consumption to C_F. Under no trade, the production and consumption would be at P_S and welfare at U_S would be below that under free trade at U_F. An appropriate production subsidy (or, alternatively tax) on the exportable good (or, alternatively on the importable good) would shift production from P_F to P_T, consumption to C_T, thus reducing the volume of trade *below* the free trade level and welfare *below* the no-trade level ($U_T < U_S$), thus demonstrating that restricted trade would, in this instance, be inferior to no trade.

restricted trade is superior to no trade can no longer be considered valid.

Further, we have discussed so far only taxes and subsidies on *production* as methods by which trade may be restricted. We may, however, also consider taxes and subsidies on *consumption* as possible methods of restricting trade. If we do so, Kemp's theorem can be shown again to be invalid, in general, for this class of policy instruments.[1]

[1] Note again that Kemp was implicitly considering restrictions of trade brought about by tariffs and equivalent restrictions. What has been demonstrated here is that the theorem is not capable of extension, in general, to restrictions of trade brought about by other policy instruments (except under restrictive assumptions).

Take the case of tax (subsidy) on the consumption of importables (exportables). In this case, even when fixed resources and absence of monopoly power in trade are assumed to simplify the analysis, restricted trade may be inferior to no trade. This is illustrated in Figure 3.5 where the trade-reducing consumption subsidy (tax) on exportables (importables) is shown to result in welfare deterioration below the no-trade level ($U_T < U_S$). Note that this possibility does not require any restriction on demand, such as inferiority of either good in social consumption, as in the case of production subsidy (tax) on importables (exportables).[1]

3. HIGHER TARIFF vs. LOWER TARIFF

A further theorem, stated by Kemp, is that for a country with no monopoly power in trade, and without any domestic distortions, a higher tariff is inferior to a lower tariff. As Kemp [2, p. 814] states it:

What can be said of the relative desirabilities of the free-trading situation, the trading situation characterized by a uniform 5% import duty, that characterized by a 10% duty, etc.?

In the special case in which a country's terms of trade are independent of that country's offer a particularly simple answer can be given: the free-trade situation is superior to the 5% situation, which in turn is superior to the 10% situation, and so on. The reason is very simple: under free trade all the necessary marginal conditions of a Paretian national optimum are satisfied. In particular, the marginal rate of transformation between commodities in production is equal to the marginal rate of transformation between commodities in international trade (the marginal terms of trade) and to their marginal rate of substitution in consumption. A tariff destroys the equality between the marginal terms of trade and the other two marginal rates of transformation. And the greater the duty, the greater the resulting inequality.

While Kemp's argument seems valid at a superficial glance, and indeed was adopted as such in my own Survey [1], it turns out that it raises certain difficulties when inferiority of the exportable good in consumption is not ruled out.

Note that the argument is certainly valid if the ranking of tariffs is

[1] On the other hand, if a trade-reducing tax (subsidy) is levied on the consumption of exportables (importables), this can be shown to result invariably in a higher welfare level than under no trade when there is no monopoly power in trade and resources are fixed in supply.

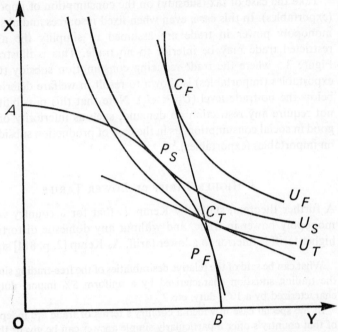

FIGURE 3.5*

* AP_SB is the domestic, production possibility frontier. Under no trade, production and consumption will be at P_S. Under free trade, at the given world price ratio measured by the slope of $C_F P_F$, production will be at P_F, consumption at C_F and social welfare at U_F. If, however, along with otherwise-free trade, an appropriate subsidy (or tax) on the consumption of the exportable good (or of the importable good) is introduced, production will continue at P_F and consumption shift to C_T, the volume of trade will have been reduced below the free trade level and welfare below the no-trade level ($U_T < U_S$), thus demonstrating that, in this instance, restricted trade is inferior to no trade.

made on grounds of (what was earlier described as) technical efficiency. However, when the question of utility-wise rankings is considered, it can be shown, as in Figure 3.6, that a higher tariff rate could produce a higher level of welfare than a lower tariff rate. It is clear that this contradiction requires that the exportables be inferior in social consumption. The *volume* of trade, in this instance, falls instead of increasing as a result of a reduction of the tariff. Readers familiar with Meade's [3] cardinalist method of evaluating the marginal changes in welfare will notice that the foregoing result can naturally

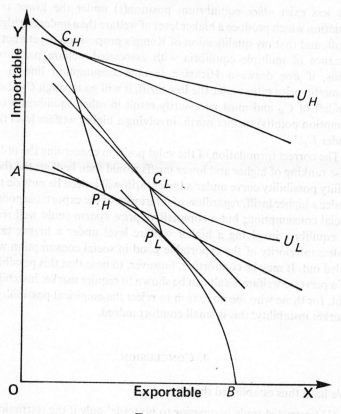

FIGURE 3.6*

* $AP_H P_L B$ is the domestic, production possibility frontier. An appropriate tariff will lead to production at P_L, consumption at C_L, trade at the given world price ratio measured by the slope of $P_L C_L$ and social welfare at U_L. An appropriate, *higher* tariff will shift production to P_H and consumption to C_H, while increasing social welfare ($U_H > U_L$), so that a higher tariff will be superior to a lower tariff in this instance. Note that this case requires the inferiority of the exportable good in social consumption; it is impossible to redraw the diagram, with the same conclusion, for the case where the exportable good is not inferior.

be reached by Meade's method as well: a reduction in the volume of imports, when there is a tariff, will produce a deterioration of welfare.

While, however, the presence of an inferior exportable good *can* result in a higher tariff producing higher social welfare than a lower tariff, Professor Samuelson has pointed out to me that there will none the less exist *other* equilibrium position(s) under the lower tariff situation which produce a higher level of welfare than under the higher tariff, and that my qualification of Kemp's proposition is yet another instance of multiple equilibria with associated welfare paradoxes. Thus, if one draws a Hicksian income-consumption line at the domestic price ratio under the low tariff, it will go through C_L and to the left of C_H and must necessarily result in other equilibrium consumption point(s) further north, involving a higher welfare level than under U_H.[1]

The correct formulation of the valid position concerning the utility-wise ranking of higher and lower tariffs would then be that: the (best) utility possibility curve under a lower tariff will indeed lie outside that under a higher tariff, regardless of inferiority of the exportable good in social consumption; but a competitive price system could well result in equilibria involving a higher welfare level under a higher tariff, unless inferiority of the exportable good in social consumption were ruled out. It may be comforting, however, to note that this possibility of a perverse welfare result can be shown to require market instability. But, for those who see no reason to reject the empirical possibility of market instability, this is small comfort indeed.

4. CONCLUSION

We have thus established that:

(1) 'restricted trade is superior to no trade' only if the restriction is brought about by tariffs, quotas or (equivalent) exchange restrictions but not if brought about by taxes or subsidies on domestic production or consumption; and

(2) 'a higher tariff is (utility-wise) inferior to a lower tariff', for a country with neither monopoly power in trade nor domestic distortions, only when inferiority of exportables in societal consumption is ruled out; if this is not done, a competitive system may well lead a reduced tariff to result in a deterioration of economic welfare, even though the possibility of improved economic welfare, at a different equilibrium position with the same reduced tariff, will always exist.

----

[1] The problems raised by inferior goods have been noted independently by J. Vanek [7] as well; his contribution came to my notice after this paper was complete.

REFERENCES

1 Bhagwati, J., 'The Pure Theory of International Trade: A Survey', *Economic Journal*, Vol. 74, March 1964.

2 Kemp, M. C., 'The Gain from International Trade', *Economic Journal*, Vol. 72, December 1962.

3 Meade, J. E., *The Theory of Customs Unions* (Amsterdam, North Holland Publishing Co., 1955).

4 Samuelson, P. A., 'The Gains from International Trade', *Canadian Journal of Economics and Political Science*, Vol. 5, May 1939; reprinted in *Readings in the Theory of International Trade*, edited by Howard S. Ellis and Lloyd A. Metzler (Philadelphia, 1949).

5 Samuelson, P. A., 'Social Indifference Curves', *Quarterly Journal of Economics*, Vol. 70, February 1956.

6 Samuelson, P. A., 'The Gains from International Trade Once Again', *Economic Journal*, Vol. 72, December 1962.

7 Vanek, J., *General Equilibrium of International Discrimination*, Harvard University Press, 1965.

4 Ranking of Tariffs Under Monopoly Power in Trade

Kemp [3] has argued that, for a country with no monopoly power in trade, a lower tariff is preferable to a higher tariff, in the sense that any distribution of individual utilities attainable with a higher tariff is attainable with a lower tariff, usually with something to spare. Subsequently, Vanek [5] and Bhagwati [1] showed that if exportables are inferior (a) competitive equilibrium may not be unique, (b) one of the low-tariff equilibria may be inferior to one of the high-tariff equilibria and, therefore, (c) a reduction in the tariff might leave a country worse off. As a result [1] [4] [5], Kemp's proposition has now been elaborated to read:

The (best) utility possibility curve under a lower tariff will indeed lie outside that under a higher tariff, regardless of the inferiority of the exportable good in social consumption; but a competitive price system could well result in equilibria involving a higher welfare level under a higher tariff, unless inferiority of the exportable good in social consumption were ruled out.[1]

Can anything be said about the ranking of tariffs when a country has monopoly power in trade? Or must one be content to know that an optimal tariff exists? This note shows that, under very modest restrictions on preferences and in spite of the necessity of ranking sub-optimal policies, it is possible to establish the following propositions. Let the optimum tariff be t_w, the zero tariff t_o, and the (just) prohibitive tariff t_p.

Proposition 1: Successive increases in the tariff from the level t_o will raise welfare until the level t_w is reached; successive increases in the tariff thereafter will reduce welfare until the level t_p is reached; higher tariffs merely involve continuing autarky and hence are partially ordered.

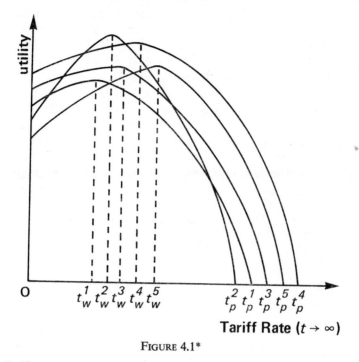

FIGURE 4.1*

* Tariff-ranking for a given country, with monopoly power in trade, under five alternative social welfare functions. Note that no cardinal significance is to be attached to the utility axis. The figure merely ranks, in terms of utility, tariffs ranging from zero to infinity for each social welfare function. It also shows the optimum tariffs, for each of the five functions, at t_w^5, t_w^4, t_w^3, t_w^2, t_w^1 and the corresponding prohibitive tariff levels at t_p^5, t_p^4, t_p^3, t_p^2, and t_p^1.

The diagram could be readily extended to the second and third quadrants, to show the effects and ranking of export subsidies.

Proposition 2: For a country with monopoly power in trade, therefore, the choice of a social welfare function will *merely* determine the magnitudes of t_w and t_p; hence one could regard tariffs as continuously laid in a chain from zero to infinity, with the social welfare function (for a specific country) serving, as it were, as a spike which lifts this chain up to the level of the optimal tariff and drops it to the floor at the level of the (appropriate) prohibitive tariff – as illustrated by Figure 1 for five hypothetical welfare functions.

These propositions are not *generally* valid. To establish the conditions under which they *are* valid, consider Figure 4.2, which shows the trade-indifference curves U_w^{I}, U_o^{I} and U_p^{I} reached by country I successively under an optimum tariff, a zero tariff and a prohibitive tariff. It is clear that Proposition 1, and hence Proposition 2, will hold *if and only if* an increase in country I's tariff will necessarily reduce the demand for imports. For, in such a case, an increase in the tariff, starting from a zero tariff at R_o, will take the economy through higher and higher trade indifference curves until it reaches R^* and then through successively lower trade-indifference curves to O and U_p^{I}.

Therefore, exceptions to Proposition 1, and hence Proposition 2, must constitute exceptions to the rule that an increase in the tariff will reduce the demand for imports. It can then be shown that this rule admits of exceptions only when the exportable commodity is inferior.[1]

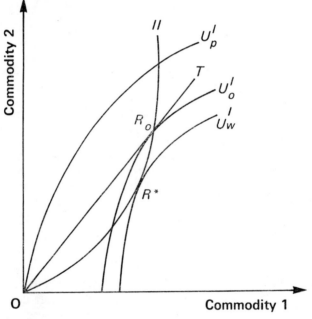

FIGURE 4.2*

---

* The figure shows the optimum-tariff welfare level U_w^{I}, the zero-tariff welfare level U_o^{I} and the self-sufficiency welfare level U_p^{I} for country I, the free-trade terms of trade OT and country II's offer curve OII.

[1] Note, therefore, that the argument sometimes made in balance of payments theory, that tariffs must be preferred to devaluation *until* the optimum tariff is reached, is valid only insofar as inferiority of the exportable good is ruled out.

Hold the terms of trade constant at unity. Suppose that Commodity 1 is imported and that Commodity 2 is the *numéraire*. The internal price ratio is, therefore, $(1 + t)$ where t is the rate of duty. The demand for imports is $E_1(1 + t, I_2)$ where

$$I_2 = (1 + t) X_1 + X_2 + t E_1$$

is income in terms of the *numéraire* commodity, X_i is the output of good i and $t E_1$ is the tariff revenue. We have

$$\frac{dE_1}{dt} = \frac{\partial E_1}{\partial t} + \frac{\partial E_1}{\partial I_2} \frac{dI_2}{dt}$$

$$\frac{dI_2}{dt} = X_1 + E_1 + \frac{t dE_1}{dt}$$

Hence

$$\frac{dE_1}{dt} = \frac{\partial E_1}{\partial t} + \frac{m_1}{1 + t} \left(X_1 + E_1 + \frac{t dE_1}{dt} \right)$$

$$= \frac{\dfrac{\partial E_1}{\partial t} + \dfrac{m_1}{1 + t} D_1}{1 - \dfrac{t}{1 + t} m_1}$$

where m_1 is the marginal propensity to consume the first or imported commodity and D_1 is consumption of the first commodity. Introducing the Slutzky decomposition,

$$\frac{\partial E_1}{\partial t} = \frac{\partial E_1}{\partial t} \bigg| - \frac{m_1}{1 + t} D_1,$$

where $\dfrac{\partial E_1}{\partial t} \bigg|$ is the pure substitution slope, we obtain, finally,

$$\frac{dE_1}{dt} = \frac{\dfrac{\partial E_1}{\partial t} \bigg|}{1 - \dfrac{t}{1 + t} m_1}$$

which is negative unless the export is very inferior.

Figure 4.3 illustrates the possibility, ruled out by our restrictions on consumption inferiority, that an increase in the rate of duty may give rise both to an increase in import demand and to a deterioration in the terms of trade of the tariff-imposing country. With the lower tariff, production takes place at P, consumption at C, and the terms of trade are indicated by the slope of PC. With the higher rate of duty,

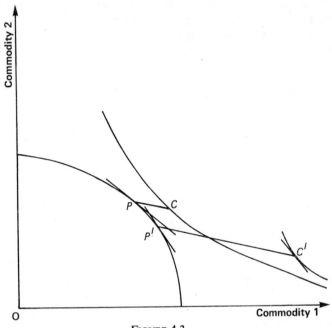

FIGURE 4.3

production takes place at P', consumption at C'; and the (worsened) terms of trade are indicated by the slope of $P'C'$.

We have already stated that the possibility illustrated by Figure 4.3 can be ruled out if very modest restrictions are imposed on the community's preferences. We now offer two observations designed to emphasize just how modest those restrictions are.[1] First, we recall that '. . . the reciprocal demand curve traced out by a higher tariff rate will always lie inside the curve traced out by a lower tariff rate. . . .' ([3], p. 34, n. 7.) It follows that the possibility illustrated by Figure 4.3 requires offer curves which yield multiple equilibria at given terms of trade, as in Figure 4.4. (Points W and W' of Figure 4.4 correspond respectively to points C and C' of Figure 3.) Second, it follows from our mathematical analysis that dE_1/dt is positive if and only if $1 - [tm_1/(1 + t)]$ is negative, that is, if and only if

$$1 + t(1 - m_1) < 0$$

[1] The first observation emerged from a long correspondence with Harry G. Johnson.

As Kemp [4] has shown, however, this is precisely the condition for market instability when the terms of trade are given.

Finally, we note that, even when an increase in the rate of duty is associated with a reduction in the demand for imports and a deterioration of the terms of trade, nevertheless there exists an alternative

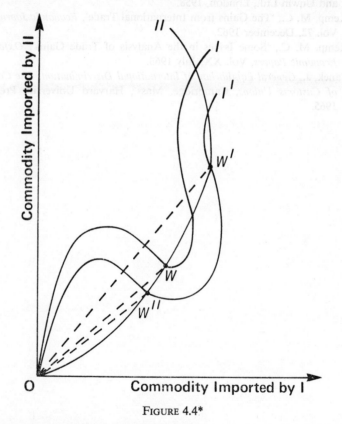

FIGURE 4.4*

* OI is the low-tariff offer curve of country I.
  OI' is the high-tariff offer curve of country I
  OII is the offer curve of country II.

high-tariff equilibrium characterized by reduced import demand and improved terms of trade. (Point W'' in Figure 4.4 illustrates.) It follows that by choosing carefully from alternative equilibria one can ensure that, as the rate of duty is raised, welfare rises steadily, reaches a maximum, then declines until the duty is prohibitive.

REFERENCES

1 Bhagwati, J., 'The Gains from Trade Once Again', *Oxford Economic Papers*, Vol. XX, July 1968.

2 Johnson, H. G., *International Trade and Economic Growth*, George Allen and Unwin Ltd., London, 1958.

3 Kemp, M. C., 'The Gains from International Trade', *Economic Journal*, Vol. 72, December 1962.

4 Kemp. M. C., 'Some Issues in the Analysis of Trade Gains', *Oxford Economic Papers*, Vol. XX, July 1968.

5 Vanek, J., *General Equilibrium of International Discrimination: The Case of Customs Unions*, Cambridge, Mass., Harvard University Press, 1965.

5 Non-Economic Objectives and the Efficiency Properties of Trade[1]

It is well known (Kemp, 1962; Samuelson, 1962; Bhagwati, 1968) that, for a country with no monopoly power in trade (or domestic distortions), free trade (in the sense of a policy resulting in the equalization of domestic and foreign prices and hence excluding trade, production and consumption taxes, subsidies, and quantitative restrictions) is the optimal policy. It follows, therefore, that free trade is superior to no trade.

It has also been argued recently (Kemp, 1962), that, even in the case where there is monopoly power in trade, so that both no trade and free trade are sub-optimal policies, it is possible to demonstrate that free trade is superior to no trade.

What of the case where the country has no monopoly power in trade but has a non-economic objective which consists in requiring production to be maintained at a certain level in a specific activity? In the standard, two-commodity case, this type of objective can be treated as requiring production to be necessarily at a particular position on the production-possibility frontier – as has been done by earlier writers, such as Corden (1957) and Johnson (1965). Can we still rank trade as superior to autarky in this case? In the following analysis, we distinguish between two sets of possible trade policies: (1) trade with consumption at international prices and (2) trade with tariffs and (trade) subsidies.

[1] The problems analysed in this paper arose from a stimulating question of my student, Harriet Zellner, when we were discussing my paper 'The Gains from Trade Once Again' (Chapter 3 above), in the International Economics Workshop Seminar at Columbia University.

1. SUPERIORITY OF TRADE (AND CONSUMPTION AT INTERNATIONAL PRICES) OVER NO TRADE

It can be shown quite readily that the stated non-economic objective can be reached at lower cost under a policy of trade (and consumption at international prices) than under autarky or no trade. Thus, even in the case of non-economic objectives of this specific variety, trade continues to be superior to no trade.

Consider two alternative cases: (1) where the desired production bundle is different from the self-sufficiency bundle under any given income distribution, and (2) where the desired bundle happens to coincide with the self-sufficiency bundle.

In the former case, analysed with the aid of Figure 5.1a, it will be necessary to adopt a tax-cum-subsidy-on-production policy to shift production under autarky to the desired bundle P^*. Assume that the commodity price ratio P_s then faces the consumers, and the welfare level resulting is at U_{NT}. Now, there are three alternative positions for the given trade price ratio, which must pass through P^*, relative

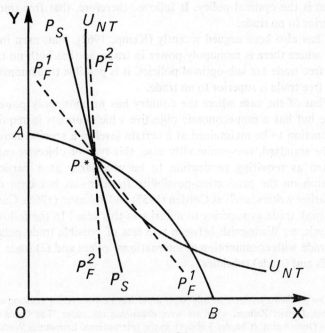

FIGURE 5.1a

to P_s. If it happens to coincide with it, then equilibrium will again take the economy to welfare level at U_{NT}, and there will be *de facto* autarky. This is the borderline case. On the other hand, if the foreign price ratio is at $P_F{}^1$ or $P_F{}^2$, the two remaining possibilities, the new welfare level can only be at a higher level than at U_{NT} (for the social indifference curves cannot intersect).

In the other case, where the desired production bundle happens to coincide with that under autarky, a similar conclusion holds. This case is analysed with the aid of Figure 5.1b, where autarky or no trade leads to production at P^* and to welfare level U_{NT}. Maintaining production at P^* with the aid of an appropriate tax-cum-subsidy-on-production policy under a situation of trade at international prices, the economy could achieve welfare level at $U_{FT}{}^1$ or at $U_{FT}{}^2$. Alternatively, there would be the third borderline case where the foreign price ratio happens to coincide with the autarkic price ratio P_s, in which case trade will not take place even though the trade opportunity exists.

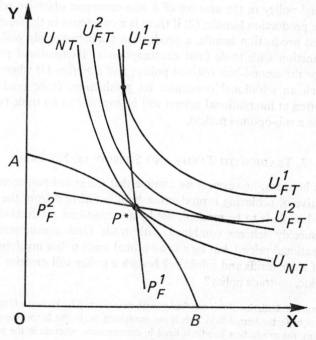

FIGURE 5.1b

Thus, the analysis shows that trade (and consumption at international prices) will be a superior policy to no trade even when there is a non-economic objective with respect to the production bundle.[1]

In fact, this proposition is readily understood when it is realized that under the assumptions made, free trade is the optimal policy *if* there is no additional constraint on production. On the other hand, shifting production to a specific bundle other than the free-trade bundle imposes a cost that can be *minimized* by adopting a tax-cum-subsidy-on-production policy which will get to the desired bundle of production without imposing any other (consumption) cost than that which is implicit in the shift to an 'inefficient' production bundle itself. Thus, for example, as Corden (1957) has shown, a tariff imposed with a view to shifting the production bundle to P^* (when the production of importables desired is higher than under free trade) will be inefficient relative to a production tax-cum-subsidy policy which will permit consumption to be undertaken at international prices.

Thus, we can conclude this section as follows: (1) Free trade is the optimal policy in the absence of a non-economic objective relating to the production bundle; (2) if there is a constraint in the form of a desired production bundle, a production tax-cum-subsidy policy, in conjunction with trade (and consumption at international prices), will be the second-best optimal policy; and *therefore* (3) when there is such an additional constraint on production, trade (and consumption at international prices) will be superior to no trade (which will be a sub-optimal policy).

2. TRADE WITH TARIFF AND SUBSIDY *vs.* NO TRADE

What happens, however, if we assume that the stated non-economic objective of achieving a production bundle different from the free-trade bundle is to be reached, *not* by a second-best production tax-cum-subsidy scheme combined with trade (and consumption at international prices), but by a sub-optimal trade policy involving the use of trade tariffs and subsidies? Is such a policy still superior to an autarkic, no-trade policy?

---

[1] Note the similarity of this conclusion with that reached by Haberler (1950) for the case of factor immobility. This is not surprising as, in the factor-immobility situation, the production bundle is fixed in consequence, whereas in the present case it is fixed *directly* as a non-economic objective.

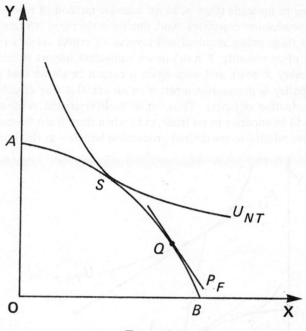

FIGURE 5.2

The answer to this question depends on where the required production bundle is relative to the free trade and no-trade bundles. In Figure 5.2, three relevant possibilities are distinguished, based on the free trade production bundle Q and the no-trade bundle S. These three possibilities are that the required production bundle will lie in the ranges AS (excluding S), SQ, and QB (excluding Q).

First, in the range SQ, it can be shown that a 'tariff-restricted' trade policy will be superior to a no-trade policy for achieving the required production objective.[1] Second, if, however, the required bundle is in the range QB (excluding Q), then it would require a trade subsidy policy, in a trade situation, to achieve it; and it can be shown that, unlike the preceding case, such a trade (subsidy) policy is *not* necessarily

---

[1] This argument excludes the two borderline cases, where the objective is to produce at Q or at S. Where Q is the objective, the free-trade policy, which is the first-best optimal policy, will naturally be superior to an autarkic policy of reaching Q. Where the objective instead is to reach S, the autarkic policy will become equivalent to the tariff policy, since the latter, in any case, will have to be prohibitive.

superior to no trade (that is, to an autarkic method of reaching the stated production objective). And, finally, in the range AS (excluding S), the trade policy required will involve an export subsidy (on the export of commodity Y now) or an equivalent import subsidy (on commodity X now), and once again it cannot be shown that such a trade policy is necessarily superior to an autarkic way of achieving the production objective. Thus, while 'tariff-restricted' trade can be shown to be superior to no trade, even when there is a non-economic objective relating to the desired production bundle – as this implicitly

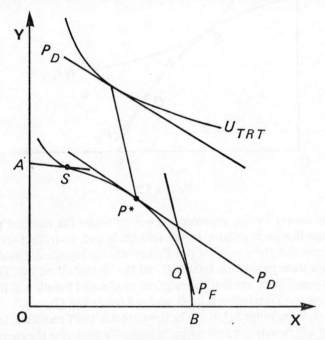

FIGURE 5.3a

involves the location of the required production bundle within the range SQ – this is *not* the case with 'trade-subsidy-assisted' trade *vis-à-vis* autarkic achievement of the required production objective, as such a comparison implicitly involves the location of the required production bundle on the range AS or QB. These propositions are demonstrated readily below.

In Figure 5.3a it is shown that, if the desired production bundle is at P^* which lies in the range SQ, and the foreign price ratio given to the economy is P_F and the tariff-inclusive domestic price ratio is P_D, then the utility level reached under this tariff-restricted policy will be indicated by the social welfare curve U_{TRT}. It is then easy to see that the social welfare curve going through P^*, which will be the level attained under autarky by a suitable tax-cum-subsidy policy on consumption, must necessarily be inferior to U_{TRT}. Hence, we have demonstrated that the utility level achieved by a policy of tariff-restricted trade will be higher than that under an autarkic policy, when the production bundle desired lies in the range SQ.

In Figure 5.3b we examine the case where the desired production bundle P^* is in the range BQ. In this case, a suitable subsidy on the

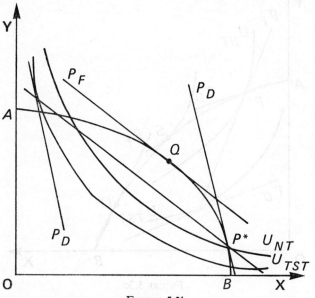

FIGURE 5.3b

export of X (for import of Y) will bring production to the desired level, with domestic price ratio at P_D and the foreign price ratio at P_F. The utility level reached will be indicated by the social indifference curve U_{TST}. On the other hand, in Figure 5.3b we have shown the case that the indifference curve passing through P^*, which will indicate the welfare level under an autarkic policy, will show an improvement ($U_{NT} > U_{TST}$). Hence, this is a case where the trade-subsidy-assisted trade policy will be inferior to an autarkic policy. However, if the indifference curve U_{TST} has been drawn so as to pass above P^*, this conclusion would have been reversed; whereas if it had been drawn so as to pass through P^*, the welfare levels reached under the two policies would have been identical. Hence, we cannot establish that a trade-subsidy-assisted trade policy is necessarily superior to an autarkic policy for achieving a stated production objective when the required production bundles lies in the range BQ.

Finally, in Figure 5.3c, we examine the case where the required production bundle is in the range SA. In the diagram, P^* is this bundle,

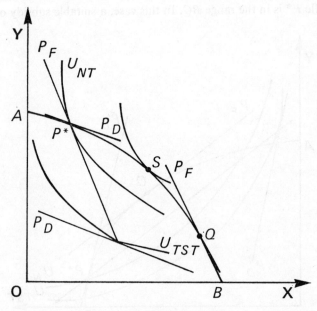

FIGURE 5.3c

with an export subsidy now on commodity Y (or an import subsidy now on commodity X), bringing production to the required point P^*, and utility level to U_{TST}. Assuming that the indifference curve passing through P^* is U_{NT}, we thus illustrate a case where the trade-subsidy-assisted trade policy results in lower welfare than an autarkic policy for reaching the same, required production bundle. We could equally well have illustrated a specific case where the ranking was the reverse: $U_{TST} > U_{NT}$. So, again, we cannot establish that a trade-subsidy-assisted trade policy is *necessarily* superior to an autarkic policy for achieving a stated production objective when the required production bundle lies in the range SA.[1]

We can then conclude with the following propositions:

1 In the case where the desired production bundle can be reached by the use of a trade tariff, rather than a trade subsidy, autarky will still be an inferior policy, thus enabling us to rank in descending order the following three policies: (*a*) trade (and consumption at international prices), (*b*) trade tariff, and (*c*) no trade or autarky.

2 Where the desired production bundle must be reached by the use of a trade subsidy, on the other hand, this strong ordering of policies will disappear, while trade (and consumption at international prices) continues naturally to be the optimal policy.

REFERENCES

1 Bhagwati, J., 'The Gains from Trade Once Again', *Oxford Economic Papers*, Vol. 20 (July, 1968).

2 Corden, W. M., 'Tariffs, Subsidies and the Terms of Trade', *Economica*, N.S., Vol. XXIV (August, 1957).

3 Haberler, G., 'Some Problems in the Pure Theory of International Trade', *Economic Journal*, Vol. LX (June 1950).

4 Johnson, H. G., 'Optimal Trade Intervention in the Presence of Domestic Distortions', *Trade, Growth and the Balance of Payments*, Chicago, Rand McNally Co., 1965.

5 Kemp, M. C., 'The Gains from International Trade', *Economic Journal*, Vol. LXXII (December, 1962).

6 Samuelson, P. A., 'The Gains from International Trade Once Again', *Economic Journal*, Vol. LXXII (December, 1962).

---

[1] In fact, for the cases where a trade subsidy is required, it is possible to state the rather stronger conclusion (pointed out to me by Michael Michaely and T. N. Srinivasan) that, where the parametric properties require that the subsidy granted to consumers under autarky exceeds the subsidy granted for export under the trade situation, autarky will be the superior policy, though no unique ranking of the two policies will be possible outside this range.

6 The Proofs of the Theorems on Comparative Advantage

This note examines critically the usual statement and proofs of the two principal theories of comparative advantage: (i) Ricardian, and (ii) Heckscher–Ohlin. While none of the analysis offered here is intrinsically novel, it is presented in a manner which has fairly important implications for a full understanding – not evident in either oral or written tradition – of the postulates underlying these theories of comparative advantage. More significantly, it is shown that (contrary to what is thought) certain restrictions on demand conditions have to be specified *even when* the two-commodity version of the Ricardian theorem and the Heckscher-Ohlin theorem (using the price definition of factor abundance) are to be proved.

1.

The proofs of the two-country, two-commodity theories of comparative advantage relating to the pattern of trade, whether one takes the Ricardian or the Heckscher–Ohlin version, depend on two successive arguments.

Argument 1.

Propositions are proven, relating to the determination of the *pre-trade* commodity price ratio: thus, in the Ricardian model, the pre-trade commodity price ratio is shown to be equal to the labour productivity ratio whereas, in the Heckscher–Ohlin model, it is demonstrated that the relative, pre-trade price of the commodity using the country's abundant factor intensively will be lower than in the other country.

Argument 2.

(i) It is argued that a country will export that commodity whose relative, pre-trade price is lower than in the other country and will import the other commodity. (ii) *Corollary:* Also usually considered implicit is the proposition that if the pre-trade prices are identical between countries no trade will occur.

The successive Arguments 1 and 2 (i) lead to the well-known theorems of comparative advantage: (1) *Ricardian Theorem,* a country will export (import) that commodity in which her comparative factor productivity is higher (lower); and (2) *Heckscher–Ohlin Theorem,* a country will export (import) that commodity which uses her abundant (scarce) factor intensively.[1] Possible corollaries to these theorems, sometimes derived from Arguments 1 and 2 (ii), are: (1) *Ricardian Corollary* – where comparative factor productivities are identical between countries, no trade will occur; and (2) *Heckscher–Ohlin Corollary* – where factor endowments are identical between countries, no trade will take place.

In Section 2, addressed to the Ricardian propositions, it is shown that the Ricardian theorem requires the specification of restrictions (albeit 'reasonable') on demand *in addition* to the postulates always

---

[1] That the traditional proofs of both Ricardian and Heckscher–Ohlin propositions rely explicitly on Argument 1 and implicitly on Argument 2 (ii) is evident not merely from oral traditions but also from the writings of various theorists.

Thus Ohlin [7, p. 29], for example, in his famous work on *Interregional and International Trade,* leads up, *via* Argument 1, to an assertion of Argument 2 (ii) and consequently to the Heckscher–Ohlin theorem: 'The first condition of trade is that some goods can be produced more cheaply in one region than in another. In each of them the cheap goods are those containing relatively great quantities of the factors cheaper than in the other regions' (Argument 1). 'These cheap goods make up exports, whereas goods which can be more cheaply produced in the other regions are imported' (Argument 2 (ii)). 'We may say, therefore, that exports are in each region composed of articles into the production of which enter large quantities of cheap factors' (Heckscher–Ohlin theorem, with price definition of factor abundance).

Similarly, a modern author such as Jones [3] on the Heckscher–Ohlin theory terminates his analysis at the point at which Argument 1 is proven; and implicitly assuming Argument 2 (ii), proceeds to the Heckscher–Ohlin theorem.

At a more general level, embracing all theories of comparative advantage, Kindleberger [4, p. 88] also assumes Argument 2 (ii) as valid and proceeds to discuss Argument 1 substantively by stating that '. . . the law of comparative costs says that a country exports those products which are comparatively cheap in price at home, and imports those which are comparatively expensive' (Argument 2 (ii)). 'But economics can say more than this' (Argument 1).

These examples could be readily multiplied but hardly need to be.

stated. Opportunity is also taken to note that the Ricardian corollary is invalid owing to the familiar multiplicity of production equilibria in the Ricardian model. Finally, in Section 3, which discusses the Heckscher–Ohlin propositions, it is argued that while the assumption that the consumption pattern be identical between countries regardless of income levels is correctly held to be required only when the *physical* definition of factor abundance (to be discussed later) is used, it is incorrect to maintain that *no* restrictions at all need to be put on demand when the *price* definition is adopted.

2. RICARDIAN PROPOSITIONS

A. *Ricardian Corollary*

The Ricardian corollary, stating that where factor productivity ratios are identical between the two countries no trade will take place, is not logically true. Indeed, not merely can trade take place but, in general, the pattern of trade will be reversible as well. This follows immediately from the well-known multiplicity of production equilibria corresponding to the commodity price ratio, which is equated, under perfect competition, with the identical factor productivity ratio in each country.

This is readily illustrated. In Figure 6.1a the production possibility curves of countries I and II are depicted as $R_I F_I$ and $R_{II} F_{II}$ respectively. Note that these show constant and identical rates of transformation at the margin, because of the one-factor, constant-returns technology and the assumption of identical factor productivity ratios.[1] Argument 1 holds in this model because the *pre-trade* commodity price ratio in each country will equal the factor productivity ratio. But the factor productivity ratios being identical in the two countries, the pre-trade price ratios in the two countries will also be equalized. Does Argument 2 (ii) then necessarily hold, leading to the Ricardian corollary?

It does not. In Figure 6.1a the contrary possibility is illustrated.

---

[1] In the Ricardian model, if labour is the factor of production and x_I and x_{II} the labour productivity ratios in commodity X in countries I and II respectively and y_I and y_{II} in commodity Y, then $x_I/y_I = (P_x/P_y) I$ (the price of X in terms of Y) and $x_{II}/y_{II} = (P_x/P_y) II$ prior to trade. Therefore, any ranking of $(P_x/P_y) I$ and $(P_x/P_y) II$ prior to trade implies a corresponding, equivalent ranking of the factor productivity ratios as well. Therefore, when the factor productivity ratios x_I/y_I and x_{II}/y_{II} are identical, so will be the pre-trade commodity price ratios in the two countries.

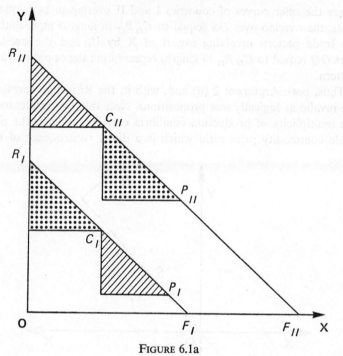

FIGURE 6.1a

Assuming that, at the commodity price ratio $R_{II}F_{II} = R_I F_I$, country II 'chooses' consumption at C_{II} and country I at C_I, the production choice is still wide open for each country. Each country can have production at *any* point on its production possibility frontier. Suppose that the production then is at C_{II} in Country II and at C_I in country I; in this case both Argument 2 (ii) and the Ricardian corollary will turn out to be valid. However, suppose that the choice of production is to the north-west of C_{II} in country II and (an identical distance, implying 'matching offers' between both countries) to the south-east of C_I in country I, then trade *will* occur with II exporting Y and importing X. On the other hand, the choice of production occurring in contrary directions, trade will again occur, but with the trade-pattern reversed. The full range of possible trade equilibria is then defined by: (i) the two identical, dotted triangles which imply export of X and import of Y by II, and (ii) the two identical, striped triangles which imply export of Y and import of X by II. The counterpart of this, in the Marshallian offer curve diagram, is shown in Figure 6.1b,

G

where the offer curves of countries I and II overlap in both quadrants, the overlap over OS (equal to $C_{II} P_{II}$ in length) representing the trade pattern involving export of X by II, and the overlap over OQ (equal to $C_{II} R_{II}$ in length) representing the opposite trade pattern.

Thus, both Argument 2 (ii) and, with it, the Ricardian corollary are invalid as logically true propositions. Note that this results from the multiplicity of production equilibria corresponding to the pre-trade commodity price ratio which is a direct consequence of the

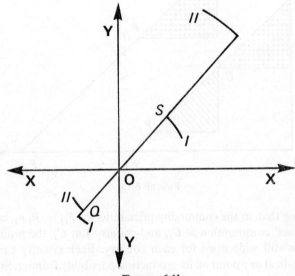

FIGURE 6.1b

Ricardian one-factor, constant returns-to-scale assumption combined with perfect competition. The correct Ricardian corollary therefore is that, where comparative factor productivities are identical between countries, the volume and direction of trade are indeterminate.

B. *Ricardian Theorem*

However, what about the case where factor productivity ratios are different between countries? In this case again, in view of Argument 1 retaining its validity, the pre-trade commodity price ratios will differ between the two countries. Does Argument 2 (i) then necessarily hold, leading to the Ricardian theorem?

It does not. The reason is that demand conditions may be such as to lead to multiple self-sufficiency equilibria. Thus in Figure 6.2, OQ_IO is the offer curve of country I and $OQ_{II}O$ of country II. Note that, under self-sufficiency, each country has two possible price equilibria: OS_I and OT for country I, OS_{II} and OT for country II. If then the pre-trade equilibrium price ratios are at OS_I and OS_{II} the equilibrium price ratio will be at OT and no trade will occur, *once free trade is*

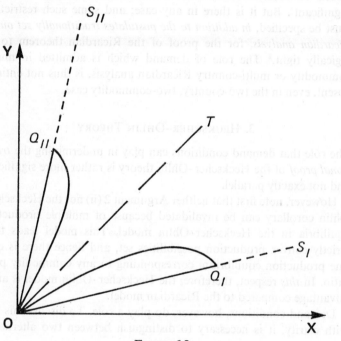

FIGURE 6.2

possible. Argument 2 (i) thus collapses: although the pre-trade prices are different between the two countries, trade will *not* take place. With Argument 2 (i), the Ricardian theorem also collapses: the factor productivity ratio in country I equals OS_I, and thus differs from that in country II, which equals OS_{II}, and yet no trade occurs.

Suitable restrictions have to be placed therefore on demand conditions to eliminate this possibility. A sufficient restriction is to assume that societal tastes enjoy the properties of well-ordered individual taste maps – as with Samuelson's social indifference curves.[1] Since, in Ricardo's model, there is only one factor of production and (at points of complete specialization) the marginal product is fixed in terms of the commodity produced, the social demands will be such as to rule out the possibility of a free-trade price equilibrium involving no trade *even when* the taste map of *each* factor-owner is alternatively assumed to be well ordered. Since the latter assumption is quite reasonable, the restriction that needs to be placed on demand conditions in Ricardian analysis is not at all 'significant'. But it is there in any case; and some such restriction must be specified, *in addition to the postulates traditionally set out in Ricardian analysis*, for the proof of the Ricardian theorem to be logically tight.[2] The role of demand which is admitted in multi-commodity or multi-country Ricardian analysis, is thus not entirely absent, even in the two-country, two-commodity case.

3. HECKSCHER–OHLIN THEORY

The role that demand conditions can play in undermining the *traditional proof* of the Heckscher–Ohlin theory is rather more significant and not exactly parallel.

However, note first that neither Argument 2 (ii) nor the Heckscher–Ohlin corollary can be invalidated because of multiple production equilibria in the Heckscher–Ohlin model. This model leads to a strictly convex production possibilities set, and hence there is only one production equilibrium corresponding to any commodity price ratio. In *this* respect, therefore, the Heckscher–Ohlin model is at an advantage compared to the Ricardian model.

Demand conditions, however, do play a role. To discuss this role with clarity, it is necessary to distinguish between two alternative

[1] Samuelson [10] proves the following theorem: '(a) If each group member's demand and indifference contours have the conventional "regular" convexity, and (b) if the social welfare function is defined to have similar regular convexity properties, and (c) if within the group optimal lump-sum transfers are always made, then it follows: (1) there will result observable demand totals that are functions of market prices and total income alone, and (2) that these demand functions will have all the Slutsky-Hicks or revealed preference properties of any single consumer's demand, and (3) there will exist a set of indifference contours relating to the totals X, Y, . . . that has all the regular properties of any individual's contours and which we can pretend a single mind is engaged in maximizing.'

[2] As H. Johnson has pointed out to me in correspondence, an alternative restriction could be to assume that some of both goods is demanded in each country at all price ratios.

versions of the Heckscher–Ohlin propositions, stemming from alternative definitions of factor abundance. Under the *physical* definition of factor abundance, if $(K/L)_I > (K/L)_{II}$, where K and L refer to the overall endowments of these two factors, country I is defined as K-abundant or L-scarce. Under the *price* definition, if $(P_K/P_L)_I < (P_K/P_L)_{II}$, where P_K/P_L stands for the price of K in terms of the price of L in the *pre-trade* situation, then I is K-abundant or L-scarce.

Where the *physical* definition is used, the proof of the Heckscher–Ohlin theorem proceeds traditionally by: (1) showing that the K-abundant country I will have, at the *same* commodity price ratio, a higher (X/Y) ratio in production than country II, where X is the K-intensive commodity;[1] (2) assuming that the consumption pattern is identical between the two countries, in the sense that the (X/Y) ratio in consumption, at the *same* commodity price ratio, is identical between the two countries; (3) therewith deducing that, for self-sufficiency, $(P_X/P_Y)I < (P_X/P_Y)II$, thus completing Argument 1, which requires that the K-abundant country will have its pre-trade relative price of the K-intensive commodity cheaper than the L-abundant country, and then (4) arguing, from Argument 2 (i), that the K-abundant country will export the K-intensive commodity and import the L-intensive commodity.

Where the *price* definition is used, the proof proceeds *directly* to Argument 1, avoiding the three specific steps involved in the case of the physical definition. The assumed technology leads to a unique relationship between commodity and factor price ratios,[2] and hence $P_X/P_Y)I < (P_X/P_Y)II$ follows immediately from $(P_K/P_L)I < (P_K/P_L)II$. Beyond that, *only* step (4), involving Argument 2 (i), is required. Note therefore that, in the case of the price definition, step (3) above does not have to be brought in. In view of this difference, we examine the two proofs, one for each definition, successively. Since the arguments are symmetrical for the theorem and the corollary, only the theorem is considered here to avoid tedious repetition.

1. *Physical Definition*

Whereas steps (3) and (4) are never explicitly stated and proved, they can be shown to be valid as soon as it is assumed [as in step (2)] that

[1] This proposition is valid for incomplete specialization, of course. For proof, see Jones [3].

[2] This is the proposition well known to trade theorists and first proved by Samuelson [8, 9] for a two-factor, two-commodity model.

the consumption pattern is identical between countries, at identical commodity prices, regardless of income level. Note that this assumption implies non-intersecting, *homothetic* social market-demand curves, which, in conjunction with the assumption of convexity, rule out any possibility of contradicting steps (3) and (4).

Thus, for example, take step (3). P_s^{II} is the self-sufficiency price-ratio for country II in Figure 6.3a, and the equilibrium consumption and production points C_{II} and P_{II} coincide. C_I and C_{II} then lie on the same ray from the origin because of the assumption in step (2); and P_I lies to the right of P_{II} by virtue of the proposition in step (1). It is then easy to see that the self-sufficiency price-ratio $(P_x/P_y) = P_s^I$ for country I will be lower than P_s^{II}. This is because a contradiction, such as shown in Figure 6.3b, requires *intersecting*, social market-demand curves which are ruled out as soon as the assumption in step (2) is made. So also for step (4).

2. *Price Definition*

While, therefore, the assumption of international identity of consumption patterns at all income levels is indeed an adequate restriction on

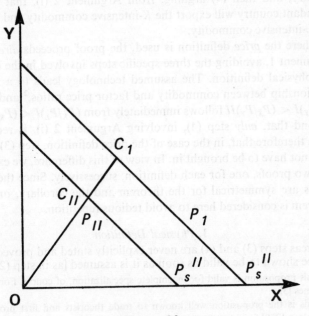

FIGURE 6.3a

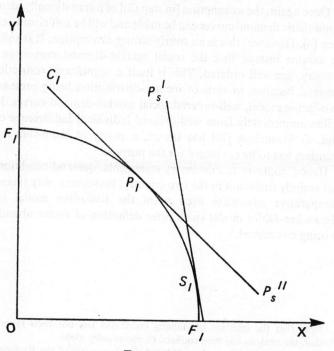

FIGURE 6.3b

demand for the Heckscher–Ohlin theorem to be valid when the physical definition of factor abundance is used, the customary presumption that no restriction at all is necessary when the price definition of factor abundance is used is not correct.

When the price definition is used, we have seen that we by-pass steps (2) and (3) and, in fact, infer *directly* that the K-abundant economy will have the K-intensive commodity cheaper under self-sufficiency. But *before* we can infer from this that the K-intensive commodity will be therefore exported [i.e., step (4)], we must again impose restrictions on demand.

What really happens is that the elimination of step (3) by virtue of the price definition still leaves step (4) intact in the chain of argument; and since *each* of the two steps (3) and (4) follows from the assumption of internationally identical, homothetic market-demand curves, *some* assumption with respect to demand continues to be necessary to sustain step (4), even when the price-definition of factor abundance is used.

Once again, the assumption [in step (2)] of internationally identical, homothetic demand curves can be made and will be sufficient to ensure step (4). However, this is an overly-strong assumption. It is sufficient to assume instead that the social market-demand curves, in each country, are well ordered. This is itself a 'significant' restriction on demand because, in view of income-distribution being present in a two-factor model, well-ordered social market-demand curves do not follow immediately from well-ordered individual indifference curves and, as Samuelson [10] has shown, a policy of lump-sum income transfers has to be envisaged for the purpose.[1]

Hence, contrary to customary statements, demand conditions are not entirely irrelevant in the two-country, two-commodity theories of comparative advantage even when the Ricardian model or the Heckscher–Ohlin model (with *price* definition of factor abundance) is being considered.[2]

---

[1] Note that the question of stability conditions has not been raised here. Further, the analysis has been confined to one country alone.

[2] The analysis in the text has accepted the framework of the Ricardian and Heckscher–Ohlin models. It is well known, however, that if either the technological or the institutional assumptions are relaxed, Arguments 1 and 2 can easily be jeopardized. For example, if increasing returns are assumed, it is known from Meade [6] and Matthews [5] that Argument 2 (ii) collapses: when the pre-trade prices are different between countries both patterns of trade may be possible.

Similarly, if there is a wage-differential between the two sectors it is no longer possible to sustain Argument 1 as logically true. This is because the equality of the commodity price-ratio with the domestic rate of transformation in production (at points of incomplete specialization) disappears [2], so that the required ranking of the pre-trade commodity price ratios in the two countries will not necessarily emerge. On the other hand, if the wage differential operates identically in the two countries, this will be a sufficient condition for sustaining Argument 1. As for Argument 2 (ii), it will continue to hold in the Ricardian case as also in the Heckscher–Ohlin model (with the assumption of internationally identical, homothetic market-demand curves), *despite* the wage-differential and the consequent divergence of the commodity price ratio from the (marginal) domestic rate of transformation in production.

Note finally that, although the assumption of identical wage differentials in the two countries will leave the comparative advantage theorems unscathed, it is *not* correct to argue, as Taussig [11] did, that the terms and volume of trade will also be the same as in the case where there is no wage differential at all.

REFERENCES

1 Bhagwati, J., and Ramaswami, V. K., 'Domestic Distortions, Tariffs and the Theory of Optimum Subsidy', *Journal of Political Economy*, Vol. 71, February 1963.

2 Hagen, E., 'An Economic Justification of Protectionism', *Quarterly Journal of Economics*, Vol. 72, November 1958.

3 Jones, R., 'Factor Proportions and the Heckscher–Ohlin Model', *Review of Economic Studies*, Vol. 24, October 1956.

4 Kindleberger, C. P., *International Economics* (Illinois, Richard D. Irwin, Inc., 1955).

5 Matthews, R. C. O., 'Reciprocal Demand and Increasing Returns', *Review of Economic Studies*, Vol. 17, February 1950.

6 Meade, J. E., *A Geometry of International Trade* (London, Allen and Unwin Ltd., 1952).

7 Ohlin, B., *Interregional and International Trade* (Cambridge, Harvard University Press, 1952).

8 Samuelson, P. A., 'International Trade and the Equalisation of Factor Prices', *Economic Journal*, June 1948.

9 Samuelson, P. A., 'International Factor Price Equalisation Once Again', *Economic Journal*, June 1949.

10 Samuelson, P. A., 'Social Indifference Curves', *Quarterly Journal of Economics*, Vol. 70, February 1956.

11 Taussig, F. W., *International Trade* (New York, Macmillan Company Ltd., 1927).

PART THREE

Tariffs, Quantitative Restrictions and Subsidies

7 Protection, Real Wages and Real Incomes[1]

1 In a recent article [5], Mr Lancaster re-examined the famous Stolper–Samuelson theorem and concluded:

This paper does not deny that protection will raise the real wage of one of the factors, but shows that no general statement about which of the factors this will be can be deduced from the relative 'scarcity' of the factors in the Stolper–Samuelson sense.

Although the Stolper–Samuelson theorem 'Protection raises the real wage of the scarce factor' is shown to be an incorrect generalisation, a restatement in the form 'Protection raises the real wage of the factor in which the imported good is relatively more intensive' has general validity.

It is proposed in Section 1 of this paper to review systematically the original Stolper–Samuelson contribution, therewith to advance a critique (distinct from Mr Lancaster's criticism, which is not accepted), of the Stolper–Samuelson formulation of the theorem and then to restate the theorem: this restatement being considered to be the only true and general statement about the effect of protection (prohibitive or otherwise) on real wages of factors in the context of the basic Stolper–Samuelson model. The logical truth of the restated theorem is briefly analysed then in the context of alternative models. Section 2 proceeds to extend the scope of the discussion with the argument that, with a non-prohibitive tariff, a sharp distinction must be drawn between the impact on the real wage of a factor and the effect on its real income; some implications of this distinction are then analysed.

[1] This paper was read to the Nuffield Economics Society. My thanks are due to Professor Hicks and J. Black for helpful suggestions. I am also happy to record my indebtedness to Professor Harry Johnson, whose suggestions have led to improvements in the paper.

1. PROTECTION AND REAL WAGES

2 In the following analysis, we shall take the *basic* Stolper–Samuelson [10] model to mean that the protecting country has two factors, two commodities enjoying different factor intensities, linear and homogeneous production functions subject to diminishing returns (along isoquants) and incomplete specialization in production. Full employment of factors, pure competition and perfect mobility of factors are also assumed.

Founded on this model, we have three alternative formulations of the theorem concerning the impact of protection on the real wages of factors:

(1) *Restrictive Stolper–Samuelson Theorem.* 'International trade necessarily lowers the real wage of the scarce factor expressed in terms of any good' [10, p. 346]. This formulation restricts itself to the comparison of the free-trade real wage with the self-sufficiency real wage of the scarce factor. The comparison is confined to the case of a prohibitive tariff and excludes non-prohibitive protection. The theorem can be rewritten as follows: prohibitive protection necessarily raises the real wage of the scarce factor.

(2) *General Stolper–Samuelson Theorem.* Protection raises the real wage of the scarce factor.[1] This formulation is clearly intended to be more general and includes non-prohibitive tariffs as well. To emphasize this, we may rewrite it thus: protection (prohibitive or otherwise) necessarily raises the real wage of the scarce factor.

(3) *Stolper–Samuelson–Metzler–Lancaster Theorem.* 'Protection

---

[1] The actual formulation of the general Stolper–Samuelson theorem is from Lancaster [5, p. 199]. While the bulk of their analysis relates explicitly to the restrictive formulation, there are several indications that Stolper and Samuelson had in mind the general formulation as well: (1) a large number of quotations they cite from other authors to outline the problem refer to tariffs in general rather than to tariffs of a prohibitive nature alone; (2) they feel it necessary to assume that 'the country in question is relatively small and has no influence on the terms of trade. Thus any gain to the country through monopolistic or monopsonistic behaviour is excluded' [10, p. 344]; this assumption is quite superfluous, as we shall later see, if we wish to sustain only the restrictive formulation of the theorem; and (3) the title chosen for the article is not 'International Trade and Real Wages' but 'Protection and Real Wages'. Lancaster [5, p. 201] also construes the Stolper–Samuelson theorem in its general form; thus witness his argument that 'Protection will cause a movement in the *general direction* $Q'Q$, away from the free-trade point towards the self-sufficiency point' (my italics).

[prohibitive or otherwise] raises the real wage of the factor in which the imported good is relatively more intensive.'[1]

In the ensuing analysis any reference to 'the Stolper–Samuelson theorems' should be taken to relate to the initial two formulations alone; reference to the last formulation will always be by its full title.

3 We can begin by setting out the basic elements in the argument leading to the twin formulations of the Stolper–Samuelson theorem:

(1) protection increases the internal relative price of the importable good;

(2) an increase in the relative price of a good increases the real wage of the factor used intensively in its production;

(3) the importable good is intensive in the use of the scarce factor. Therefore,

(4) protection raises the real wage of the scarce factor.

These arguments must each be closely examined.

4 Concerning argument (1), we must distinguish between prohibitive and non-prohibitive protection:

(i) Protection will necessarily raise the relative price of the importable good when the tariff is prohibitive; the free-trade relative price of the importable good is lower than under self-sufficiency.[2]

(ii) Non-prohibitive protection may either raise, leave unchanged or lower the internal relative price of the importable good, Metzler [7] has demonstrated that this last 'perverse' possibility will occur, in the context of our present model, when the elasticity of foreign demand for imports (n_x) is less than the domestic marginal propensity to consume exportable goods (c).[3] It follows, then, that if

[1] Lancaster [5, p. 199]. This theorem has been given its stated name on grounds which are made explicit later.

[2] This is true except in a *limiting* case where the terms of trade will not change with trade. This case, however, can be ruled out, in the context of the model used here, by assuming that the community indifference curves (used here without any welfare connotation) are strictly convex. This limiting case will henceforward be ignored.

[3] It should be emphasized that the Metzler formula for determining the impact of protection on the internal commodity price-ratio relates to the case where the initial situation is that of free trade. Where, however, the initial situation itself has a tariff and the impact of *increased* protection is the subject of analysis, the 'perverse' possibility mentioned in the text will occur, as argued in Section 2, when a slightly altered condition is fulfilled. The discussion in Section 1, however, is confined to initial situations of free trade, as with Stolper and Samuelson, Metzler and Lancaster.

imports are not inferior goods in the protecting country's consumption this case requires inelastic foreign demand; and we can ensure that the internal relative price of the importable good always rises with the imposition of a tariff by assuming *either* elastic foreign demand (sometimes done in the form of assuming a small country) *or* a big enough tariff (in the limit, a prohibitive tariff) for demand to be elastic.

5 Argument (2) follows necessarily from the basic Stolper–Samuelson model. To show this simply, we should recall the technological features of the model employed by Samuelson some years later [8] [9] to demonstrate factor–price equalization: these features are identical with those of the Stolper–Samuelson model in all respects. We propose thus to avoid altogether the use of the box-diagram and work instead with the unique relationships that Samuelson derived in these later articles between commodity price-ratios, factor price-ratios and factor proportions in the two industries in a country, from the given assumptions concerning technology alone. These are summarized in Figure 7.1, which is reproduced, with slight changes, from Samuelson's 1949 article [9].

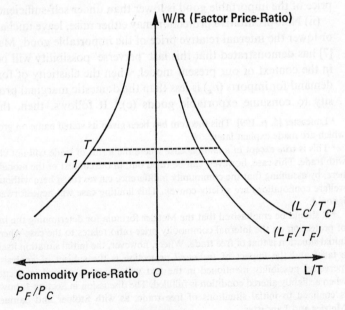

FIGURE 7.1

Let L_C and L_F represent the labour employed in producing clothing and food respectively; T_C and T_F being the quantities of land so employed. W/R represents the ratio of wages to rents; L/T the factor endowment ratio of the country; and P_F/P_C the price of food over the price of clothing. Clothing is the labour-intensive industry, food the land-intensive industry, at all relevant factor price ratios. ($L_C/T_C > L_F/T_F$ at all relevant W/R.)[1] As wages fall relatively to rents, the price of food is shown to rise relatively to that of clothing in a monotonic fashion. The factor endowment ratio of the country (L/T) fixes the range of the diagram which is relevant. This is a purely technology-determined diagram, and demand conditions are totally absent from it.

T being any given commodity price-ratio (P_F/P_C), change it to T_1 such that the relative price of food rises. With it, the labour-to-land ratios in both food and clothing will rise. The marginal physical product of land in both products will thus rise and of labour fall, so that the real wage of land will be unambiguously increased and of labour decreased. Increase in the relative price of food thus increases the real wage of land, the factor intensively used in producing food and reduces the real wage of labour (used intensively in cloth).

This argument, it should be noted, rests on the assumption, part of the basic Stolper–Samuelson model, that the rise of the relative price of food does not go so far as to make the country specialize completely on food, insofar as the fall in the real wage of labour is concerned; for, once the country is specialized completely, further increases in the relative price of food will raise the real wage of *both* labour and land, which is destructive of the full validity of argument (2).

Given the basic Stolper–Samuelson model, therefore, an increase (decrease) in the relative price of a good will necessarily increase (decrease) the real wage of the factor intensively used in its production.

6 Argument (3) that the importable good is intensive in the use of the scarce factor is really the well-known Heckscher–Ohlin theorem. The crucial question that it raises is: does the Heckscher–Ohlin theorem follow from the basic Stolper–Samuelson model? To answer this question, we should first have to define 'factor scarcity'. We may choose from three alternative definitions of factor scarcity:

[1] Although the factor-intensities of the commodities may be reversible, they *cannot* reverse for a country with a *given* factor endowment. At the present stage of our argument, therefore, we do not need to make the strong assumption that factor-intensities are non-reversible at *all* factor price-ratios.

A *Lancaster definition*. A country's scarce factor is that which is used more intensively in the production of the importable good. This definition may be described as tautological, since it turns the Heckscher–Ohlin theorem into a valid proposition by *definition*. It may also be described as an internal definition, since it excludes any comparison with the foreign country. It has been suggested by Lancaster.[1]

B *Heckscher–Ohlin definition*. A country's scarce factor is that whose relative price is higher than abroad under self-sufficiency. This may also be described as a price definition, since the country's scarce factor is that factor which is more expensive prior to trade than abroad. This definition has been used by Heckscher and Ohlin.[2]

C *Leontief definition*. A country's scarce factor is that of which there are fewer physical units per unit of the other factor than abroad. This may also be described as a physical definition, since it defines scarcity with reference to the relative physical quantities of factors.[3]

Using each of these definitions in turn, let us analyse the Heckscher–Ohlin theorem.

A If the Lancaster definition of factor scarcity is used, then the Heckscher–Ohlin theorem holds by definition.

B If the Heckscher–Ohlin definition of factor scarcity is used then the further assumptions of international identity of production functions and non-reversibility of factor-intensities of commodities

---

[1] Lancaster [5, p. 208] argues that 'the only acceptable definition' of a scarce factor is that which defines it as the factor 'which is used more intensively in the good of which more is produced in isolation than in trade'. It is of some interest to note that tariffs designed to influence distribution are probably set with reference to such internal criteria: to raise the real wage of labour, for instance, tariffs are imposed on labour-intensive industries rather than on products of industries using a factor which is scarcer at home than abroad; with the possible exception of the pauper-labour argument for such tariffs.

[2] For a convincing attribution of the authorship of this definition of factor scarcity to Heckscher and Ohlin, see the masterly article by R. Jones [3]. The definition may be also illustrated in terms of Figure 7.1: country A is labour-abundant and country B land-abundant if, under self-sufficiency, $(W/R)_A < (W/R)_B$.

[3] W. Leontief [6]. Again, country A is labour-abundant and country B land-abundant if, under self-sufficiency, $(L/T)_A > (L/T)_B$.

between the two countries will suffice to ensure the full validity of the Heckscher–Ohlin theorem.[1]

C If the Leontief definition of factor scarcity is used, then the threefold assumptions of non-reversibilities of factor-intensities of commodities between the trading countries and the international identity of both production functions and consumption patterns will ensure the validity of the Heckscher-Ohlin theorem.[2]

7 We can now sum up on the Stolper–Samuelson formulations as follows:[3]

A (1) The restrictive Stolper–Samuelson theorem is logically true if we use: (a) the basic Stolper–Samuelson model, and (b) the Lancaster definition of factor scarcity.

(2) The general Stolper–Samuelson theorem is logically true if we use the further assumption that the elasticity of foreign demand is greater than the marginal propensity to consume exportable goods ($n_x > c$).

[1] This can be seen readily from Figure 7.1. If $(W/R)_A < (W/R)_B$ and production functions with non-reversible factor-intensities are common between the countries, then we can see that $(P_F/P_C)_A > (P_F/P_C)_B$ under self-sufficiency and the labour-abundant country A will necessarily export the labour-intensive commodity, clothing. We could, of course, specify what appears to be a less restrictive condition than that set out in the text: for instance, we could sustain that Heckscher–Ohlin theorem by assuming merely that, instead of identical production functions between countries, the differences in the production functions are not large enough to outweigh the effect of differences in factor scarcity on the pre-trade commodity price-ratios. We have preferred to use the strong condition (identity of tastes) instead of the weak one on the ground that the use of the latter seems to be bad methodology, amounting to the argument that the Heckscher–Ohlin definition of factor scarcity will suffice to sustain the Heckscher–Ohlin theorem if other factors do not work to invalidate it.

[2] The Heckscher–Ohlin theorem would not hold as a logically true proposition in this case unless we also postulate now international identity of tastes (or the weak postulate that differences in tastes between countries do not affect the issue). This follows from the fact that while, with identical production functions, country A will show a bias towards the production of the labour-intensive commodity, clothing, by virtue of her physical abundance in labour, this bias in production may be more than offset by a bias in A towards the *consumption* of clothing: such that, in self-sufficiency, we find that $(P_F/P_C)_A < (P_F/P_C)_B$ and country A, although physically abundant in labour, would export the land-intensive commodity, food.

[3] The phrase 'logically true' in the following statements is used in the strict mathematical sense: 'A statement that is true in every logically possible case is said to be *logically true*' [4, p. 19].

B (1) The restrictive Stolper–Samuelson theorem is logically true if we use: (a) the basic Stolper–Samuelson model, (b) the Heckscher–Ohlin definition of factor scarcity, (c) the assumption of international identity of production functions, and (d) the assumption of non-reversibility of factor-intensities of commodities between the countries.

(2) The general Stolper–Samuelson theorem is logically true if we use the further assumption that $n_x > c$.

C (1) The restrictive Stolper–Samuelson theorem is logically true if we use: (a) the basic Stolper–Samuelson model, (b) the Leontief definition of factor scarcity, (c) the assumption of international identity of production functions, (d) the assumption of non-reversibility of factor-intensities of commodities between countries, and (e) the assumption of international identity of consumption patterns.

(2) The general Stolper–Samuelson theorem is logically true if we use the further assumption that $n_x > c$.

A tree-diagram, based on this analysis, is presented in Table 1.

8 We are now in a position to decide whether Stolper and Samuelson derived their theorems logically. Aside from their basic model:

(1) they adopt, though without complete clarity, the Heckscher–Ohlin definition of factor scarcity and the postulate concerning the non-reversibility of factor-intensities; and, quite explicitly, the assumption of international identity of production functions:[1] this establishes the restrictive Stolper–Samuelson theorem as logically true [B(1)];

(2) they further assume that 'the country in question is relatively small and has no influence on the terms of trade' [10, p. 346]; this establishes the general Stolper–Samuelson theorem as logically true [B(2)].

9 No critique of the Stolper–Samuelson formulations can thus be founded on the argument that they are not logically true, given the premises. What we could say, however, is that the theorem should be founded as closely as possible on the *basic* Stolper–Samuelson model alone; and

(1) that, if we use the Heckscher–Ohlin definition of factor

---

[1] Stolper and Samuelson [10, pp. 335–40]. Some of the argument is, of course, obscure in view of the pioneering nature of the article: a sympathetic interpretation, therefore, is called for. Metzler [7, p. 5] also adopts the Heckscher–Ohlin definition of factor scarcity in discussing the Stolper–Samuelson theorem.

TABLE 1

	Basic Stolper-Samuelson Model		Leontief
	Lancaster	Heckscher-Ohlin	
Definition of factor scarcity			
Production functions	Identical	Identical	Different
Factor-intensity	Non-Reversible	Non-Reversible	Reversible
Consumption patterns	Identical	Identical	Different
Tariffs	Prohibitive	Non-prohibitive	Non-prohibitive
Relative values of n_x and c	$n_x > c \quad n_x \leqq c$	$n_x > c \quad n \quad n_x \leqq c$	
Does protection necessarily raise the real wage of the scarce factor?	Yes Yes No	Yes Yes No No No	Yes Yes No No No

scarcity, the assumptions that we find ourselves making about the international identity of production functions and the non-reversibility of factor-intensities to sustain the twin formulations of the Stolper–Samuelson theorem are, on this criterion, *restrictive*; and

(2) that, if we use the Leontief definition of factor scarcity (as we should probably want to since it is, in a sense, the most 'objective' definition we could adopt in this context), we discover ourselves adopting the threefold restrictive assumptions [C(1)] of international identity of production functions and tastes plus the non-reversibility of factor-intensities of commodities, to sustain the Stolper–Samuelson formulations.[1]

10 It will be remembered, however, that these restrictive assumptions were made only because we wished to use argument (3) concerning the validity of the Heckscher–Ohlin theorem.[2] This may also be seen indirectly from the fact that, if we use the Lancaster definition of factor scarcity, no such restrictive assumptions are necessary [A(1)]: for the Heckscher–Ohlin theorem has been rendered valid by definition!

The suggestion follows readily from these considerations that we should formulate our theorem in terms of arguments (1) and (2) alone, while eliminating the use of the troublesome argument (3). This can be done readily: protection (prohibitive or otherwise) raises the real wage of the factor intensively employed in the production of the importable good. This theorem is logically true if we use: (a) the basic Stolper–Samuelson model, and (b) the assumption that $n_x > c$.

This theorem has been described as the Stolper–Samuelson–Metzler–Lancaster theorem on the following grounds:

(1) It is *implicit* in the Stolper–Samuelson argument, towards the end of their paper: 'It does not follow that our results stand and fall with the Heckscher–Ohlin theorem. Our analysis neglected the other country completely. If factors of production are not comparable between countries, or if production functions differ,

---

[1] The additional restrictive assumption that $n_x > c$ has not been listed here because we wish at this stage to concentrate on only those restrictive assumptions which are made to sustain argument (3).

[2] It is important to remember that these assumptions are restrictive only in so far as we wish to found our theorem exclusively on the basic Stolper–Samuelson model.

nevertheless, so long as the country has only two factors, international trade would necessarily affect the real wage of a factor in the same direction as its relative remuneration.' [10, pp. 355–6].[1]

(2) Metzler *explicitly* states it as 'the Stolper–Samuelson conclusion that tariffs benefit the factors of production which are required in relatively large amounts in the industries competing with imports.' [7, p. 13.][2]

(3) Lancaster advances this formulation directly as an *alternative* to the Stolper–Samuelson formulations considered above on the ground that it is more general than the latter.

11 Whereas, however, Lancaster's observation that the Stolper–Samuelson formulations are 'non-universal' (restrictive) is well taken, the argument by which he supports it is erroneous and different from that set out in this paper. Lancaster proceeds by establishing, with the aid of a highly ingenious model, the proposition that, in the context of the basic Stolper–Samuelson model combined with the assumption of a small country facing fixed terms of trade, differences in demand conditions ('which good is the wage-good') will affect the composition of a country's foreign trade. On this proposition he founds the following critique:

The non-universality of the [Stolper–Samuelson] theorem is due to incorrect formulation: if the scarce factor is defined as that which is used more intensively in the good of which more is produced in isolation than in trade (the only acceptable definition), then the previous analysis has shown that different wage-goods may make for different factor scarcities. In this sense, the Stolper–Samuelson formulation is meaningless, since the phrases 'real wages . . . in terms of any good' and 'scarce factor' represent incompatible concepts [5, p. 208].

The following comments on Lancaster's critique seem warranted here, in view of our preceding analysis.

To begin with, it is difficult to understand what Lancaster means by the statement that 'the previous analysis has shown that different wage-goods may make for different factor scarcities. In this sense,

[1] Homogeneity of factors between countries has not been listed separately as an assumption in this paper because it is believed that this is implicit in both the Heckscher–Ohlin and the Leontief definitions of factor scarcity.

[2] Metzler, of course, does not state it as a rival formulation, but it is abundantly clear that he is aware that this formulation is implicit in the general Stolper–Samuelson theorem.

the Stolper–Samuelson formulation is meaningless, since the phrases "real wages . . . in terms of any good" and "scarce factor" represent incompatible concepts.' Which good will be imported into a country will depend in our model on the pre-trade commodity price-ratios in the trading countries; these price-ratios are determined by domestic supply and demand; and domestic demand is affected by 'which good is the wage-good'. If the scarce factor is defined tautologously as that which is used intensively in the importable good it follows then, from elementary considerations, that 'different wage-goods may make for different factor scarcities'. But surely, how can this render the Stolper–Samuelson formulations *meaningless* or make 'real wages . . . in terms of any good' and 'scarce factor' *incompatible* concepts? And, more pertinently, why should this make the Stolper–Samuelson formulation 'non-universal'?

Indeed, if the tautologous definition of factor scarcity is adopted, as Lancaster suggests, then the general Stolper–Samuelson theorem and the Stolper–Samuelson–Metzler–Lancaster theorem are *identical*: the phrases 'scarce factor' and 'factor intensively employed in the importable good' can be used interchangeably. Lancaster cannot, therefore, claim one formulation to be 'non-universal' and the other to be 'universally true': on his own definition of factor scarcity, the two formulations come to the same thing!

To be sure, Lancaster's critique would be valid (though, as we have shown, incomplete) only if the physical, Leontief definition of factor scarcity were proven to have been adopted by Stolper and Samuelson, and were adopted by Lancaster as well; as formulated, however, the criticism is merely erroneous.[1] In failing to investigate precisely what Stolper and Samuelson assumed by way of their definition of factor scarcity, Lancaster has further by-passed the only legitimate critique that can be sustained against the actual formulation of the theorem by Stolper and Samuelson; namely, that advanced in this paper.

12 Our task is yet incomplete. Even the Stolper–Samuelson–Metzler–Lancaster formulation does not found the theorem completely and solely on the basic model. We must still make the restrictive assumption that $n_x > c$. We should, however, clearly want to go the whole way and remove all restrictive assumptions and restate the theorem to include

---

[1] Lancaster has pointed out to me, in private communication, that he really had in mind the physical definition of factor scarcity, despite the printed commitment to the tautologous definition.

the entire matrix of possibilities: such that the theorem is logically true, given only the basic Stolper–Samuelson model. This formulation is:[1]

> *Protection (prohibitive or otherwise) will raise, reduce or leave unchanged the real wage of the factor intensively employed in the production of a good according as protection raises, lowers or leaves unchanged the internal relative price of that good.*

This is really the fundamental theorem that Stolper and Samuelson contributed to our knowledge of the properties of the basic model they were using. Given the basic model, our formulation is logically true for all possible cases.

13 It should perhaps be emphasized that the preceding analysis has been centred entirely on the problem of analysing the impact of protection on real wages of factors in the context of the basic model employed by Stolper and Samuelson. It should be possible, of course, to analyse the problem afresh in terms of models employing alternative assumptions. This, however, would be mostly destructive of the full validity of our theorem.

If we allow for complete specialization with trade, for instance, we can claim only that protection will raise, lower or leave unchanged the real wage of the factor in which the *exportable* good is postulated to be intensive according as protection raises, lowers or leaves unchanged the internal relative price of the exportable good. But we cannot extend the theorem to the factor postulated to be used intensively in the production, if any, of the importable good because any increase in the internal relative price of the exportable good after complete specialization must raise the real wage of *both* factors.

On the other hand, if we allow for changing returns to scale in either or both of the two activities, clearly it becomes impossible to maintain that our theorem will be logically true.

2. PROTECTION AND REAL INCOMES

14 Our analysis has so far been concerned with the original Stolper–Samuelson problem of discovering the impact of protection on the *real wage* earned by factors in employment. It seems useful, however, to emphasize that if we are interested in finding out the net change in

---

[1] This formulation stems directly from argument (2), which is founded exclusively, as the reader will remember, on the basic Stolper–Samuelson model.

the *real income* of the factors it is only in the case of a prohibitive tariff that a complete identity obtains between change in real wage and change in the real income of a factor. Where the tariff is non-prohibitive, the complication arises from the revenue earned by the Government. If this revenue is assumed to be redistributed to the owners of factors according to some formula, factors will derive incomes *both* from the real wage in employment and from the redistributed proceeds of the tariff-revenue.

Hence arises the interesting possibility that the factor whose real wage has been damaged by protection may still find its real income improved if the formula for the redistribution of the tariff-revenue is heavily biased in its favour. Since this possibility constitutes a qualification to the generally accepted implication of the Stolper–Samuelson analysis, it should be of some interest to delimit the conditions under which it may occur.

To begin with, this possibility of over-compensating the damaged factor from the *tariff-revenue* clearly cannot arise unless the real income of the country as a whole is improved by protection. We know from the preceding analysis that where the real wage of one factor is reduced, that of the other necessarily rises; hence, if protection did not bring some gain to the country as a whole, it should be impossible to over-compensate the factor with the damaged real wage (from tariff-revenues). To rephrase the proposition, then, accrual of gain to the protecting country from the imposition of protection is a necessary, though not sufficient, condition for the possibility of over-compensating the factor with the damaged real wage.[1]

In the following brief analysis we seek to relate this proposition to Metzler's formula for determining the impact of protection on the internal commodity price-ratio: partly to establish link with Metzler's pioneering analysis in this field and largely because it enables us to define, and distinguish between, situations in which the factor with the damaged real wage will be export-intensive (intensively used in exportables) and those where it will be import-intensive. The discussion is then briefly extended to the case where the initial situation is that of a tariff instead of free trade and the effect of an *increase* in protection is the subject of inquiry.

[1] That is to say, whereas the country must have gained from protection before the damaged factor can be over-compensated from the tariff revenues (necessary condition), this gain must be large enough to permit over-compensation (sufficient condition).

15 In Figure 7.2 let O_b be the foreign reciprocal demand curve facing country A. F is the free-trade point, OF yielding the corresponding terms of trade. I_a^1 is the trade-indifference curve of A passing through F at a tangent to OF and intersecting O_b at U. Its postulated curvature derives from the assumption of strict convexity of the production frontier and community indifference curves.

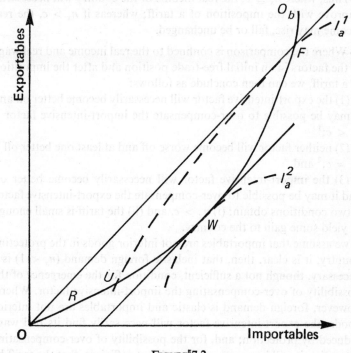

FIGURE 7.2

(1) Assume that the tariff-added offer curve of country A intersects O_b at U. The internal relative price of the importable good is then given by the slope of the trade-indifference curve I_a^1 at U, which is clearly, by virtue of the postulated curvature of I_a^1, greater than at F. We can deduce, therefore, that protection can leave the real income of the country unchanged only if the internal relative price of the importable good rises from the free-trade level with the imposition of protection (in turn, only if $n_x > c$).

(2) Similarly, by considering points on O_b to the left of U such as R, we can argue that protection can reduce the real income of the country

only if the internal relative price of the importable good rises with protection (in turn, only if $n_x > c$).

(3) However, protection can increase the real income of the country whether the internal relative price of the importable good rises, is unchanged (W) or falls with the imposition of protection (in turn, whether $n_x \lessgtr c$).

Thus, where $n_x \leq c$, the real income of the country will necessarily improve with the imposition of a tariff; whereas if $n_x > c$, the real income may rise, fall or be unchanged.

(16) Where the comparison is confined to the real income and real wage of the factors in an initial free-trade position and after the imposition of a tariff, we can then conclude as follows:

(1) the export-intensive factor will necessarily become better off and it may be possible to over-compensate the import-intensive factor if $n_x < c$;[1]

(2) neither factor will become worse off and at least one better off if $n_x = c$;[2] and

(3) the import-intensive factor will necessarily become better off and it may be possible to over-compensate the export-intensive factor if two conditions obtain: (i) $n_x > c$, and (ii) the tariff is small enough to yield some gain to the country.

If we assume that importables are not inferior goods in the protecting country, it is clear, then, that inelastic foreign demand ($n_x < 1$) is a necessary, though not a sufficient, condition for the emergence of the possibility of over-compensating the import-intensive factor. Where, however, foreign demand is elastic and importables are not inferior goods, the export-intensive factor will necessarily find its real wage reduced by protection; and, for the possibility of over-compensating it to arise, it will be necessary, though not sufficient, that the tariff be small enough to make the country better off than under free trade.

(17) If, however, we wish to compare the real incomes and wages of factors in an initial situation of a tariff and after *increase* in the tariff, the analysis must be somewhat modified.

---

[1] When $n_x < c$ we know now that: (1) the internal relative price of the importable good falls, thus increasing the real wage of the export-intensive factor and reducing that of the import-intensive factor; and (2) the country must have become better off. Hence the proposition in the text.

[2] Where $n_x = c$, we know that: (1) the internal relative price of the importable good is unchanged, thus leaving unchanged the real wages of both factors; and (2) the real income of the country must increase. Hence the proposition in the text.

To begin with, the Metzler formula must be altered so as to read: the internal relative price of the importable good will rise, be unchanged or fall according as $n_x \gtreqless \dfrac{c}{1 + ct}$ where t is the initial tariff rate. It will be seen that where the initial situation is that of free trade, t will be zero and the formula will reduce to the well-known Metzler formula.

Secondly, the impact on the real income of the country will not bear the same relationship to the shifts in the internal commodity price-ratio as in the previous analysis with the free-trade initial situation. It can be demonstrated, by a geometrical argument analogous to that used earlier, that although the internal relative price of the importable good must still rise for the country to be as well off as prior to the increased tariff, both reduction and increase in the real income of the country are now consistent with any shift in this price.

Thirdly, arguing from the optimum tariff theory, we can claim that the real income of the country will improve with increased protection if two conditions obtain: (i) the pre-increase tariff rate is less than the optimum tariff rate: $t < \dfrac{1}{n_x - 1}$; and (ii) *either* the post-increase tariff rate is also less than the optimum tariff rate *or*, if it exceeds the optimum tariff rate, it is small enough to leave some gain in real income to the country from the increase in tariff.

These considerations lead to the following conclusions:[1]

✓(1) The export-intensive factor will necessarily become better off and it may be possible to over-compensate the import-intensive factor from *increased* tariff revenues when three conditions obtain: (i) $n_x < \dfrac{c}{1 + ct}$; (ii) $t < \dfrac{1}{n_x - 1}$; and (iii) *either* the post-increase tariff rate is also less than the optimum tariff rate *or*, if it exceeds the optimum tariff, it is still small enough to leave some gain in real income to the country from the increase in the tariff.

✓(2) The import-intensive factor will necessarily become better off and it may be possible to over-compensate the export-intensive factor

---

[1] The first two propositions that follow assume that the factor stated to become necessarily better off continued to receive *at least* the same revenue as in the initial situation; this assumption being made explicit by the use of the phrase 'from *increased* tariff revenues'. This assumption is needed because otherwise improvement merely in the real wage of a factor due to increased protection could be offset by an accompanying unfavourable distribution of tariff revenues to the factor after the increase in the tariff.

from *increased* tariff revenues when three conditions obtain: (i) $n_x > \dfrac{c}{1 + ct}$; (ii) $t < \dfrac{1}{n_x - 1}$; and (iii) *either* the post-increase tariff rate is also less than the optimum tariff *or*, if it exceeds the optimum tariff, it is still small enough to leave some gain in real income to the country from the increase in protection.

(3) Where, however, $n_x = \dfrac{c}{1 + ct}$, the real wage of neither factor changes with the increase in protection. It follows, therefore, that the real income of both factors will increase, decrease or remain unchanged according as the increase in tariff raises, lowers or leaves unchanged the real income of the country: assuming, of course, that the tariff-revenues are divided among the factors in a given proportion.

18 In conclusion, it should be re-emphasized that the brief discussion presented here has been concerned only with the limited task of exploring some of the implications of the proposition that accrual of gain to the protecting country from the imposition of protection is a necessary, though not sufficient, condition for the emergence of the possibility of over-compensating, from tariff revenues, the factor with the damaged real wage.[1]

[1] A rigorous analysis of the sufficient conditions for the emergence of this possibility would call for an analysis of distribution and demand, so that factor earnings and income subsidies from tariff revenues could be related to real incomes of factors. Such analysis would preclude us from taking as given, as we have done here, the set of community indifference curves: this practice has been adopted in the present paper for strictly pedagogic reasons.

REFERENCES

1 Harrod, R. F., 'Factor-Price Relations Under Free Trade', *Economic Journal*, June 1958.

2 Johnson, H. G., 'Factor Endowments, International Trade and Factor Prices', *Manchester School of Economic and Social Studies*, September 1957.

3 Jones, R., 'Factor Proportions and the Heckscher–Ohlin Theorem', *Review of Economic Studies*, 1956–7.

4 Kemeny, Snell, and Thompson, *Introduction to Finite Mathematics*, Prentice–Hall, 1957.

5 Lancaster, K., 'Protection and Real Wages: A Restatement', *Economic Journal*, June 1957.

6 Leontief, W., 'Domestic Production and Foreign Trade: The American Capital Position Reexamined', *Proceedings of the American Philosophical Society*, 28 September, 1953.

7 Metzler, L., 'Tariffs, the Terms of Trade and the Distribution of National Income', *Journal of Political Economy*, February 1949.

8 Samuelson, P. A., 'International Trade and the Equalization of Factor Prices', *Economic Journal*, June 1948.

9 Samuelson, P. A., 'International Factor–Price Equalization Once Again', *Economic Journal*, June 1949.

10 Stolper, W., and Samuelson, P. A., 'Protection and Real Wages', *A.E.A. Readings in the Theory of International Trade*, Blakiston Co., 1949.

8 A Generalized Theory of the Effects of Tariffs on the Terms of Trade[1]

Traditional analysis of the effect of a tariff on the terms of trade of the protecting country draws a distinction between two cases: (1) where the tariff revenue is spent by the government; and (2) where the tariff revenue is redistributed as an income subsidy to the private sector. In both cases the conclusion reached is that the terms of trade of the protecting country will improve or deteriorate according as the country's elasticity of demand for imports is greater or less than the marginal propensity to consume importables (of the government or the private sector, as the case may be). By splitting the elasticity of demand for imports into the sum of the compensated elasticity of demand for imports and the private sector's marginal propensity to consume importables, it can further be shown (on the usual assumption of convex indifference and transformation curves) that the terms of trade must improve if the private sector spends the tariff revenue; and that, if the government spends the tariff revenue, the terms of trade can only deteriorate if the government's marginal propensity to consume importables exceeds the private sector's marginal propensity to consume importables by more than the private compensated elasticity of demand for imports. Normally, the terms of trade will not improve sufficiently to offset the effect of the tariff in raising the domestic price of importables; but the tariff will reduce the domestic price of importables if the marginal propensity to consume exportables of whichever sector spends the tariff revenue is greater than the foreign elasticity of demand for exportables.

[1] The major part of the work on this paper was done at the University of Chicago; the final draft was prepared at the Institute for Economic Research, Queen's University, Kingston, Ontario. We are grateful to the Institute for extending to us the use of its facilities.

This analysis, however, is founded on four restrictive postulates:

(1) *Initial free trade*. It is assumed that there is no tariff in effect in the initial situation; hence the analysis does not apply to the case of an increase in an existing tariff rate.

(2) *Independence of consumer taste and government expenditure*. Where the government spends the tariff revenue, it is assumed that the amount of government expenditure – either the total, or the amount spent on particular commodities – does not affect the way in which the private sector divides its expenditure between importables and exportables; hence the analysis does not apply to the case of dependence of consumer taste on the amount of government expenditure.

(3) *Aggregation of the private sector*. It is assumed that the private sector can be treated as a homogeneous unit with respect to its demand for imports; this ignores the effects of a change in the domestic price of importables in redistributing real income (a) between consumers with different tastes, and (b) between owners of different collections of factors of production, as well as the influence [in case (2)] of the way in which the redistributed tariff revenue is allocated among private consumers.

(4) *Inelastic supply of factors*. In dealing with the effects of a change in the domestic price of importables on domestic production, it is assumed that the supply of resources is given; hence the analysis does not take account of the effects on import demand of changes in factor supplies consequential on the change in the tariff rate.

In this paper we generalize the theory of tariffs by examining the effect of an increase in the tariff rate when these restrictive assumptions do not hold.[1] We distinguish three major cases: (1) where the government spends the tariff revenue and private demand is independent of

[1] For the traditional analysis, reference may be made to A. P. Lerner, 'The Symmetry Between Import and Export Taxes,' *Economica*, N.S., vol. iii, No. 11 (Aug. 1936), pp. 306–13; L. Metzler, 'Tariffs, the Terms of Trade and the Distribution of National Income', *Journal of Political Economy*, vol. lvii, No. 1 (Feb. 1949), pp. 1–29; and R. E. Baldwin, 'The Effect of Tariffs on International and Domestic Prices', *Quarterly Journal of Economics*, vol. lxxiv, No. 1 (Feb. 1960), pp. 65–78' In a later supplement to his classic paper, *op. cit.*, Lloyd Metzler recognized explicitly the dependence of the analysis developed by him, of the effect of tariffs on domestic prices, on the assumption of initial free trade; see his 'Tariffs, International Demand, and Domestic Prices', *Journal of Political Economy*, vol. lvii, No. 4 (Aug. 1949), pp. 345–51.

H

government expenditure; (2) where the proceeds of the tariff are consumed by the private sector; (3) where the government spends the tariff revenue and the amount of government expenditure influences the private sector's demand for imports. Section 1 analyses the first two (the traditional) cases, abandoning the restriction of initial free trade. Section 2 analyses the third case, abandoning the second restriction of independence of private demand and government expenditure. Section 3 abandons the third restriction and incorporates the effects of disaggregating consumption demand and factor ownership in the analysis of the three cases. Section 4 abandons the fourth restriction and extends the analysis to include the effects of variable supplies of factors. These four sections are concerned with the effect of the tariff increase on the terms of trade; in Section 5 we analyse the effect of the tariff increase on the domestic price of importables.

Throughout the analysis we assume that only two goods are produced and consumed, 'exportables' and 'importables'; in analysing case (3), however, we assume that the amount of government expenditure enters consumers' utility functions as a third consumption good. In dropping restrictions (3) and (4) we assume that income is shared between two individuals, each of whom owns a collection of productive factors and earns an income from the sale of their services; and that each good is produced in a linear homogeneous production function employing two factors, labour and capital, whose earnings are wages and rent respectively, these factors being employed in different ratios in the two industries. Markets for goods and factors are assumed to be perfectly competitive. In analysing the effect of the tariff increase in the various cases, we employ the simplifying device of assuming the conditions for stability in the international market; this permits the effect of the tariff on the terms of trade to be inferred from its effect on the excess demand for imports at the initial terms of trade, and its effect on the domestic price of importables to be inferred from its effect on the excess demand for imports at the initial domestic price of imports.

We employ the following mathematical symbols throughout the article; other symbols are defined when they appear in the argument:

p, the international price of the importable good in terms of the exportable good (the terms of trade); by choice of units, p is initially made equal to unity;

t, the tariff rate, defined as a proportion of the international price of importables;

π, the domestic price of importables in terms of exportables; $\pi = (1 + t)p$; because p is initially unity $d\pi/dt$ in the mathematical development below is equal to unity;

P, the quantity of importables produced domestically;

Q, the quantity of exportables produced domestically;

Y, the amount of earned income: $Y = \pi P + Q$;

C, the quantity of importables consumed out of private income; private income is equal to earned income where the government spends the tariff revenue [cases (1) and (3)], and to earned income plus tariff proceeds where the latter are redistributed to the private sector [case (2)];

M_1, the quantity of importables imported for private consumption: $M_1 = C - P$;

M_2, the quantity of importables consumed by the government out of tariff revenue; this quantity must obviously be imported, and it simplifies matters to assume that the government buys its importables abroad at the world market price;

M, the total quantity of imports: $M = M_1 + M_2$;

R, the tariff revenue: $R = tpM_1$;

c, the private sector's marginal propensity to spend on importables at the domestic price of importables; the private sector's marginal propensity to consume importables is c/π;

g, the government's marginal propensity to spend tariff revenue on imports at the international price of imports; the government's marginal propensity to consume imports is $g/p = g$;

ξ, the domestic price elasticity of private demand for imports, tariff revenue being held constant where it affects private demand [cases (2) and (3)]; $\xi = -\dfrac{\pi}{M_1}\dfrac{\delta M_1}{\delta \pi}$;

η, the price elasticity of private demand for importables, earned income and tariff revenue being held constant; $\eta = -\dfrac{\pi}{C}\dfrac{\delta C;}{\delta \pi}$

η', the compensated elasticity of private demand for importables; $\eta' = \eta - c$;

ε, the elasticity of domestic supply of importables with given supplies of factors of production; $\varepsilon = \dfrac{\pi}{P}\dfrac{\delta P}{\delta \pi}$;

ξ', the compensated elasticity of private demand for imports:

$$\xi' = \frac{C}{M_1}\eta' + \frac{P}{M_1}\varepsilon = \xi - c.$$

Barred symbols denote initial magnitudes of the variables when these might be confused with the functional relationships that determine them. The main equations in the mathematical argument have been numbered; the formulae derived have also been assigned roman numerals.

1. THE EFFECT OF AN INCREASE IN THE TARIFF ON THE TERMS OF TRADE: CASES (1) AND (2)

An increase in the tariff rate will cause an improvement or a deterioration in the terms of trade according as it gives rise to a negative or a positive world excess demand for importables at the initial international price of imports. Since the quantity of imports supplied by the rest of the world at the initial terms of trade is unchanged by the increase in the tariff, the change in the world excess demand for importables resulting from the tariff increase is equal to the change in the tariff-increasing country's demand for imports. On the usual assumptions that the private sector can be treated as an aggregate and that factor supplies are inelastic, this change, in cases (1) and (2), is the net result of two effects of the tariff increase:

(i) the effect of the increase in the domestic price of importables due to the tariff increase on the quantity of imports privately demanded;

(ii) the effect of the change in the amount of tariff revenue due to the increase in the tariff and the consequential change in the quantity of imports privately demanded under (1) above, on the quantity of imports demanded by the government or the private sector, whichever spends the tariff revenue.

(1) The change in the quantity of imports privately demanded is determined by the elasticity of private demand for imports; this change, which we denote by $\delta M_1/\delta t$ because the tariff increase also affects private demand for imports in other ways in case (2) and other cases considered below, is:

$$\frac{\delta M_1}{\delta t} = \frac{\delta M_1}{\delta \pi} \frac{d\pi}{dt} = -\frac{\overline{M}_1}{\pi} \xi.$$

The change in the quantity of imports demanded due to the increase in the domestic price of importables is actually the net result of three effects of the increase in the domestic price of importables:

(i) the change in private consumption of importables due to the increase in the price of importables, determined by the price elasticity of private demand for importables; this change is:

$$\frac{\delta C}{\delta \pi}\frac{d\pi}{dt} = -\frac{\bar{C}}{\pi}\eta;$$

(ii) the change in private consumption of importables due to the increase in income earned in domestic production resulting from the increased domestic price of importables, determined[1] by the initial amount of domestic production of importables and the marginal propensity to consume importables; this change is:

$$\frac{\delta C}{\delta Y}\frac{\delta Y}{\delta \pi}\frac{d\pi}{dt} = \frac{c}{\pi}\bar{P};$$

(iii) the increase in domestic production of importables in response to the increase in their domestic price, determined by the elasticity of domestic supply of importables; this change is:

$$\frac{dP}{d\pi}\frac{d\pi}{dt} = \frac{\bar{P}}{\pi}\varepsilon.$$

The net result of these three effects is:

$$\frac{\delta M_1}{\delta t} = -\frac{\bar{M}_1}{\pi}\left(\frac{\bar{C}}{\bar{M}_1}\eta - \frac{\bar{P}}{\bar{M}_1}c + \frac{\bar{P}}{\bar{M}_1}\varepsilon\right)$$

$$= -\frac{\bar{M}_1}{\pi}\left(\frac{\bar{C}}{\bar{M}_1}\eta' + \frac{\bar{P}}{\bar{M}_1}\varepsilon + c\right)$$

$$= -\frac{\bar{M}_1}{\pi}(\xi' + c). \tag{1}$$

(2) (a) Where the government spends the tariff revenue, the change in the quantity of imports it demands will be determined by the change in the tariff revenue from private imports and the government's marginal propensity to consume importables; this change is:

$$\frac{dM_2}{dt} = g\frac{dR}{dt} = g\left(t\frac{\partial M_1}{\partial t} + \bar{M}_1\right) = g\bar{M}_1\left(1 - \frac{t}{\pi}\xi\right). \tag{2 a}$$

[1] The effect on the value of output of the increase in production of importables [analysed under (iii) above] and the associated reduction in the production of exportables induced by the increase in the domestic price of importables can be ignored, since maximization of the value of output under competition implies that the effect of small departures of production from the equilibrium quantities is of the second order of smalls.

(b) Where the tariff revenue is redistributed to the private sector the change in the quantity of imports privately demanded will be determined by the change in the tariff revenue and the marginal propensity to consume importables of the private sector; but the change in the tariff revenue in this case is not simply the change in tariff revenue due to the change in private imports analysed under (1) above, but the product of that change and the sum of a series which is determined by the marginal propensity to consume imports of the private sector. The initial change in the tariff revenue due to the increase in the tariff rate and its effect on the quantity of imports privately demanded will change private expenditure on imports by a fraction of itself approximately equal to c, of which c/π will represent a change in the quantity of imports demanded and ct/π a further change in tariff revenue, which will lead to further changes of $c^2 t/\pi^2$ in the quantity of imports demanded and $c^2 t^2/\pi^2$ in tariff revenue, and so on. Hence the total change in redistributed tariff revenue will be:

$$\frac{dR}{dt} = \left(1 + \frac{ct}{\pi} + \frac{c^2 t^2}{\pi^2} + \cdots\right)\frac{\delta R}{\delta t} = \frac{\pi}{1 + (1-c)t}\frac{\delta R}{\delta t},$$

where

$$\frac{\partial R}{\partial t} = \frac{\delta}{\delta t}(tM_1) = \overline{M}_1\left(1 - \frac{t}{\pi}\xi\right);$$

and the change in the quantity of imports demanded due to the effect of the tariff change on the amount of redistributed tariff revenue will be:

$$\frac{\partial C}{\partial R}\frac{dR}{dt} = \frac{c}{\pi}\frac{\pi}{1 + (1-c)t}\frac{\partial R}{\partial t} = \frac{c\overline{M}_1}{1 + (1-c)t}\left(1 - \frac{t}{\pi}\xi\right). \quad (2\text{ b})$$

In *case (1)* the total effect of the tariff increase on the world excess demand for importables is [the sum of equations (1) and (2 a)]:[1]

$$\frac{dM}{dt} = -\frac{\overline{M}_1}{\pi}\xi + g\overline{M}_1\left(1 - \frac{t}{\pi}\xi\right)$$

$$= \overline{M}_1\left(g - \frac{1 + gt}{\pi}\xi\right)$$

$$= \overline{M}_1\left(g - (1 + gt)\frac{c}{\pi} - \frac{1 + gt}{\pi}\xi'\right). \quad (3)\text{ I}$$

If initially there is free trade, this reduces to $dM/dt = \overline{M}_1 g(-c - \xi')$, which yields the traditional conclusion that world excess demand for

---

[1] This result can be obtained directly by differentiating the basic equation for this case. $M \equiv M_1 + M_2 = M_1(\pi) + M_2(R)$, where $R = tM_1$ and $dM_2/dR = g$.

importables at the initial world price will be negative and the terms of trade turn in the country's favour unless the government's marginal propensity to consume importables exceeds the private sector's marginal propensity to consume importables by more than the private sector's compensated elasticity of demand for imports. This in turn requires that the government have a stronger marginal preference for importables than the private sector (a higher marginal propensity to spend on them at the same price) and that the private compensated elasticity of demand for imports be less than unity (assuming that imports are not inferior in private consumption, and that the government, having no initial revenue, cannot have a marginal propensity to spend on importables greater than unity). *If there is a tariff in effect, it remains true that the government must have a higher marginal propensity to consume importables than the private sector for the terms of trade to deteriorate; but since the tariff makes the real cost of importables to the consumer higher than to the government* (assuming that the latter chooses rationally on the basis of world and not domestic prices), *this does not necessarily imply that the government has the stronger marginal preference for importables* (in the sense defined above). *In the general case, also, the terms of trade can deteriorate even if the private compensated elasticity of demand for imports exceeds unity*; this could occur if the government's marginal propensity to consume importables (though higher than the private) were sufficiently low or the tariff rate sufficiently high to offset a compensated elasticity above unity, or if importables were inferior goods to the government at the income level represented by the initial tariff revenue.

In *case* (2) the total effect of the tariff increase on the world excess demand for importables is [the sum of equations (1) and (2 b)]:[1]

$$\frac{dM}{dt} = -\frac{\overline{M}_1}{\pi}\xi + \frac{c\overline{M}_1}{1+(1-c)t}\left(1 - \frac{t}{\pi}\xi\right)$$

$$= \frac{\overline{M}_1}{1+(1-c)t}(c - \xi)$$

$$= -\frac{\overline{M}_1\xi'}{1+(1-c)t}. \qquad (4)\ \text{II}$$

It follows that world excess demand for importables at the initial world price must be negative and the terms of trade must be improved

---

[1] This result can be obtained directly by differentiating the basic equation for this case, $M \equiv M_1 = M_1(\pi, R)$ where $\delta M_1/\delta R = c/1 + t$ and $R = tM_1$.

following an increase in the tariff rate; hence *the result of a tariff increase in case (2) is the same, whether the tariff increase is imposed on an initial free-trade situation or on an existing tariff*. This is only what one would expect, since redistribution of tariff proceeds reduces the effect of a tariff increase on the demand for imports to a pure substitution effect.

2. The Effect of an Increase in the Tariff on the Terms of Trade: case (3), Dependence

In the preceding section we have analysed the two traditional cases, (1) where the government spends the tariff revenue, and (2) where the tariff revenue is redistributed to the private sector. In analysing the latter case we have assumed that the tariff proceeds are redistributed in the form of an income subsidy, which is spent by the private sector in the same way as would be an increment in earned income.[1] But it would make no difference to the final result if it were assumed that the tariff proceeds were distributed in kind instead of in cash – that the government used the tariff revenue to purchase some collection of exportables and importables and distributed that collection to the public. For the public would merely adjust its purchases from its earned income to obtain the same total consumption of each good as it would have chosen if the tariff proceeds had been redistributed in cash. A subsidy in kind can only produce a different consumption pattern than a cash subsidy if the amount of a particular good distributed in kind is larger than the total that would have been purchased out of the subsidy-recipient's own income plus the cash subsidy, and this possibility is excluded in the present case by the fact that the amount of goods the government can distribute in kind is restricted by the amount of tariff proceeds it collects.

In analysing the former case we have made the traditional assumption that the behaviour of the private sector is unaffected by the expenditure of the tariff revenue by the government – that private-sector tastes are independent of government consumption. The case of dependence of private tastes on government consumption has recently been examined by Robert Baldwin, who reaches the rather

---

[1] This income-subsidy assumption is to be found in J. E. Meade, *A Geometry of International Trade* (London: Allen & Unwin, 1952), chap. vi. Metzler, *op. cit.*, assumes, however, a reduction in an existing income tax by this amount, which reduces to the same thing.

surprising conclusion that the results in the dependence case are the same as in the income-subsidy case. This conclusion is understandable, however, once it is realized that Baldwin identifies the general case of dependence with the special case in which consumers regard government purchases as equivalent to an addition to their own private consumption of the goods concerned. In fact, in his theoretical analysis, Baldwin explicitly treats government consumption as the provision of benefits in kind to consumers, which means that the government in effect is not consuming the tariff proceeds on its own behalf but is redistributing them in kind; and, as we have just argued, this should have the same effect as redistributing them through income subsidies.[1]

The more interesting general problem of dependence arises when the government uses the tariff proceeds for its own consumption, *and* the amount of some or all of the governmental services provided by this consumption influences the relative quantities of commodities purchased by the private sector from its earned income in a way not necessarily identifiable with the influence of a direct governmental subsidy in cash or kind. This is a more realistic case than that traditionally analysed [our case (1)] and a more general case than that analysed by Baldwin. One would expect that an increase in state expenditure on, say, police services would lead to a reduction in the amount of private expenditure on fire-arms, locks and bolts, and bodyguards, but not that the effects of the two changes on demand would exactly offset one another, since the government provides services in a different form than they would be privately provided. Similarly, the government provides collective goods which would not be privately provided if consumers had the spending of their tax contributions, and which influence the pattern of private demand.

Technically, dependence implies that the amount of some or all of the service provided by government enters the utility function of the private sector in a significant way (*i.e.* its substitute-complement

---

[1] R. E. Baldwin, *op. cit.*, especially pp. 69–71. In note 5 to p. 67, Baldwin interprets 'dependence' in the broader sense in which we discuss it: 'However, as long as the consumption by the government furnishes some utility to the private sector, it is possible for this public consumption to change the civilian offer curve of exports for imports'. But in his analysis he gives it the narrow interpretation discussed here. We are indebted to Mr Baldwin for correspondence and personal discussion which removed a misunderstanding of his argument on our part.

relationship with commodities privately consumed varies between commodities) so that the private sector's demands for goods become functions of the total or of some component of the amount of government consumption. Insofar as the composition of governmental services depends on the relative prices of commodities purchased by the government, the equilibrium of the economy will vary with the nature of the dependence of private demands on the amounts of governmental services provided; but for the present analysis, which is concerned with the effect of a tariff increase on the excess demand for importables at the given initial world price of importables and assumes that the government chooses on the basis of this price, private demands can be assumed to depend only on the total amount of governmental expenditure, since this will determine the amounts of the separate types of government service provided.[1]

Dependence means that, in addition to the price effect on private demand for imports and the revenue effect on governmental demand for imports analysed under case (1), the tariff increase will have a dependence effect on private demand for imports through its effect on the amount of government revenue and consumption. This effect will be:

$$\frac{\delta C}{\delta R}\frac{dR}{dt} = \frac{b}{\pi}\left(t\frac{dM_1}{dt} + \overline{M}_1\right), \tag{5}$$

where b, the change in private expenditure on importables associated with a unit change in government expenditure, will be positive or negative according as imports are complementary or substitutary with government expenditure in private consumption. The total change in private demand for imports is now [the sum of equations (1) and (5)]:

$$\frac{dM_1}{dt} = -\frac{\overline{M}_1}{\pi}\xi + \frac{b}{\pi}\left(t\frac{dM_1}{dt} + \overline{M}_1\right) = \frac{(b-\xi)\overline{M}_1}{1+(1-b)t}, \tag{6}$$

and the resulting change in government demand for imports is:

$$\frac{dM_2}{dt} = g\left(\frac{t(b-\xi)\overline{M}_1}{1+(1-b)t} + \overline{M}_1\right) = \frac{(\pi - t\xi)g}{1+(1-b)t}\overline{M}_1; \tag{7}$$

[1] Our problem here is analytically similar to that faced by J. R. Hicks in his analysis of the effects of a change in wants, in chap. xvii, especially pp. 162–4, of *A Revision of Demand Theory* (Oxford, At the Clarendon Press, 1956).

hence the total change in world excess demand for importables is [the sum of equations (6) and (7)]:[1]

$$\frac{dM}{dt} = \frac{\overline{M}_1}{1 + (1 - b)t} \{b + g\pi - (1 + gt)\xi\}$$

$$= \frac{\overline{M}_1}{1 + (1 - b)t} \{b + g\pi - (1 + gt)c - (1 + gt)\xi'\}. \quad (8) \text{III}$$

If initially there is free trade, this formula reduces to $\overline{M}_1(b + g - c - \xi')$. In contrast to the case of independence [case (1) above], *world excess demand for importables at the initial world price can be positive and the terms of trade deteriorate even if the private sector has a higher marginal propensity to consume importables than the government and the private compensated elasticity of demand for imports exceeds unity; this result can occur if government services are sufficiently strongly complementary with importables in private-sector consumption.* The same conclusion holds *a fortiori* for the case of an existing tariff.[2]

3. The Effect of an Increase in the Tariff on the Terms of Trade: Disaggregation of the Private Sector

In the previous two sections we have analysed the effect of an increase in the tariff rate in our three cases on the assumption that the private sector could be regarded as a homogeneous unit. Abandonment of this assumption introduces three complications:

(1) Insofar as consumers consume exportables and importables in differing proportions, as a result of either taste or income differences, a change in the domestic price of importables alters the distribution of real income between them.

---

[1] This result can be obtained directly by differentiating the basic equation for this case, $M \equiv M_1 + M_2 = M_1(\pi, R) + M_2(R)$, where $\delta M_1/\delta R = b/\pi$, $\delta M_2/\delta R = g$, and $R = tM_1$; it is necessary first to solve for dM_1/dt by differentiating M_1 alone. It should be noted that the stability of equilibrium requires that the denominator in this and similar expressions presented subsequently for cases (2) and (3) must be positive; this is assumed without further comment in the argument of the rest of this article.

[2] It should be noticed that if consumers treat government consumption as equivalent to personal consumption of the commodities concerned (the Baldwin case), with initial free trade $b = c - g$ and the formula is identical with that given earlier for case (2). With a tariff initially in effect the formulae are different because we have assumed that the government does not pay tariff revenue to itself on its imports.

(2) Insofar as consumers own factors of production in different proportions, a change in the domestic price of importables, by altering the relative prices of factors of production, alters the distribution of earned income between them.

(3) Where the tariff proceeds are redistributed to the private sector and the marginal propensities of consumers to consume importables differ, as a result of either taste or income differences, the way in which the tariff proceeds are divided among consumers will influence the effect of redistribution on the demand for importables.

To develop the analysis of the disaggregated case we assume that the private sector consists of two typical consumers, each of whom derives his earned income from the ownership of a collection of factors used in production. We begin with case (1); once the results for this case have been developed, the modifications required for the other cases are minor. The problem in case (1) is to disaggregate the elasticity of private demand for imports.

It has been shown elsewhere by one of the present writers that the income earned by a factor owner at any particular domestic price ratio between exportables and importables can be equated with the sum of the real values of the quantities (one of which may be negative) of the two commodities which would be produced with his factors at that price ratio.[1] Accordingly, let the earned incomes of the two factor owners at the initial domestic price of importables be:

$$Y_1 = \pi P_1 + Q_1 \tag{9 a}$$

and
$$Y_2 = \pi P_2 + Q_2, \tag{9 b}$$

where Y represents income and P and Q quantities of importables and exportables produced, and subscripts 1 and 2 denote the two individuals. We now write the total private-sector demand for importables as the sum of the demands of the two individuals, each of which depends on the domestic price of importables and the individual's income:[2]

$$C \equiv C_1 + C_2 = C_1(\pi, Y_1) + C_2(\pi, Y_2).$$

[1] H. G. Johnson, 'International Trade, Income Distribution, and the Offer Curve', *Manchester School of Economic and Social Studies*, vol. xxvii, No. 3 (Sept. 1959), pp. 241–60.

[2] For the analysis of case (2), demands depend on the sum of earned income and the amount of redistributed tariff proceeds received; but the latter is assumed constant in deriving the elasticities of consumption demand and the elasticity of import demand.

Differentiating by π, we obtain:[1]

$$\frac{dC}{d\pi} = \frac{\partial C_1}{\partial Y_1} \bar{P}_1 + \frac{\partial C_1}{\partial \pi} + \frac{\partial C_2}{\partial Y_2} \bar{P}_2 + \frac{\partial C_2}{\partial \pi}$$

$$= \frac{c_1}{\pi} \bar{P}_1 - \frac{\bar{C}_1}{\pi} \eta_1 + \frac{c_2}{\pi} \bar{P}_2 - \frac{\bar{C}_2}{\pi} \eta_2$$

$$= -\frac{\bar{C}_1}{\pi} \eta'_1 - \frac{\bar{C}_2}{\pi} \eta'_2 - \frac{c_1}{\pi}(\bar{C}_1 - \bar{P}_1) - \frac{c_2}{\pi}(\bar{C}_2 - \bar{P}_2), \quad (10\,a)$$

where c_1 and c_2 are the marginal propensities to spend on importables of the two individuals, η_1 and η_2 are the price elasticities of their demands for importables from their initial incomes, and $\eta'_1 (= \eta_1 - c_1)$ and $\eta'_2 (= \eta_2 - c_2)$ are their compensated price elasticities of demand for importables.

The two terms on the right-hand side of the above expression represent the net income effects of the increased price of imports on the demands of the two individuals; the terms in parentheses are the net income-losses themselves. Unless the excess of initial consumption over the amount of importables the individual's factors would produce bears the same ratio to the initial amount of income for each individual, the price increase will alter the relative real incomes of the individuals; that individual will gain relatively who initially spent the smaller proportion of his income on importables, factors being owned in equal ratios by the two individuals, or who possesses the higher proportion of factors used relatively intensively in the importable-good industry, initial consumption proportions being equal. If tastes, incomes, or factor-ownership ratios differ considerably, it is even possible that one individual's consumption of importables will be less than the amount of importables produced by his factors, so that that individual gains real income as a result of the increase in the price of imports; this must be true in the extreme case in which each individual owns the whole supply of one factor, since in that case the individual's income will comprise a negative quantity of the good which uses intensively the factor he does not own. If conditions are such that one individual gains real income, and his marginal propensity to spend on importables is higher than that of the other individual, the aggregate income effect on demand for importables may be positive rather than negative; the

[1] For each individual $\delta Y/\delta\pi = P$, since the effect on the real value of his income of changes in the relative amounts of the two goods produced by his factors induced by the change in π can be neglected for small changes.

individual gaining real income must have the higher marginal propensity to spend on importables for this to happen, since the other individual must be consuming both the excess of this individual's production of importables over his consumption and the country's imports from the rest of the world ($\overline{C}_1 - \overline{P}_1 = \overline{M}_1 + \overline{P}_2 - \overline{C}_2$). If the aggregate income effect on demand for imports is positive it may outweigh the negative effects of the compensated elasticities, so that the aggregate effect of an increase in the price of importables is to increase the quantity of imports demanded.

This possibility can be shown by re-writing $dC/d\pi$ in the form

$$\frac{dC}{d\pi} = -\frac{\overline{C}_1}{\pi}\eta'_1 - \frac{\overline{C}_2}{\pi}\eta'_2 - \left(\frac{c_2}{\pi} - \frac{c_1}{\pi}\right)(\overline{C}_2 - \overline{P}_2) - \frac{c_1}{\pi}\overline{M}_1.$$
(10 b)

If individual 2 has the higher marginal propensity to consume importables and his factors produce more importables than he consumes, the second-to-last term on the right will be positive. The quantity of importables demanded will increase when the price of importables rises if

$$(c_2 - c_1)(\overline{C}_2 - \overline{P}_2) > \overline{C}_1\eta'_1 + \overline{C}_2\eta'_2 + c_1\overline{M}_1.$$

The total change in private demand for imports resulting from an increase in the domestic price of importables is the difference between the change in consumption demand and the increase in domestic production. Hence the disaggregated elasticity of private demand for imports is:

$$\xi = \left(\frac{\overline{P}}{\overline{M}_1}\varepsilon + \frac{\overline{C}_1}{\overline{M}_1}\eta'_1 + \frac{\overline{C}_2}{\overline{M}_1}\eta'_2 + c_1 + (c_2 - c_1)\frac{\overline{C}_2 - \overline{P}_2}{\overline{M}_1}\right)$$
$$= \{\xi' + c_1 + (c_2 - c_1)m_2\},$$
(11)

where $m_2 = (\overline{C}_2 - \overline{P}_2)/\overline{M}_1$ is the proportion of the country's imports consumed, net, by individual 2. If m_2 is negative, individual 2 is a 'net supplier' of importables to the economy. For convenience we shall assume in what follows that individual 2 has the higher marginal propensity to consume importables ($c_2 > c_1$).

The formula for the effect of an increase in the tariff rate in the *disaggregated case (1)* is readily obtained by substituting the expression for the disaggregated elasticity of private demand for imports just derived into the formula [equation (3)] given in Section 1 above. The resulting formula is:

$$\frac{dM}{dt} = \overline{M}_1\left(g - (1 + gt)\frac{c_1}{\pi} - \frac{1 + gt}{\pi}(c_2 - c_1)m_2 - \frac{1 + gt}{\pi}\xi'\right).$$

(12) IV

In the initial free-trade case this reduces to

$$\frac{dM}{dt} = \overline{M}_1\{g - c_1 - (c_2 - c_1)m_2 - \xi'\}.$$

The chief modification to the preceding analysis of case (1) introduced by disaggregation which emerges from this formula is that *it is not necessary for the government to have a higher marginal propensity to consume importables than the private sector for the tariff increase to give rise to a positive excess demand for importables in the world market* and so necessitate a deterioration in the terms of trade. *Such a deterioration can occur even though the government has a lower marginal propensity to consume importables from an increment of tariff revenue than does either individual from an increment in his income*, if the individual with the higher marginal propensity to consume importables is a net supplier of importables to the economy (m_2 is negative in the above formula). Similarly, even in the case of initial free trade a deterioration of the terms of trade does not require an inelastic compensated private demand for imports.

To obtain the formula for the effect of the tariff increase in the *disaggregated case* (2) from the formula given [equation (4)] for the aggregated case (2) in Section 1, it is necessary both to substitute the disaggregated expression for the aggregate elasticity of private demand for imports and to replace the single marginal propensity to consume importables used in analysing the effect of the change in the amount of redistributed tariff proceeds by an average of the marginal propensities of the two individuals, weighted by the proportions in which they share in the redistributed tariff proceeds. The resulting formula is:

$$\frac{dM}{dt} = \frac{\overline{M}_1}{1 + (1 - \bar{c})t}(\bar{c} - \xi) = \frac{\overline{M}_1}{1 + (1 - \bar{c})t}\{(c_2 - c_1)(s_2 - m_2) - \xi'\},$$

(13) V

where s_2 is the share of individual 2 in marginal redistributed tariff proceeds, and $\bar{c}\ [= c_1 + s_2(c_2 - c_1)]$ is the weighted average marginal propensity to spend redistributed tariff proceeds on importables. This formula shows that, in contrast to the aggregated case (2), *in the disaggregated case* (2) *the tariff increase does not necessarily produce a negative world excess demand for importables* and turn the terms of trade in the tariff-increasing country's favour. *The reverse is possible*

*if the share in the redistributed tariff proceeds of the individual with the
higher marginal propensity to consume importables is larger than the
proportion of the initial quantity of imports he consumes.* This will be
the case, for example, if tariff proceeds are redistributed in proportion
to income and (for reasons discussed above) the quantity of imports
he consumes is smaller in relation to his income than is the quantity
consumed by the other individual in relation to the latter's income – so
that this individual is overcompensated for the income effect of the
increased domestic price of importables. It should be noticed also that,
since the individual with the higher marginal propensity to consume
importables may be a net supplier of importables to the economy
(m_2 negative) there may be *no* way of allocating the marginal change
in tariff proceeds between the two individuals which would compensate both of them exactly for the income effect of the tariff increase.

To obtain the formula for the effect of the tariff increase in the
disaggregated case (3) from the formula [equation (8)] given for the
aggregated case (3) in Section 2 above, it is necessary to substitute the
disaggregated expression for the elasticity of private demand for
importables in that formula and to rewrite the dependence effect as
the sum of the dependence effects on the two individuals (which may
be of different magnitudes and opposite signs). The resulting formula
is:

$$\frac{dM}{dt} = \frac{\overline{M}_1}{1 + (1 - b_1 - b_2)t} \times$$
$$\{b_1 + b_2 + g\pi - (1 + gt)c_1 - (1 + gt)(c_2 - c_1)m_2 - (1 + gt)\xi'\}.$$
$$(14)\ \text{VI}$$

The main modification introduced by disaggregation arises from the
possibility that the individual with the higher marginal propensity to
consume importables will gain real income from the increase in the
domestic price of importables; the nature of this modification has
already been discussed in connection with the disaggregated case (1).

4. The Effect of an Increase in the Tariff on the Terms of Trade: Variable Supplies of Factors of Production

In the preceding sections we have successively relaxed three of the
assumptions of the traditional analysis of the effect of a tariff on the
terms of trade – the assumptions of initial free trade, independence of
private from government consumption, and homogeneity of the private

sector. We must now relax the fourth assumption, constancy of supplies of factors of production. The analysis of the effects of a tariff when factor supplies are variable is the subject of a paper by Murray C. Kemp, which we have been privileged to read and which suggested the inclusion of the present section of this article to us. We gratefully acknowledge his priority, and also our indebtedness to R. W. Jones, who has since produced a broader study of variability of factor supplies in international trade;[1] our own analysis takes a slightly different form from theirs, better adapted to the general purpose of this article.

For simplicity of analysis we shall assume that only the quantity of labour is variable. This assumption has some economic justification, inasmuch as we may assume that the quantity of labour available for employment from a given total stock depends on the relative attractiveness at the margin of the real consumption obtainable by offering labour and of the leisure obtained by not offering it, to the owner of labour, while the total stock of capital, having no alternative utility-yielding use, is always available for employment. The real consumption enjoyed with the employment of a given quantity of labour depends on the quantity of labour employed, the quantity of capital owned, the real wage rate and real rent rate measured in terms of exportable goods, and the relative price of importables; but the real wage and real rent rates are linked through the technology of the economy to the relative price of importables, so that the latter determines the former. In cases (2) and (3), though in different ways, real consumption also depends on the amount of tariff revenue.

With leisure as the alternative to labour the quantity of labour supplied will decrease with an increase in the amount of real income that could be enjoyed with the employment of the initial amount of labour, since some (but not all, barring inferiority of real consumption) of the potential increase in real consumption will be consumed in the form of leisure. The real consumption enjoyable from the employment of the initial amount of labour remaining constant, an increase in the real wage rate will generally, but not always, increase the quantity of labour supplied. Such a 'compensated' increase in the real wage-rate has two effects: it raises the price of labour (the cost of leisure) in terms of goods, and so induces a substitution of labour, and the real

[1] M. C. Kemp, 'Tariffs, Protection, and the Distribution of National Income', and R. W. Jones, 'General Equilibrium with Variable Labour Supply'; these two papers have been merged in an excellent joint article, 'Variable Labour Supply and the Theory of International Trade', *Journal of Political Economy*, February 1962.

consumption it makes possible for leisure – an increase in the quantity of labour supplied; but it also reduces the relative price of the commodity in whose production labour is used relatively unintensively. If this commodity is substitutary with leisure, the effect is again to induce an increase in the quantity of labour supplied; but if it is complementary with leisure, the effect is to induce a decrease in the quantity of labour supplied, and this effect may be strong enough to outweigh the general tendency to substitute real consumption for leisure, and so reduce the quantity of labour supplied. This possibility we shall describe as one of strong complementarity of leisure and the capital-intensive good in consumption.

With this background, we can proceed to the analysis of the effect of a tariff increase in our three aggregative cases.

The increase in the domestic price of importables resulting from the tariff increase has two effects on the quantity of labour supplied:

(a) The loss of real income due to the increase in the price of importables increases the quantity of labour supplied. The loss of real income due to the increased price of importables is approximately equal to the increased cost of the initial volume of private imports, and the change in the quantity of labour supplied for this reason is therefore:

$$\frac{\partial L}{\partial Y'} \frac{\partial Y'}{\partial \pi} \frac{d\pi}{dt} = (-l)(-\overline{M}_1) = \overline{M}_1 l, \qquad (15\,a)$$

where Y' represents real income and l represents the marginal propensity to consume leisure when potential real income increases; l must be positive and smaller than $1/w$ (w being the real wage-rate) on the assumption that neither leisure nor real consumption is inferior.

(b) The change in the relative price of labour due to the change in the relative price of importables alters the quantity of labour supplied, the direction and extent of the change being determined by the elasticity of the real wage rate with respect to the price of importables and the elasticity of supply of labour with respect to the real wage-rate. The change in the quantity of labour supplied is:

$$\frac{\partial L}{\partial w} \frac{\partial w}{\partial \pi} \frac{d\pi}{dt} = \frac{L}{\pi} \lambda e_w, \qquad (15\,b)$$

where $\lambda \{= (w/L)\,\partial L/\partial w\}$ is the compensated elasticity of supply of labour, and is positive unless there is strong complementarity between the capital-intensive commodity and leisure, and $e_w \{= (\pi/w)\,\partial w/\partial \pi\}$ is the elasticity of the real wage-rate with respect to the price of importables. Since a rise in the price of importables will raise or lower the real wage-rate according as labour is used relatively intensively in the importable-goods or the exportable-goods industry, e_w will be positive or negative according as the importable-goods industry is labour-intensive or capital-intensive.

The change in the quantity of labour initially supplied due to these two effects of the increased domestic price of importables resulting from the tariff increase is therefore:

$$\frac{\partial L}{\partial t} = \frac{\partial L}{\partial \pi}\frac{d\pi}{dt} = \frac{\bar{L}}{\pi}\lambda e_w + \bar{M}_1 l. \tag{16}$$

This change in the quantity of labour supplied due to the increase in the domestic price of importables has two effects on the quantity of imports demanded (in addition to those analysed in Section 1):

(1) The change in the quantity of labour supplied changes the amount of income earned by the private sector and so changes the quantity of importables demanded. The change in earned income is approximately equal to the wage rate multiplied by the change in the quantity of labour supplied, and the change in the quantity of imports demanded due to a change in earned income is determined by the marginal propensity to consume importables. Hence the change in the quantity of importables demanded due to the effect of the tariff increase on the domestic price of importables is:

$$\frac{\partial C}{\partial L}\frac{\partial L}{\partial t} = \frac{cw}{\pi}\left(\frac{\bar{L}}{\pi}\lambda e_w + \bar{M}_1 l\right). \tag{17 a}$$

(2) The change in the quantity of labour supplied changes the amount of importables domestically produced. This change can be deduced from one of the established propositions of the theory of international trade and economic growth, according to which an increase in the quantity of one factor at a given domestic price ratio must be absorbed by transferring both factors out of the industry which uses that factor unintensively into the other industry, where they are combined with the new quantities of the increased factor in the more intensive ratio optimal in that industry; and conversely for a decrease in the quantity of a factor.[1] The changes in the outputs of

[1] This proposition is originally due to T. M. Rybczynski, 'Factor Endowment and Relative Commodity Prices', *Economica*, N.S., vol. xxii, No. 88 (Nov. 1955), pp. 336–41. For a recent statement, see J. Bhagwati and H. G. Johnson, 'Notes on Some Controversies in the Theory of International Trade', *Economic Journal*, vol. lxx, No. 277 (Mar. 1960), pp. 74–93, especially p. 82.

the two industries, per unit change in the total amount of a factor supplied, are determined by the factor ratios in the two industries and the average output per unit of the factor whose supply is altered in the relevant industry.[1]

It follows from this principle that the change in the output of importables due to a change in the quantity of labour supplied must be greater absolutely than the change in national income due to the same cause, so that the effect on importable goods production dominates the net effect on imports demanded of a change in the quantity of labour supplied. Also, the change in the domestic output of importable goods due to an increase in the quantity of labour supplied must be of the same sign as the change in the real wage-rate due to an increase in the domestic price of importable goods. If labour is used intensively in importable-goods production, an increase in the domestic price of importables must increase the real wage-rate, and an increase in the quantity of labour must be absorbed by an expansion of production of importables at the expense of exportables; conversely, if labour is used intensively in the production of exportables, an increase in the domestic price of importables must lower the real wage-rate and an increase in the quantity of labour supplied must increase the domestic production of exportables at the expense of importables. Accordingly, the change in the domestic production of importable goods due to the tariff increase is:

$$\frac{\partial P}{\partial L}\frac{\partial L}{\partial t} = \rho\left(\frac{L}{\pi}\lambda e_w + \overline{M}_1 l\right), \tag{17 b}$$

where ρ, the change in the quantity of importables domestically produced due to an increase in the quantity of labour supplied, must have the same sign as e_w and exceed w in absolute magnitude.[2]

[2] Let k_1 and $k_2(< k_1)$ be the capital:labour ratios in the capital-intensive and labour-intensive industries, and a_1 and a_2 be the average products of labour in those industries. The movement of a unit of labour from the former to the latter industry releases $(k_1 - k_2)$ units of capital, which will permit the employment of an additional $(k_1 - k_2)/k_2$ units of labour in the labour-intensive industry: hence employment of an additional unit of labour in the latter industry requires a transfer of $k_2/(k_1 - k_2)$ labour units (together with the capital employed with them in the capital-intensive industry). Output in the capital-intensive industry, therefore, must fall by $k_2 a_1/(k_1 - k_2)$, and output in the labour-intensive industry rise by $a_2\{1 + k_2/(k_1 - k_2)\} = k_1 a_2/(k_1 - k_2)$ when the labour supply increases by one unit.

[2] It follows from n. 2, p. 223, that $\rho = k_x a_m/(k_x - k_m)$, where the subscripts x and m refer to the exportable-goods and importable-goods industries respectively.

The net change in the quantity of importables demanded by the private sector due to the change in the quantity of labour supplied resulting from the effect of the tariff increase on the real wage-rate is therefore [the difference between (17 a) and (17 b)]:

$$\frac{\partial M_1}{\partial L}\frac{\partial L}{\partial t} = \left(\frac{cw}{\pi} - \rho\right)\left(\frac{L}{\pi}\lambda e_w + \overline{M}_1 l\right). \tag{18}$$

To allow for variability of the quantity of labour supplied in response to the increase in the domestic price of importables resulting from the tariff increase in deriving the formulae for the effect of the tariff increase on the world excess demand for importables, it is necessary to include the expression just derived in reckoning the effect of the tariff increase on the quantity of importables privately demanded. This entails adding the expression

$$-\frac{\pi}{\overline{M}_1}\frac{\partial M_1}{\partial L}\frac{\partial L}{\partial t} = (\rho\pi - cw)\left(\frac{L}{\pi\overline{M}_1}\lambda e_w + l\right), \tag{19}$$

to the elasticity of private demand for imports in the formulae derived in Sections 1 and 2. In this expression ($\rho\pi - cw$) must have the same sign as ρ, because ρ exceeds w in absolute magnitude and c, the marginal propensity to consume importables, is assumed to be less than unity and therefore less than π.

In *case (1)*, where the government spends the tariff revenue and the preferences of the private sector are independent of the amount of government expenditure, this is the only adjustment required. In *case (2)*, however, the change in the amount of tariff revenue redistributed due to the tariff increase will alter the real income obtainable with the employment of the initial quantity of labour supplied and so alter the quantity of labour supplied. The change in the amount of importables demanded resulting for this reason from the increase in the tariff rate will be:

$$\frac{\partial M_1}{\partial L}\frac{\partial L}{\partial Y'}\frac{dR}{dt} = \left(\rho - \frac{cw}{\pi}\right)l\frac{dR}{dt}. \tag{20}$$

In *case (3)* the quantity of labour supplied will depend on the amount of government services if leisure is substitutary or complementary with government services; in this case the change in tariff revenue due to the tariff increase will change the quantity of imports demanded through its effects on the quantity of labour supplied by the amount

$$\frac{\partial M_1}{\partial L} \frac{\partial L}{\partial R} \frac{dR}{dt} = \left(\frac{cw}{\pi} - \rho\right) \alpha \frac{dR}{dt}, \tag{21}$$

where α is the change in the quantity of labour supplied due to a unit increase in government expenditure, and may be positive or negative.

In the *aggregated case* (*1*) with variable labour supply, the effect of the tariff increase on the world excess demand for importables is[1] [derived from (3) and (19)]:

$$\frac{dM}{dt} = \overline{M}_1 \left\{ g - (1 + gt)\frac{c}{\pi} - \frac{(1+gt)}{\pi}\xi' - \frac{(1+gt)}{\pi}(\rho\pi - cw) \times \right.$$
$$\left. \left(\frac{\overline{L}}{\pi\overline{M}_1}\lambda e_w + l\right)\right\}. \tag{22} VII$$

If the elasticity of supply of labour λ is positive, and ρ is also positive, implying that importable-goods production is labour-intensive, the last term within the brackets must be positive, so that all the terms except g have a negative sign, and the traditional conclusion that an adverse movement of the terms of trade requires a governmental marginal propensity to consume importables greater than the private marginal propensity to consume them continues to hold. But if the elasticity of supply of labour λ is positive and ρ is negative, implying that exportable-goods production is labour-intensive, it is possible for the last term to be negative (in spite of the fact that the first half of it must be positive owing to the identity of signs of ρ and e_w), so that the traditional condition is not necessary in this case. If the elasticity of supply of labour λ is negative and ρ is also negative – implying that importables are capital-intensive in production and strongly complementary with leisure in consumption – the last term must be negative, so that the influence of variability of the labour supply is to increase the world excess demand for importables, and the traditional condition is not necessary for the terms of trade to turn against the country. Similarly, if the elasticity of supply of labour λ is negative and ρ is positive – exportables are capital-intensive in production and strongly complementary with leisure in consumption – the last term may be negative on balance, and again the traditional condition is not necessary for the terms of trade to turn against the country.

[1] This result is obtained, as explained above, by adding the expression for the effect of the tariff increase, via the labour supply, on the demand for importables to the elasticity of private demand for imports in the formula previously derived for the aggregated case with constant labour supply.

In the *aggregated case* (2), with variable labour supply, the effect of the tariff increase on world excess demand for importables is [the sum of (4), (18), and (20)]:

$$\frac{dM_1}{dt} = \frac{\partial M_1}{\partial t} + \left(\frac{cw}{\pi} - \rho\right)\frac{\partial L}{\partial t} + \left(\frac{c}{\pi}\right)\frac{dR}{dt} + \left(\rho - \frac{cw}{\pi}\right)l\frac{dR}{dt}$$

$$= -\frac{\overline{M}_1}{\pi}\left\{\xi + (\rho\pi - cw)\left(\frac{L}{\pi\overline{M}_1}\lambda e_w + l\right)\right\} +$$

$$\left\{\frac{c}{\pi} + \left(\rho - \frac{cw}{\pi}\right)l\right\}\left(\overline{M}_1 + t\frac{dM_1}{dt}\right)$$

$$= \frac{\overline{M}_1}{1 + \{1 - c - (\rho\pi - cw)l\}t}\left(-\xi' - (\rho\pi - cw)\frac{L}{\pi\overline{M}_1}\lambda e_w\right).$$

(23) VIII

Since $(\rho\pi - cw)(L/\pi\overline{M}_1)e_w$ must be positive, the tariff increase cannot turn the terms of trade against the country if the supply of labour is positively elastic with respect to the real wage rate (λ is positive). If the supply of labour is negatively elastic (strong complementarity of the capital-intensive commodity, whichever it is, with leisure in consumption) the terms of trade may turn against the country. Thus variability of the labour supply can reverse the traditional conclusion in the exceptional case of a negative elasticity of supply of labour.

In the *aggregated case* (3), with variable labour supply, the change in the amount of imports privately demanded due to the tariff increase is:

$$\frac{dM_1}{dt} = \frac{\partial M_1}{\partial t} + \left(\frac{cw}{\pi} - \rho\right)\left(\frac{\partial L}{\partial t}\right) + \left\{\frac{b}{\pi} + \left(\frac{cw}{\pi} - \rho\right)\alpha\right\}\frac{dR}{dt}$$

$$= \frac{b - \xi - (\xi\pi - cw)\{\alpha + (L/\pi\overline{M}_1)\lambda e_w + l\}}{1 + \{1 - b + (\rho\pi - cw)\alpha\}t}\overline{M}_1; \quad (24\text{ a})$$

the change in the amount of imports demanded by the government is:

$$\frac{dM_2}{dt} = g\left(\overline{M}_1 + t\frac{dM_1}{dt}\right)$$

$$= \frac{\pi - t\xi - t(\rho\pi - cw)\{(L/\pi\overline{M}_1)\lambda e_w + l\}}{1 + \{1 - b + (\rho\pi - cw)\alpha\}t}g\overline{M}_1; \quad (24\text{ b})$$

and the change in the total quantity of imports demanded, and the world excess demand for importables, is consequently [the sum of (24 a) and (24 b)]:

$$\frac{dM}{dt} = \frac{\begin{array}{l} \pi g + b - (1 + gt)\,\xi' - (1 + gt)\,c - \\ - (1 + gt)\,(\rho\pi - cw)\,\{(\overline{L}/\pi\overline{M}_1)\,\lambda e_w + l\} - (\rho\pi - cw)\,\alpha \end{array}}{1 + \{1 - b + (\rho\pi - cw)\alpha\}\,t}\,\overline{M}_1.$$

$$(25)\ IX$$

In the case of initial free trade, which we shall consider for simplicity, this reduces to:

$$\frac{dM}{dt} = \left[g + b - \xi' - c - (\rho\pi - cw)\left(\frac{L}{\overline{M}_1}\,\lambda e_w + l + \alpha\right)\right]\overline{M}_1.$$

It follows from this formula that, even with initial free trade, an inverse relation between government expenditure and private demand for importables, and a government marginal propensity to consume importables less than that of the private sector, an increase in the tariff rate can turn the terms of trade against the country. This requires the final term of the foregoing expression to be negative, which in turn requires $\left(\lambda + \dfrac{l + \alpha}{e_w}\dfrac{\overline{M}_1}{L}\right)$ to be negative. This is possible in the following cases:

(i) Negative elasticity of supply of labour ($\lambda < 0$), requiring strong complementarity of the capital-intensive good (which may be either commodity) with leisure in consumption; the necessary condition for the term to be negative in this case is $-\lambda > \dfrac{l + \alpha}{Le_w}\overline{M}_1$.

(ii) Positive elasticity of supply of labour ($\lambda > 0$) and negative elasticity of the wage-rate with respect to the price of importables ($e_w < 0$), which requires the exportable-goods industry to be relatively labour-intensive, together with ($l + \alpha$) positive, which, since l is necessarily positive, is consistent with the quantity of labour supplied either increasing or decreasing as government expenditure increases; the necessary condition for the term to be negative in this case is $\dfrac{l + \alpha}{\lambda}\dfrac{\overline{M}_1}{L} > -e_w.$

(iii) Positive elasticity of supply of labour ($\lambda > 0$) and positive elasticity of the wage-rate with respect to the price of importables ($e_w > 0$), which requires the importable-goods industry to be labour-intensive, together with ($l + \alpha$) negative, which, since l is necessarily positive, requires that an increase in government expenditure reduce the quantity of labour supplied; the necessary condition for the term to be negative in this case is $-\alpha > \dfrac{L\lambda e_w}{\overline{M}_1} + l.$

To obtain the formulae for the effect of the tariff increase on world excess demand for importables in the *disaggregated cases* it is necessary to introduce appropriately weighted averages of the expressions for the income and substitution effects of the increase in the domestic price of importables due to the tariff increase on the quantity of labour supplied, and of the effects on labour supplied of the change in the tariff revenue due to the tariff increase, for the two individuals. The resulting formulae will not be reproduced here; the general nature of the effects of allowing for differences between members of the private sector can be inferred from the argument of this and the preceding section.

5. The Effect of an Increase in the Tariff on the Domestic Price Ratio

The previous sections of this article have been concerned with generalizing the theory of the effect of a tariff increase on the terms of trade of the tariff-raising country. In this final section we consider the conditions under which a tariff increase may improve the terms of trade so much that the internal price of importable goods actually falls, a question which is of particular interest in connection with the effect of the tariff in redistributing income between the owners of factors of production. The traditional analysis concludes (as mentioned in the introduction) that such an improvement requires that the marginal propensity to spend on domestic goods of the government or the private sector, whichever spends the tariff proceeds, must exceed the foreign elasticity of demand for the country's exports (so that, barring inferiority of importables in private or government consumption, that elasticity must be less than unity).

Like the terms of trade problem, this problem can be simplified by considering the effect of the tariff increase on world excess demand for importables at a given price for them; in this case we consider the effect on excess demand at the initial domestic price of importables. World excess demand for importables is symbolized below by $M' \equiv M - M_s$, where M is the quantity of imports demanded by the tariff-imposing country and M_s the quantity of imports supplied by the rest of the world; initially $M' = 0$. The tariff increase will raise or lower the internal price of importables according as it gives rise to an excess demand for or excess supply of importables in the world market at the initial domestic price of importables. We begin with our three aggregated cases, assuming that the private sector can be treated as homogeneous and that factor supplies are constant. The effect of the tariff increase on the world excess demand for importables is then the net resultant of three effects of the tariff increase:

(1) The tariff increase reduces the price offered to foreign suppliers for imports, and so alters the quantity supplied at the initial domestic price ratio. The change in the quantity supplied is

$$\frac{dM_s}{dt} = \frac{dM_s}{dp}\frac{dp}{dt} = \frac{dM_s}{dp}\frac{d}{dt}\left(\frac{\pi}{1+t}\right) = -\frac{\varepsilon_f}{\pi}\overline{M}_s = \frac{1-\eta_f}{\pi}\overline{M}, \quad (26)$$

where ε_f is the foreign elasticity of supply of imports and η_f is the elasticity of foreign demand for the country's exports. For the quantity of imports supplied to increase when the price offered for them falls, it is necessary for the foreign import demand elasticity to be less than unity. We shall not investigate the determinants of the foreign import demand elasticity; but the analysis of the preceding sections shows that, in addition to the usual possibility of a low demand elasticity due to a low elasticity of substitution between exportables and importables in foreign consumption, the foreign elasticity of demand for imports may be less than unity, and even negative, if the factor used intensively in foreign production of exportables has the higher marginal propensity to consume exportables, or if the supply curve of that factor is backward-rising.

(2) Where the government spends the tariff proceeds, and allocates expenditure between exportables and importables on the basis of world market prices, the reduction in the world market price increases the quantity of imports it demands from a given tariff revenue. The change in the quantity of imports demanded on this account is

$$\frac{\delta M_2}{\delta p}\frac{dp}{dt} = -\eta_g\overline{M}_2\frac{d}{dt}\left(\frac{\pi}{1+t}\right) = \frac{\eta_g}{\pi}\overline{M}_2, \quad (27)$$

where η_g is the elasticity of government demand for imports.

(3) The increase in the tariff rate increases the tariff proceeds derived from the initial volume of imports and so increases the quantity of imports demanded to an extent which is differently determined in the different cases. The increase in the tariff revenue derived from the initial volume of imports is

$$\frac{\partial R}{\partial t} = \frac{\partial}{\partial t}\left(\frac{t}{1+t}\pi\overline{M}_1\right) = \frac{\overline{M}_1}{\pi}.$$

(a) Where the government spends the tariff revenue and private sector demand is independent of the level of government activity [case (1)], the increase in the quantity of imports demanded due to the increase in the tariff revenue is:

$$\frac{\partial M_2}{\partial R}\frac{\delta R}{\delta t} = g\frac{\partial R}{\partial t} = \frac{g}{\pi}\,\overline{M}_1.$$

(b) Where the tariff revenue is redistributed to the private sector [case (2)], the increase in the quantity of imports demanded is

$$\frac{dM_1}{dt} = \frac{\partial M_1}{\partial R}\frac{dR}{dt} = \frac{c}{\pi}\left(\frac{\partial R}{\partial t} + t\frac{dM_1}{dt}\right) = \frac{c}{1 + (1 - c)t}\frac{\overline{M}_1}{\pi}.$$

(c) In case (3), where the government spends the tariff revenue and private demand for importables is dependent on the amount of governmental services provided, the tariff increase has a fourth effect, which is most conveniently considered in conjunction with the third. For, in addition to increasing the level of government consumption through increasing the amount of tariff revenue, the increase in the tariff rate, by reducing the price offered to foreign suppliers, both increases the real level and alters the composition of government consumption from the initial amount of tariff revenue. These changes, as well as the increase in tariff revenue, will have a dependence effect on the private demand for importables, which effect will differ according to the precise nature of the dependence of private demand on governmental activity. The latter must accordingly be specified, whereas it could legitimately be ignored in analysing the effect of the tariff increase on the terms of trade. Three cases can be distinguished: (3 a) dependence on total real governmental consumption, (3 b) dependence on the quantity of importables consumed by the government, and (3 c) dependence on the quantity of exportables consumed by the government.

A *general formula for case* (3) which can be adapted to fit these alternative assumptions about the nature of dependence can be derived as follows: define B as the increase in quantity of importables privately demanded when government revenue (expenditure) increases by one unit, and A as the increase in government revenue that would produce the same effect on private demand for importables as the change in whatever aspect of government expenditure influences that demand that results from the tariff increase, tariff revenue being held constant.

Then the increase in the quantity of importables privately demanded due to the effect of the tariff increase on governmental consumption is

$$\frac{dM_1}{dt} = \frac{\partial M_1}{\partial R}\left(\frac{dR}{dt} + A\right) = B\left(\frac{\delta R}{\delta t} + t\frac{dM_1}{dt} + A\right) = \frac{B(\overline{M}_1/\pi + A)}{1 - Bt};$$

the increase in the quantity of imports demanded by the government due to the increase in tariff revenue is

$$\frac{dM_2}{dt} = \frac{\delta M_2}{\delta R}\frac{dR}{dt} = g\left(\frac{\delta R}{\delta t} + t\frac{dM_1}{dt}\right) = \frac{g(\overline{M}_1/\pi + ABt)}{1 - Bt};$$

and the total change[1] in the quantity of importables demanded resulting from the effect of the increase in the tariff rate on governmental expenditure and the associated dependence effect on private demand for importables is

$$\begin{aligned}\frac{dM}{dt} &= \frac{(g + B)\,(\overline{M}_1/\pi) + AB(1 + gt)}{1 - Bt}\\ &= \frac{g\overline{M}_1}{\pi} + \frac{(1 + gt)\,B(\overline{M}_1/\pi + A)}{1 - Bt}.\end{aligned} \tag{28}$$

The reduction in the price of imports due to the increase in the tariff (tariff proceeds remaining constant) increases governmental real income by $-\overline{M}_2\,dp/dt = \overline{M}_2/\pi$, increases governmental consumption of importables by $(\delta\overline{M}_2/\delta p)\,(dp/dt) = \eta_g(\overline{M}_2/\pi)$, and alters governmental consumption of exportables by $-\delta(p\overline{M}_2)/\delta t = (1 - \eta_g)(\overline{M}_2/\pi)$. Hence the parameter A in the general formula is equal to $\overline{M}_2/\pi$ in case (3 a), $(\eta_g/g)\,(\overline{M}_2/\pi)$ in case (3 b), and $\{(1 - \eta_g)/(1 - g)\}(\overline{M}_2/\pi)$ in case (3 c). The parameter B in the formula is equal to b_r/π in case (3 a), $b_m g/\pi$ in case (3 b) and $b_x(1 - g)/\pi$ in case (3 c), where the b's are coefficients relating the increase in private expenditure on importables to the increase in real government consumption, government consumption of importables, and government consumption of exportables, which induce it in the three cases. The total changes in the quantity of imports demanded resulting from the effects of the tariff increase under analysis in the three sub-cases are obtained by inserting these values in the general formula; since the results are rather cumbrous, and are contained in the formulae for the effect of the tariff increase on the excess demand for importables presented below, they are not reproduced here.

[1] This change excludes the direct effect of the lower price of imports in increasing government consumption of them from the initial tariff revenue, discussed under (2) above.

In *case* (*1*) the total effect of the tariff increase on world excess demand for importables at the initial domestic price of importables is

$$\frac{dM'}{dt} = \frac{dM}{dt} - \frac{dM_s}{dt} = \left(g + \eta'_g \frac{\overline{M}_2}{\overline{M}} - 1 + \eta_f \right) \frac{\overline{M}}{\pi}, \qquad 29 \text{ X}$$

where η'_g is the compensated elasticity of government demand for imports. For this to be negative, representing an excess supply of importables and necessitating a reduction in the world and domestic price of importables to restore equilibrium, requires[1]

$$(1 - g) - \frac{\overline{M}_2}{\overline{M}} \eta_g' > \eta_f.$$

Whether free trade ($\overline{M}_2 = 0$) or a tariff ($\overline{M}_2 > 0$) is initially in force, the internal price of imports can fall only if the government's marginal propensity to spend on exportables $(1 - g)$ exceeds the foreign elasticity of demand for imports (η_f), which in turn requires an inelastic foreign demand for imports unless importables are inferior in government consumption at the pre-existing level of tariff proceeds. Where a tariff is initially in force, an excess of $(1 - g)$ over η_f is a necessary but not a sufficient condition for the internal price of importables to fall.

In *case* (2) the total effect of the tariff increase on the world excess demand for importables is

$$\frac{dM'}{dt} = \left(\frac{c}{1 + (1 - c)t} - 1 + \eta_f \right) \frac{\overline{M}_1}{\pi}. \qquad (30) \text{ XI}$$

A decrease in the world and domestic price of importables in this case requires

$$(1 - c) > \frac{\eta_f}{\pi - \eta_f t}.$$

[1] This result differs from that derived by Metzler in the supplementary paper referred to in n. 1, p. 207 (*op. cit.*, especially equation (7), p. 439). The reason is that Metzler, in dealing with the case, writes governmental demand as a function of the tariff proceeds measured in importable goods, whereas we write it as a function of tariff proceeds measured in exportable goods. On his assumption, $\delta R/\delta t = \delta(tM_1)/\delta t = \overline{M}_1$, as contrasted with our $\delta R/\delta t = \overline{M}_1/1 + t$. In dealing with our case (2), Metzler writes private demand as a function of tariff proceeds measured in exportable goods, and obtains a result identical with ours. Metzler's technique for the former case is inferior to ours, since it means that all the income effect of an import price change on government demand falls on the exportable good.

This requires the private sector's marginal propensity to spend on exportables $(1 - c)$ to exceed the foreign elasticity of demand for imports when free trade initially prevails, but not when there is a pre-existing tariff; it is always necessary, however, for the foreign demand for imports to be inelastic (barring inferiority of importables).

In *case* (3) the total effect of the tariff increase on world excess demand for importables is

$$\frac{dM'}{dt} = \left(\frac{b_r(1 + gt)}{1 + (1 - b_r)t} + g + \eta'_g \frac{\overline{M}_2}{\overline{M}} - 1 + \eta_f \right) \frac{\overline{M}}{\pi}$$

(31 a) XII

when private demand is influenced by real government consumption;

$$\frac{dM'}{dt} = \left\{ \frac{\pi + b_m}{1 + (1 - b_m g)t} \left(g \frac{\overline{M}_1}{\overline{M}} + \eta_g \frac{\overline{M}_2}{\overline{M}} \right) - 1 + \eta_f \right\} \frac{\overline{M}}{\pi}$$

(31 b) XIII

when private demand is influenced by governmental consumption of importables; and

$$\frac{dM'}{dt} = \left(\frac{b_x(1 - g) + g\pi}{1 + (1 - b_x + b_x g)t} \frac{\overline{M}_1}{\overline{M}} + \right.$$
$$\left. \frac{b_x(1 + gt) + \pi(1 - b_x)\eta_g}{1 + (1 - b_x + b_x g)t} \frac{\overline{M}_2}{\overline{M}} - 1 + \eta_f \right) \frac{\overline{M}}{\pi}$$

(31 c) XIV

when private demand is influenced by governmental consumption of exportables.

For simplicity we consider only the case in which private demand is influenced by the level of government consumption [case (3 a), equation (31 a)]. In this case the tariff increase will lower the domestic price of importables if

$$(1 - g) - \frac{b_r(1 + gt)}{1 + (1 - b_r)t} - \eta'_g \frac{\overline{M}_2}{\overline{M}} > \eta_f.$$

(32)

If an increase in government expenditure has the indirect effect of increasing private demand for importables ($b_r > 0$) the tariff can reduce the domestic price of importables only if the government's marginal propensity to spend on exportables is greater than the foreign elasticity of demand for imports, which (barring inferior goods) must be less than unity.[1] But if an increase in government expenditure has

---

[1] An exception is possible if $b_r > 1 + t/t$.

the indirect effect of reducing private demand for importables ($b_r < 0$), the tariff can reduce the domestic price of importables even though the government's marginal propensity to spend on exportables is less than the foreign elasticity of demand for imports and even though the latter is greater than unity.

Since the analysis of the effect of a tariff increase on the equilibrium domestic price of importables obtains its results from the effect of the tariff increase on world excess demand at the initial domestic price of importables, *relaxation of the assumption that the private sector can be treated as an aggregate* makes no essential difference to the results: since domestic earned income and its distribution are unchanged if the domestic price of importables is unchanged, disaggregation requires merely the replacement of the aggregate marginal propensity to consume importables by an average of the marginal propensities of the two individuals, weighted by their shares in redistributed tariff proceeds, in case (2), and the replacement of the aggregate dependence coefficient by the sum of the coefficients for the two individuals, in case (3). For the same reason, *variability of the quantity of labour supplied* in response to changes in factor prices will make no difference to the various formulae, since the real wage-rate and real rent remain constant by the assumption of a constant internal price of importables. But variability in response to changes in the amount of tariff revenue redistributed will make a difference in case (2) and variability in response to changes in the amount and composition of real government consumption will make a difference in case (3).

In both cases, allowance for variability of the quantity of labour supplied involves introducing another effect of the tariff increase on the world excess demand for importables, the effect of the change in tariff revenue or real government consumption on the quantity of labour supplied and so on the quantity of importables domestically produced and the income available for private expenditure. These effects have already been discussed in connection with the analysis of the effect of the tariff increase on the terms of trade.

Allowing for variability of the labour supply in response to changes in the amount of tariff revenue redistributed, the total effect of the tariff increase on world excess demand for importables in case (2) is

$$\frac{dM'}{dt} = \left(\frac{c + (\pi\rho - cw)l}{1 + \{1 - c - (\pi\rho - cw)l\}t} - 1 + \eta_f \right) \frac{\overline{M}_1}{\pi}.$$

(33) XV

The corresponding condition for the tariff increase to lower the domestic price of importables is

$$(1 - c) - (\pi\rho - cw)l > \frac{\eta_f}{\pi - \eta_f t}.$$

It follows from this inequality that, even in the case of initial free trade [where the inequality reduces to $(1 - c) - (\rho - cw)l > \eta_f$] it is not necessary for the private marginal propensity to spend on exportables to exceed the foreign elasticity of demand for imports for the tariff to lower the domestic price of importables; since $\pi\rho$ is necessarily greater in absolute value than cw, a reduction of the domestic price of importables with $\eta_f > 1 - c$ requires a negative ρ, which in turn means that labour is used intensively in the exportable-goods industry. If labour is used intensively in the exportable-goods industry, the domestic price of importables can fall even if the foreign demand for imports is elastic.

Allowing for variability of the labour supply in response to changes in the amount of real government consumption – the only variant of *case* (3) we shall consider[1] – the total effect of the tariff increase on world excess demand for importables is

$$\frac{dM'}{dt} = \left(\frac{\{b_r - (\pi\rho - cw)\alpha_r\}(1 + gt)}{1 + \{1 - b_r + (\pi\rho - cw)\alpha_r\}t} + g + \eta'_g\frac{\overline{M}_2}{\overline{M}} - 1 + \eta_f \right)\frac{\overline{M}}{\pi},$$
(34) XVI

where α_r is the change in the quantity of labour supplied due to a unit increase in real government consumption. The corresponding condition for the tariff increase to lower the domestic price of importables is

$$(1 - g) - \frac{b_r - (\pi\rho - cw)\alpha_r}{1 + \{1 - b_r + (\pi\rho - cw)\alpha_r\}t}(1 + gt) - \eta'_g\frac{\overline{M}_2}{\overline{M}} > \eta_f.$$

In the initial free-trade case, this reduces to

$$(1 - g) - b_r + (\rho - cw)\alpha_r > \eta_f;$$

and it follows from this formula that even if the dependence effect of a change in government revenue is positive, the internal price of

[1] Since allowing for variability of labour supply requires merely the addition of $(cw - \rho\pi)$, multiplied by the a relating labour supply to whatever aspect of governmental consumption it depends on, to the corresponding b term in the parameter B in the general formula developed above, the interested reader can easily work out the results for the other two variants for himself.

importables may fall even though the government's marginal propensity to spend on exportables is less than the foreign elasticity of demand for imports and the latter is greater than unity. This can occur if *either* ρ is positive, implying that labour is used relatively intensively in the importable-goods industry, *and* α_r is positive, implying that the quantity of labour supplied increases when real government consumption increases, *or* ρ is negative, implying that labour is used relatively intensively in the exportable-goods industry, *and* α_r is negative, implying that the quantity of labour supplied decreases as real government consumption increases. Similar modifications apply to the general case in which a tariff is in force in the initial situation.

To allow for variability of the quantity of labour supplied in the disaggregated cases (2) and (3) it is necessary merely to replace c, b, $(\rho\pi - cw)l$ and $(\rho\pi - cw)\alpha_r$ by appropriately weighted sums of the corresponding expressions for the two separate individuals. The nature of the resulting modifications in the analysis of the effects of an increase in the tariff rate on the domestic price of importables is evident from the preceding analysis, and will not be developed further here.

9 On the Equivalence of Tariffs and Quotas[1]

This paper examines the proposition that tariffs and quotas are equivalent in the sense that an explicit tariff rate will produce an import level which, if set *alternatively* as a quota, will produce an implicit tariff equal to the explicit tariff (and, pairwise, that a quota will produce an implicit tariff which, if set *alternatively* as an explicit tariff, will generate the same level of imports).

Such a notion of the equivalence between tariffs and quotas is widespread in the literature on trade theory – particularly in discussions relating to the protective effect of quantitative restrictions.[2] On the other hand, equivalence in the sense defined obtains as a logically true proposition only in a limited class of situations.

Indeed, it is easy to construct several possible situations where the equivalence breaks down. This paper demonstrates many such possibilities and then proceeds, in the light of this analysis, to correct some of the current misconceptions about tariffs and quotas which have their origin in the equivalence proposition.

1. ALTERNATIVE POSSIBILITIES

The traditional equivalence proposition is deduced in the context of a model which assumes (a) competitive foreign supply, (b) perfect

---

[1] This revised version has profited as a result of a stimulating comment of Hirofumi Shibata [6]. The original version owed some improvements to Harry Johnson.

[2] C. P. Kindleberger [4], however, does explicitly analyse a case of non-equivalence. Kindleberger [4, pp. 621–3] concentrates on showing how a quota can create a monopoly domestically, and hence does not generalize the argument concerning non-equivalence in the way attempted here. Earlier, J. E. Meade [5, especially pp. 282–5] analysed various possibilities of monopoly arising from the administration of quota systems. The problem, as posed and analysed here, is mentioned in an earlier paper of mine [1].

competition in domestic production, and (c) a quota which is allocated so as to ensure perfect competition among the quota-holders, one consequence of which is that all quotas are used. This *universal* assumption of competitiveness ensures the equivalence which, as we shall soon see, generally breaks down with the introduction of monopoly elements in any one or more of the three listed areas.

We will begin the analysis with the case of universal perfect competition and then examine the following alternative cases: (a) perfect competition in (domestic) production replaced by pure monopoly in production; (b) perfect competition among quota-holders replaced by monopolist holding of quota; (c) simultaneous presence of monopoly in quota-holding and in domestic production; and (d) monopolistic supply of imports.

Throughout the analysis, we use the following notation:

P_F = foreign price

P_D = domestic price

t = tariff rate

S_D = domestic supply (production) of the commodity

S_F = foreign supply (production) of the commodity

D = total domestic demand for (consumption of) the commodity

D_D = net domestic demand for the commodity, available to the domestic suppliers

C = total cost of domestic production of the commodity

Case 1 Competitive supply from abroad, perfect competition in domestic production, and perfect competition among quota-holders.

We first set out the model for the case when a tariff, rather than a quota, is imposed.

$$S_D = S_D(P_D) \qquad (1)$$
$$S_F = S_F(P_F) \qquad (2)$$
$$P_F(1 + t) = P_D \qquad (3)$$
$$S_P + S_F = D \qquad (4)$$
$$D = D(P_D). \qquad (5)$$

Equation (1) states that the domestic supply is a function of domestic price; equation (2) that the foreign supply is a function of foreign price; equation (3) that the domestic price exceeds the foreign price by the amount of the tariff; equation (4) that aggregate supply must equal domestic demand; and equation (5) that domestic demand is a function of domestic price.

We thus have five equations and six unknowns: S_D, S_F, D, P_D, P_F, and t. Thus, if t is given, the remaining unknowns are determined. Corresponding to every tariff rate t, therefore, there will be some import level S_F.

In the case where an import quota is set, the system is identical to that for the tariff case. Corresponding to every import level S_F chosen as the quota, therefore, there will be some (implicit) tariff rate, *i.e.*, discrepancy between P_D and P_F. Moreover, the systems being identical, a tariff will generate an import level which, set alternatively as a quota, will generate the *same* tariff rate.

Figure 9.1 shows graphically the equilibrium in this system. The tariff rate AV/VO shifts the S_F schedule upwards. The resulting total supply schedule S_T (aggregating S_F and S_D) cuts the D schedule to give the import level BC ($= EH$), foreign price OH, and domestic price OF. Conversely, with a quota of BC, the domestic price will turn out to be OF, the foreign price to be OH, and the (implicit) tariff rate therefore to be $(FH/OH =)$ AV/VO. Equivalence thus obtains in this case.

Case 2 Competitive supply from abroad, monopoly in domestic production, and perfect competition among quota-holders.

Starting again with the case of tariffs, we find that the economic system is the following:

$$S_F = S_F(P_F) \tag{1}$$
$$D = D(P_D) \tag{2}$$
$$D_D = D(P_D) - S_F(P_F) \tag{3}$$
$$D_D = S_D \tag{4}$$
$$C = C(S_D) \tag{5}$$
$$\frac{d(P_D S_D)}{dS_D} = \frac{dC}{dS_D} \tag{6}$$
$$P_F(1 + t) = P_D \tag{7}$$

Equation (1) states that the foreign supply is a function of foreign price; equation (2) that total domestic demand is a function of domestic price; equation (3) that the net demand available to the domestic monopolist is the difference between total demand and foreign supply; equation (4) that net domestic demand equals domestic supply; equation (5) that total cost of domestic production (supply) is a function of the level of production; equation (6) that marginal revenue in domestic production is equated by the monopolist with his marginal cost; and equation (7) that the domestic price is higher than the foreign price by the amount of the tariff.

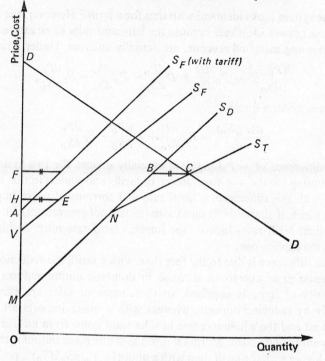

FIGURE 9.1

We have here seven equations and eight unknowns: D, D_D, S_F, S_D, P_D, P_F, C, and t. By choosing the tariff rate, t, therefore, we can determine the remaining values. Consequently, corresponding to every t there will be some level of imports, S_F.

But in contrast to Case 1, the present system shows non-equivalence. For a quota, the system is the following:

$$D = D(P_D) \tag{1}$$
$$S_F = S_F(P_F) \tag{2}$$
$$D_D = D(P_D) - S_F(P_F) \tag{3}$$
$$D_D = S_D \tag{4}$$
$$C = C(S_D) \tag{5}$$
$$\frac{d(P_D S_D)}{dS_D} = \frac{dC}{dS_D} \tag{6}$$
$$\frac{P_D}{P_F} = 1 + t \tag{7}$$

The system looks identical with that for a tariff.[1] However, the two systems are *not* identical, because the left-hand sides of equation (6), representing marginal revenue, are actually different. Under a tariff,

$$\frac{d(P_D S_D)}{dS_D} = P_D \frac{dD}{dS_D} + D \frac{dP_D}{dS_D} - P_D \frac{dS_F}{dS_D} - S_F \frac{dP_D}{dS_D};$$

whereas under a quota,

$$\frac{d(P_D S_D)}{dS_D} = P_D \frac{dD}{dS_D} + D \frac{dP_D}{dS_D} - S_F \frac{dP_D}{dS_D}$$

The difference of $- P_D(dS_F/dS_D)$ crucially divides the two systems, accounting for the non-equivalence of tariffs and quotas in this case. For, with this difference, a tariff rate will correspond to an import level which, if alternatively set as a quota, will not generate an identical (implicit) tariff rate. Indeed, the implicit tariff rate must be higher than the explicit one.

The difference is due to the fact that, with a tariff, the reduction in domestic price due to an increase in domestic output reduces the quantity of imports supplied, so that increased sales are effected partly by reducing imports, whereas with a quota imports are not reduced and the whole increase in sales must come from an increase in quantity demanded. Marginal revenue at any given output is therefore higher with the tariff than with a quota $[- P_D(dS_F/dS_D)$ is positive because (dS_F/dS_D) is negative]. Hence output will be higher, and domestic price, lower, under a tariff than it would be under a quota, for the same level of imports. This non-equivalence is easily illustrated graphically: Figures 9.2 and 9.3 show respectively the tariff and quota systems, two figures being employed instead of one to avoid confusion. In Figure 9.2, we set a tariff rate which generates an import level; in Figure 9.3, we set the *same* import level as a quota and show that a *different* (and higher) implicit tariff rate is generated.

In Figure 9.2, the tariff rate ($= AW/WO$) shifts the supply schedule S_F upwards. The net demand schedule for the domestic monopolist then is VUD, while VR is the marginal revenue schedule for the monopolist. Equilibrium exists where the latter cuts the marginal cost schedule for the monopolist, so that the monopolist's production (S_D)

---

[1] Of course, equations (2) and (7) are now to be understood differently. In the present, quota case, equation (2) gives the foreign price corresponding to the import quota set; whereas in equation (7) t is the *implicit* tariff rate, obtained merely as $(P_D/P_F - 1)$. Neither of these differences, however, affects the equivalence proposition.

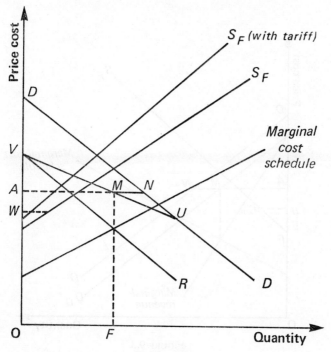

FIGURE 9.2

is at OF, the domestic price at OA, the foreign price at OW, and the import level (S_F) at MN.

We then use the *same* import level MN as the quota in Figure 9.3. The *net* demand schedule for the domestic monopolist is now D_D; it is steeper than the net demand schedule segment VU in the previous diagram. The corresponding marginal revenue schedule must lie farther below M (in Figure 9.2) than the previous marginal revenue schedule VR; it therefore cuts the monopolist's marginal cost schedule at a lower output than under the tariff, to yield OA as the domestic price and OB as the foreign price, the implicit tariff rate being AB/OB. Since OB in Figure 9.3 is equal to OW in Figure 9.2 (imports being the same in both cases), and OA in Figure 9.3 must be greater than OA in Figure 9.2, the implicit tariff rate under the quota must exceed the explicit tariff rate that would produce the same volume of imports. This demonstrates the non-equivalence between tariffs and quotas when there is monopoly in domestic production.

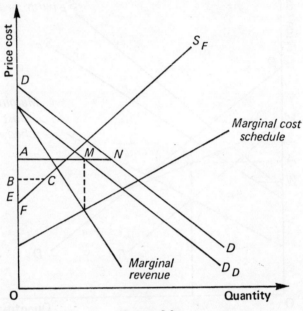

FIGURE 9.3

Case 3 Competitive supply from abroad, perfect competition in domestic production, and monopolist-holding of quotas.

Case A Assume that the imports are competitively demanded under the tariff situation. The analysis of a tariff in this case is identical with that in Case 1. With a quota, however, the system is now different. Since the quota-holder may be assumed to maximize his profits, he will vary his imports (within the quota set) so as to achieve this goal. The system then becomes the following:

$$D = D(P_D) \tag{1}$$
$$S_F = D(P_D) - S_D(P_D) \tag{2}$$
$$S_D = S_D(P_D) \tag{3}$$
$$S_F = S_F(P_F) \tag{4}$$
$$\frac{P_D}{P_F} = (1 + t) \tag{5}$$
$$\frac{d(P_D - P_F)S_F}{dS_F} \geqq 0. \tag{6}$$

The first five equations are already familiar. The last merely states the first-order, maximizing (equilibrium) condition for the monopolist quota-holder; the equality sign holds if the monopolist uses less than his full quota, the inequality if he uses all of his quota. There are thus six equations and six unknowns: P_F, P_D, S_F, S_D, D, and t. The import level which will maximize the quota-holder's profits is thus determinate;[1] and it is obvious that if this import volume is less than would occur under the tariff, the implicit tariff rate must exceed the explicit tariff rate. Since the tariff system and the quota system are different in this case, the equivalence proposition breaks down. It will hold only in the special case when the shapes of the various schedules make it most profitable for the monopolist to use his full quota.

Equilibrium in the quota system is easily illustrated in the three-quadrant Figure 9.4. The right-hand quadrant contains the usual S_D, S_F, and D schedules. The upper left-hand quadrant contains two schedules, one depicting the domestic price and the other the foreign price, corresponding to different levels of utilization of the quota $MN(= OR)$ by the quota-holder. The lower left-hand quadrant shows the level of profits corresponding to every level of utilization of the quota. $AB(= OE)$ then represents the level of quota utilization at which the profits of the quota-holder are at a maximum; and the corresponding (implicit) tariff rate is CD/DE.[2] This is necessarily greater than, or at least equal to, the tariff rate that would produce the level of imports OR.

Case B Assume, however, that imports are effected by a monopoly, such as a state trading corporation, under the tariff situation. In this variation of Case 3, monopolistic importation extends to *both* the quota and the tariff situation.[3]

---

[1] This import level will, however, be subject to an *upper bound* set by the quota.

[2] The equilibrium value of S_F can easily be shown to be:

$$\frac{P_D - P_F}{P'_F - (1/D' - S'_D)}$$

where

$$P'_F = \frac{dP_F}{dS_F}, \quad D' = \frac{dD}{dP_D},$$

and

$$S'_D = \frac{dS_D}{dP_D}.$$

[3] Case B was suggested by G. Yadav [7].

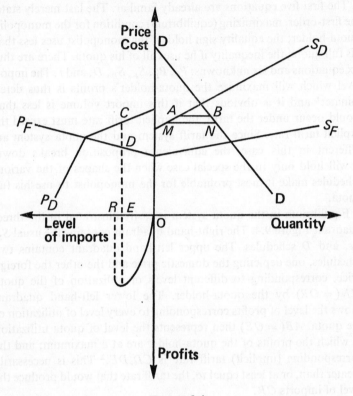

FIGURE 9.4

This case is readily analysed in Figure 9.5. Here, imports are made by a single importer, under *both* tariff and quota régimes, but competition holds everywhere else. Under tariff rate t, S_t is the foreign supply curve of imports; without the tariff, it is S. AR is the *net* demand curve for imports, the marginal revenue curve to it being MR. The intersection of the marginal cost curve MC_t, which is marginal to S_t, at F with MR, determines the maximum profit position for the monopolist importer under the tariff. The domestic price is EG, the foreign c.i.f. price is HG, the landed price is JG and hence the implicit tariff rate EH/HG exceeds the actual tariff rate JH/HG. When the quota is alternatively set at OG and the explicit tariff removed, equilibrium is again at domestic price EG, so that the implicit tariff rate is again EH/HG but this differs from, and exceeds, the explicit

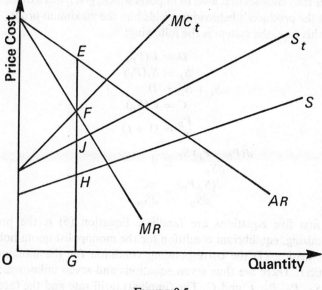

FIGURE 9.5

tariff rate JH/HG. Thus equivalence breaks down in this case as well.[1]

Case 4. Competitive supply from abroad, monopoly in domestic production, and monopolist holding of quotas.

The tariff system in this case is identical to that in Case 2 (and Figure 9.2). The quota system, however, will now differ – unless, of course, it is assumed that the quota-holder acts as a perfect competitor and fails to maximize his profits. Since the quota-holder may also be expected to maximize his profits, the problem becomes that of duopoly, and, as with that general class of problems, there are as many solutions as the behavioural assumptions one cares to make. We take only two simple cases here; they are sufficient for underlining the non-equivalence possibility.

Case A Assume that the producer maximizes his profits at every level of imports chosen by the quota-holder, and that the quota-

[1] If one takes the *pair-wise definition* of equivalence, that *a quota will give rise to an implicit tariff rate which, if alternatively set as a tariff, will generate the same level of imports as the quota,* it is again clear that equivalence breaks down when there is monopoly import under *both* tariff and quota: for, in this case, the quota *OG* will lead to an implicit tariff rate *EH/HG* which, then set alternatively as the tariff, will not lead to the same import level *OG*.

holder then chooses that level of imports which, given this assumption about the producer's behaviour, yields him the maximum profit.

In this case, the system is the following:

$$D = D(P_D) \tag{1}$$
$$S_F = S_F(P_F) \tag{2}$$
$$S_F + S_D = D \tag{3}$$
$$C = C(S_D) \tag{4}$$
$$\frac{P_D}{P_F} = (1 + t) \tag{5}$$
$$\frac{d(P_D - P_F)S_F}{dS_F} \geqq 0 \tag{6}$$
$$\frac{d(S_D P_D)}{dS_D} = \frac{dC}{dS_D} \tag{7}$$

The first five equations are familiar. Equation (6) is the profit-maximizing, equilibrium condition for the monopolist quota-holder, and equation (7) the corresponding condition for the monopolist producer. There are thus seven equations and seven unknowns: D, D_F, S_D, P_F, P_D, t, and C. The (implicit) tariff rate and the (actual) import level are thus determined simultaneously. Note further that the tariff and quota systems are again different so that non-equivalence will obtain,[1] except where conditions lead the monopolist quota-holder to use all his quota. Where the quota is not entirely utilized, the implicit tariff rate must be higher than the explicit tariff rate.

Case B Assume instead that the quota is allotted to the producer-monopolist himself.[2]

In this case, the producer becomes a pure monopolist, with two sources of supply – domestic and foreign. He will then use them in such a way as to maximize his profits. The system of equations is then the following:

$$D = D(P_D) \tag{1}$$
$$S_F + S_D = D \tag{2}$$

[1] This case could also be illustrated by adapting the three-quadrant diagram in Figure 9.4 so as to introduce monopoly instead of competition in domestic production.

[2] This is not as fanciful an assumption as it appears. In countries such as India, considerable concentration of ownership and control obtains in economic activity, owing to a variety of reasons such as strictly controlled entry and economies of scale combined with limited markets. It is thus not merely possible, but also probable, for the case described in the text to obtain in practice.

$$S_F = S_F(P_F) \tag{3}$$
$$C = C(S_D) \tag{4}$$
$$\frac{P_D}{P_F} = 1 + t \tag{5}$$
$$\frac{d(P_F S_F)}{dS_F} \lessgtr \frac{dC}{dS_D} = \frac{d(P_D D)}{dD}. \tag{6 and 7}$$

We thus have seven equations (all familiar by now) and seven unknowns: D, S_F, S_D, C, P_F, P_D and t. Thus, both the (implicit) tariff rate and the rate of quota utilization are determined. Note again the differences in the tariff and quota systems in this case, implying non-equivalence.

This case is easily illustrated in Figure 9.6, where MC is the marginal cost schedule for imports, and the aggregate marginal cost schedule, for both sources of supply, is SRA_{mc}. The latter's intersection with the marginal revenue schedule at R yields the domestic price as EO,

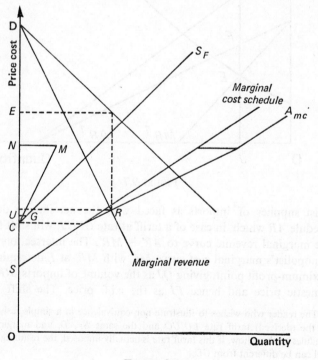

FIGURE 9.6

the foreign price as UO, the (implicit) tariff rate as EU/UO, and the level of imports as GU.[1]

Case 5 Monopolistic supply of imports from abroad, and competition elsewhere.

Consider finally the case where the foreign supply of imports is monopolistic under *both* tariff and quota.[2] In Figure 9.7, the mono-

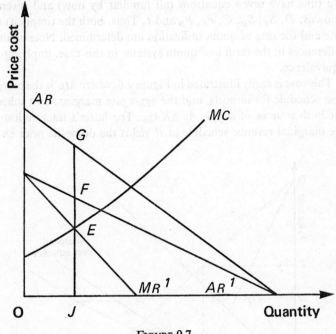

FIGURE 9.7

polist supplier of imports is faced with the net import demand schedule AR which, in case of a tariff at rate GF/FJ, will shift to AR' The marginal revenue curve to AR' is MR'. The intersection of the monopolist's marginal cost curve MC with MR' at E determines his maximum-profit point, giving OJ as the volume of imports, JG as the domestic price and hence FJ as the c.i.f. price. The shift to the

[1] The reader who wishes to illustrate non-equivalence in a simple fashion can use the (derived) tariff rate EU/UO and the same S_F, D, and marginal cost schedules to show how, if this tariff rate is actually imposed, the resulting import level can be different from GU.

[2] This is the case analysed by Shibata [6].

alternative situation where the tariff GF/FJ is removed and replaced by a quota of OJ, leads on the other hand to the same domestic price GJ, but the ci.f. price now shifts also to GJ, so that the implicit tariff rate is *zero*, and hence is *below* the explicit tariff.

The equivalence proposition thus breaks down unequivocally: an explicit tariff will not lead to an import level which, if set alternatively as a quota, will generate the same implicit tariff. (Nor will a quota lead to an implicit tariff which, if set alternatively as a tariff, will generate the same level of imports.) Hence, this case also is no exception to the presumption that equivalence will generally break down with the introduction of monopoly elements.

2. IMPLICATIONS OF NON-EQUIVALENCE

The demonstration that the equivalence of tariffs and quotas can break down, once we move away from the universally competitive model, is not merely interesting in itself but also has important implications in several areas of analysis.

1 We can now answer directly the question whether under a quota régime the observed implicit tariff rates can be treated as equivalent to identical tariff rates (levied instead of the quota) in the sense of generating the same level of imports and domestic production. This is a question that comes up frequently and the general practice is *indeed* to treat the observed, implicit tariff rate under a QR régime as the 'effective tariff rate'. Examination of the equivalence proposition, in terms of the definition used here, throws up the limitations of these deductions when monopoly elements are present.

Thus, for example, in the case when foreign supply is monopolistic, the implicit tariff rate is zero under the quota – refer back to Figure 9.7 – but setting the actual tariff rate at zero and removing the quota restriction will *not* yield the same level of imports and domestic production; the truly equivalent tariff rate is *higher*. Similarly, in the case where there is domestic, import-monopoly instead, the truly equivalent tariff is *lower* than the implicit tariff rate in the quota alternative – refer back to Figure 9.5. Similar conclusions apply to the other cases analysed here: (i) where there is monopolistic-holding of quotas, but competition elsewhere, again the implicit tariff rate will *exceed* the explicit tariff rate, thus *overstating* the truly equivalent tariff rate, when the quota is under-utilized; (ii) where there is monopoly in domestic production as well as in the holding of quotas, again the under-utlization of the quota would imply an implicit tariff rate that exceeds the explicit tariff rate and hence *overstates* the truly equivalent, effective tariff; and (iii) where there is monopoly in domestic production but competition everywhere else, the implicit tariff will exceed the explicit tariff, thus *overstating* again the truly equivalent, effective tariff that the quota represents.

2 Yet another inference from the equivalence proposition has been that when both tariffs and quotas are applied to an industry, and the discrepancy between the foreign and domestic prices exceeds the tariff rate, the tariff is redundant (except insofar as it cuts into the profits of the quota-holders and yields corresponding revenue to the state). This inference is not necessarily valid, of course, when non-equivalence obtains, and it is important to note this in view of the widespread, simultaneous use of tariffs and quotas in many developing countries.[1]

The imposition of a tariff, even when the equilibrium solution with this tariff plus a specific quota shows a greater difference between P_f and P_D than the tariff would have produced, may still have a net supplementary protective effect, in the sense of increasing domestic production above what it would otherwise be. This can readily be illustrated in the framework of Case 4, assumption B, in which the domestic monopolist also has a monopoly of the quota. A tariff on imports (at less than the implicit tariff rate) would raise their marginal cost to the monopolist, inducing him to shift toward more domestic production while at the same time curtailing total sales. Similar interactions of quotas and tariffs could be demonstrated in other frameworks as well.

3 Note further that equivalence as defined in the present paper is *not* identical with equivalence defined as follows: that, corresponding to any tariff, there will exist *some* quota which will result in the same

[1] Firms frequently ask for tariff protection for their industries, even when the tariff may in fact be 'redundant' (in the sense of the text) by virtue of import control, because import control is subject to frequent revision – semiannually in India – and hence its protective effect is 'uncertain', whereas tariffs are revised in practice only after several years and hence can be 'relied upon'. Frequently also, there are built-in leakages, even in import control, which introduce uncertainty. Thus, for example, many countries now experiment with export-incentive schemes involving 'import-replacement' licences. Under these schemes, imports of a commodity earning a higher premium could well increase, thereby reducing the 'protective' effect of import control for the domestic producers of this commodity. A tariff could then be very useful indeed in reducing such a leakage!

level of imports and importable production. And it is equivalence in the *latter* sense that is implied in the literature on balance of payments theory, as in Johnson [3], Meade [5] and Fleming [2], for example, where it is customarily argued that the use of quantitative restrictions is identical with the use of *some* equivalent tariff, that the use of (further) tariffs is justified only insofar as the country is below the optimum tariff level, and that the use of quantitative restrictions to reduce an external deficit is therefore justified, from the welfare view-point, only when the country does not already have optimal restrictions. Equivalence in this latter sense *also* breaks down, generally speaking, with the introduction of monopoly elements, *along with* equivalence in the former sense used in this paper; but not always. For example, in Case 3 B and Case 5, equivalence breaks down in the sense of this paper but *not* in the sense relevant to payments theory. As a general proposition, however, it remains correct to argue that the introduction of monopoly elements will invalidate, generally speaking, the equivalence of tariffs and quotas in *either* sense; and hence balance of payments literature which relies on equivalence must be generally qualified.

4 It is often stated that quotas are preferred to tariffs because their import-restricting effect, although in principle equivalent to that of tariffs, is certain, whereas that of tariffs is not. The reason cited is the difficulty of estimating the supply and demand schedules, both domestic and foreign. In point of fact, the possible differences in market structure (at the level of foreign supply and domestic production) under the two systems have also to be assessed accurately – and these, as well as their effects, can be far more difficult to judge.

Moreover, the impression that quotas necessarily produce certain predictions about the level of actual imports is incorrect. They frequently set only an upper bound to the level of imports – not merely because foreign or domestic supply and/or demand schedules have changed or because of administrative delays in allocations of exchange, but also because the market structure may depart from the universally competitive model (as in Case 4, for example).[1]

Before concluding, we may spell out briefly two other propositions,

[1] Non-utilization due to administrative delays and changed supply or demand conditions is, of course, quite important. The time profile of utilization within the time horizon specified also can be interesting to analyse and would involve an inter-temporal, profit-maximizing solution.

relating to quotas *per se* rather than to the equivalence proposition, which seem to be of some interest.

1 It is frequently thought that import-quota auctions would be equivalent to ordinary quotas, while the profits made by quota-holders would accrue to the state as auction premiums. On the other hand, it is clear from the preceding analysis that the issue depends on *how* the auctions are conducted. For example, if quotas are allocated to a 'large' number of holders under the ordinary system, whereas the auction permits one buyer to bid highest, the latter will bid *until* the *monopolist*-profit is exhausted by way of premium, so that the resulting situation will become one of monopoly quota-holding instead of the original competition among quota-holders.[1] In this case, therefore, the auction would convert the situation from one system to another – from Case 1 to Case 3 (if we assume competition in domestic production). The equivalence of auctions and ordinary quotas would thus break down.

2 Another interesting policy proposition relates to the widely observed association of quantitative import restrictions with monopoly (or oligopoly) in domestic production and its consequently deleterious effects on *both* the level of output and the level of efficiency (with respect to minimizing the cost of producing a specified output).[2]

The restrictive effect on the level of output is implicit in the analysis of Case 2. The effect on efficiency, however, is perhaps far more significant – and has been the concern of planners, using import control régimes, in many developing countries.

It is pertinent, therefore, to consider seriously whether the import control régime should not be modified so as to build into the system a threat of 'liberalization' of imports when there is evidence of quality deterioration, inefficiency, or restrictive output policies. (This is, of course, similar to the traditional prescription with respect to removal of tariff protection.)

This prescription, however, runs counter to the present

---

[1] This argument, of course, presumes that the monopolistic buying-up occurs under auctions but that no monopoly is obtained by purchasing from the quota-holders under the non-auction system of allocation. These assumptions, however, may be realistic.

[2] The absence of foreign competition, combined with a planning set-up which rules out new entry and the driving out of inefficient producers, has resulted in considerable inefficiency in countries such as India. It is enough to be a consumer (or a producer using domestic intermediates) in India to see the force of this observation!

indiscriminate resort to quantitative restrictions and the tendency to ignore the economic costs of import control analysed here. But there is little doubt that it is imperative to experiment with this idea in practice if a way out of the current widespread 'featherbedding' and inefficiency in sheltered markets is to be reduced to less gigantic proportions.[1]

REFERENCES

1 Bhagwati, J., 'Quantitative Restrictions and Quotas in International Trade', *International Encyclopedia of the Social Sciences*, forthcoming.

2 Fleming, J. M., 'On Making the Best of Balance of Payments Restrictions on Imports', *Economic Journal*, March 1951.

3 Johnson, H. G., *International Trade and Economic Growth*, London, Allen and Unwin, 1958.

4 Kindleberger, C. P., *International Economics*, Homewood, Illinois, Richard D. Irwin, Inc., 1958.

5 Meade, J. E., *The Theory of International Economic Policy*, Volume I, *The Balance of Payments*, London, Oxford University Press, 1951.

6 Shibata, H., 'A Note on the Equivalence of Tariffs and Quotas', *American Economic Review*, March 1968.

7 Yadav, G., 'A Note on the Equivalence of Tariffs and Quotas', *Canadian Journal of Economics and Political Science*, February, 1968.

---

[1] Under balance-of-payments pressures, more countries may be expected to slide into such economic régimes. During a consulting assignment in Turkey in the summer of 1964, I found Turkey gradually moving into such a set-up. There, as soon as a domestic industry is established, the imports of that commodity are practically automatically 'deliberalized'. Aside from the adverse effects on quality and costs which may confidently be expected from this policy, its operation has led to interesting destabilization in the short term. Thus, as soon as the industry comes into operation, there is an excessive import of the commodity in the expectation that it will be deliberalized: this happened with rubber tyres, for example.

10 Fiscal Policies, the Faking of Foreign Trade Declarations, and the Balance of Payments[1]

The interaction between fiscal and monetary policies, including foreign and domestic taxation measures, and the balance of payments has been analysed at several levels by trade theorists. The effects of changes in interest rates on the current and capital accounts are, for example, very much at the core of the classical analysis of balance of payments adjustment. So also the macro-analysis of fiscal policy, *via* budgetary surplus and deficit changes, has now been integrated into the recent absorption approach to balance of payments analysis.[2] Recently, there have also been attempts to analyse the effects of certain domestic taxes (such as the value-added tax, the Corporation tax, etc.) for balance of payments behaviour *via* their effects on costs and prices.[3]

However, there is a curious absence of systematic analysis of the effects that fiscal policies, in the nature of export and import duties

---

[1] This paper is an amalgam of two papers published in the *Bulletin of the Oxford University Institute of Statistics*, one of the same title published in February 1967 and another, earlier note 'On the Underinvoicing of Imports', November 1964. My thanks are due to V. K. Ramaswami, T. N. Srinivasan and A. Vaidyanathan for helpful comments.

[2] Numerous references could be cited in support of these statements; the following, however, are quite sufficient: H. G. Johnson, *International Trade and Economic Growth*, London, George Allen & Unwin Ltd., 1958, Chapter 6, for the absorption approach and macro-fiscal policies; and J. E. Meade, *The Balance of Payments* (*The Theory of International Economic Policy*, Vol. I), Oxford, Oxford University Press, 1955, for the classical analysis of the balance of payments.

[3] Two recent contributions of interest are: R. A. Musgrave, 'Tax Policy', *Review of Economics and Statistics*, Vol. 46 (2), May 1964; and W. B. Salant, 'The Balance-of-Payments Deficit and the Tax Structure', *Review of Economics and Statistics*, Vol. 46 (2), May 1964.

and/or subsidies, have on the balance of payments *via* the incentives they often create for faking customs declarations. These effects are important to comprehend for making policy decisions arising from balance of payments changes.

This paper makes a pioneering attempt at analysis in this area. More specifically, the paper

1 states the reasons for which *trade* tariffs and subsidies can lead to faked trade declarations;

2 discusses the techniques of examining empirically the phenomenon of faking, stating their limitations clearly; and

3 examines the implications of such faking of trade data for economic analysis and policy with respect to the balance of payments.

A further section explores similar issues from the point of view of *internal* levies and subsidies.

1. TRADE TARIFFS AND SUBSIDIES

A. *Theoretical Analysis*

The presence of tariffs and subsidies on international trade transactions generally creates immediately an incentive to overinvoice or underinvoice the value of the transactions. Which of these two possibilities obtains will depend not merely on the rate of the tariff or subsidy but also on the premium or discount at which the incremental foreign exchange, so required or acquired, is bought or sold in the foreign exchange market.

For example, if an *ad valorem* export subsidy is available and there is no exchange control so that all exchange transactions take place only within the insignificant range legally permitted around the parity value, there will immediately be an incentive to overinvoice exports. The exporter who does overinvoice will enjoy a profit of $tx\%$ on the *actual* export value, where t is the *ad valorem* subsidy rate and x the percentage by which exports are overinvoiced. Where, however, there is exchange control, and the exporter must surrender to the exchange authorities the full, *declared* value of exports, the exporter will have to purchase illegal foreign exchange in the black market to the amount of the excess of declared over actual value of exports. In this case, if the black market premium on foreign exchange is $P\%$, the incentive to overinvoice will exist only if $t > P$.[1] In practice, of course, the overinvoicing, in view of the illegality entailed both in faking the declaration and in the purchase of foreign exchange in the black market (in case of exchange control), will be practised only when t exceeds P significantly enough to outweigh the risks ensuing from the illegal transactions. Where t happens to be below P, further, the incentive will be to underinvoice exports. This will be the case, for example, when there is a tariff on exports: in this case the exporter makes a profit, via underinvoicing, both by avoiding tariff and by earning a premium on the sale of illegally acquired foreign exchange. But such underinvoicing will occur even when there is an export subsidy (at rate t) and $t < P$.

Correspondingly, on the *import* side, a similar analysis holds. If t now stands for an import tariff (rate), and P again for the premium on illegal foreign exchange there will be an incentive to underinvoice imports when $t > P$ and to overinvoice imports when $t < P$. For example, where there is an import subsidy and no exchange control or a net premium on illegal foreign exchange the incentive will clearly be to overinvoice imports; and where there is a tariff and there is no exchange control (so that $P = 0$), the incentive will clearly be to underinvoice imports.

Where there is overinvoicing of exports or underinvoicing of imports, the transaction will create a net *demand* for illegal foreign exchange (in exchange-control economies); where there is underinvoicing of exports or overinvoicing of imports, the transaction will create a net *supply* of illegal foreign exchange. In the former case, the effect will be to increase the black market premium on foreign exchange; in the latter case, to reduce it.

B. *Possibility of Empirical Analysis*

Whereas it is easy to establish the conditions under which the faking of trade values, as argued above, will occur, it is in practice extremely difficult to set about determining whether such faking is *actually* occurring. It is further *impossible* to find out *how much* faking is going on.

---

[1] Note that the formula applies equally to the case where there is no exchange control, as in the preceding case. In that case, $P = 0$ and therefore t, which is positive, will exceed P, creating an incentive to overinvoice exports. The phenomenon of faked trade declarations has thus nothing to do with whether there is exchange control or not.

One method, traditionally used by economists and now more or less out of favour, is to ask those engaged in the actual transactions whether such faking occurs and, if so, in what direction. This method *can* work to some extent, especially if the interviewees confess to themselves having indulged in these 'malpractices'. Rare, however, are such instances; the business ethos does not permit the admission of such behaviour. It is much easier, in fact, to get such admissions in respect of *other* firms in the industry; the interviewees are readier to accuse than to confess![1]

One would thus like to supplement such 'evidence' with analysis based on 'cold facts'. There *is*, in fact, a method which I have found useful and which is generally applicable to the analysis of over-invoiced exports and underinvoiced imports (although, with slight amendment, it can be extended to the analysis of underinvoiced exports and overinvoiced exports as well). It is *not* free from certain methodological limitations; but it seems to me to possess a fair degree of power in furnishing 'reasonable' evidence of overinvoicing or underinvoicing of trade figures. The method rests essentially on comparing partner-country trade data.

It is well known that, with few exceptions, import data are published at c.i.f. value and export data at f.o.b. value. As a consequence most teachers of international economics are likely, at some stage or other, to have been confronted by a research student who has looked at international trade statistics and 'discovered' that the world as a whole has a deficit on its balance of trade! Now, one would normally expect partner-country statistics to show an excess of c.i.f. import values over corresponding f.o.b. export values (relating to the *same* trade flows). If, therefore, the observed discrepancy between these data is in the 'perverse' direction, one may conclude that there is a *prima facie* evidence for *either* overinvoiced exports or underinvoiced imports (or both, of course).

Of course, either of these phenomena may obtain without being large enough to reverse the 'normal' excess of import over (partner) export values, in which case the present statistical technique will not be useful (*unless* the insurance and freight element can be reasonably approximated and adjusted for). Again, the method will not be available when one is looking for overinvoicing of imports or under-

---

[1] This statement is based on my experience with Indian exporters, several of whom were interviewed by me during June 1965 on the question of overinvoicing in their field.

invoicing of exports (*unless* again the insurance and freight margins can be reasonably adjusted for), because these would merely reinforce, rather than reverse, the 'normal' excess of c.i.f. import over (partner-country) f.o.b. export values. A yet further and more serious limitation of the method arises from the fact that it presumes the faking of invoices to occur only at one end, *or* that the incentive to fake runs in contrary directions at the two ends (so that the exporter, for example, wishes to overinvoice and the importer to underinvoice). In such cases, the invoices surrendered to partner countries, by corresponding nationals, will be different and, since no international cross-check by customs authorities is practised, the discrepancy will arise and remain unchecked. Where, however, the incentive to fake as also the direction of this faking are common to both parties – as when, for example, the exporter wishes to overinvoice in view of remunerative subsidies and the importer *also* wishes to overinvoice to export unauthorized capital to the exporter's country, as seems to be the case with some recent overinvoicing of exports in India – the proposed statistical technique for detecting faked invoicing would normally break down.

But even where the method is *prima facie* usable, there are, of course, difficulties in using it for our purpose. In fact, the statisticians have long observed *both* discrepancies in partner-country data and the occasional 'perversity' of these discrepancies.[1] And their traditional observations on these 'inconsistencies' provide clues to the possible, *alternative* explanation of the perverse discrepancies. It is *only* when these alternative explanations have been examined and dismissed as inapplicable to the specific empirical analysis, and the relative magnitudes of the premium on the black market for foreign exchange and

[1] Any random reference to a statistical publication containing data on exports, according to category and destination and a patient preparation of partner-country tables, will demonstrate this point effectively if one is not satisfied by the testimony of those who compile or use international trade statistics. Refer also to L. Allen, *Soviet Economic Warfare*, Public Affairs Press, Washington DC, 1960, pp. 268 and 284–91, for a statistical examination of discrepancies in the partner-country data for the following countries: Soviet Union, India, France, Italy, Japan, Sweden, Switzerland, United Kingdom, United States, and West Germany, for the year 1956. Allen's objective is to examine whether the discrepancies for the Soviet Union are any larger than those to be found for every country, whether Communist or not. No attention is paid by him, however, to the *direction* of these discrepancies. There is also the excellent work of Morgenstern in *The Accuracy of Economic Observation*, Princeton University Press, 1965, on partner-country trade comparisons. His explanations, however, are statistical and relate to *totals* of exports and imports.

the import tariff (or export subsidy) on the items where the 'perverse' discrepancies have been observed are such as to indicate an incentive for underinvoicing of imports (or overinvoicing of exports) that we can consider having produced 'reasonable' evidence in support of the hypothesis of underinvoicing of imports (or overinvoicing of exports). And even then, it is always possible to raise the methodological objection that one may have overlooked either some evidence in support of the alternative explanations examined and dismissed or, more pointedly still, an alternative explanation itself. 'Proof' is thus impossible; only 'plausibility' can be procured by the method proposed.

What are these alternative, possible explanations of 'perverse' discrepancies between partner-country, export and import statistics? Several exist.

(1) There can be 'misallocations' of the same traded item, by both Standard International Trade Classification (SITC) category and by country. If inconsistencies obtain between partner countries on either score, then a comparison of c.i.f. import and f.o.b. export values of the two countries with each other, by SITC categories, could well show 'perverse' discrepancies. These inconsistencies can arise from both genuine Customs mistakes and differences in conventions adopted (chiefly with respect to questions of origin and transit). An example from actual trade data is provided by the fact that Malayan exports of rubber to Turkey are attributed in Turkish import statistics to the United Kingdom because an English exporter is handling the transaction, whereas United Kingdom export statistics do not register the transaction, thus leading to a discrepancy in the partner-country statistics of United Kingdom and Turkey but *not* if the exercise of comparisons is extended to include Malaya as well.

Cross-checking with other SITC categories for the *same* pair of countries (to discover possible misallocations by category) and with similar comparisons for *other pairs of countries* is essential before one can rule out statistical misallocations as an explanation of any observed 'perversity' in discrepancies.

(2) But the discrepancies can arise also from the lag between shipment and arrival in the importing country. If the average lag remains unchanged, and the level of export values is not changing, there would of course be no discrepancy between export and import statistics from this source: the excess of import over exports owing to the preceding year's carry-over would offset the deficit owing to this year's carry-

forward. Where, however, exports are rising, and the lag is unchanged, there *would* result an excess of recorded exports over imports.[1]

(3) Some observed discrepancies are also to be attributed to inaccuracies arising from conversion calculations. More important, however, may be the general Customs practice of scaling down or up the invoices presented to them. This practice itself originates from the suspicion of the genuineness of the presented invoices. Where the scaling down takes place when overinvoicing of exports is suspected *and* is actually taking place, there is no complication from this source; nor does it matter when the scaling up occurs when underinvoicing of imports is suspected *and* is actually being attempted. Where, however, the enforced revisions occur in the opposite directions, such that scaling down for example is undertaken for fear of overinvoicing of imports when in fact the invoice is correct, the 'perverse' discrepancy can arise from the Customs revisions rather than from genuine faking of invoices!

This rather long analysis of alternative, possible explanations of perverse discrepancies shows how difficult it is, in practice, to use the statistical technique of partner-country-data comparisons for reaching any conclusions about faking of trade invoices and the direction of such faking.

However, it is interesting to note that, in an attempt at empirical use of this technique on Turkish statistics for 1960 and 1961, I have managed to find plausible evidence for the conclusion that import values of manufactures, especially in the field of transport equipment and machinery, are understated. Let me state the analysis fully.

The data for Turkey–Italy, Turkey–Germany, Turkey–United States, Turkey–France, and Turkey–Netherlands (Tables 1–9), relating to Turkey's principal trading partners, testify to substantial excesses of f.o.b. over c.i.f. values in petroleum products and in the categories of main manufactured goods (Code No. 6), machinery and transport equipment (Code No. 7) and miscellaneous manufactures (Code No. 8).

Not all of these testify to underinvoicing of imports. The

---

[1] This is unlikely, however, to be significant in normal cases. Even if trade grows at ten per cent – which is quite a generous assumption for most countries – and the carry-forward applies to a three-month period, the resulting discrepancy as a percentage of the recorded trade cannot be more than about three per cent, unless unusual and contrasting bunching of trade is assumed for the preceding and the present years.

discrepancies in petroleum products, for instance, are offsetting between France, Italy, United States and United Kingdom (Tables 10–11). They arise from this misallocation of imports among sources, resulting from confusion over the ownership of refineries and of petroleum.[1] But I have not been able to think of similar explanations for the other discrepancies.[2]

It is not valid to argue that the time-lag between exports and imports will explain the discrepancies observed.[3] Significant over-invoicing by exporters to Turkey is unlikely, given the existence of convertibility during this period for the relevant currencies and countries.[4]

We are therefore left with some significant discrepancies for which the only explanation appears to be underinvoicing. How does this explanation stand up in relation to Turkey's organization of its international trade? Quite well, as it turns out.

Turkey, during the early 1960s, was operating a substantially 'liberalized' trade system. It relied on tariffs – other price-instruments such as devaluation, licence fees, stamp duty also being used occasionally – to regulate imports. I expected, therefore, that the under-invoicing would in this case turn out to be related to tariffs, rather than to import control. This turned out to be the case.

In the statement on Turkey's tariffs in 1961 (which also adequately serves our purpose for 1960), included at the end of this paper, the reader will find that the categories of goods which show perverse discrepancies (in Tables 1–9) also generally had tariff rates ranging up to thirty per cent and rarely below ten per cent.[5]

As the black market premium for foreign exchange has rarely exceeded fifteen per cent according to official observations, and has been usually below this level, it seems reasonable to conclude that the discrepancies represent underinvoicing of imports, by and large.

---

[1] I am indebted to R. Gross, who spotted the offsetting nature of the petroleum discrepancies.

[2] In ships and boats I found that the discrepancy was to be explained by foreign registration: but this, in turn, might be linked to high tariffs on import of ships.

[3] This is for much the same reason as set out in footnote 1, p. 272.

[4] It is true that the relief from the cascading turnover taxes in some Western European countries was related, during this period, to the value of exports. Hence there could have been some overinvoicing of exports to secure greater relief. But I doubt whether much can be made of this point.

[5] Some puzzling tariffs seem to be those on non-ferrous metals – at five per cent. I have not been able to think of a suitable explanation in these cases.

This conclusion is further reinforced by the fact that understatement of value in the field of manufactures – especially machinery, which is frequently made to order and rarely carries standard prices that the Customs can readily check – is readily possible. And it is precisely in these areas that the perverse discrepancies occur in the Turkish case.

Let me emphasize again that the preceding analysis provides, not a conclusive proof, but only a strong indication of the presence of under-invoicing of imports in the Turkish case. Indeed, for many the case may appear totally convincing.

Whereas the Turkish case yielded an interesting 'confirmation' of the usability of the proposed technique for inferring the faking of trade invoices and hence trade data, my attempt at inferring over-invoicing of exports in the Indian context has had to by-pass this technique for reasons which throw the limitations of this technique into sharp focus. There are two fairly strong reasons for believing that a segment of Indian exports recently has been overinvoiced.

(a) There has been *de facto* subsidization of several new exports, via a form of 'import entitlement' (similar to 'exchange retention') schemes, and there has been general admission, by business houses and official export-promoting agencies, of the overinvoicing that has prevailed; and

(b) an examination of the premium on the (transferable) import entitlements, and the relationship of the entitlements to the export values, shows a subsidy which exceeds the black market discount on the Indian Rupee, both for currency rates and for illegal transfers, at most of the principal centres (Hong Kong, Nairobi, Mombasa, Aden and Berne), so that the incentive to overinvoice has been considerable.[1]

However, the applicability of the proposed statistical technique breaks down in certain significant ways, all of some interest.

(1) The SITC data, required for such analysis in a careful manner, are not available except for the OECD countries (with insignificant exceptions) so that the technique cannot even be a starter on much of

[1] The statement on the *de facto* subsidies, resulting from the import entitlement schemes, is based on information gathered from interviews by me, with export houses and manufacturer-exporters, during June 1965. The information on the black market discount on the rupee is regularly received officially by the central banking authorities from the different centres via 'contacts'; the information for Hong Kong is, in any case, regularly listed on the back pages of the *Far Eastern Economic Review*.

India's exports of the incentive-covered items outside the Soviet Bloc.

(2) The applicability of the technique to the OECD countries shows, in fact, that there are excessive 'normal' discrepancies which may *either* imply underinvoicing of exports (as it well may, since the items in which the serious differences occur are where there are no significant subsidies at all) *or* be a result of different conventions (which may be the case with imports of Indian goods by certain Western European countries *via* the Soviet Bloc, these being classified by the former as imports from India but by India as exports to the Soviet Bloc). Whereas there seems to be some slender evidence for the latter explanation, in the form of complaints by Indian exporters that Indian goods, purchased by the Soviet Bloc under bilateral agreements, are being resold at 'dumped' prices in India's traditional markets, it is not possible to cross-check for this 'misallocation' in trade statistics by using independent, Soviet Bloc data on direction-cum-SITC-categories trade because these data are not possible to obtain.[1] Nor is it possible to check whether the large excesses of EEC c.i.f. import values over Indian f.o.b. export data are not due to misallocations with yet other countries for whom no direction-cum-categories data are available.

(3) Further, the overinvoicing of Indian exports is suspected to have occurred largely with respect to exports to certain 'free ports' such as Hong Kong, Aden and Panama, where the 'partner-country-comparison' technique is inapplicable owing to lack of data.

(4) Finally, much overinvoicing has also allegedly taken place with East Africa and Malaysia. There, the 'Indians' are aiming to pull out capital, in violation of exchange control on capital movement. They are thus happy to fake the value of their imports, in collaboration with the Indian exporters. The resulting difference from the normal overinvoicing is that *both* import and (corresponding) export invoices are faked upwards. This being the case, the statistical technique of partner-country-comparisons breaks down as an aid to empirical analysis.

---

[1] It is possible, however, to go *some* way towards a cross-check, by examining whether the SITC groups in which the excessive discrepancies obtain with EEC countries are also the groups where India's exports to the Soviet Bloc are reasonably commensurate. If not, clearly the explanation of 're-sale' by the Soviet Bloc will not hold. Indeed, such a check shows that the 're-sale' explanation cannot explain more than a limited fraction of the excessively large, 'normal' discrepancies in EEC–India trade data.

The usability of the statistical technique suggested here is thus dependent on several favourable circumstances. In other cases, the analyst will have to rely on word-of-mouth assurances subjected only to two 'indirect' tests:

(a) Are the items, where the faking of invoices is allegedly practised, of a kind where such faking is possible in the teeth of Customs checks?

(b) Are the magnitudes of the black market premium on foreign exchange and the subsidy of tariff rates on trade transactions such as to provide a significant incentive for the alleged faking of invoices?

For most purposes, these two tests ought to provide fairly strong indication of some (though, indeterminate) amount of faking of invoices in external transactions.

C. *Economic Implications*

Whereas, however, it is difficult to secure objective and strong evidence on the prevalence of faked invoicing in foreign trade declarations, these practices undoubtedly obtain when fiscal and exchange policies combine to make them worth while. The economic implications of these practices are thus important to analyse. It will be useful to distinguish, for this purpose, among:

(a) overinvoicing of exports;
(b) underinvoicing of imports;
(c) underinvoicing of exports; and
(d) overinvoicing of imports.

Since the analysis can be readily adapted for the remaining phenomena, overinvoicing of exports alone is subjected to detailed analysis.

Further, the following analysis begins with (1) the impact on the balance of payments, distinguishing between the 'official' and the 'real' balance; and then extends the argument to the effect of overinvoicing of exports (2) on individual items in the balance of payments and *via* that on other variables and (3) on the time-lag between exports and receipts.

1 The analysis of the impact on the *balance of payments* at any point of time (and thus abstracting from long-run effects) must distinguish between what may be described as the *real* position and the *official*,

recorded position. The official balance of payments record need not necessarily reflect the real foreign exchange position and generally will not do so when faking is occurring. This real position is given by net availability of foreign exchange for use by the country *after* adjusting for all leakages into prohibited uses resulting in loss of foreign exchange to the country, these leakages being unauthorized remittances and transfers of capital abroad and tourist expenditure in foreign countries (as also possible, unauthorized import expenditure *via* smuggling).

Assume initially then that the export *volume* and *unfaked value* as well as *authorized* import *expenditure* are given. The illegal foreign exchange market is being fed by supplies from overinvoicing of imports, underinvoicing of exports, diverted remittances and foreign-tourist expenditure and foreign flight of capital. The demands for black exchange come from underinvoicing of imports, illegal tourist expenditure and transfers of capital and remittances abroad, and overinvoicing of exports. Assume further that

(a) the flight of foreign capital is channelled in through the over-invoicing of exports, and

(b) all illegal demands respond inversely to changes in the premium on black exchange and all illegal supplies respond directly to such changes.

Effect on 'real' balance of payments: The effect of any increase in overinvoicing of exports on the *real* balance of payments is then measured by the impact change in the total foreign supply of remit-tances, capital transfers and tourist expenditure (insofar as they respond to the increase in overinvoicing of exports) *plus* any change in the leakage into illegal transfers of capital and remittances to foreign countries and unauthorized tourist expenditure abroad. The change in this measures the net increment or reduction in foreign exchange availability for authorized uses. In the following analysis, two prin-cipal varieties of increments in the overinvoicing of exports are discussed:

(a) where the cause is net increase in subsidization of exports; and

(b) where the cause is an autonomous, illegal transfer of foreign capital *via* the overinvoicing of exports.

(i) It will be clear that any increase in overinvoicing of exports which reflects a policy change such as the expansion of the export-subsidization programme, will lead to an increase in the black market premium and thus have two favourable effects:

(a) it will cut into the illegal leakages into capital and remittance transfers abroad and also into unauthorized expenditure on foreign travel; and

(b) it will induce an increase in the *overall* inflow of remittances, funds-transfers and foreign tourist expenditure insofar as these are price-elastic.

Note that if we were to assume away these effects, such that these illegal leakages as also the overall inflows of remittances, etc. are now assumed not to respond to increase in the premium, then the incremental overinvoicing of exports will create a demand for black exchange that will necessarily involve a diversion from official channels. This can take different forms, among them a diversion from official receipts or a stimulation of overinvoicing of imports (owing to the rise in the black market premium). In none of these cases, however, will the real balance of payments be affected.

Thus, consider the case where the incremental, overinvoiced exports are 'financed' by diversion of official remittances. In this case, the diverted remittances *in any case* wind up eventually with the exchange authorities. [This is *not* to argue, of course, that there would be no economic 'loss' at all. For example, if an *ad valorem, cash* subsidy is given on exports, this diversion leads to an 'unnecessary' subsidy-transfer, which may jeopardize some economic objective, especially if there is a political constraint on the revenues that can be raised: or, for example, if the subsidization takes the form of *exchange retention* by exporters, overinvoicing will bias the allocation of foreign exchange earnings towards the exporters and thereby possibly distort the priorities in allocation that may have been laid down by the authorities.][1]

Alternatively, consider the other case where the illegal overinvoiced amount of foreign exchange is secured, not by diversion from 'normal' inflow of receipts (such as remittances, tourist expenditure), but by the stimulation of faking on the import side; for example, through the overinvoicing of imports which yields the illegal supply of exchange. In this case, part of the official, foreign exchange allocation for imports, in the first round, will be used up in 'financing' the overinvoiced part of

[1] This may well be considered a significant effect, especially by governments which opt for strong ordering of priorities.

imports; it will then leak into the illegal market for 'financing' over-invoicing of exports; it will therewith return to the exchange authorities and then be reallocated to the users of foreign exchange. Once again, therefore, there is no adverse effect on the real balance of payments. [The allocation of available exchange *will*, however, be affected, thereby affecting any priorities that the authorities may have concerning the use of foreign exchange.] Thus, in these and similar cases, the effect on the real balance of payments position will be neutral (although, as already discussed, *other* economic effects cannot be ruled out).

Hence, the overall effect on the real balance of payments position, when the increment in overinvoicing of exports follows upon an expanded subsidy programme, will be:

(a) favourable whenever illegal leakages and/or overall inflow of remittances, transfers and foreign-tourist expenditures are responsive to changes in the black market premium on foreign exchange, and

(b) neutral when these effects are assumed away.

In either case, internal economic effects will undoubtedly follow, which may well be adverse.[1]

(ii) On the other hand, insofar as the increase in overinvoicing merely reflects an illegal inflow of foreign capital, the overinvoicing creates its own, *net* source of foreign exchange supply and no increment in the premium need therefore be expected so that none of the favourable effects considered so far will follow. However, the illegal inflow of foreign capital *itself* will, of course, represent a *net* gain to the real balance of payments position. This phenomenon occurs, for example, when a Malaysian trader, wishing to pull capital out of Malaysia in contravention of the exchange control rules, overinvoices his imports from India, matched by overinvoiced exports from India, and the capital thus flows from Malaysia to India. To consider this net inflow of capital into India, where exports are overinvoiced, a net gain to the real balance of payments position in India would naturally involve an implicit, though normally legitimate, assumption that the capital export would not otherwise have been feasible.

Effect on official balance of payments: While therefore the *real*

---

[1] There *is* one important exception, which follows from the effect of over-invoicing on the lag between exports and export receipts. This is considered later in the text.

balance of payments will generally improve, and at worst may remain unaffected, following upon an increase in the overinvoicing of exports, the *official* balance of payments position will also generally look better – provided the illegal loss of exchange responds to the increment in the black market premium when the overinvoicing of exports increases in response to a subsidy programme (see Appendix). Where the incremental overinvoicing of exports elicits its own net inflow of capital, further, this itself constitutes the full measure of the improvement in the official balance of payments position.

Hence (under the assumptions so far made) overinvoicing of exports, though widely condemned as a malpractice, is from both the real and the official points of view as considered in this paper, advantageous to a country's overall balance of payments position.[1] The conclusion is merely reinforced if we bring in the possibility of unauthorized import expenditure (on smuggled goods and gold) being reduced as the black market premium on exchange rises. Nor does the conclusion alter if we assume that the authorized import quantities rather than authorized import expenditure are fixed (see Appendix).

2 On the other hand, the implication for *individual*, recorded entries in the balance of payments is not necessarily advantageous. The fact remains that the *composition* of the balance of payments will look different from its 'actual' position. The question then is whether this can have any adverse or favourable effects, in turn, aside from the obvious 'muddling up' that it must cause in economic policy based on balance of payments analysis. At least one important implication does, in fact, follow and needs to be spelled out. Aid inflow is frequently conditional upon the trends in the balance of payments. At the Consortium (or Aid-Club) meetings, the recipient country's foreign exchange performance usually becomes the focal point of overall evaluation, the discussion frequently turning on whether the recipient country is likely to be able to earn enough foreign exchange to become

[1] Note that we have so far not made any allowance for the fact that there may be 'secondary' effects on the balance of payments, arising from (alternative) ways in which any 'improvements' in the payments position are 'disposed of'. Also there may be 'indirect' effects on the balance of payments; for example, with exchange authorization for imports taken as fixed and overinvoicing of imports increasing and underinvoicing decreasing, the *quantum* of imports will fall and this itself may have expenditure effects affecting the balance of payments currently; or, *via* shift in pattern of availabilities, there may be effects on the future balance of payments.

eventually 'viable' *i.e.* presumably to meet her debt servicing requirements plus the 'normal' import requirements.[1]

In a country where a good (visible) export performance does make a
considerable difference and serves to impress the possibility of long-
run 'viability' on the aid-givers (as, for example, in the case of India)
inflation of export values is a psychological booster to *easier*, maybe
even bigger, aid-flow. But where the overinvoicing springs from
diverted supplies of exchange from remittances, tourist earnings, etc.,
and the aid-givers are relying upon performance in *these* areas of
invisible earnings for signs of the possibility of long-run viability (as,
for example, in Turkey), the net effect may be unfavourable rather
than favourable.

3 There is yet another significant way in which overinvoicing of
exports can affect the balance of payments behaviour and which must
be discussed here. All countries, which have exchange control on
capital movements, impose a time-limit on the (possible) *lag* between
exports and the surrender of the exchange earned therefrom; for
example, with insignificant exceptions for certain capital goods, the
permitted lag in India is currently six months. *Within* this permissible
limit, exporters have the choice of either keeping their earnings abroad
or remitting them home. The former will take usually the shape of a
trade credit or may even be an explicit, short-term investment. In
either case, the basic choice will be determined by the factors governing
the rates of return on either option. These rates of return are supposed
to be a reflection largely of respective short-term interest rates and it
seems sensible to argue, at the least, that a widening of the difference
between foreign and domestic short-term interest rates, in favour of
the former, will tend to lengthen the average lag between exports and
export receipts.

The overinvoicing of exports will also generally lengthen this lag.
The overinvoiced part of the declared value has to be secured from
illegal sources; this is likely to take time if the exporter wishes to find

---

[1] This appears to be valid certainly, in my experience, for Turkey and India.
Of course, the cynics may argue that economic arguments are only a cloak for
what are really hard, political factors governing the level of aid given, and that a
reduction in aid (for example) will follow from political considerations rather than
because viability seems dubious at higher aid levels. On the other hand, it certainly
makes it *easier* to reduce aid, if convenient economic 'excuses' can be found to do
so, so that there may well be a relationship between economic arguments and the
level of aid inflow.

out the cheapest source for illegal purchase of foreign exchange. More important, the exporter can avoid altogether any interest charge on the cost (equivalent to the premium on illegal foreign exchange) incurred by the purchase of illegal foreign exchange, by putting it off till the very end of the permissible period. Hence, he has a definite incentive, as long as the interest rate is positive, to defer (as long as possible) the return of the overinvoiced part of the export 'earnings'. This will, therefore, increase the *average* lag on total export 'earnings' insofar as such overinvoicing is a new, or an increasing, phenomenon.[1] Insofar as this happens, further, the time-profile of receipts of foreign exchange will undoubtedly be affected – and the result may well be, after taking into account the source from which the illegal exchange comes to 'finance' the overinvoicing, a net deterioration in the *immediate* availability of foreign exchange to the country.

Similar arguments can be applied, *mutatis mutandis*, to the other varieties of faked trade declarations. For those who attach any weight to the *political* aspects of economic policy, it is further pertinent to note the corruption which both follows and later prevents the elimination of the fiscal policies that lead to such faking of trade declarations.

2. OTHER, NON-TRADE FISCAL POLICIES

So far, the analysis has been confined to trade tariffs and subsidies. It applies equally to quantitative restrictions, of course. Insofar as these restrictions, on imports for example, lead to domestic premiums on imported commodities, the preceding analysis becomes relevant: thus, imports may be underinvoiced when the domestic premium on imports exceeds the premium on illegal foreign exchange (and when the import licences are issued in value terms).[2]

---

[1] This is likely to have happened in the case of India during the fiscal year 1964–5 when a very large excess of recorded exports over export earnings developed along with an intensification of the export promotion drive. For details, see my paper on 'Why Export Receipts Lag Behind Exports', *Economic Weekly*, Vol. 27, July 24, 1965. For an illuminating theoretical analysis of the effect of an extended lag, between exports and receipts, on the time profile of the difference between the two, Bent Hansen's *Foreign Trade Credits and Exchange Reserves*, Amsterdam, North-Holland Publishing Co., 1961, remains the standard work so far.

[2] This should not come as a surprise to the readers acquainted with trade theory and the proposition that to each tariff rate, there corresponds an 'equivalent' import quota in the sense that the tariff rate will generate an import level which, if alternatively set as a quota, will generate in turn an identical 'tariff' rate,

What is not so readily obvious is the implication that *domestic* fiscal policy has for the faking of trade declarations and hence of the balance of payments. [Note that this has nothing to do with the well-known equivalence proposition which states that each trade tariff (or subsidy) can be shown to be equivalent to a combination of domestic consumption and production taxes-cum-subsidies.[1] This proposition merely relates to the identity of the differences between foreign and domestic prices that will be the consequence of each policy. This equivalence will *not* extend to the incentives for faking trade declarations; the incentives for faking declarations arise at the point at which taxes are levied, so that a policy of consumption-plus-production tax-cum-subsidies will set up incentive to fake production and consumption data, *not* trade data.]

The relationship between domestic taxes (and subsidies) and the faking of trade declarations is readily illustrated. Take, for example, the accelerated depreciation allowance which is allowed to companies in many countries. This naturally amounts to an interest-free loan by the revenue authorities to the companies. Since this loan is related to the value of the fixed capital and hence, in turn, to the value of machinery and plant principally, it is clear that the availability of an accelerated depreciation allowance provides a counter-incentive to the incentive to underinvoice imports of capital goods when import duties on them exceed the premium on illegal foreign exchange.[2]

Another example, of rather greater interest, is provided by the faking of the prices at which components are sold to or purchased from subsidiary companies in one country by parent companies in *other* countries, the motive being to reduce the overall tax liability by showing profits in the country with the lower tax rate on profits. Frequently this incentive is compounded by other tax provisions.

---

i.e. discrepancy between foreign and domestic prices. The limitations of this proposition have been analysed by me in a paper 'On the Equivalence of Tariffs and Quotas', *Trade, Growth and the Balance of Payments* (Chicago, Rand-McNally and Co., 1965).

[1] For a systematic account of these equivalence propositions, refer to R. A. Mundell, 'The Pure Theory of International Trade', *American Economic Review*, Vol. 50 (March 1960).

[2] Similar arguments apply, for example, to the Wealth Tax levied on companies in India. Around July 1965, the average tariff level was around 50% and the discount on the Indian rupee abroad around 35%, so that there was undoubtedly an incentive to underinvoice *some* imports. Hence, the Wealth Tax may well have operated as a counter-incentive, working against underinvoiced imports.

Thus, for example, the oil companies, which are vertically integrated and have oilfields in the Middle East from which crude is 'sold' to virtually themselves for refining elsewhere, deliberately price the crude at artificially high rates so as to take the bulk of their profits in the Middle East and sometimes even to render their later operations 'unprofitable' in accounting terms. This is because, in view of United States and Middle East tax provisions, the profits (net of *all* tax liability) are maximized by such arbitrary and feasible splitting up of profits.[1]

This kind of 'faked' pricing of components or materials, when sold to or purchased from subsidiary companies, is a widespread phenomenon in experience with private foreign investment in the developing countries. But it is *not* all to be put down to differential profit provisions between countries.

For example, the practice of charging exaggerated prices for components sold to subsidiaries or paying unduly low prices for components purchased from subsidiaries may merely reflect an easy method of remitting capital out of the country of investment when there is either a control on straightforward profit repatriation or a stigma attached to firms repatriating 'unduly large' amounts of profits, which may seriously impede the firm's long-run prospects in a controlled economy. Simultaneously, this practice reduces the profits

---

[1] 'But there is another fact of decisive importance. The United States companies, which first adopted the device of posted prices and which first accepted the 50/50 profit-sharing arrangements, stood to gain under the United States tax laws by attributing large profits to crude oil production, in spite of the fact that they handed half of this profit over to the producing countries. Under United States law United States companies can deduct from their taxable income a depletion allowance equal to $27\frac{1}{2}\%$ of the gross income arising in crude oil production. The higher the posted price, the higher is the gross income attributed to crude and the higher the depletion allowance. Furthermore, under United States law the profits paid to the producing countries in the form of an income tax are considered a foreign tax and are treated as a credit against any US tax liability that remains. Thus the combination of "50/50", the depletion allowance, and a high posted price for crude oil virtually eliminates the tax liability of the American companies to the United States and puts their shareholder (the majors) in a much better position with respect to taxes than they would have been had their profits been shown at some subsequent stage of production and hence been subject to the United States corporate income tax of 52%.' E. Penrose, 'Middle East Oil: The International Distribution of Profits and Income Taxes', *Economica*, Vol. 27, August 1960. Also Mrs Penrose's companion paper, 'Profit Sharing Between Producing Countries and Oil Companies in the Middle East', *Economic Journal*, Vol. 69, June 1959.

shown to be made by the subsidiary firms; this dampens the enthusiasm of the powerful critics of private foreign investment who like to point to high profit rates in foreign enterprises to question, with varying degrees of sophistication, the advisability of encouraging the inflow of private foreign capital. This practice has been suspected strongly to be the case with the foreign investments in drugs and pharmaceuticals in India in the 1950–65 period – and the practice certainly has not been confined to this industrial sector.[1] In the case of drugs and pharmaceuticals, the practice appears to have been made readily possible because of the frequent unavailability, to Customs authorities, of the prices at which intermediates and components should really be invoiced; indeed, in many cases, there is no 'outside' sale of such intermediates by the firms at all so that no such information is available in any case! Unless the Customs authorities have access to technical knowledge so as to be able to link specific final products with specific intermediates and also the resources to investigate the prices of the former in foreign markets, thereby getting some kind of approximation to the 'legitimate' prices of the latter (making again due allowances for other inputs, their foreign costs, etc.), it will be impossible for them to eliminate such faking practices; and such indeed appears to have been the case in the drugs and pharmaceuticals sector.

Yet another reason for such faking by foreign investors, which is also unrelated to fiscal policy as such, seems to consist in the opportunity for higher profits that such faking provides under certain circumstances in economies with a *combined* battery of strict import, investment and price controls. In such economies, of which India has been an apt example, it is common for the scale of output to be fixed, with the help of investment and production controls, at levels where the market demand would raise the unit price significantly above that fixed by price control. There is further no question of competition with imports of similar or identical items and prices are usually controlled by fixing them at a certain percentage over cost or as a certain percentage rate of return on employed capital. In this situation, it pays the foreign firm which is operating a subsidiary, as also one

[1] This is consistent with the fact that even the profits *shown*, in this industry, have been strikingly high. *Cf.* the analysis in 'Post-War Foreign Investment in India', *Economic Bulletin for Asia and the Far East*, Vol. 13, June 1962. The 'high price' at which crude oil has been imported into India has also been an object of much critical analysis and comment in Indian discussions; *cf. Report of the Oil Price Enquiry Committee*, Government of India (Ministry of Steel, Mines and Fuel), July 1961, especially pp. 21–33.

which is selling intermediates to a local firm, to raise its price of intermediates up to the point at which the controlled price of the manufactured product is raised, in view of 'higher costs', to a level which nearly approximates the price that demand implies. This undoubtedly explains the phenomenon, for example, of Fiat components being imported into India, at one time, at a price *higher* than the c.i.f. price of a Fiat were it to be imported!

These and other similar reasons for international companies inflating or deflating the prices of traded items are probably more important and frequent than the faking that is motivated by fiscal policies whose effects have been analysed in the present paper.

APPENDIX

The arguments (in the text) concerning the balance of payments implications of the overinvoicing of exports can be readily supported by extremely elementary mathematical analysis.

Take the following system.

$$S = S_1 + S_2 + S_3 + S_4 + S_5 \tag{1}$$

where S is the total supply of illegal foreign exchange, S_1 the supply from overinvoicing of imports, S_2 the supply from underinvoicing of exports, S_3 the supply from diverted remittances, S_4 the supply from diverted expenditure of foreign tourists and S_5 the supply from flight of foreign capital (coming into this country *via* overinvoiced exports from this country to the foreign countries from where capital is illegally being taken out and *via* matching overinvoicing of corresponding imports in these foreign countries).

$$S_1 = S_1(p) \qquad (2) \qquad\qquad (S_1' > 0)$$

such that S_1 is an increasing function of the premium (p) on foreign exchange. Similarly,

$$S_2 = S_2(p) \qquad (3) \qquad\qquad (S_2' > 0)$$
$$S_3 = S_3(p) \qquad (4) \qquad\qquad (S_3' > 0)$$
$$S_4 = S_4(p) \qquad (5) \qquad\qquad (S_4' > 0)$$

Moreover,

$$S_3 + S_3^0 = \bar{S}_3 \tag{6}$$

Where $\bar{S}_3$ is the *given*, total supply of remittances from abroad to this country, with $S_3{}^0$ the *official* inflow and S_3 the *illegal* inflow; and similarly

$$S_4 + S_4{}^0 = \bar{S}_4 \qquad (7)$$

where $\bar{S}_4$ is the fixed, *total* foreign-tourist expenditure in this country, of which $S_4{}^0$ is the legal, *official* receipts.

Further,

$$D = D_1 + D_2 + D_3 + D_4 + D_5 \qquad (8)$$

where D is the total demand for illegal foreign exchange, D_1 the demand from underinvoicing of imports, D_2 the demand from illegal tourist expenditure in foreign countries, D_3 the demand from illegal capital transfers to foreign countries, and finally D_4 and D_5 are the demands from overinvoicing of exports where D_5 is that part which is related to the illegal transfer of capital from abroad.

$$
\begin{array}{lll}
D_1 = D_1(P) & \qquad (9) & \qquad (D_1' < 0) \\
D_2 = D_2(P) & \qquad (10) & \qquad (D_2' < 0) \\
D_3 = D_3(P) & \qquad (11) & \qquad (D_3' < 0) \\
D_4 = D_4(P, r) & \qquad (12) &
\end{array}
$$

(where $\dfrac{\partial D_4}{\partial p} < 0$ and $\dfrac{\partial D_4}{\partial r} > 0$ and r is the subsidy rate on the sub-

sidized exports), and

$$D_5 = S_5 \qquad (13)$$

such that it is assumed that the illegal transfer of capital from abroad to this country takes the form of, and elicits an *equal* amount of over-invoicing of exports (as in the example of overinvoiced Indian exports to East Africa and Malaysia in the text).

Finally,

$$S = D \qquad (14)$$

Altogether, therefore, the system has 14 equations, and provided r and S_5 are specified, 14 unknowns: S, D, D_1, D_2, D_3, D_4, D_5, S_1, S_2, S_3, S_4, $S_3{}^0$, $S_4{}^0$ and p. By differentiating the system with respect to r, therefore, the effect of the resulting increase in overinvoicing of exports can be readily investigated.

First, examine the impact on the *official* balance of payments.

$$d \left\{ \frac{S_3{}^0 + S_4{}^0 + D_4 + D_5 - S_2}{dr} \right\}$$

because $S_3{}^0$ represents the official remittances, $S_4{}^0$ the official receipts from foreign tourist expenditure, D_4 and D_5 represent the over-invoiced part of export receipts and S_2 represents the underinvoiced part of (other) export receipts. It is assumed that the total allocation for *imports* remains unchanged, regardless of faking.

$$\frac{dS}{dr} = \frac{dS_1}{dr} + \frac{dS_2}{dr} + \frac{dS_3}{dr} + \frac{dS_4}{dr}$$

$$= (S_1{}' + S_2{}' + S_3{}' + S_4{}') \cdot \frac{dP}{dr} \tag{15}$$

and

$$\frac{dD}{dr} = \frac{dD_1}{dr} + \frac{dD_2}{dr} + \frac{dD_3}{dr} + \frac{dD_4}{dr}$$

$$= (D_1{}' + D_2{}' + D_3{}' + D_{4P}) \frac{dP}{dr} + D_{4r}{}' \tag{16}$$

where

$$D_{4P}{}' = \frac{\partial D_4}{\partial P} \text{ and } D_{4r}{}' = \frac{\partial D_4}{\partial r} \tag{16}$$

$\therefore$ Since $\dfrac{dS}{dr} = \dfrac{dD}{dr}$ from (14), we have:

$$\frac{dP}{dr} = \frac{D_{4r}{}'}{S_1{}' + S_2{}' + S_3{}' + S_4{}' - (D_1{}' + D_2{}' + D_3{}' + D_{4P}{}')} \tag{17}$$

$$\therefore \qquad \frac{d(S_3{}^0 + S_4{}^0 + D_4 + D_5 - S_2)}{dr}$$

$$= D_{4r}{}' \frac{S_1{}' - (D_1{}' + D_2{}' + D_3{}')}{S_1{}' + S_2{}' + S_3{}' + S_4{}' - (D_1{}' + D_2{}' + D_3{}' + D_{4P}{}')} > 0 \tag{18}$$

The *official* balance of payments will thus necessarily improve, under the assumption made.

The impact on the *real* balance of payments may, however, be defined as the impact on the net accrual of all foreign exchange (legal and illegal) to the country after adjusting for leakages into unauthorized and wasteful uses such as illegal transfers of capital and tourist expenditure abroad. In this case, we wish to find out:

$$\frac{d(\bar{S}_3 + \bar{S}_4 + S_5 - D_2 - D_3)}{dr}$$

This reduces to: $\dfrac{d(-D_2 - D_3)}{dr} =$

$$= \frac{(-D_2' - D_3')D_{4r}'}{S_1' + S_2' + S_3' + S_4' - (D_1' + D_2' + D_3' + D_{4P}')} > 0 \tag{19}$$

Thus the *real* balance of payments will necessarily improve, under the assumptions made. Note further that it will improve more, the larger the size of the reduction in leakage of foreign exchange into illegal capital transfers and unauthorized expenditure abroad (*i.e.* of D_2' and D_3'). Therefore both the official and the 'real' balance of payments situations will improve following upon an increase in the export subsidy programme and hence in export overinvoicing.

These conclusions are further *strengthened* if we assume the *total* inflow of remittances ($\bar{S}_3$) and tourist expenditure ($\bar{S}_4$) to be not fixed but themselves positively responsive to higher return, *i.e.* $\dfrac{d\bar{S}_3}{dP} > 0$ and $\dfrac{d\bar{S}_4}{dP} > 0$. So will any (autonomous) change S_5 and D_5 only improve (and by the same amount) the official and 'real' balance of payments positions.[1]

A change in the assumption of *fixed*, authorized import expenditure will also not impair the (directional) conclusions reached if we assume, for example, that the authorized import *quantities* are fixed instead. In this case, the authorized, official allocations for imports will vary with the overinvoicing and underinvoicing of imports. But neither the official[2] nor the real balance of payments[3] will worsen, as a result of this.

Note finally that *individual* balance of payments entries, such as official remittances, will undoubtedly be affected and may, in turn, have economic implications insofar as they are treated by influential

---

[1] This is obvious because S^5 and D^5 represent respectively the flight of capital from foreign countries and the overinvoicing of exports in this country (matched by overinvoicing of corresponding imports in these foreign countries) which permits this flight and canalizes it to itself. Since S_5 and D_5 are identically equal, there will be no effect on the premium or any other magnitude.

[2] The change in the official balance of payments will now be:

$$D_{4r}' \frac{-(D_2' + D_3')}{S_1' + S_2' + S_3' + S_4' - (D_1' + D_2' + D_3' + D_{4P}')} \tag{20}$$

which is still greater than zero.

[3] This change in the real balance of payments will remain as in equation (19).

commentators, such as aid-giving agencies, as significant indicators of balance of payments health.[1]

[1] The analysis above has ignored the complications arising from swings in the trade credits as overinvoicing of exports increases. Yet other qualifications have been noted in footnote 1, p. 280. It would be useful also to add that, as Peter Oppenheimer has pointed out to me, the definition of the 'real' balance of payments adopted in this paper is a 'resource-allocational' one, appropriate to a planning authority, examining the availability of foreign exchange for its authorized uses, and ought not to be confused with the traditional formulations of balance of payments 'imbalance' or 'disequilibrium'.

TABLE 1 *1960 Trade between France and Turkey (000$)*

SITC Code No.	Commodities	France's exports	Turkey's imports	Discrepancy
313	Petroleum products	9,059	617	− 8,442
6	Main manufactured goods	3,212	3,196	− 16
66	Non-metallic mineral manufactures	343	266	− 77
68	Non-ferrous metals	4,412	3,464	− 948
69	Metal manufactures	3,915	544	3,371
7	Machinery and transport equipment	5,270	3,820	− 1,450
8	Miscellaneous manufactured goods	1,246	595	− 651
	Others	4,197	3,834	− 363
	TOTAL	31,654	16,336	% 15,318

TABLE 2 *1960 Trade between Italy and Turkey (000$)*

SITC Code No.	Commodities	Italy's exports	Turkey's imports	Discrepancy
313	Petroleum products	13,093	713	− 12,380
6	Main manufactured goods	3,576	3,559	− 17
65	Files, textiles, etc.	2,737	1,590	− 1,147
66	Non-metallic minerals manufactures	265	173	− 92
68	Non-ferrous metals	4,700	1,317	− 3,383
69	Metal manufactures	3,151	2,258	− 893
7	Machinery and transport equipment	18,913	15,213	− 3,700
8	Miscellaneous manufactured goods	1,591	1,035	− 556
	Others	4,391	4,176	− 215
	TOTAL	52,417	30,034	− 22,382

TABLE 3 *1960 Trade between Germany and Turkey (000$)*

SITC Code No.	Commodities	Germany's exports	Turkey's imports	Dis-crepancy
6	Main manufactured goods	4,094	4,023	— 71
66	Non-metallic minerals manufactures	3,111	1,259	— 1,852
68	Non-ferrous metals	20,623	21,357	+ 734
69	Metal manufactures	7,620	5,260	— 2,360
7	Machinery and transport equipment	62,884	51,097	— 11,787
8	Miscellaneous manufactured goods	6,916	4,043	— 2,873
	Others	9,984	10,987	+ 1,003
	TOTAL	115,232	98,026	— 17,206

TABLE 4 *1960 Trade beween USA and Turkey (000$)*

SITC Code No.	Commodities	USA's exports	Turkey's imports	Dis-crepancy
313	Petroleum products	7,130	24,660	+ 17,530
412	Vegetable oils	5,673	14,828	+ 9,155
5	Chemical products	4,414	3,894	— 530
6	Main manufactured goods	5,258	4,529	— 729
66	Non-metallic minerals manufactures	350	563	+ 213
68	Non-ferrous metals	4,599	4,108	— 491
69	Metal manufactures	1,084	922	— 162
7	Machinery and transport equipment	62,032	53,942	— 8,090
8	Miscellaneous manufactured goods	2,422	1,711	— 711
	Others	31,808	11,310	— 20,498
	TOTAL	124,785	120,467	4,318

TABLE 5 *1960 Trade between Netherlands and Turkey (000$)*

SITC Code No.	Commodities	Netherland's exports	Turkey's imports	Dis-crepancy
6	Main manufactured goods	4,298	4,062	— 236
7	Machinery and transport equipment	5,400	3,561	— 1,839
8	Miscellaneous manufactured goods	498	382	— 116
	Others	3,402	4,094	+ 692
	TOTAL	13,598	12,099	— 1,499

TABLE 6 *1961 Trade between Germany and Turkey* (000$)

SITC Code No.	Commodities	Germany's exports	Turkey's imports	Discrepancy
6	Main manufactured goods	3,726	3,170	− 16
66+	Non-metallic mineral manufactures +			
66	Iron and Steel	14,700	16,620	+ 1,920
68	Non-ferrous metals	949	1,211	+ 262
69	Metal manufactures	4,795	2,848	− 1,947
7	Machinery and transport equipment	52,629	46,158	− 6,471
8	Miscellaneous manufactured goods	4,410	3,377	− 1,033
	Others	12,079	11,152	− 927
	TOTAL	93,288	85,076	− 8,212

TABLE 7 *1961 Trade between Italy and Turkey* (000$)

SITC Code No.	Commodities	Italy's exports	Turkey's imports	Discrepancy
352	Petroleum products	15,526	592	− 14,934
6	Main manufactured goods	4,368	4,503	+ 135
65	Files, textiles, etc.	1,749	1,461	− 288
66	Non-metallic mineral manufactures	373	363	− 10
67	Iron and Steel	2,759	2,169	− 410
69	Metal manufactures	1,450	1,188	− 262
7	Machinery and transport equipment	21,801	24,465	+ 2,664
8	Miscellaneous manufactured goods	1,719	1,660	− 59
	Others	6,468	6,473	+ 5
	TOTAL	56,033	42,874	− 13,179

TABLE 8 *1961 Trade between USA and Turkey* (000$)

SITC Code No.	Commodities	USA's exports	Turkey's imports	Discrepancy
352	Petroleum products	7,167	21,722	+ 14,555
5	Chemical products	7,637	6,526	− 1,111
6	Main manufactured goods	12,850	12,161	− 689
7	Machinery and transport equipment	39,380	30,513	− 8,867
8	Miscellaneous manufactured goods	2,721	1,548	− 1,173
	Others	71,893	67,609	− 4,374
	TOTAL	141,738	140,079	− 1,695

TABLE 9 *1961 Trade between France and Turkey (000$)*

SITC Code No.	Commodities	France's exports	Turkey's imports	Discrepancy
332	Petroleum products	8,601	127	− 8,474
6	Main manufactured goods	6,355	6,050	− 305
7	Machinery and transport equipment	9,063	6,874	− 2,189
	Others	5,409	4,648	− 761
	TOTAL	29,428	17,699	−11,729

TABLE 10 *Turkey's Imports of Petroleum Products, 1960 (000$)*

Exporting Country	Exporting Country's Statistics	Turkey's Statistics	Discrepancy
France	9,059	617	− 8,442
Italy	13,093	713	− 12,380
United Kingdom	2,166	8,819	+ 6,653
United States	7,130	24,660	+ 17,530
TOTAL	31,448	34,809	+ 3,361

TABLE 11 *Turkey's Imports of Petroleum Products, 1961 (00$) (SITC 332)*

Exporting Country	Exporting Country's Statistics	Turkey's Statistics	Discrepancy
France	8,601	127	− 8,474
Italy	15,526	592	− 14,934
United Kingdom	1,339	10,030	+ 8,691
United States	7,167	21,722	+ 14,555
TOTAL	32,633	32,471	− 162

Note: Turkish Tariffs During 1961

There was a stamp duty (*i.e.* a *de facto* tariff) of 5 per cent on all visible imports. Moreover, the tariff rates on the items covered in our analysis ranged up to 30–40 per cent, in some cases going even higher. The only exceptions among the items which appear to have been understated in value were nickel, aluminium and zinc, which carried a duty of only 5 per cent, and copper for which the duty was 10 per cent.

Among transport equipment and different kinds of machinery, the following may be taken as illustrative:

20 per cent on locomotives, trains, buses and wagons,
25 per cent on tractors,
40 per cent on automobiles, buses and pick-ups,
50 per cent on ships and other craft,
20–25 per cent on generators, motors and transformers,
20–30 per cent on other machinery (including agricultural).

Some 'protective' duties were quite high and obviously related to categories of imports for which underinvoicing of imports seemed to be important. Examples are:

60 per cent on knives,
70 per cent on spoons and forks,
100 per cent on lamps,
50 per cent on bells,
50 per cent on mirrors,
100 per cent on metal necklaces, etc.,
100 per cent on decorative sculpture (figurines, etc.).

There is a minor complication in interpreting these duties. It was possible, in several cases, to get exemption from these duties and pay *lower* duties under certain circumstances. I have found it difficult to judge how important this exemption was, but my impression is that its effect was not significant from the viewpoint of the present analysis.

11 Domestic Distortions, Tariffs and the Theory of Optimum Subsidy[1]

There is confusion of varying degrees in the current literature on trade theory concerning the desirable form of intervention in foreign trade when the economy is characterized by domestic distortions (divergences of the commodity price ratios from the corresponding marginal rates of transformation). For instance, the age-old debate over whether tariffs or subsidies should be used to protect an infant industry is still carried on in terms of the respective political and psychological merits of the two forms of protection while their relative economic advantages are assumed not to point in the direction of a definite choice.[2]

Three questions about the use of tariffs when domestic distortions exist need to be distinguished here. (1) Is a tariff necessarily superior to free trade (that is, can a tariff rate always be found that yields a welfare position not inferior to that produced by free trade)? (2) Is a tariff policy necessarily superior to any other form of *trade* policy? (3) If the choice can be made from the entire range of policy instruments, which is the optimal economic policy?

In Section 1 we state the general theory that provides the answers to these three questions. In the light of this theory, we examine the propositions advanced in the two central contributions to trade theory in this field: Haberler's justly celebrated 1950 *Economic Journal* paper [5] and Hagen's recent analysis [6] of wage differentials. Sections

[1] An early draft of this paper was read to seminars at Massachusetts Institute of Technology, the University of Chicago, and Stanford University. C. P. Kindleberger and H. G. Johnson have made useful suggestions.

[2] For instance, C. P. Kindleberger [8], as does also G. Haberler [4], states the economic argument in favour of subsidies and tariffs without stating definitely that one is invariably superior to the other from the economic viewpoint.

2 and 3 examine these two analyses. Section 4 concludes with some observations concerning the relative advantages of tariffs and subsidies from the practical viewpoint.

1. GENERAL THEORY

The three questions posed here can be effectively answered by analysing the characteristics of an optimum solution. Thus, for instance, the optimum tariff argument can be stated elegantly in terms of these characteristics. The achievement of an optimum solution is characterized by the equality of the foreign rate of transformation (FRT), the domestic rate of transformation in production (DRT), and the domestic rate of substitution in consumption (DRS). If the country has monopoly power in trade, a competitive free trade solution will be characterized by DRS = DRT ≠ FRT. By introducing a suitable tariff, a country can achieve DRS = DRT = FRT. A subsidy (tax) on the domestic production of importables (exportables) could equalize DRT and FRT but would destroy the equality of DRS with DRT. Hence it is clear that a tax-cum-subsidy on domestic production is necessarily inferior to an optimum tariff. Moreover it may be impossible in any given empirical situation to devise a tax-cum-subsidy that would yield a solution superior to that arrived at under free trade.

By analogy we can argue that, in the case of domestic distortions, DRS = FRT ≠ DRT under free trade. A suitable tariff can equalize FRT and DRT but would destroy the equality between DRS and FRT. Hence it is clear that no tariff may exist that would yield a solution superior to that under free trade. A suitable tax-cum-subsidy on domestic production, however, would enable the policy-maker to secure DRS = FRT = DRT and hence is necessarily the optimum solution. Hence a tariff policy is also necessarily inferior to an optimum tax-cum-subsidy policy. And the same argument must hold true of trade subsidies as well since they also, like tariffs, are directed at *foreign* trade whereas the problem to be tackled is one of *domestic* distortion.

Three propositions, therefore, follow in the case of domestic distortions. (a) A tariff is not necessarily superior to free trade. (b) A tariff is not necessarily superior to an export (or import) subsidy. (c) A policy permitting the attainment of maximum welfare involves a tax-cum-subsidy on domestic production. Just as there exists an optimum tariff policy for a divergence between foreign prices and

FRT, so there exists an *optimum subsidy* (or an equivalent tax-cum-subsidy) policy for a divergence between domestic prices and DRT.

2. HABERLER ON EXTERNAL ECONOMIES

A divergence between the domestic commodity price ratios and the marginal rates of transformation between commodities may arise from what are usually described as 'external economies'. These may take various forms.[1] It is most fashionable at the moment to discuss the external economies arising from the interdependence of investment decisions.[2]

Haberler analyses this problem in terms of the standard two-good, two-factor model of trade theory, using geometrical methods. Haberler is aware that a tariff is not necessarily superior to free trade. However, he is in error concerning the relative advantages of tariffs and trade subsidies. Further, he does not discuss the optimum economic policy under the circumstances.

Haberler distinguishes between two situations according to whether the domestic production of importables rises or falls (what he calls the direction of 'specialization'). We shall analyse each case separately.

Case 1 In the former case, illustrated here in Figure 11.1a, *AB* is the production possibility curve. The discrepancy between the domestic price ratio and the domestic rate of transformation (DRT) leads to self-sufficiency equilibrium at *S*. Free trade, at the *given* international price *PF*, leads to production at *P*, consumption at *F*, export of agricultural goods, and a deterioration in welfare.[3]

The following comments are warranted. First, although Haberler does not state this explicitly, it can be shown that prohibitive protection may make the country worse off (Figure 11.1b). Second, it follows from Section 1 that *no* tariff may be superior to free trade (this is implicit, we think, in Haberler's statements elsewhere in his paper).

---

[1] According to Haberler [5, p. 236], 'there may be a deviation between social and private cost due to external economies or diseconomies, *i.e.* due to certain cost-raising or cost-reduction factors which would come into play if one industry expanded and the other contracted – factors which for some reason or other are not, or not sufficiently, allowed for in private cost calculations'.

[2] This has been analysed in the context of international trade by J. Bhagwati [1].

[3] Haberler wrongly seems to imply that the country must export agricultural goods in this case. There is no reason, *once there is a domestic distortion*, why a country should necessarily export the commodity that is cheaper than abroad in the absence of trade.

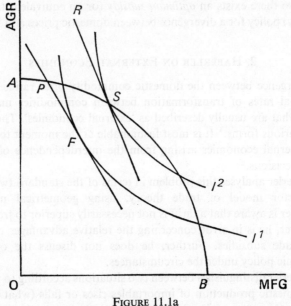

FIGURE 11.1a

Finally, the optimum result could be achieved by a policy of tax-cum-subsidy on domestic production. Such a policy is illustrated in Figure 1c where the tax-cum-subsidy eliminates the divergence between commodity prices and DRT and brings production to P' and consumption to F'.

Case 2 Haberler distinguishes the other case by arguing that the self-sufficiency price ratio RS may be less steep than the *given* foreign price ratio PF. Here the production point is shifted to the right by free trade.[1] In this case, Haberler argues that 'the country would specialize in the "right" direction but not sufficiently. *It would after trade be better off than before, but it would not reach the optimum point. . . . In that case an export or import subsidy (rather than a tariff) would be indicated.*'[2]

[1] This, of course, is erroneous, as noted in n. 3, p. 298. Haberler implies that under free trade manufactures will now become the exported good. Haberler also describes this case as characterized by specialization in the 'right' direction. He is right if, by this, he means that the movement of the production point to the right of S, caused by free trade, will necessarily improve welfare. He is wrong, however, if he means that the commodity exported will be that which would have been exported if the divergence did not exist.

[2] Haberler [5, p. 237]. Our italics.

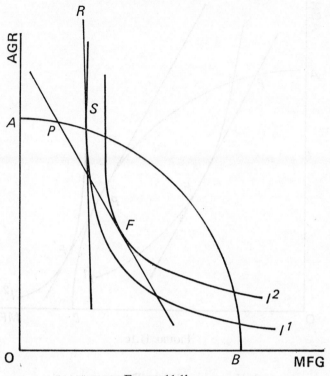

FIGURE 11.1b

While Haberler is right in arguing that a movement to the right of S, when free trade is introduced, will necessarily be beneficial, his conclusion that an export (or import) subsidy is indicated and would be preferable to a tariff is erroneous in every rigorous sense in which it may be understood. First, it cannot be argued that the optimal solution when the policy used is an export (or import) subsidy will be necessarily superior to that when the policy used is a tariff. As argued in Section 1, both policies are handicapped as they seek to affect *foreign* trade whereas the distortion is *domestic*; there is no reason why one should necessarily be better than the other. Second, nor can one maintain that an export (or import) subsidy will necessarily exist that will be superior to free trade, just as one cannot maintain that a tariff necessarily will be available that is superior to free trade. Third, the optimum solution again is to impose a tax-cum-subsidy on domestic production.

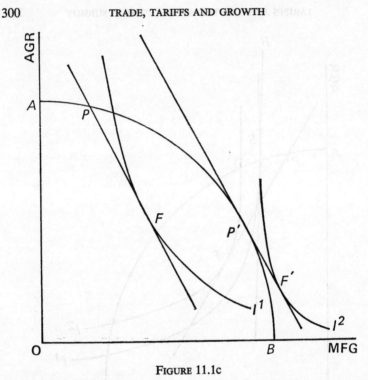

FIGURE 11.1c

3. HAGEN ON WAGE DIFFERENTIALS

A divergence between DRT and the domestic price ratio, arising from factor-market imperfections in the form of intersectoral wage differentials, has been discussed in relation to trade policy by Hagen. Before we proceed to Hagen's analysis, certain observations concerning the circumstances in which differential remuneration causes a distortion are in order.

The observed wage differentials between the urban and rural sector may *not* represent a genuine distortion. For instance, they may reflect (1) a utility preference between occupations on the part of the wage-earners, or (2) a rent (on scarce skills), or (3) a return on investment in human capital (by training), or (4) a return on investment in the cost of movement (from the rural to the urban sector). There *would* be a distortion, however, where the differential is attributable to (5) trade-union intervention, or (6) prestige-cum-humanitarian grounds ('I must pay my man a decent wage') that fix wages at varying levels in different sectors. Two other types of explanations may also be discussed: (7) Hagen argues that the differential occurs in manufacture because this is the advancing sector and growing activities inevitably have to pay higher wages to draw labour away from other industries. While this 'dynamic' argument appears to provide support for the distortionary character of the differential, there are difficulties with it. For instance, the fact that a differential has to be maintained to draw labour away may very well be due to the cost of movement.[1] (8) A more substantive argument is that the rural sector affords employment to non-adult members of the family whereas, in the urban sector, the adult alone gets employment (owing to institutional reasons such as factory acts). Hence, to migrate, an adult would need to be compensated for the loss of employment by the non-adult members of his family.[2] If this is the case, there is certainly a market imperfection (assuming that individual preferences rather than collective preferences, expressed in legislation, are relevant) and hence distortion.[3]

In the following analysis, we shall assume that the wage differential represents a genuine distortion while remaining sceptical about the degree to which such distortions obtain in the actual world.[4] We will also adopt Hagen's analytical framework of a two-commodity, two-factor model and a *constant* wage differential. The assumption of constancy of the wage differential raises some difficulties, probably with reasons (3) and (6) but certainly with reason (7), on which Hagen mainly relies. As will be seen presently, Hagen's analysis involves the *contraction* of manufactures after the introduction of trade; if the wage differential is due to the fact that manufactures are expanding and drawing labour away, it should surely reverse itself during the transition from autarchy to free trade. The difficulty is that Hagen, in relying upon reason (7) while using traditional trade analysis, is

[1] Other difficulties also arise when the argument is used in conjunction with a static analysis. These will be discussed later.

[2] This hypothesis was suggested by D. Mazumdar.

[3] This 'distortion', unlike the others, involves a contraction of the labour force as labour moves from one sector to another. Hence, the following analysis does not apply and a fresh solution, incorporating a changing labour supply, is called for. Note here also that the wage differential variety of distortion is quite distinct from the distortion caused when, although the wage is identical between sectors, it differs from the 'shadow' optimal wage. This distortion has been blurred by recent analysts, especially W. A. Lewis [9] and H. Myint [10]. Also see Bhagwati [1].

[4] A. Kafka [7].

illegitimately superimposing a dynamic argument upon a comparative statics framework. To analyse the distortion arising from reason (8) one needs an explicitly dynamic analysis. Hence, the following analysis applies, strictly speaking, only to distortions produced by reasons (5) and (6).

Hagen concludes that a tariff is superior to free trade when the *importable manufacturing* activity has to pay the higher wage.

As a result of the wage disparity, manufacturing industry will be undersold by imports when the foreign exchanges are in equilibrium. Protection which permits such industry to exist will increase real income in the economy. However, a subsidy per unit of labour equal to the wage differential will increase real income further, and if combined with free trade will permit attaining an *optimum optimorum*.[1]

Hagen works successively with two models that differ only in the assumption concerning the number of factors of production. Since the first model has only one factor and is only a special case of the second, two-factor model, we shall concentrate here on the latter. It is assumed that all the standard Paretian conditions obtain except for the wage differential. We begin with Hagen's analysis and then comment on it.

In Figure 11.2a AQB is the production possibility curve on the assumption of a wage uniform between the two sectors. APB is the production possibility curve, assuming the given wage differential.[2]

---

[1] [6, p. 498]. Hagen himself does not state explicitly that he is confining the analysis to the case where the differential operates against the importable activity. If the differential were to work in the contrary direction, the results would naturally have to be modified radically.

[2] The reader can satisfy himself as to the 'shrinking in' of the production possibility curve by manipulating the Edgeworth box diagram. The careful reader of Hagen's paper will note that Hagen draws the 'shrunk-in' production possibility curve so that it is convex (in the mathematical sense). This, however, is a property that does not necessarily follow from the assumptions made, and it is possible to produce counter-examples of concavity, although we have not been able to produce a general mathematical proof. (When this paper was read at Stanford, Paul David drew attention to A. Fishlow and P. David [3] for a proof of this proposition. These writers have also anticipated our criticism concerning Hagen's confusion of statics and dynamics.) We shall use the convex curve, however, as it enables us to state our propositions in terms of equalities and without bothering about second-order conditions; the substance of the propositions *that interest us here* is unaffected by this complication. The divergence between the commodity price ratio and the domestic rate of transformation, which also results from the wage differential, needs a rigorous proof, which can be found by the reader in Hagen [6, pp. 507–8].

The wage differential against manufactures, aside from reducing the production feasibilities, will make the commodity price ratio, at any production point on *APB*, steeper than the rate of transformation along *APB* so that the price ratio understates the profitability of transforming agriculture into manufactures. *PT* being the foreign price ratio, the economy produces at *P* and consumes at *F* under free trade.

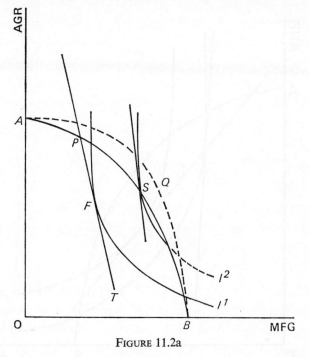

FIGURE 11.2a

Under self-sufficiency, however, the relative price of manufactures being higher, the economy would produce and consume at *S* and be better off. From this, Hagen [6, p. 510] concludes: 'Protection of manufacturing from foreign trade will increase real income.'

However, the conclusion must be rectified. First, as illustrated in Figure 2b, where the contrary possibility is shown, prohibitive protection is not necessarily superior to free trade. Second, it may further be impossible, as argued in Section 1, to find any level of tariff (or trade subsidy) that is superior to free trade. Third, a tax-cum-subsidy on the domestic production of the commodities, which eliminates the divergence between the price ratio and DRT (along

APB) would necessarily yield a better solution than protection. In Figure 11.2c, *F'* represents the consumption and *P'* the production reached by the pursuit of such a tax-cum-subsidy policy.[1] Finally, a policy of tax-cum-subsidy on labour use would achieve equilibrium production at *P"* and consumption at *F"* in Figure 11.2c and produce the 'first-best' result, as recognized by Hagen.

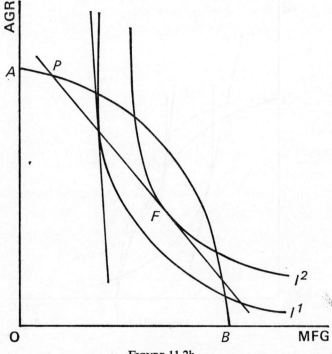

FIGURE 11.2b

Note that, in contrast to the case of external economies, the optimum tax-cum-subsidy on domestic production, while superior to protection or trade subsidy, does not yield the *optimum optimorum* in the wage-differential case. The reason is straightforward. The wage differential

[1] In relation to this point, it is also worth noting that the standard procedure adopted by several tariff commissions, of choosing a tariff rate that just offsets the differential between the average domestic cost at some *arbitrary*, given production of the existing units and the landed (c.i.f.) cost, is not necessarily correct. There is no reason why the tariff rate which just offsets this differential is necessarily the tariff rate which is optimum from the viewpoint of economic policy.

causes *not merely* a domestic distortion but *also* a restriction of the production possibility curve. A tax-cum-subsidy on domestic production measure will, therefore, merely eliminate the domestic distortion but not restore the economy to the Paretian production possibility curve (AQB). It will thus achieve the equality of FRT and DRS with DRT along *the restricted production possibility curve (APB)* and hence

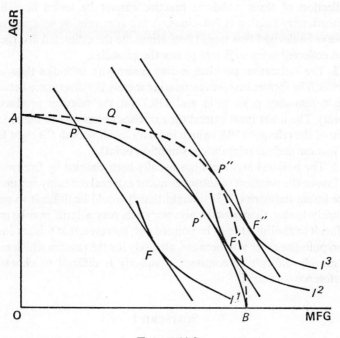

FIGURE 11.2c

constitute the optimal solution when the wage differential cannot be directly eliminated. Where, however, a direct attack on the wage differential is permitted, the fully optimal, 'first-best' solution can be achieved by a policy of tax-cum-subsidy on factor use.

4. CONCLUSION

We have argued here that an optimum subsidy (or a tax-cum-subsidy equivalent) is necessarily superior to any tariff when the distortion is domestic. It may be questioned, however, whether this advantage would obtain in practice. This question, of course, cannot be settled purely at the economic level. A fully satisfactory treatment of this issue would necessarily involve disciplines ranging from politics to psychology. However, by way of conclusion, we think it would be useful to consider a few arguments that are relevant to the final, realistic choice of policy.

1 The contention that the payment of subsidies would involve the collection of taxes which in practice cannot be levied in a non-distortionary fashion is fallacious. A tax-cum-subsidy scheme could always be devised that would *both* eliminate the estimated divergence and collected taxes sufficient to pay the subsidies.

2 The estimation problem is also easier with subsidies than with tariffs. The former involves estimating merely the divergence between the commodity price ratio and DRT (at the relevant production point). The latter must extend the exercises necessarily to the estimation of the relevant DRS (which involves locating both the right level of income *and* the relevant consumption point).

3 The political argument has usually been claimed by free traders to favour the payment of subsidies under external economy arguments like infant industries. It is thought that it would be difficult to pay a subsidy longer than strictly necessary whereas a tariff may be more difficult to abolish. It must be pointed out, however, that this argument also pulls the other way because, precisely for the reasons which make a subsidy difficult to continue, a subsidy is difficult to choose in preference to a tariff.

POSTSCRIPT

Further analysis has shown that the following two propositions stated in this chapter are invalid:

(1) no tariff may exist that would yield a solution superior to that under free trade, in the presence of a domestic distortion; and

(2) no production tax-cum-subsidy may exist that would yield a solution superior to that under free trade, in the presence of monopoly power in trade.

Kemp and Negishi [12] have correctly pointed out subsequently that such a tariff and a production tax-cum-subsidy will necessarily exist, in each respective case. Bhagwati, Ramaswami and Srinivasan [11] have generalized these results to prove the following two theorems:

Theorem 1 If the relationship between the variables DRS, DRT and FRT under *laissez-faire* is characterized by one equality and one inequality, and the policy measure that will secure equal values of the three variables cannot be applied, some second-best policy measure will exist that will raise welfare above the *laissez-faire* level though it destroys the equality.[1]

Theorem 2 If the relationship in the absence of intervention between the variables DRS, DRT and FRT is characterized by two inequalities, and *both* the policy measures that will secure equal values of the three variables cannot be applied, feasible intervention may not secure greater welfare than under *laissez-faire*.[2]

REFERENCES

1 Bhagwati, J., 'The Theory of Comparative Advantage in the Context of Underdevelopment and Growth', *Pakistan Development Review*, Autumn, 1962.

2 Chenery, H., 'The Interdependence of Investment Decisions', Moses Abramovitz (ed.) *The Allocation of Economic Resources*, Stanford University Press, 1959.

3 Fishlow, A., and David, P., 'Optimal Resource Allocation in an Imperfect Market Setting', *Journal of Political Economy*, December 1961.

4 Haberler, G., *Theory of International Trade*, Glasgow, William Hodge & Company, 1936.

5 Haberler, G., 'Some Problems in the Pure Theory of International Trade', *Economic Journal*, June 1950.

6 Hagen, E., 'An Economic Justification of Protectionism', *Quarterly Journal of Economics*, November 1958.

---

[1] Domestic distortions without monopoly power in trade would, for example, be a situation with one equality and one inequality, as defined here, insofar as $DRT \neq DRS = FRT$. Similarly, under monopoly power in trade but no domestic distortions, we would have $FRT \neq DRT = DRS$. For a consumption tax or subsidy, there would be DRS $\neq$ DRT = FRT if there were neither domestic distortions nor monopoly power in trade.

[2] The presence of *both* domestic distortions and monopoly power in trade would involve two inequalities, as defined, insofar as DRT $\neq$ DRS $\neq$ FRT in this case, generally speaking.

7 Kafka, A., 'A New Argument for Protectionism', *Quarterly Journal of Economics*, February 1962.

8 Kindleberger, C. P., *International Economics*, Homewood, Illinois, Richard D. Irwin, Inc., 1958.

9 Lewis, W. A., 'Economic Development with Unlimited Supplies of Labour', *Manchester School of Economic and Social Studies*, May 1950.

10 Myint, H., 'Infant Industry Arguments for Assistance to Industries in the setting of Dynamic Trade Theory', Roy Harrod (ed.) *Trade In A Developing World*, London, Macmillan, 1963.

11 Bhagwati, J., Ramaswami, V. K., and Srinivasan, T. N., 'Domestic Distortions, Tariffs and the Theory of Optimum Subsidy: Further Results', *Journal of Political Economy*, December 1969.

12 Kemp, M. C., and Negishi, Takashi, 'Domestic Distortions, Tariffs and the Theory of Optimum Subsidy', *Journal of Political Economy*, December 1969.

PART FOUR

Growth and Less Developed Countries

12 International Trade and Economic Expansion[1]

The recent literature on the effects of economic expansion on international trade has been concerned with two principal problems: the impact of the expansion on the terms of trade; and the resultant change in the welfare of the trading nations. The solutions offered, however, are not fully satisfactory. Thus H. G. Johnson [5] and W. M. Corden [3], who attempt to tackle the first problem, succeed only in establishing the *direction*, as distinct from the *extent*, of the consequential shift in the terms of trade. Insofar as the full impact of the expansion on the terms of trade must be known prior to determining the change in the welfare of the countries involved, it is not surprising that the second problem has received scant attention.[2]

It is intended in this paper to resolve principally the problem of bringing the different factors that affect the terms of trade into a single formula to determine the extent of the shift in the terms of trade consequent upon economic expansion. The analysis is further rendered geometrically by translating the usual textbook back-to-back partial diagram, depicting international trade equilibrium in a single commodity, into a general equilibrium framework. The argument is then extended, in a brief section, to the welfare effects of the expansion. To the gain from growth must be added the gain or loss from the resultant shift, if any, in the terms of trade; conditions are derived to determine whether the growing country will experience a net gain or loss from the expansion. The final section of the paper is concerned with the concept

[1] This paper was read at Roy Harrod and Donald MacDougall's seminar on international economics at Oxford.

[2] It should be mentioned, however, that Johnson [5] has an excellent analysis of this problem in the context of a model of complete specialization, although the concern of the article is principally to evolve a criterion to determine the impact of expansion on the terms of trade.

L

of the 'output elasticity of supply' (to be used in the paper) and the analytical methods that can be employed to investigate the output elasticity of supply of different activities under specified varieties of expansion.

1. FORMULA TO DETERMINE CHANGE IN THE TERMS OF TRADE

The model used here is the familiar two-country (I and II), two-commodity (X and Y), 'real' model with continuous full employment of all factors. Transport costs and intercountry factor movements are absent. To simplify the analysis, economic expansion, defined as the country's capacity to produce extra output at constant relative commodity prices, is confined to country I. We wish to determine the consequent impact on I's commodity terms of trade. The analysis is conducted in terms of I's importable good (Y); it is one of the advantages of our two-good model that the analysis can be couched entirely in terms of one good and yet will hold generally.

The total impact on the terms of trade of country I as a result of the expansion is compounded of six effects:

1 *Change in the Output of Y due to Economic Expansion.* The change in the output of importables (Y) in country I, at constant relative commodity prices, as a result of the economic expansion, is given by:

$$\frac{\delta Y}{\delta K} . dK = Y . E_{SY} . \bar{K} \tag{1}$$

where Y is the domestic production of importables in I prior to the expansion; K is I's productive capacity which is assumed to be kept fully employed and is measured by the value, in terms of exportables (X), of the output the country would produce at the initial terms of trade;

$$\bar{K} = \frac{dK}{K}; \text{ and } E_{SY} = \frac{K}{Y} . \frac{\delta Y}{\delta K}$$

is the output elasticity of supply of importables at constant relative commodity prices. This represents, therefore, the change in the domestic production of importables directly as a result of expansion, at constant terms of trade. If (1) is positive, the supply of Y is increased; if it is negative, the supply of Y is reduced.[1]

[1] Formula (1) may be negative under certain circumstances. This possibility is outlined again in Section 3 and is actually demonstrated, in the context of our highly simplified model, in Section 4. Also see Bhagwati [1].

2 *Change in the Demand for Y due to Economic Expansion.* We must now consider the change in the demand for importables, at constant relative commodity prices, as a direct result of the expansion. This is given by

$$\frac{\delta C}{\delta K}.dK = C.E_{DY}.\overline{K} \tag{2}$$

where C is the pre-expansion consumption of importables (Y) in I and

$$E_{DY} = \frac{K}{C}.\frac{\delta C}{\delta K}$$

is the output elasticity of demand for importables at constant relative commodity prices.[1] If (2) is positive, there is an increase in the demand for Y; if it is negative, the demand for Y is decreased.

It follows that the net change in the demand for imports, at constant terms of trade, will be given by $[(1) - (2)]$. If this expression is positive, there is a net decrease in I's demand for imports at the pre-expansion terms of trade and hence the terms of trade will tend to improve for I (unless II's offer curve is infinitely elastic); if the expression is negative, there is a net increase in I's demand for imports and the terms of trade will tend to deteriorate for I.[2] In order to determine the extent of the shift in the terms of trade which will be necessary to restore equilibrium, however, we must introduce the following four factors, three domestic and one foreign. Each of them measures one aspect of the changes in the supply of and demand for importables induced by a shift in the terms of trade.

3 *Change in the Demand for Y due to Price Shift.* The change in the demand for Y due to the shift in the terms of trade may be measured by the following expression:

$$\frac{\delta C}{\delta p}.dp = -\frac{C}{p}.\varepsilon.dp \tag{3}$$

where p is the terms of trade, measured as the number of units of exportables required to buy a unit of importables; and

$$\varepsilon = -\frac{p}{C}.\frac{\delta C}{\delta p}$$

[1] Output elasticity of demand is used in preference to income elasticity to describe the behaviour of aggregate consumption as aggregate income rises, to include the effects of population changes, growth of *per capita* incomes, and resultant changes in income distribution.

[2] This is, in effect, Johnson's [5] central argument.

is the income-compensated or constant-utility demand-elasticity for importables (Y), representing movement *along* the indifference curve in response to the price-shift. If (3) is positive, there is an increase in the demand for Y; if it is negative, there is a reduction in the demand for Y. The demand for Y will be negatively correlated with changes in the price of Y relative to the price of X.[1]

4 *Change in the Supply of Y due to Price Shift.* The change in the domestic supply of Y due to the shift in the terms of trade is:

$$\frac{\delta Y}{\delta p}.dp = \frac{Y}{p}.\sigma.dp \tag{4}$$

where

$$\sigma = \frac{p}{Y}.\frac{\delta Y}{\delta p}$$

is the supply-elasticity of importables based on movement along the transformation curve in response to the price-shift. When (4) is positive, the supply of Y is increased; when it is negative, it is decreased. The supply of Y will normally be positively correlated with changes in the price of Y relative to the price of X.[2]

5 *Change in the Demand for Y due to Change in Real Income resulting from Shift in the Terms of Trade.* A change in the terms of trade leads to a consequent change in real income. This income change is approximated here by the usual method employed widely in the theory of international trade and based on the theory of value, namely, by the difference in the cost of the initial quantity of imports. The resultant change in the demand for Y is:

$$-\frac{\delta C}{\delta K}.M.dp = -\frac{C}{K}.M.E_{DY}'.dp \tag{5}$$

where $M \equiv C - Y$ is the quantity of initial imports; and

$$E_{DY}' = \frac{K}{C}.\frac{\delta C}{\delta K}$$

is the elasticity of demand for Y with respect to a change in income resulting from changed terms of trade. If (5) is positive, there is an increase in the demand for Y; if it is negative, there is a reduction in the demand for Y.

[1] This is so because we normally assume, for well-known reasons, that the substitution effect, with which (3) is concerned, is negative.

[2] This holds again because we normally assume that the transformation curve is a convex set.

6 *Change in the Supply of Y by Country II due to Price Change.* As a result of the shift in the terms of trade, the supply of Y by II to I changes. This is given by:

$$\frac{\delta S_m}{\delta p} \cdot dp = \frac{M}{p} \cdot r_m \cdot dp \qquad (6)$$

where $S_m \equiv M$ and

$$r_m = \frac{p}{M} \cdot \frac{\delta S_m}{\delta p}$$

is the *total* elasticity of II's supply of its exports (commodity Y) to I, in response to a shift in the terms of trade. II's supply of Y to I increases or decreases according as (6) is positive or negative.[1]

The total impact on the terms of trade is then derived from the simple proposition that, in equilibrium, the excess demand for Y should be zero. Thus we can collect all the effects into two groups: those on the supply side, $[(1) + (4) + (6)]$; and those on the demand side, $[(2) + (3) + (5)]$. We subtract the latter from the former and set the expression equal to zero. Solving for dp, we get the magnitude of the shift in the terms of trade consequent upon economic expansion:

$$dp = \frac{(C \cdot E_{DY} - Y \cdot E_{SY}) \cdot \overline{K}}{\left[\dfrac{Y}{p} \cdot \sigma + \dfrac{M}{p} \cdot r_m + \dfrac{C}{p} \cdot \varepsilon + \dfrac{C}{K} \cdot M \cdot E_{DY}'\right]}, \qquad (7)$$

which may be rewritten as:

$$dp = \frac{p \cdot dM}{M\left[\dfrac{Y}{M} \cdot \sigma + r_m + \dfrac{C}{M} \cdot \varepsilon + p \cdot \dfrac{C}{K} \cdot E_{DY}'\right]}, \qquad (8)$$

provided it is remembered that *dM* refers to the income effect of expansion on imports at constant terms of trade.

We have thus succeeded in bringing together into a single formula, and thereby establishing the relative significance of, the different factors (elasticities) which simultaneously determine the impact of expansion on the international commodity terms of trade. The analysis can be readily extended to the case of simultaneous growth in *both* countries. This can be done by replacing

[1] The elasticity r_m will be negative, for instance, when the exports of I are Giffen goods in II; though this is by no means a necessary condition for r_m to be negative.

$$\left[\frac{M}{p}.r_m.dp\right]$$

by an elaborate expression derived by extending to country II an analysis exactly analogous to that we have applied to country I.[1]

Some interesting results follow from our analysis. Thus in order for the terms of trade to turn adverse to the growing country it is not sufficient that the income effects of the expansion should be unfavourable and should create an increased demand for imports (that is, $C.E_{DY} > Y.E_{SY}$). It is also necessary that the expression

$$\left[\frac{Y}{M}.\sigma + r_m + \frac{C}{M}.\varepsilon + p.\frac{C}{K}.E_{DY}'\right],$$

which constitutes the denominator in (8), should be positive. Since both σ and ε are normally positive, and since E_{DY}' is also positive (unless either the commodity Y is an inferior good in the strict Hicksian sense or the expansion is accompanied by a redistribution of income biased strongly against the consumption of Y), it follows that r_m will have to be not merely negative but also sufficiently large in magnitude in order that the entire expression should be negative. The converse is also true: where the income effects are favourable and lead to a reduction in the demand for imports, the terms of trade may still worsen for the growing country I if the total elasticity of II's supply of its exports (Y) to I is sufficiently large and negative to make the denominator in (8) negative. These conclusions are, no doubt, intuitively plausible, which is perhaps an advantage; what is chiefly claimed is that the precise relation in which the different operative factors stand *vis-à-vis* one another, which has been attempted here, lends a needed element of rigorousness to these qualitative results. Besides, it enables us to investigate more satisfactorily the related problem of the impact of economic expansion on the welfare of the growing country (Section 3).

2. GEOMETRICAL ANALYSIS

Using the familiar partial equilibrium back-to-back diagram determining the flow of exports of a single commodity from one country to another, we propose now to: (1) show how this partial diagram can be transformed into a general equilibrium diagram; and (2) relate the diagram to, and thereby illustrate, the argument algebraically presented in Section 1.

[1] Nothing substantive is gained by carrying out this exercise.

Figure 12.1 shows the usual partial equilibrium diagram for depicting international trade equilibrium in a two-country model. Transport costs are assumed to be zero. $D_1 D_1$, $S_1 S_1$ and $D_2 D_2$, $S_2 S_2$ are the domestic demand and supply curves of countries I and II respectively. ES_1 and ES_2 are the excess-supply functions, as Samuelson [11] calls them, of I and II respectively. Equilibrium is at Z where the exports of Y from II match the imports of Y into I; the equilibrium price of Y is OW.

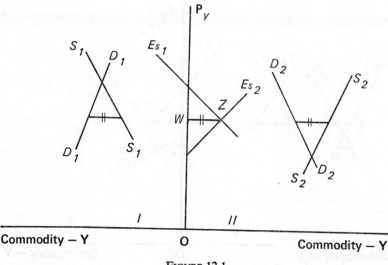

FIGURE 12.1

Now this diagram can be readily converted into a general equilibrium diagram in the following fashion. Relabel the vertical axis $p = p_y/p_x$, the terms of trade, instead of p_y, the price of Y. Further, instead of regarding $D_1 D_1$, $D_2 D_2$, $S_1 S_1$ and $S_2 S_2$ as partial curves,[1] treat them as general equilibrium or total curves. Thus $S_1 S_1$ and $S_2 S_2$ now represent schedules of varying supply of Y as the change in the terms of trade shifts production along the transformation curve. The reinterpretation of $D_1 D_1$ and $D_2 D_2$ is slightly more involved as the schedules are now compounded of two effects: (1) the shift in the demand for Y caused by the real-income change resulting from the change in the terms of trade; and (2) the change in the demand for Y

[1] See an interesting note by Hicks [4] on how the Marshallian supply curve, corresponding to Marshall's demand curve, should be derived.

as the change in the terms of trade shifts consumption along the indifference curve (*i.e.* the substitution effect).

The reader may still doubt whether the transformation of the partial into a general equilibrium diagram has been accomplished. Equilibrium in the diagram, as now interpreted, is still in the Y market. What about the X-market? The answer is straightforward. As argued before, it is one of the advantages of a two-good model, such as the one employed here, that the argument can be couched entirely in

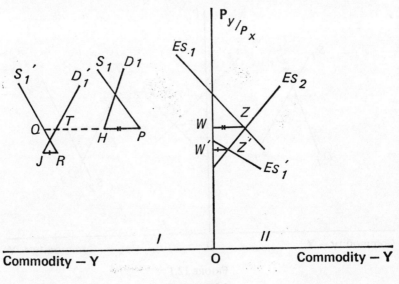

FIGURE 12.2

terms of one good. Equilibrium in the Y-market implies equilibrium in the X-market as well.

We have thus accomplished our first task of transforming the partial into a general equilibrium diagram. We can now proceed to derive geometrically the argument and result of Section 1. In Figure 2 we assume that, as a result of economic expansion, $S_1 S_1$ and $D_1 D_1$ shift to $S_1'S_1'$ and $D_1'D_1'$ respectively. ES_1 correspondingly shifts to ES_1' and the new equilibrium terms of trade are at OW'. Country II now exports $W'Z'$ of Y and I imports JR (= $W'Z'$) of Y. The total impact on imports and exports can then be analysed as follows:

1 *Total Effect on Demand for Y in I.* (a) The movement from H to T is the income effect of expansion, measured by (2) in Section 1.

(b) The movement from T to J is compounded of the income effect on consumption of Y due to the shift in the terms of trade and the substitution effect on consumption of Y due to the same shift. It is measured therefore by (5) and (3) in Section 1. (c) The movement from H to J, representing the total effect on the demand for Y in I, is thus measured by $[(2) + (3) + (5)]$.

2 *Total Effect on Supply of Y in I.* (a) The movement from P to Q is the income effect on production of the expansion, measured by (1). (b) The movement from Q to R is the substitution effect on production of Y due to the shift in the terms of trade and is measured by (4). (c) The movement from P to R, representing the total effect on the supply of Y in I, is thus measured by $[(1) + (4)]$.

3 *The Net Effect on the Excess Supply of Y in I.* This is then given by: $(1) + (4) - [(2) + (3) + (5)]$. This corresponds to the difference between HP $(= WZ)$, the old volume of imports, and JR $(= W'Z')$ the new volume of imports. If the expression is positive, there is a net reduction in the demand for imports into I; if it is negative, there is a net increase.

4 *The Net Effect on the Excess Supply of Y in II.* This is similarly given by (6). It corresponds to the difference between WZ and $W'Z'$. If it is positive, there is a net increase in the supply of imports to I; if it is negative, there is a net decrease.

The formula for determining the shift in the terms of trade is now easily derived. In equilibrium, the net changes in the excess supplies of Y in I and II must match each other and also add up to zero:

$$(1) + (4) + [(2) + (3) + (5)] + (6) = 0.$$

Solving the above for dp, we can derive formula (7). The geometrical construction not only represents the transformation of a useful diagram of partial analysis into a general equilibrium framework but also serves the purpose of deriving the results of Section 1 visually. There is an additional advantage that follows from our transformation; this is a direct result of Samuelson's ingenious use of this diagram (in a partial framework) to convert the international trade problem involved into a maximum problem, thereby enabling the analyst 'to make rigorous predictions as to the qualitative direction in which the variables of the system will change when some change is made in the data of the problem' [11, p. 299] and to derive generalized reciprocity relations.

3. EXPANSION AND ECONOMIC WELFARE

Having derived an expression to measure the precise impact of expansion on the commodity terms of trade, we can now analyse the net effect of expansion on the welfare of the growing country. Economic expansion, while increasing output, might lead to a deterioration in the terms of trade and a corresponding reduction in the growth in real income of the country experiencing the expansion. Where expansion leads to deterioration in the country's commodity terms of trade, there are three possible outcomes for the country's economic welfare:[1] net gain, no gain, or actual loss. We propose now to investigate the conditions under which these possibilities will respectively materialize.

Let dK denote the gain in real income that results from growth of output, at constant relative commodity prices. From this we must subtract the loss of real income that arises from the attendant deterioration in the terms of trade by approximating this loss with the familiar expression: $M.dp$. Using formula (8), we can say that the growing country, I, will, as a result of growth, experience net gain, make neither gain nor loss, or actually suffer immiserizing growth according as:

$$dK \gtreqless p.dM \left[\frac{Y}{M}.\sigma + r_m \times \frac{C}{M}.\varepsilon + p.\frac{\delta C}{\delta K} \right]$$

which simplifies to:

$$\left[\frac{Y}{M}.\sigma + \frac{C}{M}.\varepsilon + y \right] \gtreqless -r_m \tag{9}$$

where $y = p.(\delta Y/\delta K)$ and it is assumed that $E_{DY}' = E_{DY}$, so that a change in real income due to a reduction of import prices has the same effect on the demand for importables as a change in real income due to growth.[2]

It may be of interest to note that, since ε and σ are necessarily positive,[3] the possibility that growth might be immiserizing would arise only if either the demand for the growing country's exports is inelastic (r_m is negative) or growth actually reduces the domestic

---

[1] The analysis outlined here is subject to all the familiar caveats attending on discussions of social welfare.

[2] For a similar assumption, see Bhagwati [1]. For further observations and an able discussion of related issues, see Johnson [7].

[3] This argument is again based on the assumption of convex indifference and transformation curves, convexity being defined in the strict mathematical sense.

production of importables at constant relative commodity prices (y is negative). (Neither of these conditions, it should be noticed, is sufficient for immiserizing growth to occur.[1]) Although, as indicated in Section 1, y will normally be positive, it is possible to postulate assumptions under which it will be negative; this possibility is demonstrated in Section 4 where the concept of the output elasticity of supply is further explored.

4. INCREASED FACTOR SUPPLY AND OUTPUT ELASTICITY OF SUPPLY

Our formulae for determining the change in the terms of trade and the impact of growth on the welfare of the growing country draw upon elasticity concepts that are familiar to economists from the modern theory of value.[2] The concepts of output elasticity of supply and of demand (at constant relative commodity prices), E_{SY} and E_{DY}, however, are fairly recent concepts although they have already been widely used [2] [3] [5] [6]. They would appear far more familiar if they were described as yielding respectively Engel's curves of production and consumption of the commodity in question. Whereas, however, Engel's curves of consumption are respectable in the literature, those for production are still a sufficiently rare phenomenon to justify a sketch of the analytical techniques by which they may be derived. Of the two major sources of economic growth, namely expansion of factor supply and technical progress, the former is analysed in our simple model, and the output elasticities of supply of the two activities X and Y implied thereby are investigated.

Let a and b be the amounts of the two factors employed in industry X and a', b' the amounts employed in industry Y. The prices, p_x and p_y of X and Y respectively, are assumed to be constant throughout the analysis. $a + a' = A$ and $b + b' = B$ where A and B are the total factor endowment enjoying full employment. It is assumed that B is constant. Therefore, $db + db' = 0$. A is assumed to change

---

[1] This is best seen by rewriting the criterion thus:

$$\left[\frac{Y}{M} \cdot \sigma + \frac{C}{M} \cdot \epsilon + y + r_m \right] < 0$$

For further discussion of the economic implications of this criterion, see Bhagwati [1].

[2] Our substitution elasticities are not identical with, though similar to, the elasticities of substitution in the literature. See Morrissett [8].

infinitesimally so that $dA + da' = dA$. The production functions are assumed to be linear and homogeneous and remain unchanged throughout the analysis. We can now proceed to analyse the impact of the change in A on the output of Y as follows:

From equilibrium conditions, we have

$$p_x \cdot \frac{\delta X}{\delta a} = p_y \cdot \frac{\delta Y}{\delta a'} = \Pi_a$$

$$p_x \cdot \frac{\delta X}{\delta b} = p_y \cdot \frac{\delta Y}{\delta b'} = \Pi_b$$

Differentiating these, with p_x and p_y constant, and then using the relations $da + da' = dA$ and $db + db' = 0$, we get:

$$\left(p_y \cdot \frac{\delta^2 Y}{\delta a'^2} + p_x \cdot \frac{\delta^2 X}{\delta a^2} \right) \cdot da' + \left(p_y \cdot \frac{\delta^2 Y}{\delta a' \delta b'} + p_x \cdot \frac{\delta^2 X}{\delta a \delta b} \right) db' =$$
$$p_x \cdot \frac{\delta^2 X}{\delta a^2} \cdot dA \qquad (10)$$

$$\left(p_y \cdot \frac{\delta^2 Y}{\delta a' \delta b'} + p_x \cdot \frac{\delta^2 X}{\delta a \delta b} \right) \cdot da' + \left(p_y \cdot \frac{\delta^2 Y}{\delta b'^2} + p_x \cdot \frac{\delta^2 X}{\delta b^2} \right) \cdot db' =$$
$$p_x \cdot \frac{\delta^2 X}{\delta a \delta b} \, dA \qquad (11)$$

Using equations (10) and (11) and the identity

$$p_y \cdot \frac{dY}{dA} = \Pi_a \frac{da'}{dA} + \Pi_b \frac{db'}{dA}$$

and choosing units such that all prices are equal to unity, we arrive at the following formula:[1]

---

[1] Since the change in A is assumed to be infinitesimal, formula (12) can be derived much more readily by using the Samuelson theorem [12] that the relationship between commodity and factor price ratios is unique under the conditions postulated. J. Black informs me that the following alternative proof is available, if the Samuelson theorem is used: Assume, by choice of units, that all prices equal unity.

$$da + da' = dA . \quad da' = \frac{a'}{(a' + b')} \cdot dY.$$

Similarly,

$$dY = \frac{(a' + b')}{b'} \cdot db' = -\frac{(a' + b')}{b'} \cdot \frac{b}{(a + b)} \cdot dX . \ (db = -db')$$

Therefore,

$$da = \frac{a}{(a + b)} \cdot dX = -\frac{ab'}{b(a' + b')} \cdot dY.$$

$$dY = \frac{b \cdot Y}{(a'b - ab')} \cdot dA. \tag{12}$$

Some interesting conclusions emerge from this formula. First, the formula has the property that the output elasticity of supply of Y (as also X) is independent of the scale of the two activities, X and Y, and depends exclusively on the factor proportions in the two activities. This is easily demonstrated by rewriting the formula thus:[1]

$$dY = \frac{1 + \dfrac{a'}{b'}}{\left(\dfrac{a'}{b'} - \dfrac{a}{b}\right)} \cdot dA \tag{13}$$

Further, the familiar Rybczynski [10] proposition that the output of the B-intensive industry will contract, under the assumptions made here, when the supply of A increases, at constant relative commodity prices, follows quite readily from (12). If Y is B-intensive, it follows that

$$\frac{a'}{b'} < \frac{a}{b}$$

and thus $a'b < ab'$. Under our assumptions, therefore, it can be established that dY/dA is negative if Y is B-intensive. It follows then that E_{SY} (and y) may be negative, indicating that the domestic output of importables declines absolutely, at constant terms of trade, as a result of the expansion.

The analytical technique outlined above is perfectly general and can be utilized for determining the output elasticities of supply under other types of expansion as well, such as neutral technical progress in an

---

Therefore,

$$dA = da + da' = -\frac{ab'}{b(a' + b')} \cdot dY + \frac{a'}{(a' + b')} \cdot dY.$$

Therefore,

$$dY = \frac{b(a' + b')}{(a'b - ab')} \cdot dA = \frac{b \cdot Y}{(a'b - ab')} \cdot dA.$$

The analytical method employed in the text, however, is more general and can be used for other similar problems where nothing comparable to the Samuelson theorem is available.

[1] This property is geometrically demonstrated in a different context by Mundell [9].

activity. It would thus be feasible to undertake an interesting taxonomic exercise: to consider different varieties of expansion and investigate the output elasticities of supply (and of demand) implied by them; and to relate them with different values for the substitution elasticities to discover the full impact on the terms of trade of expansion under different circumstances. Such an analysis, however, cannot be attempted here as the task would take us far afield.[1]

REFERENCES

1 Bhagwati, J., 'Immiserizing Growth: A Geometrical Note', *Review of Economic Studies*, June 1958, **25** (3), 201–5.

2 Black, J., 'Economic Expansion and International Trade: A Marshallian Approach', *Review of Economic Studies*, 1955–6, **23** (3), 204–12.

3 Corden, W. M., 'Economic Expansion and International Trade: A Geometric Approach', *Oxford Economic Papers*, June 1956, **8**, 223–8.

4 Hicks, J. R., 'A Note on the Elasticity of Supply', *Review of Economic Studies*, 1934–5, **2**, 31–7.

5 Johnson, H. G., 'Economic Expansion and International Trade', *Manchester School of Economics and Social Studies*, May 1955, **23**, 95–112.

6 Johnson, H. G., 'A Mathematical Note on Immiserizing Growth', Unpulished Manuscript, 1956.

7 Johnson, H. G., 'The Transfer Problem and Exchange Stability', *Journal of Political Economy*, June 1956, **64**, 212–25.

8 Morrissett, I., 'Some Recent Uses of Elasticity of Substitution – A Survey', *Econometrica*, January 1953, **21**, 41–62.

9 Mundell, R. A., 'International Trade and Factor Mobility', *American Economic Review*, June 1957, **47**, 321–35.

10 Rybczynski, T., 'Factor Endowments and Relative Commodity Prices', *Economica*, November 1955, **22**, 336–41.

11 Samuelson, P. A., 'Spatial Price Equilibrium and Linear Programming', *American Economic Review*, June 1952, **42**, 283–303.

12 Samuelson, P. A., 'Prices of Factors and Goods in General Equilibrium', *Review of Economic Studies*, 1953–4, **21** (1), 1–21.

---

[1] See Johnson [5] for a very able taxonomic exercise of this nature.

13 Immiserizing Growth:
A Geometrical Note

The effect of economic expansion on international trade has been receiving increasing attention from economic theorists since the publication of Professor Hicks' stimulating analysis of the 'dollar problem'.[1] It has, however, been insufficiently realized that under certain circumstances, economic expansion may harm the growing country itself.[2] Economic expansion increases *output* which, however, might lead to a sufficient deterioration in the terms of trade to offset the beneficial effect of expansion and reduce the *real income* of the growing country. It is the purpose of this note to formulate the conditions under which immiserizing growth will occur. Section 1 sets out the analysis geometrically and arrives at the criterion for immiserizing growth. Section 2 discusses some of the implications of this criterion.

1.

In the ensuing analysis we assume the traditional two-country, two commodity 'real' model where full-employment always obtains. We also assume, to simplify the analysis, that growth is confined to a single country so that the other country (*i.e.* the rest of the world) is not experiencing any growth in *output*; this assumption enables us to assume the offer curve of the rest of the world as 'given' during the course of our analysis. Finally, we simplify the problem by beginning with an investigation of the conditions under which growth would leave the country just as well off as before, and then determining whether the equilibrium actually realized would involve still less

[1] J. R. Hicks [3]. The following are of interest: H. G. Johnson [5]; E. J. Mishan [6]; and W. M. Corden [1].

[2] Exception must be made, however, in the case of Professor Johnson [4] [5].

favourable terms of trade; this approach has the convenience of avoiding the need for an explicit analysis of the income effect of growth.

Consider now Figure 13.1 which represents the growing economy. C_0 is the pre-expansion consumption, P_0 the pre-expansion production point, $P_0 C_0$ the pre-expansion terms of trade or price-line, $C_0 R_0$ the imports of Y into the country and $R_0 P_0$ the exports of X from the

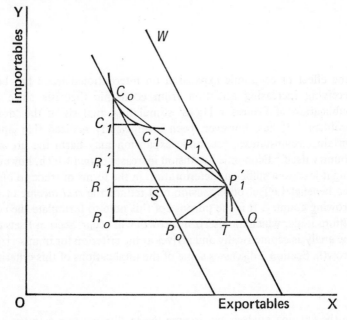

FIGURE 13.1

country. The production possibility curve tangential to $P_0 C_0$ has not been drawn in to avoid cluttering up the diagram; the indifference curve through C_0 is tangential to $P_0 C_0$ at C_0 and has been drawn partially. Consider now growth which pushes the production possibility curve outwards and which, at *constant terms of trade*, would bring production from P_0 to P_1'. Now assume that the terms of trade are changed just enough to offset the gain from growth; the relevant price line being $C_1 P_1$ which is tangential to the old indifference and the *new* production possibility curve. We later assume, legitimately for infinitesimal changes, that $C_1 P_1$ coincides with $C_0 P_1'$.

The combined effect of the expansion and the compensating

adjustment of the terms of trade is to reduce the demand for imports from $C_0 R_0$ to $C_1' R_1'$. This reduction can be analysed into the sum of three effects:

1. *The increase in production of importables due to economic expansion*
This increase ($R_0 R_1$ in the diagram) may be analysed as follows. Let p_0 and p_1 be the original and the zero-gain prices respectively, measured as the number of units of exportables required to buy a unit of importables. Then the change in total output, valued at *initial* prices, is:

$$P_0 T + TQ = P_0 Q = S P_1'$$

and

$$S P_1' = \frac{P_1' R_1 - R_1 S}{C_0 R_1} \cdot C_0 R_1 = (p_1 - p_0) \cdot C_0 R_1$$

The change in the production of importables is:

$$R_0 R_1 = P_1' T = \frac{\partial Y}{\partial K} \cdot P_0 Q = \frac{\partial Y}{\partial K} \cdot S P_1'$$

where K is defined to be the country's productive capacity which is assumed to be kept fully employed and is measured by the value in terms of exportables of the output the country would produce at the initial terms of trade and Y is the domestic output of importables. Then,

$$R_0 R_1 = C_0 R_1 \cdot \frac{\partial Y}{\partial K} \cdot (p_1 - p_0)$$

Since we have assumed the changes to be infinitesimal, it follows that we can assume $C_0 R_1 = C_0 R_0$, the initial volume of imports, so that

$$R_0 R_1 = M \cdot \frac{\partial Y}{\partial K} \cdot dp \qquad (S_m \equiv M) \qquad (1)$$

where M is the quantity of imports.

This shows the change in the production of importables due to the economic expansion itself. The expression is normally positive, indicating that the output of importables increases, consequent on economic expansion, at constant terms of trade. It should be noted here, however, that, as argued in Section 2, the output of importables may actually contract due to the expansion.

2. *The decrease in consumption of importables due to the price-change*
The price-change (from p_0 to p_1) shifts consumption *along* the

indifference curve to C_1. The consumption of importables is then reduced by:

$$C_0 C_1' = -\frac{\partial C}{\partial p}.dp \qquad (2)$$

where C is the total demand for importables.

3. *The increase in production of importables due to the price-change*
The price-change shifts production *along* the production possibility curve to P_1. The production of importables is then increased by:

$$R_1 R_1' = \frac{\partial Y}{\partial p}.dp \qquad (3)$$

The total decrease in the domestic demand for *imports*[1] is the sum of the three effects (1), (2) and (3):

$$\left(M.\frac{\partial Y}{\partial K} + \frac{\partial Y}{\partial p} - \frac{\partial C}{\partial p}\right).dp \qquad (4)$$

This expression measures the decrease in demand for imports when the effect of growth on real income is exactly offset by an adverse movement of the terms of trade. In the abnormal case where output of importables *falls* as a result of growth, the expression may be negative, indicating an *increase* in the demand for imports.

Whether the country will actually be made worse off or not depends on what would happen to the quantity of imports supplied if the terms of trade were adjusted as assumed. The change in imports supplied as a result of such a price change is:

$$\frac{\partial S_m}{\partial p}.dp \qquad (5)$$

The sum of (4) and (5) constitutes the excess supply of imports at the zero-gain terms of trade: if it is positive, the terms of trade will not move against the growing country enough to deprive it of all gain from growth; but if it is negative, the price of imports will have to rise still further to preserve equilibrium, and the growing country will actually be made worse off by growth.

The economic meaning of this criterion for immiserizing growth will be considered in the next section; for this purpose a neater formulation of the criterion is desirable, and this can be derived by subjecting it to some algebraic manipulation.

---

[1] As distinguished from *importables*.

Multiplying (4) and (5) by $\dfrac{p}{M.dp}$, we get our criterion for immiserizing growth as:

$$\left(\frac{C}{M}.\varepsilon + \frac{Y}{M}.\sigma + y + r_m\right) < 0 \tag{6}$$

which may be written as:

$$\left(\frac{C}{M}.\varepsilon + \frac{Y}{M}.\sigma + y\right) < -r_m \tag{7}$$

where

$$\varepsilon = -\frac{p}{C}.\frac{\partial C}{\partial p}, \quad r_m = \frac{p}{M}.\frac{\partial S_m}{\partial p} \quad (S_m \equiv M)$$

$$\sigma = \frac{p}{Y}.\frac{\partial Y}{\partial p} \text{ and } y = p.\frac{\partial Y}{\partial K}.$$

This criterion is also expressible in the alternative equivalent form:

$$\left(\frac{C}{M}.\varepsilon + \frac{Y}{M}.\sigma + y\right) < 1 - n_x \tag{8}$$

where $n_x = \dfrac{p}{X^0}.\dfrac{\partial X^0}{\partial p}$ and X^0 is the quantity of exports. This follows from the fact that n_x and r_m are the *total* elasticities of the rest of the world's offer curve; n_x being the elasticity of the rest of the world's demand for imports (into the rest of the world) in response to an infinitesimal change in the terms of trade and r_m being the elasticity of the rest of the world's supply of (its) exports (to the growing country) in response to an infinitesimal shift in the terms of trade. It is a well-known proposition in the theory of international trade that $n_x - r_m = 1$; hence, $1 - n_x = -r_m$.

2.

What are the implications of the criterion that we have derived in Section 1? It will be remembered that $\varepsilon = \dfrac{p}{Y}.\dfrac{\partial Y}{\partial p}$ and is thus necessarily positive and $\sigma = -\dfrac{p}{C}.\dfrac{\partial C}{\partial p}$ which again, being the constant-utility or expenditure-compensated demand-elasticity with respect to a change in the price of importables, is necessarily positive.[1] We can see from (6), (7) or (8) that the *possibility* of immiserizing growth is increased if:

(i) $\frac{Y}{M}$, the ratio of domestic production to import of importables is small. Since $\frac{C}{M} = 1 + \frac{Y}{M}$, it follows that $\frac{C}{M}$ will also be small when $\frac{Y}{M}$ is small;

(ii) ε, the constant-utility demand-elasticity for importables with respect to a change in the price of importables, is small; this would depend on the substitution effect against importables being negligible when the price of importables rises; and

(iii) σ, the elasticity in supply of importables when production shifts along the production possibility curve in resopnse to a change in the price of importables, is small.

These are, neither singly nor in combination, sufficient conditions for immiserizing growth. In fact, the *possibility* of immiserizing growth arises only when, with these conditions favourably fulfilled, either or both of the following crucial conditions are fulfilled:

(a) the offer of the rest of the world is inelastic (i.e. r_m is negative, which may be for the *extreme*, and by no means necessary, reason that the growing country's exports are Giffen goods abroad); and

(b) growth actually reduces the domestic production of importables at constant relative commodity prices (*i.e.* y is negative).

Stringent as the latter condition may appear at first sight, recent analyses have shown that it is feasible under relatively simple assumptions. Thus the Rybczynski proposition states that under a two-commodity, two-factor model where, say, labour and land being the factors, one good is labour-intensive and the other land-intensive, if labour (land) increases in supply, then the output of the land-intensive (labour-intensive) industry must actually contract if the relative commodity prices are maintained constant.[2] Professor Johnson has recently advanced the proposition that under neutral technical

---

[1] This argument obviously rests on the assumption of 'well-behaved' (convex) indifference curves and (concave) transformation curves, concavity being defined with reference to the origin and *not* in the strict mathematical sense.

[2] Rybczynski [7]. Linear homogeneity of the production functions and diminishing returns are *sufficient* conditions for the proposition to hold. The strong Samuelson notion of factor-intensity is not necessary.

progress in one industry, the technology of the other and the total factor endowment remaining unchanged, the output of the other industry must actually fall under constant relative commodity prices.[1] It may be of interest to note that under biased progress as well it is possible to establish conditions under which the output of the non-innovating industry will contract.[2]

REFERENCES

1 Corden, W. M., 'Economic Expansion and International Trade: A Geometric Approach', *Oxford Economic Papers*, June 1956.

2 Findlay, R., and Grubert, H., 'Factor Intensity, Technological Progress, and the Terms of Trade', *Oxford Economic Papers*, February 1959.

3 Hicks, J. R., 'An Inaugural Lecture', *Oxford Economic Papers*, June 1953.

4 Johnson, H. G., 'Equilibrium Growth in an Expanding Economy', *Canadian Journal of Economics and Political Science*, November 1953.

5 Johnson, H. G., 'Economic Expansion and International Trade', *Manchester School of Economic and Social Studies*, May 1955.

6 Mishan, E. J., 'The Long-Run Dollar Problem: A Comment', *Oxford Economic Papers*, June 1955.

7 Rybczynski, T., 'Factor Endowments and Relative Commodity Prices', *Economica*, November 1955.

---

[1] Johnson [5]. Diminishing returns are *sufficient* for this proposition to hold. The proposition can be readily extended to more than two goods and factors.

[2] The conditions under which this result will obtain have been investigated in a brilliant paper by Findlay and Grubert [2].

14 Distortions and Immiserizing Growth: A Generalization

In the previous chapter I analysed the case of 'immiserizing growth', where growth (due to technical progress and/or factor accumulation) leads to a sufficiently acute deterioration in the terms of trade which imposes a loss of real income outweighing the primary gain in real income due to the growth itself.[1] Recently Harry Johnson has shown that the phenomenon of immiserizing growth, involving reduction in social welfare below the initial pre-growth level, can arise also in the case of a small country without any monopoly power in trade if technical progress occurs in a *tariff-protected* import-competing industry or if the factor in whose use this industry is intensive is augmented.[2]

In point of fact, both these cases belong to a *general* class of immiserizing-growth phenomena which can arise in the presence of distortions. In the traditional case where gains from growth are outweighed by the loss from worsened terms of trade, the distortion is foreign: the average terms of trade differ from the marginal terms of trade. In the tariff situation for a small country, analysed by Johnson now, the distortion is policy-imposed: the tariff results in sub-optimality. In either case, the essential point is that the gain which would accrue from growth, *if optimal policies were followed*, is outweighed by the incremental loss of real income which the distortion imposes in the post-growth situation *vis-à-vis* the pre-growth situation Thus, the phenomenon of immiserizing growth can occur in principle, whenever distortions obtain in an economic system.

[1] See Bhagwati [1]. This case was also noted independently by Harry Johnson.
[2] See Johnson [5].

1. DISTORTIONARY WAGE DIFFERENTIALS

Take, for example, the case of distortionary wage differentials in the traditional two-factor, two-commodity model of trade theory. It is known that such a differential will result in (i) a shrinking-in of the feasible production possibility curve and (ii) a non-tangency between the commodity price-ratio and the feasible production possibility curve.[1] Suppose that this differential operates against commodity X in Figure 1 where the case of a small country with no monopoly power

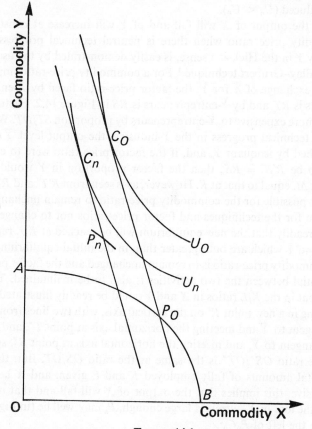

FIGURE 14.1

[1] These propositions have been discussed by Hagen [4]. The conditions under which the wage differential will be distortionary, as also the possibility of the feasible production curve losing convexity, are discussed in Bhagwati and Ramaswami, chapter 11 [2].

in trade is depicted. AB is the shrunk-in, feasible production possibility curve. P_0C_0, parallel to P_nC_n, is the fixed international price ratio. In the initial situation, P_0 is the production bundle and C_0 the consumption bundle. Next, assume that neutral technical progress takes place in industry Y.

It can then be shown, as is done below, that the output of X will fall and that of Y will increase. If, then, the production bundle shifts to a point such as P_n, to the left of P_0C_0, the availability line will become P_nC_n, consumption will be at C_n and social welfare will have been reduced ($U_n < U_0$).

That the output of X will fall and of Y will increase at constant commodity price ratio when there is neutral technical progress in industry Y in the Hicksian sense, is easily demonstrated by the use of the Findlay–Grubert technique.[1] For a commodity price-ratio implying the exchange of $\bar{X}$ for $\bar{Y}$, the factor price-ratio faced by X-entrepreneurs is RT and by $\bar{Y}$-entrepreneurs is RS in Figure 14.2. Factor L is thus more expensive to X-entrepreneurs by proportion ST/OT. With neutral technical progress in the Y-industry, the output level $\bar{Y}$ can be reached by isoquant $\bar{Y}_n$ and, if the factor price-ratio were to continue to be $R'S' = RS$, then the factor proportion in Y would be given at M, equal to that at K. However, as is seen from $R'T'$ and $R'S'$, it is not possible for the commodity price-ratio to remain unchanged and also for the techniques and factor price-ratios not to change. It is seen readily that the new equilibrium will be reached at K/L ratios for X and Y which are both greater than in the initial equilibrium, if the commodity price-ratio is to remain unchanged and the factor price differential between the two activities is also to be maintained. This increment in the K/L ratios in X and Y could be readily illustrated by sketching in a new point R'' on the vertical axis, with two lines from it, one tangent to $\bar{Y}$ and meeting the horizontal axis at point T'', and the other tangent to $\bar{Y}_n$ and meeting the horizontal axis at point S'', such that the ratio OS''/OT'' is the same as the ratio OS/OT. But, then, with total amounts of fully employed K and L given, and X being K-intensive, this implies that the output of X will fall and that of Y rise. If the loss in X-output is large enough, P_n may well lie (in Figure 14.1) to the left of P_0C_0.

---

[1] The same result would hold for augmentation of the factor L in which industry Y is assumed to be intensive, or for labour saving technical progress in industry Y. See Findlay and Grubert [3].

Thus, the possibility of immiserizing growth may arise also when there is a domestic distortion resulting from a wage differential.

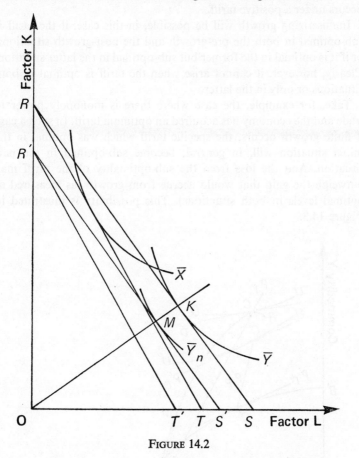

FIGURE 14.2

2. TARIFFS AND MONOPOLY POWER IN TRADE

I have already noted that the possibility of immiserizing growth has earlier been demonstrated in the cases where (1) for a country, with monopoly power in trade, growth occurs under a zero tariff and (2) for a country, with no monopoly power in trade, growth occurs under a positive tariff.[1] Both these propositions, however, can be

[1] See Bhagwati [1] and Johnson [5] respectively. Note also that the second case would equally hold for a production tax-cum-subsidy policy, as distinct from a tariff policy.

generalized and the phenomenon of immiserizing growth shown to be possible when, for a country with monopoly power in trade, growth occurs under a positive tariff.

Immiserizing growth will be possible, in this case, if the tariff is sub-optimal in both the pre-growth and the post-growth situations, or if it is optimal in the former but sub-optimal in the latter situation. Clearly, however, it cannot arise when the tariff is optimal in both situations or only in the latter.

Take, for example, the case where there is monopoly power in trade and the economy has acquired an optimum tariff. In such a case if finite growth occurs, the specific tariff which was optimal in the initial situation will, in general, become sub-optimal in the new situation. And the loss from the sub-optimality of the tariff may outweigh the gain that would accrue from growth (as measured at optimal levels in both situations). This possibility is illustrated in Figure 14.3.

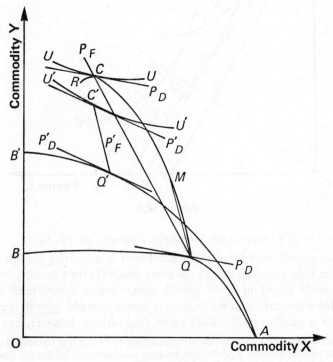

FIGURE 14.3

AQB is the pre-growth production possibility curve, $QMCR$ the given foreign reciprocal demand curve, QC the international price-ratio (P_F), and P_D the domestic price-ratio under an optimum tariff. $AQ'B'$ is the post-growth production possibility curve and $Q'C'$ the new international price ratio (P_F') – which yields a volume of trade, with production Q' and consumption C' at domestic price-ratio P_D', that is consistent with the foreign reciprocal demand curve, as seen by reference to QM. Note that, with the tariff rate assumed to be unchanged in post-growth situation, $P_D' = P_F'(1 + t_m)$ and $P_D = P_F(1 + t_m)$, at identical t_m and with the relative price defined as the price of the importable divided by the price of the exportable. The resulting welfare levels show that $U' < U$, which implies immiserizing growth.[1]

Note further that this case does not depend on 'freakish' phenomena such as inferiority of either good in social consumption; it does however require that the growth be ultra-biased against the production of the exportable commodity X, such that the output of X falls at constant commodity price-ratio. Thus, the case can arise when there is: (i) neutral technical progress in the importable industry, or (ii) the factor in which the importable industry is intensive increases, or (iii) biased technical progress occurs in the importable industry, with the bias in favour of (i.e. increasing the relative use of) the factor in which the exportable industry is intensive.[2]

REFERENCES

1 Bhagwati, J., 'Immiserizing Growth: A Geometrical Note', *Review of Economic Studies*, 25 (June 1958).
2 Bhagwati, J., and Ramaswami, V. K., 'Domestic Distortions, Tariffs and the Theory of Optimum Subsidy', *Journal of Political Economy* (February 1963).

[1] It may be stressed that immiserizing growth would necessarily be precluded if the post-growth tariff was changed to the optimal level. The economy would then, in Figure 14.3, be able to operate on the necessarily-superior envelope of consumption possibilities generated by the unchanged foreign reciprocal demand curve and the improved domestic production possibilities.

[2] *Cf*. Findlay and Grubert [3].

15 Trade Liberalization among LDCs, Trade Theory and GATT Rules[1]

Political attitudes change rapidly and astonishingly in the field of international, commercial policy. To those accustomed to the protectionist policies of the LDCs in the decade and a half since the war, it is remarkable that the LDCs today are actively discussing the issue of trade liberalization among themselves.

Not merely are they discussing it, but several of them have actively engaged in mutual negotiations to get action started. The most striking developments have undoubtedly been those in South America, where the Treaty of Montevideo represented the formal inauguration of LAFTA (The Latin American Free Trade Area),[2] of which Ecuador,

[1] This paper has grown out of my having been a member of two United Nations 'Expert Groups', in November 1964 at ECAFE and in February 1966 at UNCTAD, on this general subject. It is really an academic economist's attempt at discovering the rationale, if any, behind the attempts of the developing countries to liberalize trade in certain specific ways which do not 'square with' what economic analysis would predict as 'rational'. Throughout the paper, LDC's mean less developed countries, an identifiable bloc of countries at the UNCTAD now, and GATT stands for the General Agreement on Tariffs and Trade. I should like to record my general indebtedness to the numerous colleagues on the two United Nations Groups as also to members of a Seminar at IBRD for their comments. My thanks are also due to Harry Johnson for incisive comments on the penultimate draft of this paper and for drawing my attention to his own work [6]. Recent work of Linder, Cooper and Massell also relates to some of the questions touched upon in this paper.

[2] As far as tariff reductions are concerned, Sidney Dell records in his *A Latin American Common Market?* [4] that '. . . the LAFTA countries achieved a certain initial measure of success following the entry of the Treaty of Montevideo into force. The first round of negotiations was held in Montevideo from 24 July to 12 August 1961, the second in Mexico City from 27 August to 21 November 1962, the third in Montevideo again from 5 October to 31 December 1963, and the fourth in Bogota from 20 October to 11 December 1964' [4, p. 70]. For details and evaluation, see Dell [4, Chapter V].

Colombia, Peru, Chile, Argentina, Uruguay, Paraguay, Brazil and Mexico are already members, and the Treaty of Managua on Central American Economic Integration which has already accelerated significantly the integration process among the member countries Salvador, Guatemala, Costa Rica, Honduras, and Nicaragua.[1]

Elsewhere, the current picture is not as much in character, but the outlook points the same way. The East African Federation, comprising Tanganyika, Uganda and Kenya, and the UDEAC (Union Douanière et Economique de l'Afrique Centrale), with Congo (Brazzaville), Gabon, the Central African Republic, Chad and the Federal Republic of Cameroon in French Equatorial Africa as its members, are two of the conspicuous examples in the African continent. But they trace their ancestry to colonial periods and their 'integrated markets' have recently been witness to disruption by measures such as *inter-member* QRs, tariffs and surcharges.[2] However, the measures taken by the members to review these developments and *retain* the framework of a generally reduced and low level of trade barriers between member countries, rather than follow post-independence policies of industrialization behind universal trade barriers, themselves signify an implicit decision to liberalize trade among themselves.

There have also recently been developments such as the Regional Co-operation for Development between Pakistan, Iran and Turkey, which aims explicitly to create 'regional' division of labour with attendant liberalization of mutual trade barriers, and the still-undefined moves towards a Middle Eastern Common Market. Asia, however, has witnessed little concrete efforts or ideas in this direction, despite ECAFE's efforts to initiate regional liberalization of trade.[3]

---

[1] Dell [4] has a most useful account in Chapter IV of the background to this Treaty and subsequent development.

[2] A useful account of the disruptionist trends, immediately after independence of the three East African Territories, is contained in a contribution of Arthur Hazlewood to a forthcoming publication, of the Royal Institute of International Affairs, on Integration in Africa, edited by Hazlewood himself.

[3] The ASA (between Malaya, Thailand and Philippines) and the Maphilindo (between Malaya, Philippines and Indonesia) have remained politically utopian in their concept altogether. Several ECAFE conferences have also resulted in Ministerial resolutions on trade liberalization with practically no concrete results. On the other hand, the recent establishment of the Asian Development Bank, with the contribution mainly of Japan and the United States, may lead to the beginning of a more active interest in region-oriented tariff cuts or quota liberalization.

REASONS FOR TRADE LIBERALIZATION

The reasons for these efforts at trade liberalization among LDCs are several.

(1) There is a growing appreciation of the simple fact of inefficiency of specialization which industrialization behind indiscriminate, high trade barriers involves. Many LDCs, *especially in the ECAFE region*, feel that starting from the present position of QRs, it is possible to relax restrictions on a mutual basis with other LDCs and reduce 'overlapping' import substitution or industrialization, (provided that balance of payments difficulties resulting, if any, are not excessive and payments arrangements are forthcoming to assist in the short-run). The emphasis here is on *economic inefficiency arising from producing things which could well be imported more cheaply from others who are better placed, by natural resources or otherwise, to produce them.*

(2) This argument, however, is eclipsed by the more recent emphasis on *the inefficiency which arises from the inability to exploit economies of scale in industrial activities if one has to industrialize within essentially national markets.* This argument has come up in both African and Latin American contexts and there are three ways in which it can be encountered.

(i) It is often presented, in the African and Central American contexts, in the strongest conceivable terms as a *sine qua non* of industrialization. Individual countries are absolutely non-viable because it is impossible to conceive of any industrial activity which can be set up even remotely within sight of its optimum scale in view of the extremely small, effective demand. Thus, industrialization cannot be conceived of at all *unless* the markets are widened through trade. Hence the case for international trade liberalization.

(ii) The preceding argument overstates the case. The real point is that, if scale economies cannot be exploited, the real return to investment in industrial activity will fall, raising thereby the resources necessary to achieve the same level of industrialization. The scale of the effective demand in many African countries, for example, is perhaps so small in relation to achievable economies that the increase in costs may be significant; but it is not meaningful to describe the resulting situation as one of 'non-viability'. In the reformulated version, therefore, the argument merely amounts to stating that industrialization, with access to extra-national markets, would be achievable by an LDC at lower cost *via* the resulting exploitation of economies of scale.

(iii) Indeed, the 'non-viability' argument comes up, in a different version, in Latin America, among the industrialized countries of Brazil, Argentina and Mexico. They discuss their problems of industrialization in a Fraserian, evolutionary framework and argue that they have 'completed the first stage of industrialization, involving the production of consumer goods', reasonably adequately within national markets. But the 'next stage', involving the establishment of heavy industry, is impossible to contemplate, in view of the scale economies involved, within national frontiers and is conditional upon access to international markets.[1]

(3) Finally, there is the traditional argument that foreign trade can be an instrument for increasing competitiveness and hence the efficiency of industrial activity.[2] The experience of the LDCs has underlined the inefficiencies which arise from domestic monopolies sheltering behind trade barriers. This has been a powerful argument, in Latin America especially, for initiating reductions from very high tariff levels so as to reintroduce some 'measured degree' of competition. Note, however, that this argument presupposes that investment *is* forthcoming; since in most LDCs this itself is frequently a result of fenced-off, national markets, the concern with efficiency of investment is something which comes at a *later* stage in the process of industrialization; after all, the LDCs cannot be expected to worry about efficiency unless there is something to be efficient about!

These arguments for trade liberalization are quite sensible, of course, and familiar to economists. Not that they are always used to advantage or with a correct appreciation of their limitations. For example, the fact that economies of scale operate in industrial activities should not make the LDCs, operating a customs union and

---

[1] This 'two-stage' method of argument is absolutely 'classical', based on historical observation of industrialization, and has frequently been used to 'establish' the inadvisability of beginning *first* with heavy industry *à la* the Soviet Union. It is now well recognized, of coures, that no such 'laws' can be derived and the 'Soviet model', which reverses the stages, *can* make considerable sense. See, for example, Maurice Dobb [5].

[2] The inefficiency here relates to the lack of incentive, in a sheltered market, for reducing costs to the minimum at *whatever* level of output is chosen by the entrepreneur.

an industrial allocation policy in harness (as in East Africa, Equatorial Africa and Central America) forget that (i) the spatial distribution of demand, (ii) transportation costs, (iii) the intertemporal growth of demand at different points of consumption and (iv) the external economies obtaining *via* the geographical clustering of certain industries are *also* factors to be considered and that the optimal solutions, even when trade barriers are absent, may still demand that 'uneconomic scale' plants be constructed in different member countries in the same activity.[1]

DISTINGUISHING FEATURES OF LDC TRADE LIBERALIZATION

However, the most interesting aspect of the LDC effort at trade liberalization is that they are characterized by certain patterns which are both readily discernible and difficult to reconcile with what traditional trade theory would predict as the behaviour of governments 'rationally' pursuing economic welfare. The most notable of these features may be listed here at the outset.

(1) The trade expansion efforts are sought to be on a *preferential* basis, among a few or all LDCs but *excluding the developed countries*. Where the preferential groupings fall within the purview of GATT's Article XXIV (exempting 100 per cent preferential arrangements from the contractual commitment to extending MFN treatment to all other GATT members), there is no institutional change involved in this demand. But the LDCs clearly would like to extend the operation of such an exemption to less-than-100 per cent preferential arrangements among LDCs. They are thus demanding really the suspension of automatic MFN rights by the developed GATT members with respect to the LDC members.

(2) Furthermore, the experience in Latin America in particular shows that the LDC efforts at tariff cuts and trade liberalization are oriented very clearly towards *trade diversion*. Looked at from the viewpoint of traditional trade theory, therefore, the LDC efforts seem to be directed at the wrong kind of tariff cuts altogether! The acceptance of the increment in intra-regional trade in LAFTA as an index of its success, without any attempt at separating out trade diversion from this figure, as also the impatience exhibited in Latin American circles

---

[1] Not merely are these qualifications infrequently appreciated but also there is danger that the industrial allocations among members of a union may, in practice, be the product of 'horse trading'.

with the requirement of GATT's Article XXIV[1] that the average external tariff must not be greater after a customs union or free trade area (which would among other things, make trade diversion *via* the raising of external tariffs impossible) are pointed reminders of this divergence between LDC demands and behaviour on the one hand and traditional predictions and prescriptions on the other.

(3) The LDC negotiations and literature are unanimous in insisting upon 'reciprocity' of benefits. This is familiar from the history of tariff negotiations anywhere. The reciprocity takes the form, quite acutely in most LDC cases, of balancing of *incremental* trade flow rather than demands of identical tariffs cuts or any other method. Both the strict insistence on reciprocity and the specific form taken by it are not readily reconciled with what traditional trade theory, as analysed below, would indicate as the likely pattern of LDC behaviour.

(4) As a corollary to this concern with this form of reciprocity, there is also discernible among many LDCs a preference for negotiations and action on trade liberalization among smaller rather than larger groups. As a consequence, there is already discernible a growing conflict of opinion on whether any *sub*-set of LDCs should be allowed to discriminate against the other LDCs when a less-than-100 per cent programme of tariff cuts, outside the purview of GATT's Article XXIV, is involved. The dominant trend, however, seems to be in favour of the more 'liberal' version which would permit discriminatory tariff cuts applicable even within a sub-set of LDCs.

There are broadly two sets of issues that arise from these patterns of LDC behaviour and demands.

(1) Is it possible to 'explain' them in terms of the traditional theory of preferential trade liberalization – associated mainly with Viner, Meade and Lipsey[2] – if one makes the additional assumption that the

---

[1] 'With respect to a free-trade area, or an interim agreement leading to the formation of a free-trade area, the duties and other regulations of commerce maintained in each of the constituent territories and applicable at the formation of such free-trade area or the adoption of such interim agreement to the trade of contracting parties not included in such area or not parties to such agreement shall not be higher or more restrictive than the corresponding duties and other regulations of commerce existing in the same constituent territories prior to the formation of the free-trade area, or interim agreement, as the case may be'.

[2] The main literature is: J. Viner [12]; J. Meade [9]; and R. Lipsey [8]. There is also the 'monetary' theory of trade discrimination, associated with the names of Frisch, Fleming and Meade, which is not touched upon in this paper, but which would be relevant in understanding *payments* problems and assessing current *IMF rules*.

LDC governments act 'rationally' in pursuit of economic welfare? Or do we have to modify the theory itself so that it leads to predictions of behaviour which are consistent with those observed? It is argued, later in this paper, that we indeed require a modified, new theory which fits the observable facts very much better and that such a theory can be obtained by modifying the LDC governments' assumed 'utility function'.

(2) In light of such an 'explanation' of LDC behaviour and demands, the question immediately arises as to what attitude economists *ought* to take concerning the amendments proposed by LDCs in the GATT rules. The following analysis formulates a conceptual framework which provides a possible case for accepting such amendments, while also examining its limiting assumptions.

EXPLANATION OF DISTINGUISHING FEATURES OF LDC TRADE LIBERALIZATION

It is possible, of course, to say that the LDCs are 'muddled' and 'irrational'; such views are not as uncommon as one would imagine. They are in fact held especially by those who have not reconciled themselves to the exercise of governmental action and hence cannot admit of its possible rationality.

On the other hand, purely *political* explanations are both possible and undoubtedly relevant. Thus for example the desire to liberalize trade *within* the LDC group, to the exclusion of the developed countries, could be explained, partly at least, by reference to a desire to attain 'solidarity' within the LDC group. There are most certainly overtones of such notions as 'solidarity', 'bargaining power', 'political cohesion and strength' and the like in some of the regional LDC groups such as LAFTA and in Central America; they are to be traced to the political dominance of the United States in the area as also the example of the European Common Market which too was enveloped in a political cloak of similar cloth.

There also seems to have been considerable interest shown by some of the *developed* countries themselves in getting the LDCs to liberalize trade *among* themselves as an 'act of self-help'. This too is to be explained, at least partially, in political terms as an attempt to (i) divert LDC attention away from pressing on with their claims at UNCTAD for concessions from the developed countries, (ii) create predictable dissensions among the LDCs (on issues such as that of discrimination among themselves) and thus break the LDC-block (such as it is) at UNCTAD, and (iii) promote, in particular, *regional* groupings of LDCs which would then be easier to attract into preferential groupings with the developed countries in the region, thus reinforcing the traditional economic and political ties[1] (as with United States and Latin America or EEC and French Africa).[2]

Similarly, the interest in trade-diverting trade expansion may be explained in terms of a *political* inability to lower tariffs on protected, domestic industries. Since producers typically tend to turn into articulate and powerful pressure groups, it is plausible to argue that the politics of democratic systems will reflect producer interests more readily than any others, so that trade-diverting trade expansion is certainly likely to be preferred to trade-creating trade expansion.

While such explanations are certainly relevant, it is also of equal interest to note that practically the entire range of LDC behaviour can be 'explained' by recasting traditional trade theory into a somewhat different mould. This is, in fact, readily done.

A. *Traditional Analysis*

The traditional analysis classifies preferential tariff reduction into two ideal categories: (i) trade diverting and (ii) trade creating. Each of these well-known types may be considered, in turn, from the viewpoint of predictions of behaviour that they would generate on the assumption of 'rational' behaviour in the sense discussed earlier.

1. *Trade-diverting tariff reduction*
Looked at from the viewpoint of a tariff-cutting country (M), and

---

[1] That Raul Prebisch, Secretary General of UNCTAD, has been worried by this aspect of the problem is clear from his address to the United Nations Trade and Development Board, stating: 'Unfortunately, there are some symptoms that the spirit of Geneva is not being applied, and that on the contrary there is an aggravation of the tendency towards a system of discriminatory preferences in certain parts of the world. I cannot hide from the Board my great concern at signs in certain Latin American circles, which are manifesting themselves with increasing force in requests to the United States for a preferential system to be exclusive to Latin American countries'. [4, p. 34.] Indeed, the fact that LAFTA exists now is likely to make both the demand for, and grant of, such discriminatory preferences by the United States a significant possibility.

[2] Economists are particularly prone to scoffing at such 'fears'. They would be well advised to read, in case they *are* sceptical, E. H. Carr's brilliant account of the inevitable interaction of economic philosophy and rational, political interest in his *The 20 Years' Crisis: 1919–1939* [2].

the partner-country (P) in whose favour the tariff is cut, a trade-diverting tariff cut leads to the following situation according to the traditional theory:[1]

(a) country M will lose from the trade diversion shifting the source of imports to the higher cost supplier, country P;

(b) on the other hand, the cheapening of the commodity, on which the tariff is cut preferentially, may lead to a net consumption gain;[2]

(c) country M can therefore be left as before, or may gain or lose from a trade-diverting tariff cut;

(d) as for country P, it will *either* gain from opening trade with country M or by improving its terms of trade with it *or* have its welfare position unchanged if it is a 'large' country (in the Samuelson sense).

The matrix of welfare possibilities from a preferential tariff cut by country M in favour of country P, according to traditional theory, is thus the following.

MATRIX (1) *Welfare Possibilities under a Trade-Diverting Tariff Cut by One Country (M) – on Traditional Theory*

Possibility	Country	
	M	P
(1)	Gains	Gains
(2)	Gains	Unchanged
(3)	Loses	Gains
(4)	Loses	Unchanged
(5)	Unchanged	Gains
(6)	Unchanged	Unchanged

[1] Note that, in the analysis that follows, only the *simpler* analytical models of Viner and Lipsey [8] are used. Complications can arise, however, if this is not done. For example, as Lipsey [8] has pointed out, even the consumption effect can be negative if one takes a *three-good* model. Also, as Mundell has shown recently, unless gross substitutability is assumed between the goods of each country in a *three-good*, three-country model, the terms of trade of the partner country (P) with the third country can worsen, thus presumably opening up the possibility of a loss to it.

[2] This was shown by Lipsey [7]. Note, however, the qualifications noted in the previous footnote.

Note that, in two cases at least (1 and 2), there seems to be a clear reason why reciprocity by country P does not represent a *sine qua non* for a tariff cut by country M; whereas, only in three cases (3–5) would it seem that country M could not be induced to cut its tariff on country P without demanding some measure of reciprocity from it. Note also that whereas reciprocity would not be necessary in the cases where trade diversion leads to welfare gains, the insistence on reciprocity would arise most compellingly only in cases where the trade diversion leads to a loss (as will happen in cases 3 and 4) where again all that reciprocity may lead to is a loss to *both* countries instead of one. Thus we *either* fail to provide rationale for reciprocity at all or provide it in cases where the possibility of there being preferential tariff cuts at all is dismal.

So far, therefore, the theory fails to explain why the LDCs seem to prefer trade-diverting tariff cuts and simultaneously to insist on reciprocity (of incremental trade flows). We can, however, go somewhat further than we have. Within the framework of this analysis itself, there are two ways in which the reciprocity demands may be justified even in cases where country M gains from a unilateral, preferential tariff cut causing trade diversion:

(a) On the one hand, we could introduce a game-theoretic formulation into the analysis. For example, in the two cases 1 and 2, where country M stands to benefit unambiguously from a preferential tariff cut, its insistence on a reciprocal tariff cut *could* lead perhaps to a mutual, simultaneous tariff cut which may make country M even *better off than under a unilateral, discriminatory tariff cut.*[1]

(b) At the same time, we could well argue that the alternative to a unilateral, preferential tariff cut by country M is not merely the *status quo* but could well be a unilateral *non-discriminatory* tariff cut. Thus it could be argued that the willingness to cut a tariff preferentially in favour of country P involves a *potential* loss (or reduction in gain) as compared with a situation where country M would

[1] This aspect of tariff bargaining, which may rationalize certain reciprocity demands even within the *traditional* theoretical framework, has always been ignored by those who voice puzzlement as to the insistence of many countries on reciprocity of one kind or another in tariff negotiations. See, for example, Harry Johnson [6] whose elegant analysis neglects altogether this line of argument. Failure to see this line of argument can be traced to many liberal writers, such as Lionel Robbins who in *The Economist in the Twentieth Century* [10, pp. 137–8] recognizes the problem explicitly and tries to account for reciprocity by arguing that the burden of adjustment with unilateral tariff cuts would be greater.

have cut its tariff non-preferentially, and therefore the reciprocity demand follows from the consequential (implicit) loss to country M.[1]

We can somewhat strengthen therefore the case for expecting 'rational' governments to press for reciprocity. Note, however, that while reciprocity may be explained along these lines, we cannot so explain the desire for balancing the incremental trade flows – *i.e.* the *specific form* that reciprocity demands take. Moreover, the analysis does not really explain why the sub-set of countries M and P are interested in negotiations for trade liberalization with each other and not with others. To make this implicit but important assumption plausible, we would have to bring in some extraneous, political argument; as argued earlier, a sub-set of countries may well decide to undertake liberalization among only themselves consequent upon a

---

[1] This point can be readily seen from Lipsey's, *op. cit.*, well-known diagram. Assume that country M, specialized on producing OR of Y, has an initial, non-discriminatory tariff which leads to trade with country C at price-ratio OC, and consumption at Q with domestic, tariff-inclusive price ratio being P_t and welfare at U_i. If the tariff is eliminated altogether, welfare will increase to U_c. If the tariff is cut only for country P, trade will occur along price-line RP and welfare will be at U_p. Note that $U_p > U_i$ but $U_p < U_c$.

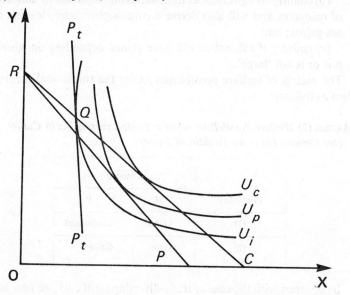

Therefore, in terms of U_c, there *is* a loss from a preferential tariff removal, even though it is a case where trade diversion increases welfare ($U_p > U_i$).

political decision to 'integrate their political and economic systems'. Indeed, some such political assumption would be necessary even to explain why it is that, since *both* countries M and P can lose from such trade-diverting trade liberalization despite reciprocity, and such possibilities do not seem to be excluded by any means by recent LDC experience, the LDCs in fact seem to opt none the less for such trade liberalization. Unless, therefore, one relies on such political arguments at a crucial stage of the analysis, the traditional theory will not be able to come to grips with even the most obvious features of LDC attempts at trade liberalization.

(i) *Trade-creating tariff reduction*

When we analyse the case of trade-creating tariff cuts, the inability of traditional theory to come to grips with LDC behaviour seems even more evident. Assuming that country M is preferentially cutting its tariff again, if it is a trade-creating tariff cut it will lead to the following situation according to traditional theory:

(c) country M will lose its inefficient industry, partially or wholly, to country P;

(b) country M will consider itself as having improved its allocation of resources and will also derive a consumption gain, leaving it a net gainer; and

(c) country P will not or will have gained depending on whether it is or is not 'large'.

The matrix of welfare possibilities under the traditional theory is then as follows:

MATRIX (2) *Welfare Possibilities under a Trade-Creating Tariff Cut by One Country (M) – on Traditional Theory*

	Country	
Possibility	M	P
(1)	Gains	Unchanged
(2)	Gains	Gains

By contrast with the case of trade-diverting tariff cuts, we now have one case of harmony of interests and another where the tariff-cutting country gains anyway. In neither case, therefore, would reciprocity appear to be a prime requisite before country M would cut its tariff.[1]

Traditional analysis would then also imply that trade creating tariff cuts will be profitable whereas trade diverting tariff cuts would not be so except where the consumption gain is decisive. Hence we would infer from traditional analysis that trade creating tariff cuts are more likely to occur in practice than trade diverting tariff cuts. This is yet another conclusion which seems to contradict LDC experience.

B. *Modified 'Utility Function'*

Consider, however, the following modification to each LDC's objective or utility function:

(i) let each LDC attach intrinsic significance to the level of import-competing industrial output that trade diversion attracts to each country and trade creation attracts to one country 'at the expense of' the other; and

(ii) let each country ignore the significance of any possible consumption gain from the cheapening of products in domestic markets subsequent on tariff cuts.[2]

Note further that the addition of these new arguments in the LDC objective function seems quite plausible because, in particular:

(i) the LDCs typically wish to industrialize and hence use tariffs (and/or quantitative restrictions) for this purpose, so that the attraction of import-competing industrial production would be considered a desirable result *in itself*; and

(ii) in most cases, the trade pattern of the LDCs involves imports of components, materials and machines, to which the notion of a *consumption* gain is only indirectly applicable.[3]

---

[1] Again, as with the analysis of trade diversion, we could strengthen somewhat the case for reciprocity by using a game-theoretic formulation or by pointing out the *potential* loss from discriminatory, as distinct from a possible non-discriminatory, tariff cut.

[2] For this reason, though more so by virtue of the difficulty of accepting the notion of 'given preferences' on which the whole theory rests, I have found it useful to develop the welfare theory of trade in my lectures in Delhi in terms of technological efficiency rather than utility rankings. For details on this, see my forthcoming paper [2].

[3] There is also an associated 'revenue' problem. Where LDCs have levied tariffs for earning revenue, their removal or reduction, on other LDCs, could well result in a loss of revenue in case of trade diversion, if the increment in imports from the resulting cheapening of the item in domestic consumption is not large enough to offset the reduction in the tariff rate. Experience in East Africa and

If these modifications are made, consider what happens in the case of trade diversion examined earlier on traditional lines. The matrix of welfare possibilities will change radically. Country M will now feel that it has 'lost' through having to import the commodities from country P at a higher cost whereas, in its opinion, country P has registered a definite 'gain' because it has now started or expanded production of these commodities. Given therefore this change in the objective function, the matrix reduces to a simple, conflict situation where the tariff-cutting country M feels it has lost and the other country P has gained. Reciprocity thus becomes extremely important and no trade-diverting tariff cuts or free-trade areas/customs unions may therefore be expected to make progress unless reciprocity is built into the arrangements from the beginning.

At the same time, it becomes easy to see that reciprocity would ensure that, by satisfactory distribution of trade-diverted industrialization, both countries could emerge feeling that they have gained from the reciprocal, discriminatory tariff cuts.[1] Again, it is easy to see now that the LDCs would prefer to liberalize trade with one another rather than with the advanced countries. Since industrial production has value in itself, the LDCs would consider it disadvantageous to negotiate tariff cuts (on industrial products) with advanced countries (whose competitive strength in manufactures is assumed to be greater) *unless* they are one-way, in their favour, thus ruling out reciprocal tariff cuts (including customs unions and free trade areas) except among the LDCs (who are presumed to be at more comparable or 'similar' stages of development *vis-à-vis* one another) and also explaining their well-known insistence on 'non-reciprocity' by LDCs for tariff cuts made by the advanced countries.[2]

For similar reasons, trade-creating tariff cuts would, under the modified theory, equally exhibit demands for reciprocity *and* would appear less attractive than under traditional theory, thus corresponding again more closely to observable facts about LDCs. Thus, for

---

French Equatorial Africa, in particular, suggests that this possible loss of revenue is considered an important 'loss' factor by LDCs in continuing or entering upon integration schemes.

[1] It is assumed, in the following analysis, that a decisive weight will usually be attached by LDCs to the question of whether industrial activity expands or contracts in the economy.

[2] This 'principle' of non-reciprocity has been brought up even *within* preferential groupings, as in the special treatment meted out to the 'less developed' members of EEC and LAFTA, with respect to implementation of tariff cuts.

example, the matrix of welfare possibilities from such a unilateral tariff cut (Matrix 2) will now be changed. Country M will reduce its estimate of gain (by the amount of the consumption gain, if any) and, more significantly, has a new 'loss' factor because the contraction or elimination of its import-competing manufactures will be considered undesirable *per se*. At the same time, country P will be thought to have *definitely* gained because it has attracted to itself or expanded the manufacturing activity which has declined in country M. The matrix of welfare possibilities thus reduces again to a simple conflict situation where country P is supposed to have gained and country M to have lost. A unilateral tariff cut by country M is thus ruled out and reciprocal tariff cuts by country P become a *sine qua non* of country M's tariff cuts even in trade-creating situations. Moreover, since value is attached to industrial production *per se*, the LDCs fail to see any rationale in contracting the output of existing manufactures, so that trade-creating tariff cuts seem to them to be 'unnecessary' or 'unfruitful' and hence inferior to trade-diverting tariff cuts which bring more industrial activity to the members LDCs.

If therefore the new theory is accepted, it is possible to explain practically all the puzzling features of LDC negotiations, from reciprocity to preference for trade-diverting tariff cuts. The most interesting of these implications may now be brought together and further spelled out:

(1) trade liberalization will *inevitably* be accompanied by considerable interest in 'reciprocity' arrangements, even though traditional theory does not so imply;

(2) trade-diverting tariff cuts, provided reciprocity is worked out, are far more likely to be acceptable than traditional theory would imply (the creation or expansion of import-competing, industrial production being a desirable objective in itself);

(3) trade-creating tariff cuts will be far less likely to be acceptable, even when reciprocity is worked out, than traditional theory would imply (the decline of import-competing, industrial production being an undesirable objective in itself);

(4) trade-diverting tariff cuts, in consequence, are more likely to occur in practice than trade-creating tariff cuts, again contrary to what traditional theory would imply;

(5) the 'reciprocity' requirement is further likely to take the form of attention to whether the resulting, *incremental trade flows* between the participating countries are balanced: this, in turn, would be an

indication of the degree of the production 'advantage' which the new theory stresses as a significant source of gain;[1]

(6) the new theory would also reinforce political explanations in predicting that LDCs would turn to one another for tariff-cutting exercises: trade diversion is more readily practised against the developed countries which still continue overwhelmingly to be the major exporters of industrial manufactures to the LDCs;

(7) the new theory would simultaneously explain the demand to have GATT's Article XXIV amended so as to allow the *raising* of the average, external tariff in a preferential tariff cut (in a 100 per cent programme); if tariffs were to be preferentially cut only from existing levels, and if these tariffs may be expected to be higher on items where trade creation rather than trade diversion is likely,[2] the effort at preferential tariff cuts could be jeopardized by having to concentrate on trade-cutting rather than trade-diverting cuts;

(8) further, in view of the insistence on reciprocity, the preference is likely to be for tariff cuts among smaller groups of LDCs rather than larger groups; reciprocity is easier to work out within smaller group, especially when it takes the specific forms outlined earlier *and* is so important to the participants, whereas smaller groups also make it easier to supplement an 'unpredictable' trade mechanism by a 'more direct' and simultaneous policy of 'industrial allocations' among members;[3] and

[1] Evidence of such behaviour by LDC members of common markets and free trade areas is to be found in the experience in LAFTA and in East Africa. The Kampala Agreement of 1964 explicitly argues along the lines of *balanced trade flows* within the East African Federation, for example.

[2] This appears to have been the case in LAFTA countries; see Dell [4, Chapter V].

[3] Indeed, one of the important features of all LDC attempts at trade expansion, to date, has been the unwillingness to initiate tariff cuts and trust them to result in efficient, industrial division of labour in the classical, textbook manner. Even where the classical method was initially adopted, as in East Africa and with LAFTA, direct, industrial allocations of one kind or another among the member countries have now been envisaged and machinery actually set up to deal with the question. There are two major reasons for this: (i) the LDCs recognize, from experience, that wasteful duplication, or even multiplication, of industrial capacity, which the enlargement of markets *via* tariff cuts is intended to avoid, cannot frequently be eliminated in practice without governmental intervention, and (ii) the LDCs feel that market forces would tend to gravitate industrial activity towards the already industrialized areas within the group, so that interference with the market mechanism would be necessary to direct part of the industrialization towards the 'weaker' members. On the other hand, the offsetting disadvantages of such industrial allocations by political agencies, unless managed with reference to economic criteria, could also be significant.

(9) the preference for trade diversion is likely to accentuate still further the tendency to prefer smaller groups, for the simple reason that there are more outsiders to divert trade from when the group is smaller.

Indeed, these are all very distinctly the special features of LDC attempts at trade liberalization and of their consequential demands for GATT revision.

SHOULD GATT RULES BE CHANGED?

The logical question then is whether it makes economic sense to amend the GATT rules so as to accommodate the LDC patterns of behaviour and demands. There are three main types of position which can be taken on this general issue.

(1) Either one can be cynical and argue that, after all, countries act exactly as they want to *despite* GATT membership, so that there is little point in amending these rules. While there is force in the contention that actual practice manages frequently to by-pass international obligations – as, for example, with the GATT rules on export subsidies which are widely flouted in devious ways – their nuisance value is very evident and they frequently involve resort to indirect and inefficient ways of achieving legal consistency between international obligations and national action. The very fact that LDCs want GATT rules changed implies that they must, at least sometimes, be constrictive. So this cynical dismissal of the question must be rejected.

(2) Alternatively, one may argue the opposite case: that, if a sufficient number of countries want a change in the GATT rules, it will go through and there is no point in arguing the matter any further. Such a cynic may well point to the insertion of Article XXIV, undoubtedly to accommodate an impending European economic community which enjoyed equally the support of the United States while the LDCs were apathetic or reconciled to impotence in influencing events; after all, even traditional theory cannot show that a 100 per cent tariff cut, on a preferential basis, is invariably superior to a partial cut or no cut at all and yet that is exactly what Article XXIV implicitly asserts! If LDCs manage to muster enough bargaining strength, eventually they may well succeed in changing GATT rules around to suit their demands. But again, unless the developed countries can be persuaded to acquiesce in these amendments, the progress towards them would

be inevitably slow and halting. So this form of cynical dismissal of the question must also be rejected.

(3) Indeed, even from an intellectual standpoint, it is necessary to argue through the question whether the LDC demands *ought* to be supported.

In answering this question, one has to be clear about what exactly is the *alternative* to *not* amending the GATT rules in accordance with LDC demands. This, in turn, amounts to asking what is really the alternative to LDCs' not being allowed to liberalize trade *among* themselves and whether, from an economic point of view, that alternative is superior.

Emphasis is being placed here quite deliberately on defining the most realistic alternative, *in comparison with which* the possibility of amending GATT rules in the LDC-suggested direction must be judged. Much too often economic issues are misjudged because the alternatives considered are really irrelevant. Thus, for example, devaluation was widely considered to be inflationary in its impact because the alternative implicitly considered was that of utilization of reserves to ease the deficit. It was later realized that the correct comparison, from a policy viewpoint, was with alternative adjustment policies *all* being evaluated subject to non-availability of reserves, and that once this was done it was by no means obvious that devaluation would be inflationary by comparison with, for example, QRs.[1]

The starting point in finding the right alternative to answer our present question seems to be the fact that *industrialization* is among the primary, immediate objectives of the LDCs. One may debate whether this is a desirable, legitimate 'economic' objective or whether it is to be classified as a 'non-economic' objective. Regardless of the precise reasons for considering industrialization as an LDC objective, that the LDCs so consider it is the essential fact to be noted.

If then industrialization is to proceed in an LDC, the immediate consequence of such a decision for most LDCs would be for the imports, of the items in which the import-substitution occurs, to shrink below their level otherwise.[2] *Trade diversion*, in this sense, *is*

[1] Credit for this insight goes to Egon Sohmen [11] who, to my knowledge, was the first to reformulate the question of the impact of devaluation upon the price level in this manner.

[2] This argument presupposes, of course, that industrialization will lead to the imposition of tariff (or quivalent QR) protection and that the level of industrialization which free trade will permit falls short of the desired level. *Both* of these seem to be realistic assumptions, of course, about LDCs.

already implicit in the decision to industrialize. Nothing in current GATT rules can effectively block an LDC member from undertaking such trade diversion in pursuit of its policy of industrialization.

A. *Case for GATT Revisions*

From this way of looking at things, the most favourable case for accepting the LDC behaviour and demands emerges as follows.[1]

If the LDCs could be allowed to reduce tariff barriers *among* themselves, this could permit the given trade diversion (implicit in *each* LDC's decision to industrialize) to be carried out at *lower cost* because the trade diversion, while continuing against the non-members, would be eliminated or reduced as among the (member) LDCs. To put it yet differently, and more illuminatingly, the tariff cuts (among the LDCs) would in fact be permitting trade creation among the LDCs in relation to the situation where they would have industrialized behind national tariff walls. The contention then is that, regarded in this light, the apparently trade-diverting attempts by LDCs at mutual tariff preferences turn out really to be effectively trade-creating.

On this line of argument, several arguments for modifying GATT rules seem to become persuasive. For example, the automatic extension of MFN treatment by LDCs to the developed members could be removed on the ground that the trade diversion away from the developed countries will take place anyway, thanks to *individual* LDC action, so why hold up the (implicit) trade creation among the LDCs that such an amendment would facilitate?

Similarly, why not modify Article XXIV of GATT so as to permit the raising of the external, average tariff when entering a 100 per cent, preferential agreement: if the alternative again is the raising of *national*, LDC tariff barriers which GATT cannot effectively prevent (except when the duties are 'bound'), why not consider the suggested modification of Article XXIV as permitting a less undesirable, alternative procedure which would reduce the LDC-cost of industrialization?

Again, if LDCs will not as readily wish to dismantle *existing* lines of industrialization and would rather concentrate instead on ensuring that the *future* doses of industrialization are efficiently made by

[1] At the IBRD seminar, where this paper was presented, Bela Balassa pointed out to me that my way of presenting the strongest case in favour of accepting LDC demands is implicit in the writings of Raul Prebisch, Cooper and Massell and Balassa, although the formulation of the argument is different.

having wider markets among the LDCs – thus concentrating on the gains from *implicit* trade creation, as defined here – it would appear that the alternative to not letting them discriminate between tariffs on existing and on new industries (to come), as Article XXIV would require, is likely to make the LDCs continue the present policies of industrialization in small, domestic markets and thus forgo even the advantages that could accrue from implicit or potential trade creation. By this argument, therefore, there would again be a good case for letting LDCs, even in Article XXIV situations where the LDCs would commit themselves to eventual, full integration, discriminate in their progressive tariff cuts between existing and newer industries (much as there is now accepted an asymmetry between manufactures and agriculture).[1]

B. *Arguments against GATT Revisions*

The above case is, in fact, the most favourable one that can be built up for making some of the GATT revisions that the LDCs have been demanding. But it rests on two crucial assumptions which need to be spelled out very clearly, for it is around them that economists are likely to divide in their judgment of what changes in GATT are desirable.

(i) The first crucial assumption (already stated explicitly) is that the LDCs would, in fact, if GATT rules are not changed, raise their tariffs (QR barriers) in pursuit of industrialization. While this assumption is plausible, in the light of LDC experience, it *could* be challenged on the dubious argument that the increased cost of the resulting attempt at industrialization behind national tariff walls would itself reduce the degree of trade diversion (and hence economic inefficiency) which LDCs are willing to undertake in pursuit of industrialization.[2]

---

[1] This could be done quite readily by permitting a different rate of progressive tariff cuts on these two classes of products and thus effectively lengthening considerably the time over which the existing industries would have to adjust. The fact of growing industrialization and incomes, as also the prospect of eventually integrated market, would then both induce and permit an orderly decline in the relative and/or absolute level of the industry in the LDC where it is inefficient.

[2] This is, in fact, the type of argument which has long been used by the opponents of foreign aid, such as Milton Friedman, who claim that foreign aid feather-beds many inefficiencies which would become insupportable if the countries receiving aid had to make do with their own resources. This argument, of course,

(ii) The second crucial assumption is more serious. The preceding case for GATT revisions really presupposes that the LDCs will undertake tariff negotiations in a way which, while discriminatory, does in fact reduce (if not minimize) the mutual cost of any given degree of industrialization among the member countries. There is an important difference between arguing that discriminatory arrangements among LDCs *could* reduce the mutual cost of member-LDC industrialization and asserting that it would necessarily do so.[1] Indeed, from the analytical point of view, this way of posing the problem leads to at least three questions of importance and relevance to the present discussion.

(a) If an *arbitrarily-defined* sub-group of LDCs desires to achieve a *given* level of industrialization, within *each* country, what is the *optimal* level and structure of the external tariff which will permit this to be done at *least cost* within the framework of an integrated market? (No such solution need exist, of course, if the level of industrialization within any member cannot be sustained without protecting *against* the *other* members, thereby violating the presence of an integrated market within the sub-group.)

(b) Within the same, arbitrarily-defined sub-group of LDCs, what is the optimal set of policy instruments for achieving the required level of industrialization within each LDC? Here, the range of policy instruments being considered extends beyond tariff policy.[2]

(c) Given a set of LDCs, each with its own target of industrialization, what is the *optimum sub*-set of LDCs from any *one* LDC's

---

presupposes that the recipient countries agree with these commentators in regarding certain policies as 'inefficient', an assumption which is notoriously invalid – there is a well-known law of intransitivity which operates in these matters: X thinks his economics is better than Y's and Y thinks the other way around. The effect of withdrawal of aid is more likely to be the reinforcing of the very same policies that these opponents of foreign aid dislike.

[1] The experience in LAFTA, where the tariff cuts seem to have been *indiscriminatingly* trade-diverting, can only make one sceptical with respect to the second assumption being discussed here.

[2] Cooper and Massell [3] raise also the somewhat more limited question of whether the LDCs could *reduce* their mutual cost of industrialization through preferential arrangements. They use a constant-cost model, which is somewhat limited for dealing with the questions of importance to LDCs (such as economies of scale); but it is none the less a useful device, exploited with great skill by the authors.

point of view, which will permit it to achieve its objective at least cost, assuming for example that the sub-set will act so as to minimize cost for the group as in (i) or (ii) preceding?

It is not clear that LDCs would, in fact, examine their possibilities of preferential arrangements in the careful way that is necessary, so that it is inevitable that economists would be divided on the set of rules that they would like to see at GATT on the question of preferential tariff arrangements.

The questions concerning GATT revisions are thus not easily answerable; they involve resort to judgments of a fairly crucial type about what is likely to happen in response to the changes. Even the framework devised in this paper, to strengthen the case for these revisions, cannot make the case for them definitive.

Ultimately, the issue is likely to be judged also in the light of the views which economists have concerning whether the possibility of preferentially reducing trade barriers among LDCs is likely to constitute the only feasible route by which the world will move closer towards freer trade or whether it will only lead to a sustained and strengthened fragmentation of the world economy.

REFERENCES

1 Bhagwati, J., 'The Gains from Trade Once Again', *Oxford Economic Papers*, July 1968; chapter 3.

2 Carr, E. H., *The 20 Years' Crisis: 1919–1939*, London, Macmillan, 1946.

3 Cooper, C., and Massell, B. F., 'Customs Union Theory and Less Developed Countries', *Journal of Political Economy*, October 1965.

4 Dell, S., *A Latin American Common Market?*, Oxford University Press, 1966.

5 Dobb, M., *Economic Growth and Underdeveloped Countries*, London, Lawrence and Wishart, 1962.

6 Johnson, H. G., 'An Economic Theory of Protectionism, Tariff Bargaining and the Formation of Customs Unions', *Journal of Political Economy*, June 1965.

7 Lipsey, R., 'The Theory of Customs Unions: Trade Diversion and Welfare', *Economica*, February 1957.

8 Lipsey, R., 'The Theory of Customs Unions: A General Survey', *Economic Journal*, September 1960.

9 Meade, J. E., *The Theory of Customs Unions*, Amsterdam, North-Holland Publishing Co., 1955.

10 Robbins, L., *The Economist in the Twentieth Century*, London, Macmillan, 1954.

11 Sohmen, E., 'The Effect of Devaluation on the Price Level', *Quarterly Journal of Economics*, May 1958.

12 Viner, J., *The Customs Union Issue*, London 1950.

Index